STRATEGIC
MANAGEMENT

FIFTH EDITION

IN ACTION

Mary Coulter

Missouri State University

Prentice Hall

Boston   Columbus   Indianapolis   New York   San Francisco   Upper Saddle River
Amsterdam   Cape Town   Dubai   London   Madrid   Milan   Munich   Paris   Montreal   Toronto
Delhi   Mexico City   Sao Paulo   Sydney   Hong Kong   Seoul   Singapore   Taipei   Tokyo

Editorial Director: Sally Yagan
Editor in Chief: Eric Svendsen
Acquisitions Editor: Kim Norbuta
Manager, Product Development: Ashley Santora
Editorial Project Manager: Claudia Fernandes
Director of Marketing: Patrice Lumumba Jones
Marketing Manager: Nikki Jones
Marketing Assistant: Ian Gold
Senior Managing Editor: Judy Leale
Project Manager: Ana Jankowski
Senior Operations Supervisor: Arnold Vila
Senior Art Director: Kenny Beck
Text and Cover Designer: Laura C. Ierardi
Cover Art: istockphoto/Ewa Wysocka-Galka
Media Project Manager, Editorial: Denise Vaughn
Media Project Manager, Production: Lisa Rinaldi
Full-Service Project Management/Composition: TexTech International Pvt, Ltd.
Printer/Binder: Edwards Brothers
Cover Printer: Demand Production Center
Text Font: 10/12 Minion

Credits and acknowledgments borrowed from other sources and reproduced, with permission, in this textbook appear on appropriate page within text.

If you purchased this book within the United States or Canada you should be aware that it has been wrongfully imported without the approval of the Publisher or the Author.

10 9 8 7 6 5 4 3 2

Prentice Hall
is an imprint of

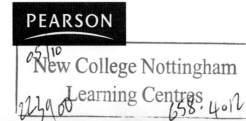

ISBN 10: 0-13-704286-8
ISBN 13: 978-0-13-704286-9

To Ron, Sarah and James, and Katie and Matt

Brief Contents

Contents

Chapter 4: Assessing Strengths and Weaknesses: Doing an Internal Analysis   101

Case #1: Caring Enough to Be the Very Best   101

Preface

Strategy Theory + Strategy Practice = Strategic Management in Action, Fifth Edition

Competitive advantage. It's a concept that's fundamental to the study of strategic management and one you'll be quite familiar with after reading this text. What is competitive advantage? It refers to what sets something (an organization, a team, a job applicant, a book, etc.) apart. And what sets this book apart? What is its competitive advantage? This is a strategic management book that *effectively integrates strategy theory and strategy practice.* As one professor who uses the book so clearly said, "It's the right stuff compactly and clearly presented." The fifth edition of *Strategic Management in Action* continues to do what it does best—presenting current strategic management theories and practices in an interesting, engaging, and easy-to-read format.

New to the Fifth Edition

Here is a chapter-by-chapter list of the changes in the fifth edition.

Chapter 1
- New case on Disney
- Role of board of directors
- World Bank and International Monetary Fund
- Today's economic climate
- 5 end-of-chapter cases
- Updated boxes, examples, and cases

Chapter 2
- Revised chapter structure
- New case on Toys R Us
- New case on Timberland
- Today's economic climate
- 5 end-of-chapter cases
- Updated boxes, examples, and cases

Chapter 3
- Reversal of offshoring/outsourcing decisions
- E-waste

- Today's economic climate
- Updated boxes, examples, and cases

Chapter 4
- New case on Hallmark
- 5 end-of-chapter cases
- Updated boxes, examples, and cases

Chapter 5
- Ins and outs of layoff strategies
- New case on Blue Nile
- Updated boxes, examples, and cases

Chapter 6
- New boxes on competition, smartphone market
- Selling luxury in today's economic climate (differentiation strategy)
- New cases on Coke and Chico's
- 5 end-of-chapter cases
- Updated boxes, examples, and cases

Chapter 7
- New material on global horizontal integration
- New box on "thinking small"
- Totally re-written cases on Nascar and WaMu
- Updated boxes, examples, and cases

Chapter 8
- Updated information on Global Entrepreneurship Monitor (GEM) study
- New case on United States Postal Service
- Totally re-written case on Eclipse Aviation
- Updated boxes, examples, and cases

Finally, this edition continues to discuss contemporary strategic management theories and practices including, for example, corporate reputations, the ethics of profits, global corporate governance, offshoring versus outsourcing, employee layoff strategies, the hourglass phenomenon, and born-global firms. Of course, traditional strategy concepts such as competitive advantage, SWOT analysis, corporate growth, and strategy implementation are covered as well.

Emphasizes Strategy in Action

This book illustrates strategic managers and strategic management in action. How? By describing real managers and real organizations using strategic management. These "strategy in action" examples are featured throughout the chapters in the various boxed features. For instance, the "Strategic Management in Action" boxes describe organizations (all types and all sizes) and the unique strategies they're using. The "Strategic Management in Action—Global Perspective" boxes describe global organizations and the unique challenges they're facing and the unique strategies they're using. And additionally, strategic management concepts being discussed throughout the various chapters are "brought to life" through descriptions of organizations using those concepts as they do what they're in business to do.

Opportunities to Practice Strategic Management

I believe that *everyone* in an organization (not just the top management team) deals with strategy and as such needs to know what's involved with strategic management. What better way to do that than by "practicing" it? And this book provides several opportunities for students to do that.

Case analysis is an important part of most strategy courses, but not every case assignment needs to be a comprehensive case for students to learn something from it. At the beginning of each chapter, there's a "Strategic Management in Action" mini-case, which describes a company facing a strategic decision. (Some of these companies are MTV, Zara, Disney, Coke, JetBlue, Netflix, and 1-800-Got-Junk.) Using the discussion questions posed at the end of the chapter, students can analyze this company. It's a way for them to "practice" strategic management by evaluating what these companies have done, as well as a way to practice different parts of the strategic management process. In addition, three or four other mini-cases and discussion questions are found at the end of each chapter. With these four to five mini-cases at the end of every chapter, there's ample opportunity for students to work with the concepts and theories that are presented in each chapter and to apply them to an organizational situation.

In addition, most of the chapter boxes have suggestions for further research, review, or discussion. Another chapter feature—The Grey Zone—emphasizes the ethical dilemmas that strategic

decision makers often face and asks students to come up with suggestions about how they would handle that dilemma.

Finally, at the end of each chapter, there are several "You As Strategic Decision Maker: Building Your Skills" exercises that provide students with opportunities to practice strategic management by doing additional research, analysis, and writing.

Discussion of Strategies

When strategic decision makers must change the strategic direction of an organization and choose a different strategy, making that decision isn't enough. There are more steps to the process. That strategy also needs to be put into action (implemented) and the results of the strategy evaluated. This strategy book discusses that process of formulation, implementation, and evaluation as each strategy level (functional, competitive, and corporate) is presented. So, for instance, when discussing competitive strategies, you'll find information on *what* strategies strategic decision makers can choose from (for instance, cost leadership, differentiation, etc.), *how* those strategies are implemented (by using the organization's resources and capabilities and by using offensive and defensive moves), and *how* results are evaluated (what performance measures might be used to evaluate the effectiveness of the competitive strategies). This approach makes sense because students need to see all the aspects of a strategy from start to finish—from formulation to implementation to evaluation.

Writing Style

An academic textbook doesn't have to be boring. This book is unique in the market because it isn't boring. Its conversational and highly readable writing style makes learning about strategic management interesting and fun. Although an author's writing style is difficult to describe (especially your own!), I did write this text in a way that I hope makes the concepts and theories of strategy and strategic management clear and understandable—yet enjoyable! My teaching philosophy (and I've been teaching now for over 25 years, have won teaching awards at my university, and am consistently ranked toward the top of my department based on student evaluations) has been that learning *can be* fun. So, I write like I teach. But only you, the reader, can ultimately judge how well I've written the material.

Student Supplements

CourseSmart eTextbook

CourseSmart is an exciting new choice for students looking to save money. As an alternative to purchasing the print textbook, students can purchase an electronic version of the same content and save up to 50 percent of the suggested list price of the print text. With a CourseSmart e-textbook, students can search the text, make notes online, print out reading assignments that incorporate lecture notes, and bookmark important passages for later review. For more information, or to purchase access to the CourseSmart e-textbook version of this text, visit www.coursesmart.com.

Companion Web site

This text's Companion Web site at www.prenhall.com/coulter contains valuable resources for students, including an online study guide with multiple-choice, true/false, and Internet-based essay questions that accompany each chapter in the text.

Acknowledgments

I need to thank a number of people for their contributions to this book. Without them, you wouldn't be holding *Strategic Management in Action, Fifth Edition* in front of you. First of all are my students—current and past. Through my experiences teaching our Strategic Management course (most of them enjoyable!), I've developed my own personal philosophy of what seems to work and what doesn't. I learn things every semester from my students and love when they challenge me on topics (even if I am the textbook author!). And I hope they're learning from me. I'd also like to say "Thank You" to my department head, Barry Wisdom, and my now-retired college dean, Ron Bottin. Thank you for your ongoing support and encouragement of my authoring efforts. And then, of course, there are my departmental secretaries, Carole Hale and Anita Looney. Thank you for all you do to make my "school" life efficient and stress-free.

I would also like to recognize the individuals who provided me with thoughtful, intelligent, and thorough reviews of the first four editions of this book. I appreciate your willingness to provide your comments and ideas. I know the fifth edition is better because of the suggestions you have provided. Thank you. These individuals are:

Dr. Augustus Abbey, Morgan State University
Moses Acquaah, University of North Carolina at Greensboro
Dr. Yusaf H. Akbar, Southern New Hampshire University
Hamid Akbari, Northeastern Illinois University
Dr. A. D. Amar, Seton Hall University
Dr. William P. Anthony, Florida State University
Dr. Richard D. Babcock, University of San Francisco
Eugene Baten, Central Connecticut State University
Laquita Blockson, University of Northern Iowa
David T. Cadden, Quinnipiac University
Laurie Dahlin, Worcester State College
Roy D. Iraggi, New York City College of Technology
Dr. Jeryl L. Nelson, Wayne State College
Don Otto, Lindenwood University

Louis P. Panetta, California State University Monterey Bay
Richard Potter, University of Illinois at Chicago
Clint Relyea, Arkansas State University
Frederick R. Richards, Sacred Heart University
David F. Robinson, Indiana State University
Patrick L. Schultz, Texas Tech University
Ram Submaranian, Grand Valley State University
Jerry Thomas, Arapahoe Community College
Marvin Washington, Texas Tech University
Jack Wheeler, Indiana Wesleyan University
Andrzej Wlodarczyk, Concordia College

I'd also like to thank the management team at Prentice Hall. As usual, all of you have been super to work with. A big THANK YOU to my editor, Kim Norbuta, Acquisitions Editor for Management. Kim, thanks for all you've done and for your support and encouragement. I'd also like to especially thank Claudia Fernandes, who has been so amazing and just a joy to work with. Thank you Claudia for all you do. Then, there's the person who is responsible for the marketing of my book, Nikki Jones. Nikki . . . you're so creative and so energetic. Thank you for all of your hard work. Some of the other people who have been important to making this book come to life include Ana Jankowski, Bharath Parthasarathy, Charles Morris, and Kenny Beck. Thank you for all your diligent efforts in making this book what it is!

Next, I'd like to say a special thank you to a good friend and outstanding mentor—Steve Robbins, a textbook author icon. Steve, your friendship and advice continue to mean a lot to me. As I've said before, thanks for taking a chance on me and for showing me the ropes of textbook publishing. I know I'm a better writer because of you. Thanks!

Finally, I can't forget the three people in my life who mean the world to me—my wonderful and truly supportive husband Ron, and my now expanded family that includes two sons-in-law: Katie and Matt, and Sarah and James. Sarah and Katie, you have become the most amazing young women and I am so proud of you as I am of your "new" husbands! Although it's hard for a mom to "turn loose" of her kids, even adult "kids," I couldn't ask for two better young men to be part of our family. To all of you . . . thank you for being patient with me when I was focused on writing and for not complaining about the many take-out meals we've consumed and the many times I've not been able to go do something because I had a deadline. You all provide that much-needed balance to my life. And what I've been able to do is because of you ... my family. Thank you and I love you all!

Mary Coulter
Missouri State University

Introducing the Concepts

LEARNING OUTCOMES

1.1 *Explain why strategic management is important.*

1.2 *Explain what strategic management is.*

1.3 *Explain who's involved with strategic management.*

1.4 *Discuss the three important factors impacting strategic management today.*

Making Magic Happen

Magic happens at the happiest place on earth.[1] At least that's what the folks at the Walt Disney Company (Disney) work hard to make us believe. In fact, when Walt Disney, the company's founder and namesake, dedicated the original Disneyland on July 17, 1955, his first words were, "To all who come to this happy place, welcome." And that heartfelt "welcome" to guests, customers, and audiences encompasses its four major business units: studio entertainment, parks and resorts, consumer products, and media networks. However, the difficult business climate in 2008 and 2009 challenged Disney, as it did many other well-managed companies. CEO Bob Iger and his top management team are looking to conjure up their own magic; that is, to find the best way to strategically maneuver the company to prosper despite the environmental uncertainties.

As one of the world's largest entertainment and media companies, Disney has had a long record of successes. From the *High School Musical, Hannah Montana,* and *Jonas Brothers* phenomena to the ever-popular Mickey Mouse characters, the "Disney Difference" is noticeably apparent. What is the Disney Difference? It's "high-quality creative content, backed up by a clear strategy for maximizing that content's value across platforms and markets." From books, toys, and games to online media, sound tracks, and DVDs, Disney exploits its rich legacy of products through quality creative content and exceptional storytelling. Some of these products include, among many others, *The Lion King, Toy Story, Snow White and the Seven Dwarfs, The Jungle Book, Cars,* Disney-ABC Television, and ESPN programming. Although Disney is a U.S.-based company, its businesses span the globe, with operations in North America, Europe, Asia-Pacific, and Latin America. Its latest push is Russia, a large untapped media market, where it's planning a broadcast version of the Disney Channel. The president of Walt Disney International says, "We believe there is vast growth to come out of this market, despite the near-term economic turmoil." Despite its magical touch on all these different products and markets, just a few short years ago, Disney wasn't such a happy place.

When Bob Iger was named CEO in 2005, analysts believed that the Disney brand had become outdated. The perception: too much Disney product in the marketplace lacking the quality people expected. Iger said, "That combination—lack of quality and too much product—was really deadly." At that time also, the Disney brand was more tied to its history than it was to being contemporary and innovative. And, there was this sense that Disney's target audience was young and that its products couldn't possibly be of interest to older kids. Iger, who views himself as the steward of the entire Disney brand, immediately recognized the importance of leveraging the company's vast media content on different platforms. His strategic approach—the Disney Difference—had been working well until the economy slowed. The decline in global consumer spending made 2008 a tough year and 2009 even more precarious. Now, Iger and his top management team will have to use all the strategic tools they have to guide the company and keep the magic coming.

This chapter-opening case illustrates many of the complexities and challenges that today's managers face in doing strategic management, that is, in *managing strategically*. Disney's strategic initiatives will affect what its managers and employees do. Even managers at other entertainment and media companies such as Time Warner, Fox Entertainment, Paramount Parks, and Carnival Corporation have to decide whether and how to respond to Disney's strategic moves. Such strategic decisions are common in today's competitive environment for all types and sizes of organizations. Understanding the how and why of strategic management is what this book is about. By studying strategic management, you can begin to understand how employees manage various strategic issues. Then, whether you're a sales assistant in Orlando, an e-commerce manager in Paris, an account manager in Tokyo, or a human resources executive at Disney's headquarters in Burbank, California, you'll be able to recognize and understand strategic decisions. What kinds of changes might be needed? How might these changes affect my work or my team?

In this introductory chapter, you'll get a taste of what strategic management is about. It's divided into three major sections: why is strategic management important, what is strategic management, and who's involved with it. The one thing not included is the *how* aspect. Don't worry! That's what the rest of the text covers—how you actually *do* strategic management. First, though, we want to look at why strategic management is important.

LEARNING OUTCOME 1.1
Explain Why Strategic Management Is Important

You may be asking yourself, "Why is this stuff important to organizations and, even more to the point, why is it important to me? I'm majoring in accounting, and my goal is to make partner in an accounting firm. What do I care about strategic management?" Or, you may be a computer graphics major who wants to design e-business applications for an online retailer. You may feel that strategic management and managing strategically have little to do with you. However, one of the assumptions we make in this book is that *every*one in an organization plays a role in managing strategically. Because life after school for most of you means finding a job in order to have an income, this means you'll be working for some organization. (Even if you choose the entrepreneurial path, managing strategically is important, as we'll discuss in Chapter 8.) The very fact that you'll be working in some organization means you'll need to know about strategic management. Why? Because understanding how and why strategic decisions are made is important so you can do your job well and have your work valued and rewarded accordingly. But, strategic management also is important for other reasons that pertain more directly to the organization.

One significant reason why strategic management is important is that it does appear to make a difference in how well an organization performs. The most fundamental questions in strategy are why firms succeed or fail, and why firms have varying levels of performance. These questions have guided strategic management researchers for years.[2] Do we have answers to those questions? Does strategic management make a difference? Yes, it appears to! Studies have shown that organizations that use strategic management tend to have higher levels of performance, usually measured as the "bottom line" or profits.[3] So if it affects organizational performance, that would seem to be an important reason to know something about strategic management.

FOR YOUR INFORMATION

Corporate Reputations

Is having a good corporate reputation important? According to a global survey of financial analysts, it is. Over 90 percent agreed that if a company doesn't take care of the reputational aspects of its performance, it will suffer financially. These reputational aspects of performance included executing company strategy, transparent disclosure of information, and strong corporate governance. So what companies have "good" corporate reputations?

An annual survey conducted by the Reputation Institute assesses the reputations of the world's largest companies and identifies those with the best corporate reputations. The latest list (2008) includes:

Companies with the Best Corporate Reputations by Country [Overall Global Reputation Leader: Toyota Motor Corporation (Japan)]

Company	Country	Company	Country
Aceitera General Deheza	Argentina	Cosmote	Greece
		Tata Group	India
		Ferrero	Italy
Qantas Airways	Australia	Toyota Motor Corporation	Japan
Petrobas	Brazil	Grupo Bimbo S.A.	Mexico
Jean Coutu Group	Canada		
		Royal Philips Electronics	Netherlands
Empresas Copec S.A.	Chile		
		Coop	Norway
Haier	China	Grupa LOTOS	Poland
Novo Nordisk	Denmark	Grupo Sonae	Portugal
Kone Corp	Finland	Lukoil	Russia
L'Oreal	France	Sasol	South Africa
Bosch	Germany	LG Electronics Inc.	South Korea

Company	Country	Company	Country
El Corte Inglés	Spain	Marks & Spencer Group	United Kingdom
Ikea	Sweden		
Migros Cooperatives	Switzerland	Google	United States

A different ranking by *BusinessWeek* described those "influential companies that have devised winning strategies in their industries. The ones with the game-changing ideas, the greatest impact on consumers, and the bold tactics rivals emulate." That list of 10 companies is given below:

Company	Country
Apple	United States
JP Morgan Chase	United States
News Corp.	United States
Saudi Aramco	Saudi Arabia
Huawei	China
Unilever	United Kingdom
Wal-Mart	United States
Toyota	Japan
Monsanto	United States
Google	United States

Considering that there are thousands of businesses around the world, how did these companies "make these lists"? What will keep them there? Although they do many things well, strategic management is one thing they excel at.

Select one of these companies and research what it does and how it manages strategically.

Sources: Based on J. McGregor, "The World's Most Influential Companies," BusinessWeek, December 22, 2008, pp. 43–53; Reputation Institute [www.reputationinstitute.com/knowledge-center/hall-of-fame], "Most Respected Companies," December 22, 2008; R. G. Eccles, S. C. Newquist, and R. Schatz, "Reputation and Its Risks," Harvard Business Review, February 2007, pp. 104–114; R. Alsop, "How Boss's Deeds Buff a Firm's Reputation," Wall Street Journal, January 31, 2007, pp. B1+; and D. K. Basdeo, K. G. Smith, C. M. Grimm, V. P. Rindova, and P. J. Derfus, "The Impact of Market Actions on Firm Reputation," Strategic Management Journal, December 2006, pp. 1205–1219.

Another reason for studying strategic management is that organizations of all types and sizes face continually changing situations both externally and internally. Being able to cope with these uncertainties *and* achieve expected levels of performance is a real challenge. However, this is where strategic management comes in. The deliberate structure of the strategic management process guides organizational decision makers in examining important issues in order to determine the most appropriate strategic decisions and actions. In fact, studies of the strategy decision process suggest that the *way* strategy is developed can make a difference in performance. For instance, one study found that strategic decision makers who collected information and used analytical techniques made more effective strategic decisions than those who did not.[4] And that's what strategic management is all about—analyzing the situation and then developing and implementing appropriate strategies. Another study found that organizations that used several approaches to developing strategy outperformed those that used a single approach.[5] These studies show that having a structured, systematic approach—that is, the strategic management process—to cope with uncertain environments can positively affect organizational performance.

The final reason strategic management is important is because an organization's various divisions, departments, and work activities need to be coordinated and focused on achieving the organization's goals. The strategic management process fills this purpose. Employees from any organizational area—operations, marketing, accounting, and so on—*and* from any level or location formulate, implement, and evaluate strategies that they believe will help the organization perform at desired levels. Strategic management can ensure that their actions are coordinated.

Although strategic management is important, it may not solve all an organization's problems. Yet, given the fact that it's increasingly difficult to achieve high performance levels, the structured nature of the strategic management process forces organizational decision makers to at least think about relevant variables.

Learning Review: Learning Outcome 1.1

- State four reasons why strategic management is important.
- Describe what studies have shown about the relationship between strategic management and an organization's performance.

LEARNING OUTCOME 1.2
Explain What Strategic Management Is

The study of strategic management *is* one of the most exciting of all the traditional business areas! That's because everything done by an organization's employees has strategic implications. Whether it's the National Basketball Association looking to expand its market reach globally, Kodak's attempts to compete with digital technology, your local library's decision to use self-checkout procedures like those used in Wal-Mart, or Disney's global expansion plans, strategic management is involved. But, what *is* strategic management? Let's take a closer look.

The Basics of Strategy and Strategic Management

To begin to understand the basics of strategy and strategic management, simply look at the discount retail industry. Two of the industry's competitors—Wal-Mart and Kmart—have battled for market dominance since 1962, the year both companies were founded. The two chains have other similarities as well: names, store atmosphere, markets served, and organizational purpose. Yet, Wal-Mart's performance (financial and otherwise) has far surpassed that of Kmart. Wal-Mart is the world's largest and most successful retailer, and Kmart was the largest retailer ever to seek Chapter 11 bankruptcy protection (from which it emerged in 2003). Why the difference in performance? Remember our earlier statement of the two fundamental questions in strategy: why firms succeed or fail and why firms have varying levels of performance. Although researchers have examined different factors in trying to answer these questions, it boils down to the fact that organizations vary in how well they perform *because of differences in their strategic positions and differences in how they've used strategic management.*[6]

Definition of Strategy

Strategy has been defined in various ways. Early efforts ranged from defining strategies as integrated decisions, actions, or plans designed to set and achieve organizational goals to defining strategy as simply the outcome of the strategy formulation process.[7] We're defining **strategies** as an organization's goal-directed plans and actions that align ("match") its capabilities and resources with the opportunities and threats in its environment. Let's look at some key parts of this definition. First of all, strategy involves an organization's goals. The chosen strategy (or strategies) should help an organization achieve its goals. But just deciding on (formulating) a goal-directed strategy isn't enough. Strategy also involves goal-directed actions—that is, implementing the strategy. In other words, an organization's strategy involves not only *what* it wants to do, but *doing* it. Finally, the organization's strategies should take into account its key internal strengths (capabilities and resources) and external opportunities and threats. We consider this "matching" idea important to the concept of strategy and strategic management and you'll see it frequently referred to throughout the book.

Definition of Strategic Management

Strategic management is a process of analyzing the current situation, developing appropriate strategies, putting those strategies into action, and evaluating and changing those strategies as needed. We call these activities situation analysis, strategy formulation, strategy implementation, and strategy evaluation. (See Figure 1.1.)

Strategic Management in Action

IDEO, the design firm based in Palo Alto, California, is well known for its design innovations created for some of corporate America's best-known companies . . . the first computer mouse for Apple, the Leap chair for Steelcase, the I-Zone fun camera for Polaroid, a needle-free vaccine patch for biotech company Iomai, and the Swiffer CarpetFlick and stand-up toothpaste tube for Procter & Gamble, to name a few. And the company consistently wins global design awards for its innovative products. One strategy that IDEO uses to keep the innovative design ideas flowing is an unusual lending library called "the tech box, a freezer-size chest of drawers" where designers can find gadgets, materials, textiles, and artifacts to help them brainstorm and to come up with applications or materials they may not have thought of. The cocreators of the tech box, Dennis Boyle and Rickson Sun, say, "It's not a typical lending library, but people will use the tech box to cross-pollinate every new project."

In today's globally competitive environment, what might other companies learn from IDEO's unusual strategic approach?

Sources: *Based on L. Tischler, "A Designer Takes on His Biggest Challenge," Fast Company, February 2009, pp. 78+; P. Dvorak, "Businesses Take a Page from Design Firms," Wall Street Journal, November 10, 2008, p. B4; J. Wiscombe, "IDEO: The Innovation Factory," Workforce Management Online, February 13, 2007* [**www.workforce.com**]; *P. Kaihla, "Best-Kept Secrets of the World's Best Companies," Business 2.0, April 2006, p. 83; and C. Taylor, "School of Bright Ideas," Time Inside Business, April 2005, pp. A8–12.*

Figure 1.1

Basic Activities of Strategic Management

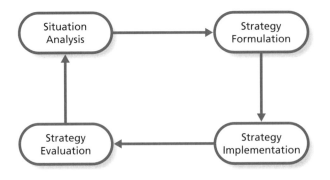

Strategic management has four characteristics. First, it is, by nature, *interdisciplinary*.[8] It doesn't focus on any one specific organizational area—such as human resources or production or marketing—but instead encompasses all the functional areas. Second, strategic management has an *external focus,* that is, it involves the interactions of the organization with its external environment. As organizational employees manage strategically, they look at the external environment to see how factors such as the economy, competitors, or market demographics might impact strategic decisions and actions. The third characteristic of strategic management is that it also has an *internal focus,* meaning it involves assessing the organization's resources and capabilities. Again, as organizational employees manage strategically, they're looking at the resources the organization has or doesn't have and at its capabilities—what it does or doesn't do well. Finally, strategic management involves the *future direction* of the organization. That "future" can mean weekly manufacturing decisions, yearly financial planning cycles, or significant long-term shifts in the organization's products and markets. Now, look back at our chapter-opening case on the Walt Disney Company. How is strategic management illustrated? As Bob Iger and his top management team evaluate the changing situation (assessing both external and internal information) and decide future actions to take, they'll be using strategic management. Let's look closer at how organizational employees do strategic management.

The Strategic Management Process

A process implies sequential and interrelated activities leading to some outcome. In the strategic management process, the interrelated activities—situation analysis, strategy formulation, strategy implementation, and strategy evaluation—result in a set of strategies

Strategic Management in Action

French toast stuffed with melted cream cheese. Yum! When CEO Julia Stewart first took over the top spot at IHOP, that's one of the first strategic changes she made. A small one, for sure, but the first of many that contributed to a successful turnaround of a struggling company. Now, Stewart has a much bigger challenge: turning around the nation's largest casual dining chain—Applebee's. With IHOP's acquisition of Applebee's in late 2007, Stewart, who used to be president of Applebee's before taking on the top job at IHOP, is on a mission to rebuild the company. Using many of the same strategies used in the IHOP transformation—better food, better advertising, and better atmosphere—she hopes to revive Applebee's reputation as the "friendly, neighborhood bar and grill it once was."

Go to Applebee's Web site **[www.applebees.com]** and look for the section on "Investors." Do some research on the strategies it's pursuing. Make a bulleted list of these strategies and be prepared to share your list with the class. What do you think of these strategies?

Source: *Based on E. B. York, "BK Menu Give Casual Dining Reason to Worry,"* Advertising Age, *November 17, 2008, p. 12; M. Sanson, "It's Time to Make Your Place Special,"* Restaurant Hospitality, *September 2008, p. 6; J. Adamy and J. S. Lublin, "Investors Bruise Applebee's Parent,"* Wall Street Journal, *September 10, 2008, p. B1; and B. Horovitz, "New CEO Puts Comeback on the Menu at Applebee's,"* USA Today, *April 28, 2008, pp. 1B+.*

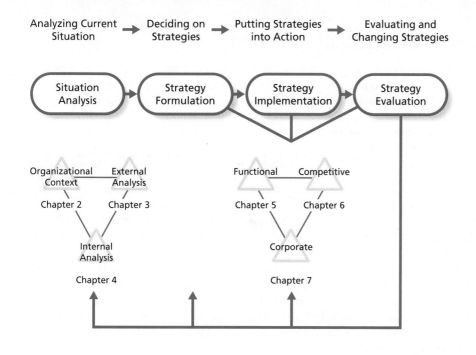

Figure 1.2

Strategic Management in Action

the organization uses in doing its business. Figure 1.2 illustrates this process. As organizational members manage strategically, these are the activities they're doing. What's involved with each?

Situation Analysis

Before deciding on an appropriate strategic direction or response, organizational employees need to analyze the current situation. A **situation analysis** involves scanning and evaluating the current organizational context, external environment, and organizational environment. In Chapter 2, we'll explore the organizational context by looking at the new economy, the role of stakeholders, the dynamics of change, and the role of organizational culture and mission. In Chapter 3, we'll look at what an external analysis is and how it's done. Finally, in Chapter 4, we'll study the steps involved in doing an internal analysis and look at an organization's resources, distinctive capabilities, and core competencies. Each of these—the context, the external environment, and the internal environment—provides important clues to the organization's current situation.

Strategy Formulation

Strategy formulation is developing and then choosing appropriate strategies (as guided by the results of the situation analysis). Figure 1.3 summarizes the three main types of strategies.

Functional strategies (also called **operational strategies**) are the goal-directed plans and actions of the organization's functional areas. The most common functional areas include production-operations (manufacturing), marketing, research and development, human resources, financial-accounting, and information systems technology and support. But keep in mind that each organization has its own unique functions. For instance, your school's functional areas might include academics, student services, financial services, facilities management, alumni relations, and athletics. A retail store's functional areas might include purchasing, merchandising display, floor sales, personnel, and store operations. We'll discuss functional strategies in Chapter 5.

The **competitive strategies** (also called **business strategies**) are the goal-directed plans and actions that are concerned with how an organization competes in a specific

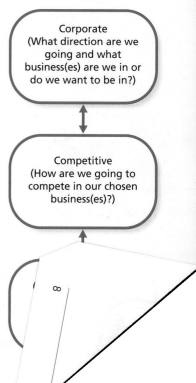

Figure 1.3

Types of Strategies

Corporate
(What direction are we going and what business(es) are we in or do we want to be in?)

Competitive
(How are we going to compete in our chosen business(es)?)

The grocery industry is extremely competitive! From online grocery stores to "destination supermarkets" to the aggressive pricing strategies of the world's largest retailer (Wal-Mart), each industry competitor is looking for the strategic approaches that will keep customers browsing the aisles and filling the cash registers. Talk about the need for some effective competitive strategies! And no one knows that better than The Kroger Company **[www.kroger.com]**, the nation's largest "pure" grocery chain.

Go to Kroger's Web site and find the "About the Company" section. Browse through the information for the various store formats, company beliefs, mission, and so on. What types of things is Kroger doing to compete in the grocery industry? Make a bulleted list describing its strategies.

Sources: Based on C. Rohwedder, "Tesco Studies Hard for U.S. Debut," Wall Street Journal, June 28, 2007, pp. B1+; D. Koenig, "Grocery Merger Issue Heats Up," USA Today, June 20, 2007, p. 5B; G. McWilliams, "Not Copying Wal-Mart Pays Off for Grocers," Wall Street Journal, June 6, 2007, pp. B1+; D. Leonhardt, "Filling Pantries Without a Middleman," New York Times Online, November 22, 2006; J. Hibbard, "Put Your Money Where Your Mouth Is," BusinessWeek, September 18, 2006, pp. 61–63; and M. Puente, "Aisles and Aisles of Good Times," USA Today, April 17, 2006, pp. D1+.

business or industry. For instance, Abercrombie & Fitch has strategies to compete with American Eagle Outfitters, Gap, J. Crew, and other specialty clothing retailers. Look back at our chapter-opening case and consider how Disney might compete with other entertainment and media companies. The competitive strategies address the competitive advantages an organization currently has or wants to develop. All aspects of competitive strategies and actions are explored in Chapter 6.

Corporate strategies are goal-directed plans and actions that are concerned with the choices of what business(es) to be in and what to do with those businesses. For instance, FedEx's decision to acquire Kinko's is an example of a corporate strategy. Other examples would be decisions PepsiCo makes regarding its various divisions—PepsiCo Beverages North America (Pepsi Cola, Aquafina, Mountain Dew, Tropicana, Gatorade, etc.), Frito-Lay North America (snack foods), Quaker Oats North America (prepared foods), and PepsiCo International. When PepsiCo changed its portfolio of businesses—as it did when it spun off its fast-food division (Taco Bell, Pizza Hut, and KFC) as a separate business in 1997 or when it acquired sparkling beverage companies IZZE and Naked Juice in 2006—these actions involved corporate strategy. But what about organizations like Pepsi's major competitor, the Coca-Cola Company, that don't have a portfolio of different businesses? What do their corporate strategies entail? In those instances, corporate strategy isn't so much concerned with the optimal mix of business(es) as it is with plans and actions regarding the future direction of the organization. Corporate strategy will be discussed in Chapter 7.

Strategy Implementation

It's not enough to formulate great strategies. Those strategies have to be implemented. **Strategy implementation** is putting the various strategies into action. Because *how* a strategy is implemented should be considered as it's formulated, we'll be looking at that as we discuss each type of strategy.

Strategy Evaluation

Strategy evaluation involves evaluating both the outcomes of the strategies and how they've been implemented. If they don't measure up to expectations or strategic goals, then the strategy itself or its implementation may need to be modified. We'll also cover evaluation as we discuss each type of strategy.

Strategic Management Process in Action

You need to understand that although we've described the strategic management process by isolating each step in order to study it, in reality it's a continual cycle that may not always follow the stated sequence. That usually only happens when strategic decision makers pursue an entirely different strategy or new strategic direction. Otherwise, strategic management in action involves adjustments to organizational strategies currently in effect. That may mean evaluating the strategy first, then analyzing the situation before formulating and implementing a new strategy. The point is that the way organizations actually do strategic management doesn't always happen according to a prescribed sequence, but that doesn't minimize the importance of the specific steps in the process.

Looking at Strategic Management's Past

We look at the history of strategic management to help us better understand how and why today's managers do strategic management and perhaps even for clues as to why organizational performance levels vary. Strategic management's history is quite interesting, ranging from great military battles to current research to better understand why firms succeed or fail.

Strategy's Military Roots

Strategy can be seen in historical decisions and actions used by military organizations. (The word *strategy* itself comes from the Greek word *strategos,* or military commander.) Historical accounts tell us that a country's military decision makers designed battlefield strategies to gain an edge on the enemy. They would try to exploit the enemy's weak spots and attack them where they were most vulnerable, thus giving the aggressor the best chance of succeeding. Even today, military historians enjoy analyzing great battles in terms of the

The United States' leading military academies teach the "nine principles of war." These principles have stood the test of time even though the environment of war has changed dramatically. The marketplace is often viewed as a "battleground," meaning these principles might be useful in developing an organization's competitive strategy. What are these nine principles?

- **The objective:** Direct every operation toward a clearly defined, decisive, and attainable objective.
- **The offensive:** Seize, retain, and exploit the initiative.
- **Unity of command:** Forces must be under one commander with full authority and responsibility.
- **Mass:** Concentrate combat power at the decisive place and time.
- **Economy of force:** Allocate only the essential minimum of forces to secondary efforts.
- **Maneuver:** Place the enemy in a position of disadvantage through the flexible application of combat power.

- **Surprise:** Strike at the enemy at a time or a place that's unexpected.
- **Security:** Never allow the enemy to acquire an unexpected advantage.
- **Simplicity:** Prepare clear, uncomplicated plans and clear, concise orders to ensure thorough understanding.

Relate these nine "war" principles to what an organization does as it "battles" in the marketplace. Can they be applied? Explain. Some military experts are now proposing 12 principles of war that better reflect today's environment. Do some research on these and relate them to business organizations. (Hint: see citations below.)

Sources: *Based on Department of Military Science, Worcester Polytechnic Institute* **[http://www.wpi.edu/Academics/Depts/MilSci/Resources/prinwar.html]**, *"Nine Principles of War," December 30, 2008; Lt. Cmdr. C. E. van Avery, "12 New Principles of War,"* Armed Forces Journal **[http://www.armedforcesjournal.com]**, *July 2007; W. C. Finnie, "A Four Cycle Approach to Strategy Development and Implementation,"* Strategy & Leadership, *January/February 1997, p. 28; and C. von Clausewitz, The Most Important Principles of the Art of War to Complete My Course of Instruction for His Royal Highness the Crown Prince (<u>German</u>: Die wichtigsten Grundsätze des Kriegführens zur Ergänzung meines Unterrichts bei Sr. Königlichen Hoheit dem Kronprinzen), 1812; translated and edited by Hans W. Gatzke as "Principles of War," September 1942, The Military Service Publishing Company.*

strategies that each side used and trying to interpret why some were successful whereas others failed. And popular games such as Battleship, chess, tic-tac-toe, and checkers are based on the idea of a "strategy." Most involve figuring out what your opponent is doing and taking actions based on that information. The process of analyzing the situation and crafting, implementing, and evaluating an appropriate response is common, although we may not specifically think of it in strategy terms.

Academic Origins of Strategic Management.[9]

As a field of study, strategic management is relatively young. Much of its theoretical foundation comes from economics and organization studies. Although mainstream economic theory, with its emphasis on rationality, predictability, and similarity, may not quite fit the realities of strategic management, it has provided a way to explore the role of management decisions and strategic choices. In addition, early organizational studies by Frederick Taylor (scientific management), Max Weber (bureaucratic organizations), and Chester Barnard (administrative functions and the organization as an open system) provided important knowledge about efficient and effective organizations and the role that managers played.

Strategic Planning and Strategic Management Emerge.[10]

During the 1960s, organization theorists searched for explanations of organizational differences in functioning and performance. The belief that there was one correct way to manage in all situations was replaced by contingency approaches, which proposed that each organizational situation was different and that the best way of managing depended on the situation. Also, during this time, three classic strategy books—Alfred Chandler's *Strategy and Structure*, Igor Ansoff's *Corporate Strategy*, and a Harvard textbook, *Business Policy: Text*

Six of the colorful, rectangular LEGO bricks can be combined to create over 915 million different arrangements. Yes, these simple, durable, and low-tech toys that most children probably have played with at one time or another, are quite versatile . . . and quite traditional. LEGOs were named "Toy of the Century" by *Fortune* magazine and by the British Toy Retailers Association in 2000. Despite the numerous imaginative ways children can play with them, such a traditional toy has found it tough going in today's toy market that's dominated by videogames and computer wizardry. Company CEO Jørgen Vig Knudstorp—the first executive to come from outside the founding family—recognized that the survival of LEGO depended on his making some radical changes. One change was cutting jobs (more than 1,000 at company headquarters in Billund, Denmark). Another was outsourcing manufacturing to cheaper locations such as the Czech Republic.

But Knudstorp also recognized that while the familiar LEGO bricks were the company's past *and* its future, the company could not ignore the digital age. Now, kids use the LEGO Digital Designer to create their own 3D models. And its Mindstorm Robotics Invention Kit is also popular with kids. Another challenge facing the company is the downturn in toy sales in the current economic climate.

What do you think of LEGO's strategies? How might strategic management be useful?

Sources: *Based on K. Oliver, E. Samakh, and P. Heckmann, "Rebuilding LEGO, Brick by Brick," Strategy & Business Online, Autumn 2007 [**www.strategy-business.com**]; C. W. Boynton, "LEGO Picks Up the Pieces After Layoffs and Moves," New York Times Online, April 15, 2007; J. Pisani, "The Making . . . of a LEGO," BusinessWeek.com, November 29, 2006; J. Scanlon, "Invasion of the DIY Robots," BusinessWeek Online, September 7, 2006; N. D. Schwartz, "One Brick at a Time," Fortune, June 12, 2006, pp. 45–46; A. D'Innocenzio, "1,200 Jobs to Go as LEGO Restructures," Springfield, Missouri, News-Leader, June 1, 2006, p. 5B; "For LEGO, An Online Lifeline?" BusinessWeek Online, August 23, 2005; and J. M. Olsen, "Toy Maker LEGO Moves Production to Czech Republic," USA Today Online, September 1, 2005.*

and Cases by Learned, Christensen, Andrews, and Guth—were instrumental in establishing many basic concepts of strategic management and in distinguishing strategic management as a separate academic field.

A dichotomy developed during the 1970s and 1980s as researchers tried to understand and describe strategic management.[11] Process researchers studied strategic management from the perspective of "how" strategy is formed, that is, the process. Content researchers studied the "what," or the content, of a strategic decision. Despite their differences in perspective, both process and content researchers continue to try to understand the relationship between strategic decisions and organizational performance.

Learning Review: Learning Outcome 1.2

- Define strategy and strategic management.
- Describe the strategic management process.
- Describe the three types of organizational strategies.
- Explain the historical evolution of strategic management.

LEARNING OUTCOME 1.3
Explain Who's Involved with Strategic Management

As we said earlier, one assumption we make is that strategic management isn't simply the responsibility of an organization's top managers. People at *all* organizational levels play a role in developing, implementing, and changing strategy. Strategic management is just as important for the bank teller at a drive-through facility as it is for the bank's executive vice president who's in charge of commercial loans. Think back to our definition of strategic management—analyzing the current situation, deciding strategies, putting those strategies into action, evaluating those strategies, and then modifying or changing those strategies as needed—and you can begin to see how each and every person is involved. The difference is the scope of the individual's strategic actions. For instance, the bank teller is concerned with issues (functional strategies) that arise at the drive-through facility; the bank's executive vice president is more concerned with strategic issues that arise at the competitive or corporate level (or both). Let's look at the three main groups who play key roles in the strategic management process: the board of directors, the top management team, and other strategic managers and organizational employees.

The Board of Directors

The **board of directors** is an elected group that represents a company's shareholders. A board's legal obligation is to represent the shareholders (stockholders) and protect their interests. It is empowered to act on the shareholders' behalf in overseeing the management of the company and plays a significant role in corporate governance—that is, in governing the decisions and actions of the organization. Because this is an important issue for today's strategic managers, we'll discuss it extensively in the last section of this chapter. Table 1.1 lists some of the responsibilities of a board of directors. Even not-for-profit organizations often have a board of advisers. In fact, your college may have a governing board that evaluates top management decisions and perhaps even makes recommendations as far as future strategic decisions and actions.

How much a board is involved in formulating and implementing strategy has always been a thorny issue.[12] The board's role has been approached from two opposing perspectives. In those organizations in which the board acted in an *approving role,* the top management team would keep board members informed of strategies, on which the board might have given limited input, but the board's role was primarily to "approve" the strategies. However, that's not what we're seeing with today's boards. Significant changes in legal mandates, investor activism, and corporate strategy have changed the role of many boards in the strategic management process. Today's board members often find themselves taking a much more *involved role* in the strategic management process by initiating strategies as well as overseeing the implementation and evaluation of the strategies.

The Role of Top Management

There's no doubt that an organization's top managers play a significant role in the strategic management process. An organization's top manager is typically the chief executive officer (CEO). This person (Bob Iger in our chapter-opening case) usually works with a top

Table 1.1

Typical Board Responsibilities

- Review and approve strategic goals and plans
- Review and approve organization's financial standards and policies
- Ensure integrity of organization's financial controls and reporting system
- Approve an organizational philosophy
- Monitor organizational performance and regularly review performance results
- Select, evaluate, and compensate top-level managers
- Develop management succession plans
- Review and approve capital allocations and expenditures
- Monitor relations with shareholders and other key stakeholders

Other responsibilities may be assigned depending on the unique culture and needs of the organization.

Source: *Based on K. McG. Sullivan and H. J. Gregory, "Board Self-Assessment," The Corporate Board, November–December 1995, p. 7.*

"Heat shield." That's the new role of Bonnie G. Hill, the longest-serving director on Home Depot's board. Company shareholders had been quite vocal about their unhappiness with the previous CEO's pay and performance. Upon his departure, Hill met with dozens of stockholders, listened to them, and eased their anger by persuading fellow directors to link the pay of current CEO Frank Blake more closely to the company's performance. Her approach characterizes an emerging breed of directors who want a closer connection with shareholders. Board members at Pfizer, Hewlett-Packard, and UnitedHealth Group, among other companies, have also taken similar approaches. Some executives still think that such increased dialogue is a bad idea as board members "run the risk of having discussions that undermine the CEO." However, with increased shareholder activism and changed corporate governance, such arguments may not carry much weight.

What do you think of this idea of directors reaching out to shareholders? What advantages and drawbacks might there be from such a practice for both the company and board members?

Sources: Based on J. S. Lublin, "New Breed of Directors Reaches Out to Shareholders," Wall Street Journal, July 21, 2008, p. B4; and J. Weber, R. O. Crockett, M. Arndt, B. Grow, and N. Byrnes, "How the Best Boards Stay Clued In," BusinessWeek, June 27, 2005, p. 40.

management team that includes other executive or senior managers such as a chief operating officer (COO), chief financial officer (CFO), chief information officer (CIO), and other individuals who may have various titles. Traditional descriptions of the CEO's role in strategic management include being the "chief" strategist, structural architect, and developer of the organization's information/control systems.[13] Other descriptions of the strategic role of the chief executive include key decision maker, visionary leader, political actor, monitor and interpreter of environment changes, and strategy designer.[14]

No matter how the top management's job is described, you can be certain that from their perspective at the organization's upper levels, it's like no other job in the organization. By definition, top managers are ultimately responsible for every decision and action of every organizational employee. One important role that top managers play is that of strategic leader. As you're probably well aware, leadership is a perennially popular management topic. Libraries and bookstores have numerous books on the subject. Type *leadership* in a Web search engine and you'll get millions of hits (157 million at Google). Organizational researchers study leadership in relation to strategic management because an organization's top managers must provide effective strategic leadership. What is **strategic leadership?** It's the ability to anticipate, envision, maintain flexibility, think strategically, and work with others in the organization to initiate changes that will create a viable and valuable future for the organization.[15] How can top managers provide effective strategic leadership? Six key dimensions have been identified.[16] (See Figure 1.4.) These dimensions include determining the organization's purpose or vision, exploiting and maintaining the organization's core competencies, developing the organization's human capital, creating and sustaining a strong organizational culture, emphasizing ethical organizational decisions and practices, and establishing appropriately balanced organizational controls. Each dimension describes an important part of the strategic management process.

Other Managers and Organizational Employees

Although an organization's top managers have several important strategic leadership responsibilities in the strategic management process, managers and employees at other levels throughout the organization also are important to the process. What are some of

Figure 1.4

*Effective Strategic
Leadership*

their strategic responsibilities?[17] One is strategy implementation. They're the individuals putting the strategies into action. They might be supervising or managing the work of others and even may be personally doing work as well. For example, think back to our opening case. Someone had to design the stage set for the *Hannah Montana* show. Someone had to oversee the creation of the characters in *Toy Story*. And, someone had to hire employees for the new Russian version of the Disney Channel. As Disney continues to adjust to its changing environment, new strategies will have to be put into action. That's another role that managers and organizational employees play.

The other thing that these individuals likely do is evaluating whether the strategies are working. If the strategies aren't helping an organization achieve its goals, then they need to be changed. Although top management may establish the guidelines for evaluating performance, it's often the managers and organizational employees who do the evaluating and follow-up.

- Explain the role of the board of directors in strategic management.

- Discuss how top managers can be effective strategic leaders.

- Describe the role of other managers and organizational employees in strategy.

LEARNING OUTCOME 1.4
Discuss the Three Important Factors Impacting Strategic Management Today

Managing strategically in today's world isn't easy! We want to look at three important issues affecting strategic management. These include the global economy and globalization, corporate governance, and e-business.

The Global Economy and Globalization

Over the last quarter century, globalization has been an important component of many company's strategies. National borders became irrelevant. For instance, over two-thirds of Avon's revenues come from outside North America. Nissan, a Japanese firm, makes cars in the United States and in Mexico. Lend Lease Corporation, Australia's leading real-estate company, built the Bluewater shopping complex in Kent, England, and contracted with Coca-Cola to build all its bottling plants in Southeast Asia. McDonald's, a U.S. business, now has more than 1,000 outlets in China. Korea's largest car company, Hyundai, chose to build its first American plant in Georgia. Swiss company ABB Ltd. constructed power-generating plants in Malaysia, South Korea, China, and Indonesia. Although globalization has offered significant business opportunities, today's economic climate is challenging even the best-managed global companies. Doing business globally has never been easy, but the next few years are likely to be even more difficult as the World Bank forecasts a world economy on the brink of a rare global recession.[18] In addition to the challenges of managing strategically in an economic climate fraught with reduced consumer demand, restricted access to capital, and severe pressures to cut costs, strategic decision makers face two additional ones: the openness of globalization and significant cultural differences.

The push to go global has been widespread. Advocates praise the economic and social benefits that come from globalization. Yet, it has created challenges because of the openness that's necessary for it to work. For instance, the public outcry when a Dubai company proposed acquiring certain U.S. ports highlighted the concerns and fears (real or perceived) that having an open economy and open borders entails.[19] Some have wondered whether the "openness" of globalization has made people more sensitive to political and cultural differences and thus increased the threats of attack by those who misunderstand or disagree. Although globalization is meant to open up trade and to break down the geographical barriers separating countries, opening up means just that—being open to the good *and* the bad. Current realities illustrate another challenge from the openness of globalization— the economic interdependence of trading countries. When one country's economy falters, it can have a domino effect on other countries with which it does business. There are mechanisms in place for dealing with such situations, but they may not always be able to prevent a crisis. One such mechanism is the **World Trade Organization (WTO),** which is a global organization of 153 countries whose goal is to help organizations conduct business by enacting trade agreements that are negotiated and ratified by the vast majority of the world's trading nations.[20] Another is the **World Bank Group,** which is a cooperative of 185 member countries that provides vital financial and technical assistance to developing countries around the world. The goal of the World Bank Group is to promote long-term economic development and poverty reduction by providing members with technical and financial support.[21] Finally, the **International Monetary Fund (IMF)** is an organization of 185 countries that promotes international monetary cooperation and provides member countries with policy advice, temporary loans, and technical assistance to establish and maintain financial stability and strengthen economies.[22]

The challenges from openness aren't the only ones that strategic managers face globally. Serious challenges also come from fundamental cultural differences between countries—differences that encompass traditions, history, religious beliefs, and deep-seated values. Capitalism's emphasis on profits, efficiency, and growth may be generally accepted in the United States, Australia, and Hong Kong, but isn't nearly as popular in places like France, the Middle East, or the Scandinavian countries. There are those who think that globalization is simply a euphemism for "Americanization"—that is, U.S. cultural values and business philosophy slowly taking over the world.[23] Proponents of Americanization hope others see how progressive, efficient, industrious, and free U.S. society and businesses are and want to emulate that way of doing things. However, critics claim that this attitude of the "almighty American dollar wanting to spread the American way to every single country" has created many problems.[24] Although history is filled with clashes between civilizations, what's unique about this time period is the speed and ease with which misunderstandings and disagreements erupt and escalate. The Internet, television and other media, and global air travel have brought the good and bad of American entertainment, products, and behaviors to every corner of the globe. For those who don't like what Americans do, say, or believe, this may lead to resentment, dislike, distrust, and even outright hatred. Successful strategic management under such conditions requires being sensitive to cultural and political differences. Strategic decision makers need to be aware of how their decisions and actions will be viewed, not only by those who may agree, but more important, by those who may disagree. Organizations are likely to have to adjust their strategies to accommodate increasingly diverse views.

Strategic Management in Action   THE GLOBAL PERSPECTIVE

As the world's number one food company, Switzerland - based Nestlé has revenues of more than $95.9 billion a year from the global sales of its over 8,000 brands—brands ranging from Nescafé instant coffee and Alpo dog food to KitKat candy bars and Jenny Craig weight loss centers. Nestlé's global strategy has been to concentrate on value-added products. In addition, Chairman Peter Brabeck-Letmathe has implemented some strategic changes including streamlining worldwide operations by improving information technology and centralizing purchasing and other corporate activities; strengthening key segments by acquiring competitors such as Finnish dairy company

Valid's Valiojäätelöö's ice cream business and Greece's Delta Ice Cream; eliminating less profitable activities such as tomato canning and pasta production and cocoa processing; and developing new products such as nutritionally enhanced cosmetics and toothpastes. Brabeck hopes that these strategies will deliver robust sales growth and cost savings that will give Nestlé stronger operating margins.

However, as a global company, what types of strategic challenges might Brabeck face in today's economic climate?

Sources: Based on "World's Largest Corporations," Fortune, July 21, 2008, pp. 165–174; and C. Matlack, "Nestlé is Starting to Slim Down at Last," BusinessWeek, October 27, 2003, pp. 56–57.

Corporate Governance

Enron. Tyco. Worldcom. These are just a few of the more notorious names from the corporate financial scandals that destroyed billions of dollars in shareholder value during a time span of approximately 18 months in 2001 and 2002. Because directors at these companies missed or ignored organizational problems, many involving fraudulent accounting schemes, U.S. legislators vowed to reform corporate governance. A significant part of this reform was the passage of the **Sarbanes-Oxley Act,** a U.S. law designed to protect investors by improving the accuracy and reliability of corporate disclosures.

What is **corporate governance?** It's the way a corporation is governed or the "determination of the broad uses to which organizational resources will be deployed and the resolution of conflicts among the myriad participants in organizations."[25] In other words, corporate governance involves how a corporation uses its resources and protects stakeholders' interests. Sarbanes-Oxley mandated two areas of corporate governance reform: the role of the board of directors and the type and scope of financial reporting.

The Role of Boards of Directors

The original purpose of a corporate board of directors was to ensure that there was a group, independent from management that looked out for the interests of the owners (i.e., the shareholders) who were not involved in the day-to-day operations of the corporation. What actually happened in too many organizations was that board members often enjoyed a cozy relationship in which board members "took care" of the CEO and the CEO "took care" of board members. With the passage of Sarbanes-Oxley, this arrangement changed and demands on board members of publicly traded companies increased considerably.[26] The Business Roundtable, an association of CEOs of leading corporations, outlined a set of governance principles for boards and top managers (see Table 1.2) that it feels are critical "to the functioning of the modern public corporation and the integrity of the public markets."[27]

Financial Reporting

In addition to expanding the role of board members, Sarbanes-Oxley also called for more disclosure and transparency of financial information. One requirement was the certification of the accuracy of financial statements, which senior managers now must do by signing off on them. Another aspect of the financial reporting requirement, which has created some special problems for companies, especially smaller public companies, is Section 404.[28] This brief passage (a mere 168 words) dealt with the establishment and auditing of internal

---

Strategic Management in Action   THE GLOBAL PERSPECTIVE

Corporate governance isn't a concern just for U.S. companies. Governance Metrics International (GMI), a corporate governance research and ratings agency **[www.gmiratings.com]**, rates countries on their governance structures and procedures. It uses six broad categories of analysis: board accountability, financial disclosure and internal controls, executive compensation, shareholder rights, ownership base, and takeover provisions. In addition, GMI looks at corporate behavior and social responsibility. What countries were rated on top? Ireland had the highest overall average rating, followed by Canada, United Kingdom, Australia, and the United States. Chile had the lowest overall average rating, followed by Indonesia, Mexico, China, and Japan.

Source: *Based on GMI, GMI Country Rankings, Governance Metrics International (New York), September 23, 2008,* **[www.gmiratings.com]**.

Table 1.2

Guiding Principles of Corporate Governance

1. The primary duty of a board of directors is to *select a CEO* and to *oversee the CEO and senior management* in the competent and ethical operation of the corporation on a day-to-day basis.
2. It is the responsibility of the management to *operate the corporation in an effective and ethical manner* to produce value for shareholders.
3. It is the responsibility of management to *produce in a timely manner financial statements that fairly represent* the financial condition and results of corporate operations.
4. It is the responsibility of the board to *engage an independent accounting firm to audit the financial statements,* issue an opinion that those statements are in accordance with Generally Accepted Accounting Principles, and oversee the corporation's relationship with the outside auditor.
5. It is the responsibility of the board to *play a leadership role in shaping the corporate governance of the corporation.*
6. It is the responsibility of the board to *adopt and oversee the implementation of compensation* policies, establish goals for performance-based compensation, and determine the compensation of the CEO and senior management.
7. It is the responsibility of the board to *respond appropriately to shareholders' concerns.*
8. It is the responsibility of the corporation to *deal with its employees, customers, suppliers, and other constituencies* in a fair and equitable manner.

Source: *Based on Principles of Corporate Governance,* Business Roundtable *(Washington, DC),* November 2005.

financial controls. Creating the control systems and hiring independent auditors to attest to managers' internal controls have proved to be very expensive. Businesses claim that countless employee hours and millions of dollars have been spent documenting things that many felt had nothing to do with the integrity of their financial statements. In response to a push by business lobbyists, securities and accounting regulators have proposed more flexible guidelines to help companies and auditors interpret Section 404 in a way that saves them time and money.[29]

Strategic Management in an E-Business World

6.3 million. That's the record number of items sold on one day in December 2008 at Web retailer Amazon.com.[30] Although overall online spending declined in 2008's tough retail climate, e-commerce and e-business are not dead (or dying). Each of us—including strategic decision makers—functions in an e-business world today. Although critics have questioned the viability of Internet-based companies, especially after the dot-com collapse in 2000 and 2001, e-business is here to stay and offers many strategic advantages.[31]

E-business is using information and communication technologies to support all the activities of a business. It includes **e-commerce,** which is essentially the retailing side of e-business. For instance, organizations such as Dell and Blue Nile are engaged in e-commerce because they sell items over the Internet.

Not every organization is, or needs to be, a total e-business. Instead, strategic decision makers might use any of three different strategic approaches to e-business. The first approach is an e-business *enhanced* organization, a traditional organization that sets up e-business capabilities, usually e-commerce, while maintaining its traditional structure. Many *Fortune 500*-type organizations have evolved into e-businesses using this approach. They use information and communication technology to *enhance* (not to replace) their traditional ways of doing business. For instance, the online division of Wal-Mart Stores, a traditional bricks-and-mortar retailer with thousands of physical stores worldwide, is intended to expand, not replace, the company's main source of revenue.

Another approach to e-business is an e-business *enabled* organization that uses information and communication technology to perform its traditional business functions better, but not to sell anything. In other words, this technology *enables* organizational members to do their work more efficiently and effectively. Numerous organizations use electronic linkages to communicate with employees, customers, or suppliers and to support them with information. For instance, Levi Strauss uses its Web site to interact with customers, providing them the latest information about the company and its products, but not to sell the jeans. It also uses an **intranet,** an internal organizational communication system that uses Internet technology and is accessible only by organizational employees, to communicate with its global workforce.

The last approach to e-business involvement is when an organization becomes a total e-business. Organizations such as Amazon.com, Google, Yahoo, and eBay are total e-business organizations. Their whole approach to business is based on the Internet and other information and communication technologies. When an organization is (or becomes) a total e-business, it completely transforms the way it does its work.

Concluding Thought

No matter where in an organization you work or what your job is, you'll find yourself involved in some way with strategic management. Whether your career goal is to be part of a top management team or whether you plan to apply your academic training in some functional area of the organization, you'll be affected by and have an effect on the organization's strategic management process. This chapter is just the beginning of your exciting journey to understand strategic management!

Learning Review: Learning Outcome 1.4

- Discuss how the global economy and globalization affect strategic management.
- Explain the concept of corporate governance and how it impacts strategic management.
- Describe the three approaches to e-business.

the bottom line

Learning Outcome 1.1: Explain why strategic management is important.

- *Individually:* you will be evaluated on and rewarded for doing your job well, which means understanding how and why strategic decisions are made.
- *Organizationally:* can make a difference in how well an organization performs; helps deal with continually changing situations; and helps in coordinating various divisions, functions, and work activities.

Learning Outcome 1.2: Explain what strategic management is.

- *Strategies:* an organization's goal-directed plans and actions that align its capabilities and resources with the opportunities and threats in its environment.
- *Strategic management:* a process of analyzing the current situation; developing appropriate strategies; putting the strategies into action; and evaluating, modifying, or changing the strategies as needed.
- *Four characteristics:* interdisciplinary, external focus, internal focus, and future-oriented.
- *Strategic management process: situation analysis* (scanning and evaluating the current organizational context and external and internal environments); *strategy formulation* (developing and then choosing appropriate strategies); *strategy implementation* (putting strategies into action); and *strategy evaluation* (evaluating the implementation and outcomes of strategies).
- *Types of organizational strategies: functional* or *operational* (goal-directed plans and actions of the organization's functional areas); *competitive* or *business* (goal-directed plans and actions concerned with how an organization competes); and *corporate* (goal-directed plans and actions concerned with the choices of what businesses to be in and what to do with those businesses).
- *Reality:* process may not always follow the stated sequence, but activities are still completed.
- *Background:* military strategies (exploiting enemy's weak spots and attacking them where most vulnerable); academic origins (economics and organizational theory).
- *Emergence of strategic planning and strategic management:* 1960s, when researchers began looking for explanations of organizational differences in performance and functioning; 1970s and 1980s, with focus on process (how strategies were formed) and content (relationship between strategic choices and performance).

Learning Outcome 1.3: Explain who's involved with strategic management.

- *Assumption:* everyone in organization plays an important role.
- *Three main groups: board of directors* (elected group that represents a company's shareholders), whose involvement ranges from approving strategy to initiating strategy; top management, whose role involves *strategic leadership* (the ability to anticipate, envision, maintain flexibility, think strategically, and work with others in the organization to initiate changes that will create a viable and valuable future for the organization); and other managers and organizational employees, whose primary tasks include strategy implementation and strategy evaluation.

- *Six key dimensions of strategic leadership:* determining organization's purpose or vision; exploiting and maintaining the organization's core competencies; developing the organization's human capital; creating and sustaining a strong organizational culture; emphasizing ethical organizational decisions and practices; and establishing appropriately balanced controls.

Learning Outcome 1.4: Discuss the three important factors impacting strategic management today.

- *Global economy and globalization:* provides both economic and social benefits; challenges come from current state of global economy; from openness, which has made countries more vulnerable to political and cultural differences; and from economic interdependence of trading nations.

- *Challenges of openness and economic interdependence have been countered by:* the *World Trade Organization* (a global organization of 153 countries that deals with monitoring and facilitating the rules of trade among nations); the *World Bank Group* (a cooperative of 185 member countries that provides financial and technical assistance to developing countries); and the *International Monetary Fund* (an organization of 185 member countries that promotes international monetary cooperation and provides financial advice, temporary loans, and technical assistance).

- *Challenges of cultural and political differences:* requires sensitivity to those differences.

- *Corporate governance* (the way a corporation is governed or the "determination of the broad uses to which organizational resources will be deployed and the resolution of conflicts among the myriad participants in organizations"): reform brought about by *Sarbanes-Oxley Act* (a U.S. federal law designed to protect investors by improving the accuracy and reliability of corporate disclosures); reform mandated in two areas—role of boards of directors and financial reporting.

- *E-business* (using information and communication technologies to support all the activities of a business): includes *e-commerce* (the retailing side of e-business); three different strategic approaches to e-business are (1) e-business enhanced (using information and communication technologies to enhance, not replace, traditional ways of doing business), (2) e-business enabled (using information and communication technologies to enable organizational members to do their work more efficiently and effectively including such things as an *intranet,* which is an internal organizational communication system that uses Internet technology and is accessible only by organizational employees), and (3) a total e-business (whole approach to business is based on electronic technologies).

YOU
as
strategic
decision
maker:
building
your
skills

1. Research the strategic leader(s) of Pepsi-Cola, Amazon.com, and Toyota Motor Company. Use paper-based sources (business periodicals, books, etc.) or Web-based information. In a brief paper, describe how each of these strategic leaders fulfills the characteristics of effective strategic leadership (see Figure 1.4).

2. "Making strategy, once an event, is now a continuous process." Explain what you think this statement means.

3. Boards of directors and top managers are being scrutinized more than ever. Complete the following assignments having to do with these two groups of strategic decision makers.

   a. *Fortune* publishes an annual ranking of the most admired companies, both global and U.S. Choose either ranking and get the most recent listing of the top 10. Look up financial information on the top three companies on the list. Look up information on the boards of directors of these companies. Report what you find. What conclusions might you draw about the role of the board in the strategic management of these most admired companies?

   b. Top executive compensation has been a controversial topic recently because of floundering company performance. Do some research on executive pay. What issues are being raised? How do you feel about these issues? What things are happening in response to these issues?

4. "With respect to business, the Internet represents one of the most important innovations of this generation for firms to cut costs, improve services, and expand markets." Do you agree with this statement? Why or why not? What are the implications for strategic decision makers?

5. The term *business model* became extremely popular during the dot-com craze—everyone was searching for that Web-based business model that promised unimaginable profits. However, as the dot-com craze imploded, the concept lost its luster. But we shouldn't be so quick to dismiss it. A good **business model,** which is simply a strategic design for how a company intends to profit from its broad array of strategies, processes, and activities, should answer four questions: (1) Who is our customer? (2) What does the customer value? (3) How do we make money in this business? and (4) What underlying economic logic explains how we can deliver value to customers at an appropriate cost?

   With this in mind, describe the business model each of the following companies is using: eBay, Carnival Cruise Lines, Domino's Pizza, and Dell Computer.

Strategic Management in Action Cases

CASE #1 Making Magic Happen

This Strategic Management in Action case can be found at the beginning of Chapter 1.

1. What is the Disney Difference and how will it affect the company's corporate, competitive, and functional strategies?

2. What challenges do you think Disney might face in doing business in Russia? How could Iger and his top management team best prepare for those challenges?

3. "The steward of the entire Disney brand." What do you think it means that Iger views himself as this? Is this part of being an effective strategic leader? Explain. How might it affect the company's strategy formulation, implementation, and evaluation?

4. How might Iger and his top management team use the strategic management process to "keep the magic coming" in the current economic climate?

CASE #2: MTV's New Reality

MTV. Is there any college student today that hasn't at least heard of MTV? The cable TV icon has "proved one thing over time . . . it knows where the kids are." In its early years (the company was founded in 1981), MTV was a radical newcomer in an industry filled with conventional approaches. With its suggestive language and racy images, teens and young adults loved the edgy content and presentation. CEO and chairperson Judy McGrath (who has been with MTV since its inception and whose first job was writing on-air promotions) has overseen some significant strategic initiatives. The company pioneered reality television in 1992 with *The Real World*, in which seven young adult strangers lived together in a house and had their lives—the good, the bad, and the downright weird—videotaped. MTV's cutting-edge real-life programming has been, and still is, widely copied. Although ratings for the MTV channel have stagnated for years, its audience is massive. The network remains "far and away the premier address for advertisers seeking to reach its coveted 18–34-year-old audience." As a subsidiary of Viacom (the film production and cable television company), MTV Networks owns and operates cable networks MTV, VH1, Nickelodeon, CMT (Country Music Television) Spike TV, and other channels including Comedy Central, TV Land, and LOGO. It also operates MTV films in conjunction with Paramount Pictures, another subsidiary of Viacom. MTV Networks continues to be the "financial engine" of Viacom. It accounted for some 60 percent of the company's annual revenue in 2007 and nearly all of its operating profit. Despite its long history of knowing what an elusive and fickle audience finds interesting, McGrath must continually juggle the strategic challenges of guiding this $8 billion-plus company as it looks for ways to continue its success. "As a brand, MTV has moved beyond durable, managing to reinvent itself continuously and in doing so presenting a fast-moving target that left many would-be rivals in its wake." Today, McGrath's primary challenges are the company's digital and global strategies.

Pointing to the popularity of social networking sites such as MySpace and Facebook, industry analysts criticized MTV's digital strategy, claiming that its "lock" on the youth culture was in danger. Those criticisms escalated when MTV didn't buy MySpace when it was for sale. It made other blunders in digital media as well. Its Web video site (Overdrive) never really took off nor did its digital music store (Urge). However, McGrath counters those criticisms by noting the company's plans to "mine deep vertical slices of pop culture, rather than attempting to build wide horizontal platforms." For instance, at the Web site dance.mtv.com, which is based on the show *America's Best Dance Crew*, amateur dancers can upload video showing off their moves. At mysupersweetparty.com, which is based on the show *My Super Sweet 16*, users can plan their own parties with the coolest pages shown on TV every week. One analyst says that, "What they're doing with these smaller properties is very smart. And the way they market it with a chance to get on TV is a huge draw." MTV now has some 50 such vertical sites. So far, the results of its digital online strategy seem to have been working. The number of unique users for MTV Networks' Web sites grew by 13 percent during the first half of 2008 and the average time spent at the sites grew by 20 percent to almost half an hour. Even as the media business continues to rapidly change, McGrath feels that her company is prepared. She says, "The talent's here. We have a plan. We're moving."

MTV Networks has an extensive global presence, reaching over 520 million households in 160 countries. Using a first-in-the-market strategy that focuses on channels with broad appeal (such as MTV Asia, MTV Latin America, MTV Turkey, and its latest entry, MTV Arabia), MTV is the world's most ubiquitous TV network with over 120 channels worldwide. Now the company is expanding in key global markets with more MTV Networks brands, like Nickelodeon, by using a range of technologies such as cable, satellite, and cell phones. Analysts caution that the key to MTV's global strategy, however, is "sticking with a winning approach that mixes universal youth sensibilities with local tastes. That way the company won't come across as a cultural imperialist." Despite MTV's far-ranging global reach and a 20 percent-a-year international growth rate, the U.S. division still accounts for 73 percent of overall revenue, which means there's still a lot of upside potential in the global market. But McGrath and her executive team appear ready to tackle the strategic challenges of both the global and the digital media environments.

Discussion Questions

1. Explain how strategic management and the strategic management process are illustrated in this case.

2. What are some performance measures that MTV's strategic decision makers might use as they evaluate the results of their digital and global strategies?

3. Go to MTV Network's corporate Web site [www.mtv.com/sitewide/mtvinfo/faq] and look for information about MTV Networks and its various business units (hint: look at job opportunities). Describe the strategic approach of MTV Networks. Then, select four businesses from its portfolio of entertainment brands and describe the strategic approach each appears to be using.

4. Using Figure 1.4, evaluate Judy McGrath's strategic leadership.

Sources: Based on T. Arango, "Make Room Cynics : MTV Wants to Do Some Good," *New York Times Online,* April 19, 2009; R. Levine, "MTV's Digital Makeover," *Fast Company,* November 2008, pp. 67–70; T. Lowry, "The Game's the Thing at MTV Networks," *BusinessWeek,* February 18, 2008, pp. 51–52; K. Cappell, "The Arab World Wants Its MTV," *BusinessWeek,* October 22, 2007, pp. 79–81; B. Keveney, "How TV Started Getting Real," *USA Today,* October 10, 2007, pp. 1D+; D. Carr, "Do They Still Want Their MTV?" *New York Times Online,* February 10, 2007; E. Pfanner, "Who Needs Europe, Anyway? Turkey Has Its Own MTV," *New York Times Online,* December 11, 2006; D. Barboza, "Viacom to Send Video to China's Internet," *New York Times Online,* October 18, 2006; R. Silkos, "Not in the Real World Anymore," *New York Times Online,* September 18, 2006; M. Karnitschnig and B. Barnes, "Does MTV Still Rock?" *Wall Street Journal,* September 7, 2006, pp. B1+; M. Karnitschnig, "Unplugged: Viacom Discovers Kids Don't Want Their MTV Online," *Wall Street Journal,* August 29, 2006, pp. A1+; and C. Clark, J. Deerwester, T. Hartman, K. Lopez, W. Matheson, and A. Maxwell, "25 Years of MTV," *USA Today,* July 28, 2006, pp. E1+.

CASE #3: Making Over Avon

As the world's largest direct seller of cosmetics and beauty-related items, Avon Products wants to continue building its global reach (more than two-thirds of Avon's sales revenues come from outside North America) and attracting younger customers. To do so, however, Andrea Jung, chairman and CEO, must continually juggle the strategic challenges of guiding this almost $10.7 billion company and its worldwide army of over 5.4 million independent representatives.

Jung was named Avon's first female CEO in 1999. Since that time, she has overseen some significant strategic initiatives. One of these was the company's $100 million investment in a state-of-the-art product research facility outside of New York City. Avon had always lagged behind its competitors in R&D (research and development), spending less than 1 percent of sales while Esteé Lauder Companies was spending over 1.3 percent of sales and L'Oreal SA about 3 percent of sales. Because this industry is one in which customers continually look for new products that make them look good and that are also good for the skin, R&D is critical. In addition, Avon is primarily a direct sales company whose representatives pitch new products to customers every two weeks, so it's important to invest in new product development.

Another of Jung's strategic moves was a revamp of Avon's old-fashioned image through new marketing and advertising. Avon—best known for its troops of mostly middle-aged women selling skin creams and cosmetics to their neighbors from catalogs—needed a serious overhaul of that dated image. Jung ordered a new design for the company's all-important sales brochure using heavier, glossier paper that was more visually appealing. Also, the company is "going Hollywood." MTV star Lauren Conrad, Patrick Dempsey of the TV drama *Grey's Anatomy,* and actress Reese Witherspoon (who is Avon's Global Ambassador) are a few of the celebrity relationships that Avon has initiated. Even with its revamped marketing strategies, Avon has work to do. In a study of mass-market cosmetics brands, it lagged behind seven others in terms of customer loyalty, while one of its main competitors, Mary Kay Cosmetics, topped the list.

Another strategic initiative was a line of cosmetics for young women aged 16–24. The company's first push into the youth market was a dramatic change from its core customer group that was aged 35 and older. Deborah Fine (who has since left the company) was president of the company division responsible for the line. She said, "We wanted to capture a younger customer, bring in new reps, and create a new global youth brand." According to Avon, 17 million young women in the United States spend at least $75 billion a year on beauty and fashion. If Avon could capture part of that spending with appealing products, it had the potential to add significantly to its bottom line. Avon's "young" brand, called *mark,* launched in summer 2003. Thousands of career-savvy young women signed on as representatives and have helped propel mark to the number two trend brand in the world. Jung is confident that mark will continue to help the company "pass the makeup brush" to a new generation of Avon customers. The strategic challenge, obviously, will be to keep mark's customers and sales force (a notoriously fickle age group) excited and hooked.

Despite these actions, Avon's sales during 2005 slowed significantly as U.S. revenues sagged, and even the previously strong overseas markets slowed. Jung's response—a multiyear restructuring program aimed at saving at least $300 million a year. This restructuring involved downsizing (eliminating corporate positions); doubling advertising spending; focusing R&D resources on product innovation in an attempt to make its brands more competitive; simplifying the manufacturing structure; outsourcing some services to low-cost countries; and improving the attractiveness of the representatives' earnings potential in the United States, Russia, and Brazil. In addition, the company implemented a zero-overhead-growth philosophy targeted at offsetting inflation through productivity improvements. At this time, Avon's greatest market potential appears to be in China. It was the first company to be granted a direct selling license there and the number of active sales representatives has increased significantly. One analyst says, "Avon has a great brand; they've got a product lineup that's appealing . . . Its [business] model is not broken." The turnaround that Jung put into place seems to be working.

Discussion Questions

1. Explain how strategic management and the strategic management process are illustrated in this case.

2. What are some performance measures that Avon's strategic decision makers might use to evaluate the results of the restructuring initiatives?

3. Andrea Jung is Avon's first female CEO, which you might find surprising considering that Avon's target market is overwhelmingly female. Do some research on the number of female CEOs and female board members in U.S. companies. (Check out Catalyst, an organization that researches women's workplace issues.) Have these numbers changed over time? What conclusions might you draw from these data?

4. Go to Avon's Web site [www.avoncompany.com]. What are Avon's vision and mission? How might these statements affect strategic decisions and actions? Check out the company's executive team. Select one top manager other than Andrea Jung. Describe that individual's job responsibility. Finally, select one of the company's brands and describe what strategies are being used for that brand.

Sources: Based on K. Nolan, "Avon Unveils New Cost Cuts," *Wall Street Journal,* February 20, 2009, p. B2; J. A. Tarquinio, "Selling Beauty on a Global Scale," *New York Times Online,* November 1, 2008; E. Byron, "Lean Times Swell Avon's Sales Force," *Wall Street Journal,* October 15, 2008, p. B1; P. Gogoi, "Why Avon Is Going Hollywood," *BusinessWeek,* July 28, 2008, p. 58; D. Sewell, Associated Press, "Beauty Requires Researching," *Springfield, Missouri, News-Leader,* May 3, 2008, p. 10A; K. Kennedy, Associated Press, " Men Are a Growing Part of Avon's Sales Empire," *Springfield, Missouri, News-Leader,* October 29, 2007, pp. 11A+; E. Byron and K. Richardson, "Avon Makeover Isn't Cosmetic," *Wall Street Journal,* October 22, 2007, pp. C1+; E. Byron, "Is Avon's Latest Scent Sweet Smell of Success?" *Wall Street Journal,* October 15, 2007, pp. B1+; N. Byrnes, "Avon: More Than Cosmetic Changes," *BusinessWeek,* March 12, 2007, pp. 62–63; A. Bert, "Avon Updates Its Look, Strategy," *USA Today,* September 11, 2006; C. C. Berk, "Avon Reorganizes in a Bid to Revive Its Sales by 2007," *Wall Street Journal,* November 16, 2005, p. B4; and M. Esterl, "Avon Works Out the Wrinkles," *Wall Street Journal,* August 31, 2005, p. B3.

CASE #4: Fighting Grime

Look in your pantry, your laundry room, your bathroom, or under your kitchen sink. Chances are, you have at least one of the Clorox Company's many cleaning products in your household. The Clorox Company [www.thecloroxcompany.com], a $5.2 billion company, manufactures and markets household cleaning and grocery products in more than 100 countries around the globe. Some of its most recognizable product names include Clorox Bleach, Glad bags, Soft Scrub bathroom cleaner, Tilex shower cleaner, STP automotive products, Kingsford charcoal, Brita water filters, S.O.S. cleaning pads, Hidden Valley Ranch dressings, and many others. It's the worldwide leader in the bleach market and added to that lead with its purchase of Colgate-Palmolive's bleach businesses. Despite its name being synonymous with bleach, that isn't even the company's biggest brand. That distinction belongs to its Glad line of food storage and disposal products. Like many consumer-products companies that have large product lines, Clorox found that close to 30 percent of its products were falling short of their sales and profit goals. Company executives responded by developing a formal product evaluation process to help them decide which products to cut. The outcome? More than 90 percent of Clorox's products now meet volume and profit goals. Despite the success of this strategic initiative, Clorox executives have to walk a fine line. They don't want to discontinue products that customers want, so product lines are frequently reviewed with customers.

The Clorox Company is facing other strategic challenges. A critical one is commodity costs (primarily oil and chemicals), which have risen significantly. To offset these costs, Clorox increased prices of many of its products. However, there are market risks associated with continually raising prices. In addition, when one of your biggest customers is the world's largest and most powerful retailer, you're vulnerable to its strategic changes. When Wal-Mart decided to "adjust" its inventories in 2006, several consumer-products giants took a hit . . . including Clorox. One analyst noted, however, that Wal-Mart actually may have done those companies a favor by making them more efficient and thus more competitive globally. Finally, Clorox had to deal with the unexpected retirement of its popular CEO (Jerry Johnston) who suffered a heart attack in early 2006. During his tenure, Jerry had set the bar high. He challenged the entire organization to understand its connection to the consumer and to recognize this as its most significant source of competitive advantage. The current CEO, Donald Knauss (who was previously head of Coke's North American business), is the first outsider to run Clorox and has continued pushing the company in new directions, the most important of which is a "going green" strategy. In late 2007, Clorox bought Burt's Bees, the company that produces lip balms and soaps from natural ingredients. In addition, Knauss oversaw the launch of a collection of natural-cleaning products called Green Works. This product line has been one of the most successful product launches in recent memory.

However, challenges still remain. In addition to the rising commodity costs—which Knauss says is the biggest challenge—he faces intensified competition from much bigger rivals such as Unilever PLC (over $59 billion in revenues) and the Procter & Gamble Company (over $83.5 billion in revenues). However, Clorox's board believes that Knauss's global and big-brand expertise and his strong bonds with major retailers have helped the company's global and product expansion. Knauss said he was "attracted by Clorox's market-leading brands and an ambition to lead a public company." He said that global markets would be a "key area of focus because there's a tremendous amount of growth potential there." In addition, Knauss hoped to continue exploiting Clorox's strong brand portfolio (most are number 1 or 2 in their product categories) by maintaining its commitment to innovation. He said, "I think there is a unique opportunity at Clorox to focus on consumer trends and to broaden the footprint of an already great stable of brands."

Yes, these are strategic challenges that Knauss and the management team at the Clorox Company welcome. After all, if they can effectively fight the grime and dirt found in some customers' homes, the marketplace wars might not seem so bad after all!

Discussion Questions

1. Do you think strategic management has contributed to the Clorox Company's success? Why or why not?

2. Given the information included in this mini-case about the Clorox Company, at what step in the strategic management process do you think it excels? Explain your choice.

3. How might Donald Knauss use strategic management to manage the challenges facing his company?

4. Update the information on the Clorox Company by logging on to the company's Web site. How big is Clorox now in terms of sales? In terms of number of employees? What new strategies is it pursuing, if any?

Sources: Based on Reuters, "Clorox Exceeds Expectations Despite Posting Lower Profit," *New York Times Online,* February 5, 2009; Clorox Company Web site [www.thecloroxcompany.com], December 31, 2008; A. Kamenetz, "Cleaning Solution," *Fast Company,* November 2008, pp. 120–125; L. Story, "Can Burt's Bees Turn Clorox Green?" *New York Times Online,* January 6, 2008; The Associated Press, "Clorox to Buy Colgate Bleach Business," *BusinessWeek Online,* December 20, 2006; Reuters, "Clorox Posts Gain in Profit," *New York Times Online,* November 2, 2006; R. Berner, "From Coke to Clorox," *BusinessWeek Online,* September 5, 2006; J. S. Lublin and E. Byron, "Clorox Picks a Top Coke Officer as New Leader," *Wall Street Journal,* August 31, 2006, p. A3; M. Baron, "Clorox CEO Retires, Citing Health," *Wall Street Journal,* May 4, 2006, p. B7; P. Bhatnagar, "Wal-Mart Puts the Squeeze on Vendors," *CNN Money Online,* April 10, 2006; and R. Van Hoek and K. Pegels, "Growing by Cutting SKUs at Clorox," *Harvard Business Review,* April 2006, p. 22.

Case #5: In the Zone

Like that other illustrious retail chain started in Arkansas, AutoZone is also known for its clean floors, friendly clerks, and spirited corporate culture featuring a rousing cheer performed by employees. Now based in Memphis with over 4,100 stores in the United States and Puerto Rico, AutoZone is the nation's number one auto parts chain. The $6.5 billion-a-year company enjoys profit margins of close to 10 percent (almost triple that of Wal-Mart, that other famous Arkansas company) and a 279 percent return on equity. And the company is doing for auto parts what Wal-Mart did for discount retailing. Yet, it has not achieved the level of brand recognition that Wal-Mart has. So, what has contributed to the company's enviable track record?

One important element in AutoZone's success is its attention to detail. It has made its stores appealing to anyone who drives a car. From the hard-core NASCAR buffs and car accessorizers to the grandma looking for new wiper blades, AutoZone is customer-friendly. The company's pledge states: "AutoZoners [that's the name company employees use to refer to themselves] always put customers first. We know our parts and products. Our stores look great! We've got the best merchandise at the right price." It's a strategic formula that has proved to be a winner. Another recent strategic change was the implementation of a task management system. Store-level associates are responsible for a variety of tasks from resetting stores and assortments to updating pricing, signs, and fixtures. However, if some tasks were to be done simultaneously, invariably some didn't get done. Thus, the corporate information technology group created a store-level plan using a task management system for dealing with those issues. Now, store associates know which tasks are most important to do each day.

Before being named to the CEO position, Bill Rhodes had served in various capacities within the company. Named to the top post in 2005, Rhodes continues to reposition the company to succeed in the future. One thing he did was to do an extensive consumer research study. This research "confirmed what we have always known. The most compelling reason we give our customers to shop at AutoZone is our continuing passion for providing trustworthy advice. We were reminded we must have the right merchandise, at the right price, at the right time in order to deepen our relationship with our customers." How did this information affect the company's strategic initiatives? In the 2008 Letter to Shareholders, Rhodes outlined key points to guide the company's strategies: (1) Capitalize on the incredible opportunity in the commercial side of the business. (2) Continue our professional sales training efforts to equip AutoZoners with more sales tools than ever before. (3) Continue to focus on providing great customer service. (4) Continue to grow sales in both retail and commercial. (5) Continue to improve inventory productivity by refining our category management initiatives and improved utilization of our hub store network. (6) Continue to be good stewards of the environment and look for additional ways to reduce fuel consumption and conserve energy in other ways.

Rhodes and his employees obviously have figured out what it takes to manage strategically. They're "in the zone" and are doing whatever it takes to ensure that they stay there!

Discussion Questions

1. In this brief description of AutoZone, how is strategic management illustrated?

2. What examples of functional strategy do you see? Describe. What factor(s) do you think AutoZone might use in its competitive strategy?

3. AutoZone is committed to "playing it clean" in terms of the way it does business. Go to the company's Web site [www.autozone.com]. Find the section on corporate governance. Describe what the company has done in terms of corporate governance. Evaluate what they're doing.

4. What types of strategic challenges might Rhodes and the company face as it pursues its strategic initiatives? How might strategic management help them deal with these challenges?

Sources: Based on T. Demos, "In the Zone," *Fortune*, April 13, 2009, pp. 78–80; AutoZone Web site [www.autozone.com]. December 31, 2008; J. D. Opdyke, "Down the Road a Bit, AutoZone Looks Good," *Wall Street Journal*, December 9, 2008, p. C1; D. Amato-McCoy, "Task Management: Check!" *Chain Store Age*, October 2008, p. 53; Corporate News, "AutoZone Net Rises 12% on Solid Sales," *Wall Street Journal*, September 23, 2008, p. B6; R. M. Murphy, "7 Ways to Join the Billion-Dollar Club," *CNNMoney.com*, April 28, 2006; and J. Boorstin, "An Auto-Parts Store Your Mother Could Love," *Fortune*, November 10, 2003, pp. 163–168.

Endnotes

1. P. Sanders, "Disney Angles for Cash, Loyalty," *Wall Street Journal,* March 11, 2009, p. B4; The Associated Press, "Walt Disney Plans to Lay Off Workers," *New York Times Online,* February 19, 2009; R. Siklos, "Bob Iger Rocks Disney," *CNN Online,* [www.cnnmoney.com], January 5, 2009; B. Barnes, "Disney Plans a Channel for Russian TV," *New York Times Online,* December 17, 2008; P. Sanders, "Disney Net Slips as Slump Hits Home," *Wall Street Journal,* November 17, 2008 pp. B1+; B. Barnes, "Disney and Pixar: The Power of the Prenup," *New York Times Online,* June 1, 2008; R. Siklos, "Q&A: The Iger Difference," *Fortune,* April 28, 2008, pp. 90–94; R. Grover, "A Star is Born, Disney Style" *BusinessWeek,* April 21, 2008, pp. 50–51; and The Walt Disney Company *2007 Fact Book,* [http://corporate.disney.go.com/investors/fact_books.html].

2. T. C. Powell, "Varieties of Competitive Parity," *Strategic Management Journal,* January 2003, pp. 61–86; M. Farjoun, "Towards an Organic Perspective on Strategy," *Strategic Management Journal,* July 2002, pp. 561–594.

3. C. Zott and R. Amit, "The Fit Between Product Market Strategy and Business Model: Implications for Firm Performance," *Strategic Management Journal,* January 2008, pp. 1–26; J. C. Short, D. J. Ketchen, Jr., T. B. Palmer, and G. T. M. Hult, "Firm, Strategic Group, and Industry Influences on Performance," *Strategic Management Journal,* February 2007, pp. 147–167; F. T. Rothaermel, M. A. Hitt, and L. A. Jobe, "Balancing Vertical Integration and Strategic Outsourcing: Effects on Product Portfolio, Product Success, and Firm Performance," *Strategic Management Journal,* November 2006, pp. 1033–1056; D. J. Miller, "Technological Diversity, Related Diversification, and Firm Performance," *Strategic Management Journal,* July 2006, pp. 601–619; J. J. Ebben and A. C. Johnson, "Efficiency, Flexibility, or Both? Evidence Linking Strategy to Performance in Small Firms," *Strategic Management Journal,* December 2005, pp. 1249–1259; C. B. Shrader, T. I. Chacko, P. Herrmann, and C. Mulford, "Planning and Firm Performance: Effects of Multiple Planning Activities and Technology Policy," *International Journal of Management and Decision Making,* vol. 5, no. 2/3, 2004, pp. 171–195; A. B. Desai, "Does Strategic Planning Create Value? The Stock Market's Belief," *Management Decision,* December 2000, pp. 685–693; P. J. Brews and M. R. Hunt, "Learning to Plan and Planning to Learn: Resolving the Planning School/Learning School Debate," *Strategic Management Journal,* vol. 20, 1999, pp. 889–913; D. J. Ketchen, Jr., J. B. Thomas, and R. R. McDaniel, Jr., "Process, Content and Context: Synergistic Effects on Performance," *Journal of Management,* vol. 22, no.2, 1996, pp. 231–257; C. C. Miller and L. B. Cardinal, "Strategic Planning and Firm Performance: A Synthesis of More Than Two Decades of Research," *Academy of Management Journal,* December 1994, pp. 1649–1665; and N. Capon, J. U. Farley, and J. M. Hulbert, "Strategic Planning and Financial Performance: More Evidence," *Journal of Management Studies,* January 1994, pp. 105–110.

4. J. W. Dean, Jr. and M. P. Sharfman, "Does Decision Process Matter? A Study of Strategic Decision-Making Effectiveness," *Academy of Management Journal,* April 1996, pp. 368–396.

5. S. Hart and C. Banbury, "How Strategy-Making Processes Can Make a Difference," *Strategic Management Journal,* May 1994, pp. 251–269.

6. W. P. Barnett, H. R. Greve, and D. Y. Park, "An Evolutionary Model of Organizational Performance," *Strategic Management Journal,* Winter 1994, pp. 11–28.

7. A. D. Chandler, Jr., *Strategy and Structure: Chapters in the History of the Industrial Enterprise* (Cambridge, MA: MIT Press, 1962); and C. W. Hofer and D. Schendel, *Strategy Formulation: Analytical Concepts* (St. Paul, MN: West, 1978).

8. O. E. Williamson, "Strategy Research: Governance and Competence Perspectives," *Strategic Management Journal,* 20, 1999, pp. 1087–1108.

9. S. P. Nerur, A. A. Rasheed, and V. Natarajan, "The Intellectual Structure of the Strategic Management Field: An Author Co-Citation Analysis," *Strategic Management Journal,* March 2008, pp. 319–336; D. C. Hambrick and M-J Chen, "New Academic Fields as Admittance-Seeking Social Movements: The Case of Strategic Management," *Academy of Management Review,* January 2008, pp. 32–54; R. Nag, D. C. Hambrick, and M-J Chen, "What Is Strategic Management, Really? Inductive Derivation of a Consensus Definition of the Field," *Strategic Management Journal,* September 2007, pp. 935–955; B. K. Boyd, S. Finkelstein, and S. Gove, "How Advanced Is the Strategy Paradigm? The Role of Particularism and Universalism in Shaping Research Outcomes," *Strategic Management Journal,* September 2005, pp. 841–854; and R. P. Rumelt, D. E. Schendel, and D. J. Teece, "Fundamental Issues in Strategy," in R. P. Rumelt, D. E. Schendel, and D. J. Teece, (eds.), *Fundamental Issues in Strategy: A Research Agenda* (Boston, MA: Harvard Business School Press, 1994), pp. 9–47.

10. R. E. Hoskisson, M. A. Hitt, W. P. Wan, and D. Yiu, "Theory and Research in Strategic Management: Swings of a Pendulum," *Journal of Management,* vol. 25, no. 3, 1999, pp. 417–456; and R. P. Rumelt, D. E. Schendel, and D. J. Teece, 1994.

11. D. J. Ketchen, J. B. Thomas, and R. R. McDaniel, Jr., 1996.

12. K. Whitehouse, "Move Over CEO: Here Come the Directors," *Wall Street Journal,* October 9, 2006, pp. R1+; J. S. Lublin and E. White, "Drama in the Boardroom," *Wall Street Journal,* October 2, 2006, pp. B1+; J. Jusko, "Beefed Up Boards," *Industry Week,* August 2005, pp. 53–56; D. A. Nadler, "Building Better Boards," *Harvard Business Review,* May 2004, pp. 102–111; E. Iwata, "Judges Signal Boards to Take Duties Seriously," *USA Today,* March 29, 2004, p. 1B; and N. Donaldson, "A New Tool for Boards: The Strategic Audit," *Harvard Business Review,* July–August 1995, pp. 99–107.

13. S. Ghoshal and C. A. Bartlett, "Changing the Role of Top Management: Beyond Structure to Process," *Harvard Business Review,* January–February 1995, pp. 86–96.

14. R. Calori, G. Johnson, and P. Sarnin, "CEO's Cognitive Maps and the Scope of the Organization," *Strategic Management Journal,* July 1994, pp. 437–457.

15. R. D. Ireland and M. A. Hitt, "Achieving and Maintaining Strategic Competitiveness in the 21st Century: The Role of Strategic Leadership," *Academy of Management Executive,* February 1999, pp. 43–57.

16. Ibid.

17. S. W. Floyd and P. J. Lane, "Strategizing Throughout the Organization: Managing Role Conflict in Strategic Renewal," *Academy of Management Review,* January 2000, pp. 154–177.

18. E. L. Andrews, "World Bank Offers Dire Forecast for World Economy," *International Herald Tribune* [http://www.iht.com], March 8, 2009; and M. Landler, "Dire Forecast for Global Economy and Trade," *New York Times Online,* December 10, 2008.

19. D. J. Lynch, "Some Would Like to Build a Wall Around U.S. Economy," *USA Today,* March 16, 2006, p. 1B+; D. E. Sanger, "A Bush Alarm: Urging U.S. to Shun Isolationism," *New York Times Online* [www.nytimes.com], March 13, 2006; G. Ip and N. King Jr., "Ports Deal Shows Roadblocks for Globalization," *Wall Street Journal,* March 11, 2006, p. A1+; and M. A. Stein, "A Big Deal Overshadowed by the Politics of Ports," *New York Times Online* [www.nytimes.com], March 11, 2006.

20. World Trade Organization Web site [www.wto.org], December 31, 2008.

21. World Bank Group Web site [web.worldbank.org], December 31, 2008.

22. International Monetary Fund Web site [www.imf.org], December 31, 2008.

23. P. Gumbel, "Branding America," *Time,* March 2005, pp. A13–A14; T. Purdum, "Survival of the Fittest," *Industry Week,* October 2003, pp. 23–25; D. Yergin, "Globalization Opens Door to New Dangers," *USA Today,* May 28, 2003, p. 11A; K. Lowrey Miller, "Is It Globaloney?" *Newsweek,* December 16, 2002, pp. E4–E8; L. Gomes, "Globalization Is Now a Two-Way Street— Good News for the U.S.," *Wall Street Journal,* December 9, 2002, p. B1; J. Kurlantzick and J. T. Allen, "The Trouble With Globalism," *U.S. News and World Report,* February 11, 2002, pp. 38–41; and J. Guyon, "The American Way," *Fortune,* November 26, 2001, pp. 114–120.

24. Guyon, "The American Way."

25. C. M. Daily, D. R. Dalton, and A. A. Cannella, Jr., "Corporate Governance: Decades of Dialogue and Data," *Academy of Management Review,* July 2003, p. 371.

26. S. Liebs, "New Terrain," *CFO,* February 2004, pp. 40–47; C. Hymowitz and J. S. Lublin, "Boardrooms Under Renovation," *Wall Street Journal,* July 22, 2003, pp. B1+; and D. Salierno, "Boards Face Increased Responsibility," *Internal Auditor,* June 2003, pp. 14–15.

27. *Principles of Corporate Governance 2005,* Business Roundtable (Washington, DC), November 2005, p. 3.

28. D. Raths, "Backlash Against Sarbanes-Oxley," *CRO,* Winter 2006, pp. 40–41; K. Scannell and D. Solomon, "Business Wins Its Battle to Ease a Costly Sarbanes-Oxley Rule," *Wall Street Journal,* November 10, 2006, pp. A1+; S. Labaton, "Panel to Propose Exceptions to Governance Rules," *New York Times Online,* April 19, 2006; A. Borrus, "Learning to Love Sarbanes-Oxley," *BusinessWeek,* November 21, 2005, pp. 126–128; "Special Report on Corporate Governance," *Wall Street Journal,* October 17, 2005, pp. R1+; and T. Reason, "Feeling the Pain: Are the Benefits of Sarbanes-Oxley Worth the Cost?" *CFO,* May 2005, pp. 50–60.

29. Scannell and Solomon , ibid.

30. M. Marcus, "Amazon's Christmas Miracle," *Forbes.com Online,* December 26, 2008.

31. N. Timiraos, "Web Can Pay Off for Traditional Retailers," *Wall Street Journal,* December 23–24, 2006, p. A7; R. Banham, "Old Dogs, New Clicks," *CFO-IT,* Summer 2005, pp. 20–26; T. J. Mullaney, H. Gree, M. Arndt, R. D. Hof, and L. Himelstein, "The E-Biz Surprise," *BusinessWeek,* May 12, 2003, pp. 60–68; R. D. Hof and S. Hamm, "How E-Biz Rose, Fell, and Will Rise Anew," *BusinessWeek,* May 13, 2002, pp. 64–72; and "Companies Leading Online," *IQ Magazine,* November–December 2001, pp. 54–63.

The Context of Managing Strategically

2

LEARNING OUTCOMES

2.1 *Describe the different perspectives on competitive advantage.*

2.2 *Explain the driving forces, implications, and critical success factors of the business environment.*

2.3 *Discuss two organizational elements that guide strategic decision makers in managing strategically in today's context.*

Fast Fashion

Strategic Management in Action

Case #1

When Amancio Ortega, a former Spanish bathrobe maker, opened his first Zara clothing store, his business model was simple: sell high-fashion look-alikes to price-conscious Europeans.[1] After succeeding in this, he decided to tackle the outdated clothing industry in which it took six months from a garment's design to consumers being able to purchase it in a store. What Ortega envisioned was "fast fashion"—getting designs to customers quickly. And that's exactly what Zara has done!

The company has been described as having more style than Gap, faster growth than Target, and logistical expertise rivaling Wal-Mart's. Zara, which is owned by the Spanish fashion retail group Inditex SA, recognizes that success in the fashion world is based on a simple rule—get products to market quickly. Accomplishing this, however, isn't so simple. It involves a clear and focused understanding of fashion, technology, and their market, *and* the ability to adapt quickly to trends.

Inditex, one of the largest fashion retail groups worldwide, runs five chains: Zara, Pull and Bear, Massimo Dutti, Stradivarius, and Oysho. The company has over 4,200 stores in 70 countries although Zara pulls in almost two-thirds of the company's revenues. Despite its global presence, Zara is not yet a household name in the United States, with just over 41 stores open, including its new prototype store in New York City.

What is Zara's secret to excelling at fast fashion? It takes just two weeks to get a new design from drawing board to store floor. And stores are stocked with new designs twice a week as clothes are shipped directly to the stores from the factory. Thus, each aspect of Zara's business contributes to the fast turnaround. Sales managers at "the Cube"—what employees call their futuristic-looking headquarters—sit at a long row of computers and scrutinize sales at every store. They see the hits and the misses almost instantaneously. They ask the in-house designers, who work in teams, sketching out new styles and deciding which fabrics will provide the best combination of style and price, for new designs. Once a design is drawn, it's sent electronically to Zara's factory across the street, where a clothing sample is made. To minimize waste, computer programs arrange and rearrange clothing patterns on the massive fabric rolls before a laser-guided machine does the cutting. Zara produces most of its designs close to home—in Morocco, Portugal, Spain, and Turkey.

Finished garments are returned to the factory within a week. Finishing touches (buttons, trim, detailing, etc.) are added, and each garment goes through a quality check. Garments that don't pass are discarded while those that do pass are individually pressed. Then, garment labels (indicating to which country garments will be shipped) and security tags are added. The bundled garments proceed along a moving carousel of hanging rails via a maze of tunnels to the warehouse, a four-story, 5-million-square-foot building (about the size of 90 football fields). As the merchandise bundles move along the rails, electronic bar code tags are read by equipment that send them to the right "staging area," where specific merchandise is first sorted by country and then by individual store, ensuring that each store gets exactly the shipment it's supposed to. From there, merchandise for European stores is sent to a loading dock and packed on a truck with other shipments in order of delivery. Deliveries to other locations go by plane. Some 60,000 items each hour—more than 2.6 million items a week—move through this ultrasophisticated distribution center. And this takes place with only a handful of workers who monitor the entire process. The company's just-in-time production (an idea borrowed from the auto industry) gives it a competitive edge in terms of speed and flexibility.

Despite Zara's success at fast fashion, its competitors are working to be faster. But CEO Pablo Isla isn't standing still. To maintain Zara's leading advantage, he's introducing new methods that enable store managers to order and display merchandise faster and is adding new cargo routes for shipping goods.

The challenges faced by Zara in giving customers what they want, when they want, it is a good example of why it's important to consider, understand, and interpret the context in which an organization's employees do strategic management. Strategic decision makers need to know their competitive advantage *and* the dynamic context they're operating in. Why? Because the context determines the "rules" of the game and what actions are likely to work best. Just as the coach of a baseball team analyzes the specific context (looking at factors such as the condition of the playing field, the team's cohesiveness, player injuries, or maybe even the team's current rankings) in deciding what game strategies might work best, so too should organizational decision makers. You can see how the context of managing strategically fits into the overall strategic management process in Figure 2.1.

LEARNING OUTCOME 2.1
Describe the Different Perspectives on Competitive Advantage

Managing strategically means formulating and implementing strategies that allow an organization to develop and maintain a **competitive advantage**—what sets an organization apart or what is its competitive edge. When an organization has a competitive advantage, it has something that competitors don't, it does something better than other organizations do, or it does something that others can't. A key concept in strategic management, competitive advantage is necessary for an organization's long-term success and survival. Even not-for-profit organizations (such as governmental agencies, educational institutions, community arts organizations, or social service groups) need something that sets them apart—something unique that they offer in order to keep their programs and services going. Getting and keeping competitive advantage is what managing strategically is all about. It's not easy to do and an organization will either succeed or fail at it. Most managers would prefer that their organizations succeed; they don't deliberately choose to fail. Instead, failure usually can be traced to not recognizing the impact of important external

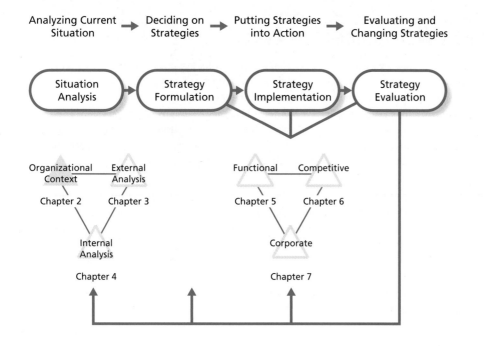

Figure 2.1

Strategic Management in Action

factors or not capitalizing on organizational resources and capabilities. Both represent different perspectives on what it takes to capture competitive advantage—that is, to manage strategically. The first view suggests organizations look at the impact of external factors and is called the industrial organization (I/O) view.[2] The second perspective—called the resource-based view (RBV)—emphasizes exploiting organizational resources in order to develop and maintain competitive advantage.[3] In addition to these two traditional approaches, another, more contemporary perspective is the guerrilla view of competitive advantage, so called because it proposes that an organization's competitive advantage is temporary and can be gained only by peppering the competitive marketplace with rapid radical surprises.[4] Because you need to understand where an organization's competitive advantage comes from, we're going to look more closely at these three perspectives. Table 2.1 summarizes the main points of each view.

Table 2.1 *Comparing the I/O, Resource-Based, and Guerrilla Views of Competitive Advantage*

	I/O View	**RBV**	**Guerrilla View**
Competitive Advantage	Positioning in industry	Possessing unique organizational assets or capabilities	Temporary
Determinants of Profitability	Characteristics of industry, firm's position within industry	Type, amount, and nature of firm's resources	Ability to change and radically surprise competitors with strategic actions
Focus of Analysis	External	Internal	External and internal
Major Concern	Competition	Resources–capabilities	Continual, radical, and chaotic conditions
Strategic Choices	Choosing attractive industry; appropriate position	Developing unique resources and distinctive capabilities	Rapidly and repeatedly disrupting current situation and surprising competitors

Strategic Management in Action

As women everywhere will attest . . . pantyhose are not a wardrobe must-have. According to industry analysts, the sales decline of pantyhose that started in the mid-1990s "still has legs." Reasons for the declining popularity include relaxed office dress codes, more natural-looking and affordable self-tanning sprays and creams, the uncomfortable feel when wearing them, and popular media attention—also known as "the *Sex and the City* effect" because the show's four women helped make going without pantyhose fashionable. One industry competitor, Hanesbrands Inc., has seen declines in its hosiery segment for a couple of years. However, Hanes and other pantyhose makers aren't walking away. The president of Hosiery Association (an industry trade group) says, "The industry is not dead. Forward-thinking companies are diversifying their product offerings."

What might the I/O view say about the pantyhose industry? Where might competitive advantage come from in this industry? Go to Hanesbrands' Web site [**www.hanesbrands.com**]. What strategies is it pursuing to get and keep a competitive advantage in this industry?

Sources: *Based on Hanesbrands Annual Report 2008, p. 11* [**www.hanesbrands.com**]; L. Petrecca, "Hope for Sagging Pantyhose Sales?" USA Today, January 2, 2007, p. 3B; "Bare-Legs Trend Still Making Strides," Springfield, Missouri, News-Leader, January 2, 2007, p. 5B; and I. M. Augstums, "Pantyhose Sales Sag As Trends Change," BusinessWeek Online (Associated Press), December 10, 2006.

The I/O View

The **I/O view** focuses on the structural forces within an industry, the competitive environment of firms, and how these influence competitive advantage. Most of what we know about the I/O approach comes from Michael Porter of the Harvard Business School. According to Porter, five industry forces (which we'll cover in detail in Chapter 3) determine the average profitability of an industry, which in turn influences the profitability of firms within the industry. His approach emphasizes choosing the "best" industries and within those industries, the most advantageous (or competitive) positions.

The I/O approach proposes that getting and keeping competitive advantage means analyzing external forces and basing strategic decisions on that analysis. Thus, the focus of strategic analysis in the I/O view is external. Because all firms within an industry face essentially the same external forces, a major concern of the I/O view is how the firm stacks up against its competitors. Keep in mind the I/O view proposes that competitive advantage relates to competitive positioning in the industry. Also, the I/O view suggests that both a firm's position within the industry and the underlying industry characteristics determine its potential profitability. If there are significant negative forces in the industry or if the firm has a weak position within the industry, then its profitability will be lower than average. But if the industry is characterized by significant opportunities or if the firm has a strong position within the industry, then its profitability will be above average. According to the I/O view, managers make sound strategic choices by understanding what makes an industry attractive, choosing an attractive industry in which to compete, and then choosing an appropriate competitive position within that industry.

The I/O view makes important contributions to understanding how to manage strategically, but critics say it doesn't tell the whole story. Although Porter's ideas don't ignore the characteristics of individual companies, the emphasis is clearly on understanding what is happening at the industry level. Several researchers believed that a complete understanding of competitive advantage also required looking at the role a firm's resources played.

Resource-Based View

The **RBV** says that a firm's resources are most important in getting and keeping a competitive advantage. It sees organizations as different collections of assets and capabilities; that is, none have had the same set of experiences, acquired the same assets or capabilities, or

Strategic Management in Action

RealNetworks is known as the leading creator of online digital media services and software. Its RealPlayer application is a common fixture found on computers. In 2006, RealNetworks' Rhapsody® digital music service was awarded the "Best Downloadable or Subscription Music Service Award" at the annual Digital Entertainment Media and Marketing Excellence Awards ceremony. At the 2009 Consumer Electronics Show, RealNetworks announced a new alliance with Vizio, Cisco, and Yahoo for streaming its Rhapsody music products to the home. However, the biggest "award" in the company's brief history may well be No. 6,985,932—the patent it received in April 2006 for a way to stream multimedia content over the Internet. CEO and founder Robert Glaser called it a "foundation patent, giving RealNetworks a strong position that it would use to help it sell its Helix media server product, which streams video and audio in several formats." Company executives said its technology differed from similar systems in the way it permitted "intelligent streaming of data in potentially congested networks." As other companies expand their efforts at turning the Internet into a broadcast medium, this patent may well give RealNetworks the competitive edge it needs.

What do you think? How important do you think this patent might be in getting a competitive edge? What type of resource is it, and would you call it unique? Explain.

Sources: Based on RealNetworks, "Rhapsody Teams with Vizio, Cisco and Yahoo! on New Streaming Music Products for the Home," 2009 Press Release [**www.real-networks.com**], January 8, 2009; J. Markoff, "Patent Awarded to RealNetworks May Give It a Competitive Edge," New York Times Online, April 24, 2006; and S. Kessler, "Finding Value on the Net," BusinessWeek Online, December 2, 2005.

built the same organizational cultures. According to the RBV, there are some key assets (resources) that can give a firm a competitive advantage. Therefore, an organization will be positioned to succeed if it has the best and most appropriate resources for its business.

Managing strategically, according to the RBV, involves developing and exploiting an organization's unique resources and capabilities. But, what exactly are "resources" and what makes them "unique"?

Resources include all of the financial, physical, human, intangible, and structural/cultural assets used by an organization to develop, produce, and deliver products or services to its customers.[5] Financial assets include the financial holdings of an organization (cash reserves, investments, etc.), the actual and available debt and equity used by the organization, and any retained earnings. Physical assets include equipment, office buildings, manufacturing or sales facilities, raw materials, or other tangible materials an organization has. Human resources include the experiences, characteristics, knowledge, judgment, wisdom, skills, abilities, and competencies of an organization's employees. Intangible assets include such things as brand names, patents, reputation, trademarks, copyrights, registered designs, and databases. Finally, structural/cultural assets include an organization's history, culture, work systems, organizational policies, working relationships, level of employee trust, and the formal structure being used.

Although every organization has resources it needs and uses to do its work, not all those resources will lead to a sustainable competitive advantage. The RBV suggests that resources must be unique to be a source of potential competitive advantage. Figure 2.2 illustrates what makes resources unique. Because these characteristics are important, let's look at them more closely.

Value

An organizational resource is unique if it adds value. Adding value means that the resource can be used to exploit external circumstances that are likely to bring in organizational revenues or that it can be used to neutralize negative external situations that are likely to keep revenue from flowing in. An organization's resources aren't valuable by themselves but only when they exploit those external opportunities or neutralize the threats. As environmental factors such as customer tastes or technology change, resources can become more

Figure 2.2

*What Makes Organizational
Resources Unique?*

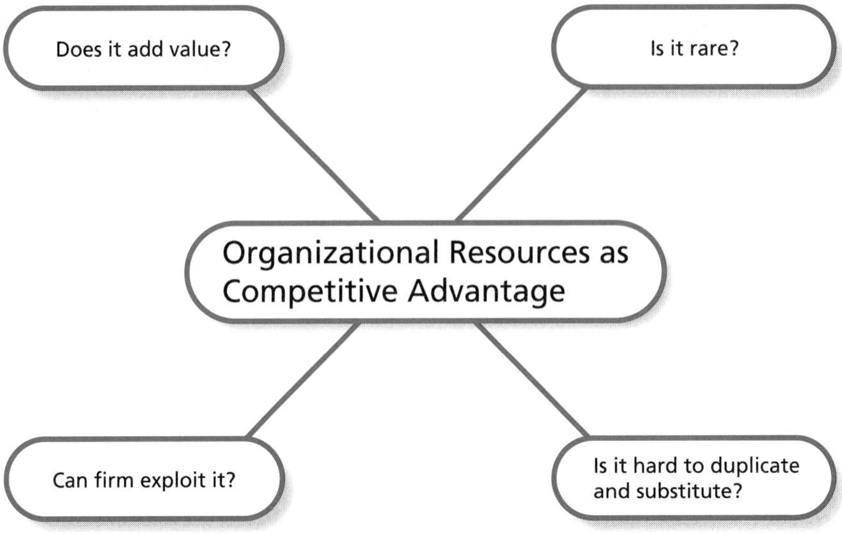

valuable or less valuable. So, a resource is valuable in the context of what's happening in the external environment.

Rare

For a resource to be rare, ideally no competing firms should already possess it. If more competitors acquire certain resources that have been a source of competitive advantage, then it becomes a less likely source of sustainable competitive advantage for an organization. Keep in mind, though, that even commonly held resources may be valuable if for no other reason than the firm's survival in a competitive environment. But, in order to gain a competitive advantage, a resource should be both valuable *and* rare.

Hard to Imitate (Duplicate) and Substitute

Obviously, if a resource can't be imitated or substituted by a competitor, then any revenues it generates are more likely to continue flowing in. Organizations want resources that are hard to imitate and substitute. Imitation (duplication) is when a competitor builds the same kind of resource as the firm it's imitating. Substitution is when a firm substitutes an alternative resource for the specific resource currently being used to gain competitive advantage and achieves the same results. So, in order to keep resources unique, you want them to be hard to imitate and substitute. Some resources are harder to imitate and substitute—for instance, such things as company reputation, employee trust, teamwork, and organizational culture.

Ability to Exploit

Not only must organizational resources be valuable, rare, and hard to imitate or substitute, the organization must be able to exploit them. Are the formal structure, systems, policies, procedures, and processes in place to use the resources it has to develop a sustainable competitive advantage? In other words, is it able to exploit the full competitive potential of its resources? Without these abilities, it will be difficult for an organization to create and maintain a competitive advantage.

All four of these characteristics are important indicators of a resource's ability to be a source of sustainable competitive advantage. The popular business press is filled with stories of companies that have unique and valuable resources they're able to exploit. But, there are also many examples of organizations that have not been able to get and keep a

W. L. Gore & Associates [**www.gore.com**] is known for its high-quality and revolutionary outdoor wear products and was recently named one of *Fortune* magazine's 100 Best Companies to Work For (its eleventh straight year of being named in the list). The kinds of innovative efforts exhibited by Gore's associates (they're not called employees) are made possible by a unique organizational culture that unleashes creativity and fosters teamwork. Being an associate at Gore requires a commitment to four basic principles articulated by company founder Bill Gore: fairness to each other and everyone you come in contact with; freedom to encourage, help, and allow other associates to grow in knowledge, skill, and scope of responsibility; the ability to make your own commitments and keep them; and consulting with other associates before undertaking actions that could impact the reputation of the company.

Go to the company's Web site. What other examples of resources do you see? Do you think any of these resources are unique? Explain.

Sources: Based on W. L. Gore & Associates [**www.gore.com**], January 8, 2009; and R. Levering and M. Moskowitz, "100 Best Companies to Work For," Fortune, February 2, 2009, pp. 67–78.

competitive edge because they have no unique resources or they haven't been able to exploit the unique resources they do have. According to the RBV, managing strategically means continually building and maintaining organizational resources—capitalizing on the "crown jewels" of the firm. However, a question facing strategic decision makers is this: Do the unique resources that are sources of competitive advantage today remain so over time? According to the next view, not always.

Guerrilla View

What do you think of when you hear the term *guerrilla*? Do you envision brief and covert attacks on an enemy position by a well-trained, competent, and skilled unit? That's the analogy behind the **guerrilla view,** which is the view that an organization's competitive advantage is temporary. Why? Because the environment is characterized by continual and often revolutionary changes. For instance, disruptions in technology, market instabilities, and other types of significant, but unpredictable changes challenge strategic managers' attempts at creating a sustainable competitive advantage. For instance, think about the environment the recorded music industry faced over the past few years and how difficult it has been to get and keep a competitive advantage. (See the end-of-chapter case on pp. 57–58 about this industry.) According to the guerrilla view, successful organizations must rapidly and repeatedly disrupt the current situation and radically surprise competitors with strategic actions designed to keep them off balance—in other words, act like a guerrilla unit. Successful organizations will repeatedly create new competitive advantages based on how the context is changing.

Which View Is Best?

We know competitive advantage is important to how an organization ultimately performs, so which view is best? Each brings a unique perspective to understanding competitive advantage. The I/O view addresses the need to look at the external environment, particularly the industry and competitors, and emphasizes the importance of understanding competitive positioning. The RBV considers the need to look inside the organization for the unique resources and capabilities that can be exploited. And, the guerrilla view forces strategic decision makers to recognize that the dynamic nature of the external environment can affect what is considered a competitive advantage and how long that competitive advantage can last.

Strategic Management in Action

What if customers said they no longer needed packages shipped "absolutely, positively overnight?" That's the position FedEx, the world's largest express transport company and a company that prided itself for being consistently on the cutting edge of product delivery, found itself in. Overnight, its market turned upside down, and the competitive advantage FedEx had developed was no longer valuable. Customers no longer wanted fast, but pricey, delivery service. External changes such as instantaneous e-mail delivery of information, discount carriers that provided package tracking information online, and competitive rivals that copied FedEx's elaborate information system that once distinguished the company have all contributed to its strategic management challenges. The company's strategic decision makers aren't just sitting back, however. To bolster the number of package pick-up locations and to give them a stronger retail presence, they acquired copy company Kinko's (now FedEx Office). In addition, the company is focusing more on long-haul global and domestic cargo markets by buying new planes and acquiring a domestic trucking company.

Take a look at the company's Web site. What other strategic options are they pursuing, especially in light of the rising fuel costs and retail slump (meaning fewer packages being delivered)? Do FedEx's actions reflect the guerrilla view of competitive advantage? Discuss.

Sources: Based on A. Roth, "FedEx Threatens to Cancel Jet Orders," Wall Street Journal, March 25, 2009, p. B1. C. Dade and S. Tibken, "FedEx Swings To a Rare Loss On Fuel Costs, Retail Slump," Wall Street Journal, June 19, 2008, p. B1; Reuters, "Kinko's Is Now FedEx Office," New York Times Online, June 3, 2008; and B. Hagenbaugh, "FedEx Moves Record 9.8M Packages Monday," USA Today, December 20, 2006, p. 4B.

Managing strategically involves looking both externally and internally to come up with strategies that have a chance of creating a sustainable competitive advantage, even if for only a brief period of time. In this way, unique resources and capabilities can be "matched" to changing external circumstances. Because the external environment is continually changing (new competitors come and go, customers' tastes change, technology changes, current competitors start a price war, etc.), the source of sustainable competitive advantage *is* probably found in different places at different points in time. So, how can strategic decision makers ever hope to develop a sustainable competitive advantage—that is, manage strategically? The answer is by continually analyzing both the external and internal organizational environments and then taking advantage of any positive changes (or buffering against negative changes) with the organization's unique resources and capabilities. One of the most important changes strategic managers must contend with is the business environment. That's what we'll look at next.

Learning Review: Learning Outcome 2.1

- Define competitive advantage and explain why it's important.
- Describe the different perspectives on competitive advantage.
- Explain what makes a resource unique.

LEARNING OUTCOME 2.2
Explain the Driving Forces, Implications, and Critical Success Factors of the Business Environment

The business context or environment that organizations operate in today is a lot different than what it used to be. Even not-for-profit organizations feel the impact of the changing context because they, too, need resources such as labor, technology, and funding to operate. We need to examine important characteristics of this business environment: What forces are "driving" it? What are the implications? And, what will it take to be successful in this context? Figure 2.3 provides an overview.

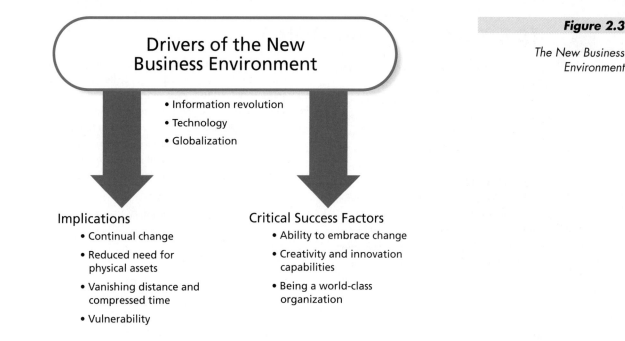

Figure 2.3

*The New Business
Environment*

**Drivers of the New
Business Environment**

- Information revolution
- Technology
- Globalization

Implications

- Continual change
- Reduced need for
  physical assets
- Vanishing distance and
  compressed time
- Vulnerability

Critical Success Factors

- Ability to embrace change
- Creativity and innovation
  capabilities
- Being a world-class
  organization

Drivers of the Business Environment

The three critical driving forces in this new business environment are: (1) the information revolution, (2) technology, and (3) globalization. Let's discuss each more thoroughly.[6]

The Information Revolution

If there's one driving force that has set the tone for this business environment, it's the information revolution. This revolution is not just continuing, it's accelerating. A recent study showed that the amount of new information saved in a single year alone would fill half a million libraries the size of the Library of Congress. Another showed that the amount of digital information is 3 million times all the books ever written. And another showed that the amount of information being created, captured, and replicated in a digital format is growing at a rate of 57 percent a year.[7] Any way you look at it, that's a lot of information! And this information is readily available to practically anyone from anywhere on the globe at any hour of the day and pretty much in any format. The instant availability of information has radically changed the nature of the business environment, which, in turn, affects the context of strategic management.

Information (knowledge) has always been used in producing goods and services, primarily to design work tools, organizational processes, management systems, and products, as organizations searched for ways to be more efficient and effective. However, a fundamental shift has occurred in which information is now *the* essential resource of production, not simply a means to an end. Knowledge is no longer viewed only as a way to make sure other resources are used efficiently. Land, labor, and capital have become supporting, not the main factors in production.[8] This means that organizations can no longer rely on the traditional factors of production to provide a sustainable competitive advantage but must look to how information and knowledge can be exploited. In addition to knowledge, technology is also one of the driving forces of this business environment.

Technology

All organizations use some form of technology to do their work. What is **technology?** It's using equipment, materials, knowledge, and experience to perform tasks. Some industries

FOR YOUR INFORMATION

All Service All the Time

"The war between the tangible and intangible sectors of the U.S. economy is over, and the intangibles have won." When Wal-Mart Stores first topped the list of *Fortune's* Global 500 in 2002 (and remains there), it was the culmination of a major economic shift that had been taking place for years—that is, the shift from producing goods to producing services. Manufacturing's share of U.S. employment, which peaked in 1953 at 35 percent, has steadily declined ever since. This is also true in all other developed economies (Germany, Canada, Japan, etc.) as well. The Bureau of Labor Statistics predicts that through the year 2014, production jobs will continue to decline while occupations in service-providing industries will continue to expand. Or put another way, the service-providing industries are expected to account for approximately 18.7 million of the 18.9 million new wage and salary jobs generated. One explanation for this shift is that as Americans got richer, consumption got more sophisticated. With more income to spend, people started purchasing more services—movies and travel, massages and facials, mortgages to buy houses, insurance to protect those houses and possessions, and so on. Economists call this a shift in the demand pattern. It's also a reason why so many top global companies are service companies.

How has the information revolution impacted service businesses? Choose a couple of service businesses and do some research to answer this question.

Sources: M. Mandel, "They Make Jobs, Not Widgets," BusinessWeek, December 22, 2008, p. 32; "World's Largest Corporations," Fortune, July 21, 2008, pp. 165–174; W. J. Holstein, "And Now a Syllabus for the Service Economy," New York Times Online, December 3, 2006; J. Scanlon, "Keeping America Competitive," BusinessWeek Online, November 15, 2006; A. Lustgarten and C. Tkaczyk, "Global 500," Fortune, July 24, 2006, pp. 66–70 and 89–98; and T. Aeppel, "U.S. 'Birthrate' For New Factories Is Steadily Falling," Wall Street Journal, March 15, 2006, p. A4.

are more technology intensive than others (for instance, think of electronics, software, telecommunications, and pharmaceuticals). But even organizations such as the American Red Cross, your neighborhood grocery store, utility companies, and steel mills use technology. Technology significantly changed the nature of competition in the last part of the twentieth century. Work approaches and tools that may have been effective in the past weren't anymore and new ones were rapidly being developed. Technology continues to have far-reaching effects on how organizations do their work—effects we can see in three different areas: innovation, bottom-up capability, and organizational performance.

Strategic Management in Action   THE GLOBAL PERSPECTIVE

Safe. Secure. Reliable. Dependable. Impenetrable. Powerful. All things that we think of when we think about information technology. However, even IT can't escape a natural disaster. Rewind to late December 2006. Computer screens at Reuters financial information company in Singapore suddenly went blank. International telephone conversations suddenly went silent. Access to international Web sites was spotty. Even international transactions at automated teller machines were lost. An "earthquake off Taiwan had damaged undersea cables, jamming Internet services as voice and data traffic vied for space on smaller cables and slower satellite links." Because most of Asia is separated by water, the most efficient option for carrying data is undersea cable systems. This earthquake took out six of seven existing systems. The service disruption was most directly experienced in Taiwan, Singapore, Hong Kong, South Korea, and Japan, but it didn't take long for a "ripple effect" to be felt in other parts of the world. Even those businesses so reliant on technology that they had a backup source found that a backup was useless when it was gone also. As one reporter said, this "disruption exposed our global networks' fragility." Executives at some telecommunication companies said the problems highlighted a need to "beef up their backup systems even more."

What does this scenario tell us about the importance of knowing the context?

Sources: D. Greenlee and W. Arnold, "Asia Scrambles to Repair Quake Damage to Data Cables," New York Times Online, December 29, 2006; C. Hang-Sun and W. Arnold, "Asian Quake Disrupts Data Traffic," New York Times Online, December 28, 2006; and J. Dean, "Asian Quake's Telecom Disruption Exposes Global Networks' Fragility," Wall Street Journal, December 28, 2006, p. A1+.

The gambling industry has embraced the wonders of technology—especially in player surveillance. For instance, although blackjack may be a simple game, the blackjack tables have become quite technologically sophisticated. Casinos now monitor cards using invisible codes, track chips with radio frequency identification (RFID) tags, and scrutinize players using facial recognition software. When players take a seat at the tables, electronic eyes scan faces and compare them with a database of known cheaters. If the database finds a match, the person is escorted out of the casino by security. European casinos pioneered the use of RFID chips, which make it easier to track inventory, betting patterns, and customer status.

Other industries such as sporting goods are embracing technology as well. For instance, German engineers have been working on a "smartball" technology that will determine whether a soccer ball has crossed the goal line.

Can you think of some other ways that casinos or sporting goods companies might use technology in their business?

Sources: I. Wylie, "This Ball Has Brains," Fast Company, July/August 2006, p. 42; and D. Terdiman, "The New Deal," Wired, February 2004, p. 38.

Technology impacts **innovation,** which we define as turning a creative idea into a product or process that can be used or sold. Innovation *is* more than just being creative—it's developing, making, and marketing something that can generate revenue. At a global innovation conference, IBM's CEO Sam Palmisano said, "The way you will thrive in this environment is by innovating—innovating in technologies, innovating in strategies, innovating in business models."[9] One company that has exploited the power of an innovative business model is Indian telecom Bharti Airtel Limited. The company, led by Sunil B. Mittal (CEO), outsources everything but marketing and customer management, charges two cents a minute for calls, and has over 67 million customers.[10]

So how important is innovation to companies? Research on the most innovative companies in the world found that these innovators have achieved a profit margin growth of 3.4 percent a year since 1995, compared to 0.4 percent growth for a company on Standard & Poor's Global 1200 list.[11] Although the majority of these "masters" of innovation were U.S. companies, statistics show that the United States lags in research and development spending. The United States still leads the world in scientific research, but six countries now devote a larger share of their economy to R&D spending, leading some experts to sound a cautionary note regarding future breakthroughs.[12]

Another area where technology has had an impact on organizations is in terms of what can be called a "bottom-up" or mass collaboration capability. Through technology such as the Internet, personal messaging systems, and social networks, power is shifting from institutions to individuals. Take, for example, the popularity of Fox Network's reality show *American Idol,* in which the audience decides who "wins." Or look at what eBay has done. The company's founder said that managers don't control the brand or customer experience: the customers do.

One final area technology affects is organizational performance. High-performance companies (e.g., Wal-Mart, McDonald's, Southwest Airlines, Toyota, Samsung, IKEA) are leaders in technology. But simply having the latest and best technology isn't their goal. Instead, these great companies realize that technology is a powerful tool that enhances their business. They realize that it's not a replacement for understanding the economics of their business and creating a business model that allows them to be the best at what they do, but that it can help them perform better.

The increasing pace of technological change and the importance of continual innovation are quite evident. Within the context of managing strategically, technology and innovation do influence an organization's sustainable competitive advantage. The challenge is capturing and exploiting the unique advantages of technology by using the organizational innovation process to create valuable products and processes—and doing so globally. The challenges and opportunities of globalization are the final driving force we're going to look at.

Globalization

In Chapter 1, we discussed how globalization and the global economy are impacting strategic management. Globalization has been around for so long now (you undoubtedly hear about it in every business class you take) that it almost seems a cliché. However, globalization has transformed and continues to transform the business environment.[13] More than ever, organizations must strategically manage global issues. The days when all our consumer products were produced in the United States are long gone. Now, it's common for these products to be provided by a foreign company or by a domestic company that also does business globally. Even small businesses feel the effects of a global business environment. Globalization influences strategic management in two ways: (1) global markets and (2) global competitors.

Creating sustainable competitive advantage may entail looking globally for customers and resources. Although any location may be a potential market, strategic decision makers

FOR YOUR INFORMATION

Offshoring and Outsourcing: The Good, the Bad, and the Reality

This is a story about the global economy. It's about markets, politics, and public opinion. And as jobs—especially white-collar and professional jobs—continue to be outsourced and offshored, the story hits closer and closer to home. Although the terms *offshoring* and *outsourcing* are often used interchangeably, they do mean different things. **Offshoring** is relocating business processes (production and services) from one country to another. **Outsourcing** is moving noncore activities from being done internally to being done externally by an entity that specializes in that activity.

One of the realities of a global economy is that to be competitive, strategic decision makers must look for the best places to do business. If a car can be made more cheaply in Mexico, maybe it should be. If a telephone inquiry can be processed more cheaply in India or the Philippines, maybe it should be. And if programming code can be written more cheaply in China or Russia, maybe it should be. Almost any professional job that can be done outside the organization is up for grabs. There's nothing political or philosophical about the reason for shipping jobs elsewhere. The bottom line is that it can save companies money. But there's a price to be paid in terms of angry and anxious employees. So, are offshoring and outsourcing bad?

Critics say "yes." It's affecting jobs once considered "safe" across a wider range of professional work activities. And the offshoring and outsourcing are taking place at a breathtaking pace. What this means is that the careers college students are preparing for probably won't sustain them in the long run. This structural change in the U.S. economy also means that the workforce is likely to face frequent career changes and downward pressures on wages.

Proponents say "no." Their argument is based on viewing economic development as a ladder with every country trying to climb to the next rung. And it's foolish to think that in the United States, we've reached the top of the ladder and there's nowhere else to go. Although people fear that educated U.S. workers will face the same fate as blue-collar workers whose jobs shifted to lower-cost countries, the truth is that the United States currently still has a competitive advantage in innovation, although, as discussed earlier, that may be in jeopardy. The biggest danger to U.S. workers isn't overseas competition; it's worrying too much about other countries climbing up the economic ladder and not worrying enough about finding that next higher rung.

Who's right? We probably can't answer that question just yet. Only time will tell. However, we do know that what we're seeing with offshoring and outsourcing is another example of why strategic decision makers need to be aware of the context within which their organizations are doing business.

Do some research on this issue and come up with arguments for and against it.

Sources: P. Engardio, M. Arndt, and D. Foust, "The Future of Outsourcing," *BusinessWeek*, January 30, 2006, pp. 50–58; J. Thottam, "Is Your Job Going Abroad?" *Time*, March 1, 2004, pp. 26–36; L. D. Tyson, "Outsourcing: Who's Safe Anymore?" *BusinessWeek*, February 23, 2004, p. 26; A. Fisher, "Think Globally, Save Your Job Locally," *Fortune*, February 23, 2004, p. 60; "The New Job Migration," *The Economist*, February 21, 2004, p. 11; O. Thomas, "The Outsourcing Solution," *Business 2.0*, September 2003, pp. 159–160; and K. Madigan and M. J. Mandel, "Outsourcing Jobs: Is It Bad?" *BusinessWeek*, August 25, 2003, pp. 36–38.

must recognize that the global economic climate and those of individual markets, can, and do, have an impact. In addition, financial, material, human, and knowledge resources are available globally and should be acquired wherever it strategically makes sense to do so. In other words, globalization means that geographic boundaries don't constrain an organization's strategic decisions and actions.

As global markets open up, competitors can come from anywhere. They, too, are looking for a sustainable competitive advantage. Although doing business globally can be rewarding, competing in a global marketplace is challenging because now you're dealing with organizations that have their own unique set of experiences and resources, making it much more difficult to understand their strategic approach and intent. However, global competitors don't have to be a threat. Strategic decision makers might find that the most effective strategy for achieving a sustainable competitive advantage is to partner with a global competitor to create or market products. In fact, in Chapter 7, in which we discuss corporate strategy, we'll look at how organizations are using global alliances.

Each of these driving forces—information revolution, technology, and globalization—is affecting the context within which strategic decision makers manage strategically. What are the implications for strategic decision makers?

Implications of These Driving Forces

Look back at Figure 2.3, and you'll see that there are four major implications of these driving forces: continual change, the reduced need for physical assets, vanishing distance and compressed time, and increased vulnerability. Let's look at each.

Continual Change

Change is the order of business in today's context as *all* organizations deal with changing conditions. These changing conditions (externally or even internally) stimulate the need for **organizational change,** which is defined as a structured transition in what an organization does and how it does it. For example, greeting card companies had to change the way they did business as people began sending electronic greeting cards (a changing external condition). Or consider how other changing external conditions—such as increasing levels of obesity—have forced organizations to change the products they offer and how they're packaged and sold.

Reduced Need for Physical Assets

The business environment of a few years ago was one in which the more physical assets you had (manufacturing facilities, office buildings, equipment, inventory, etc.), the more economically powerful you were. However, success in today's economy isn't reliant simply on physical assets. Instead, value is found in intangible factors such as information, people, ideas, and knowledge. Companies such as Google, Amazon.com, Apple, American Express, and even Toyota are finding that they can achieve a sustainable competitive advantage with nonphysical assets such as customer databases, online ordering systems, continual product and process innovation, and employee knowledge sharing.

Vanishing Distance and Compressed Time

Physical distance and time constraints on an organization's strategic decisions have all but disappeared! Although geography traditionally played an important role in determining customers and competitors, that's no longer so. An organization's potential markets and competitors can be found anywhere. As the limitations of physical distance have disappeared, so too have the limitations of time. The ability to instantly interact (e-mail, text messaging, interactive Web sites, etc.) means staying on top of changes or finding your marketplace advantage temporary, at best. Although it isn't easy, it's important.

Steve Ming-Jang Chang, CEO and president of Trend Micro, Inc., a high-tech transnational company, believes that "borders are so twentieth century." As a provider of computer network antivirus and Internet security software, Trend Micro has spread its executives, engineers, and support staff around the world in order to improve its response time to new virus threats. It's routinely the first to go on the offensive when a new virus strikes, often 30 minutes before market leader Symantec (maker of the popular Norton Antivirus software) reacts. Although Trend Micro's corporate and financial headquarters are in Tokyo, its computer virus response center is based in Manila (where costs are low), product development is based in Taiwan (where there's a plentiful supply of Ph.D.s), and sales are centered in California's Silicon Valley (where there's easier access to the vast American market). No competitor has such an international reach. The company has succeeded because it's set up its business in a way that takes advantage of the realities of today's context.

Explain how using Figure 2.3.

Sources: *Company information from Hoover's Online* [**www.hoovers.com**], *January 5, 2007; B. Grow, "The Mind Games Cybercrooks Play," BusinessWeek, April 17, 2006, pp. 54–58; and S. Hamm, "Borders Are So Twentieth Century," BusinessWeek, September 22, 2003, pp. 68–73.*

Vulnerability

Although their names are usually quite innocent and often very clever—SoBig, The Love Bug, BugBear—global computer viruses can be destructive. They illustrate the final implication of the driving forces in today's context—the increased vulnerability that organizations face from interconnectedness and openness.[14] Threats from computer virus attacks, terrorist attacks, and biological attacks should be enough to make strategic decision makers realize that their information, facilities, and employees are vulnerable. Protecting valuable resources against such potential attacks is no longer a "maybe"—it's a strategic certainty and one that shouldn't be ignored.

Critical Success Factors

Three factors critical to success in this new business environment are (1) ability to embrace change, (2) creativity and innovation capabilities, and (3) being a world-class organization (see Figure 2.3). Let's look at each.

Ability to Embrace Change

If there's one word that captures the essence of this business environment, it's *change*—from technological advances, from resource vulnerability, or from information availability. Do you like change? Probably not. Few people enjoy or even seek out change. Most of us think change is annoying, scary, or both. We like the old and comfortable, not the new or unknown. But change is a given in today's business environment. Being successful in such an environment means not only being tolerant of change, but seeking it out and embracing it. Change brings opportunities to exploit and challenges in dealing with the changes. In any type of change efforts, the quality of strategic leadership can spell the difference between success and failure.

Strategic decision makers play an important role as change agents. Effective change doesn't just happen. Someone must initiate and oversee the change efforts. These individuals are called **change agents.** Whether the change is big or small, change agents are needed, and strategic decision makers can play this important role. Ideally, an organization's top managers provide a sense of long-term direction and offer support and rationale for needed changes.[15] But, strategic leaders at any organizational level play an important role in the change process.

Change is difficult. (Think about how you react if you have a substitute professor in class one day or if your professor changes the course assignment schedule to accommodate a change in plans. You may be anxious or even annoyed.) Although strong strategic leadership can't eliminate all the challenges associated with change, it can smooth the process and facilitate successful implementation of the change. Considering the number of dynamic forces facing today's organizations, strong strategic leadership can create an appropriate and supportive organizational environment in which employees are encouraged to take responsibility for problems and solutions.[16]

Creativity and Innovation Capabilities

Here's an abbreviated statement of how critical this factor is: "Create and innovate or fail!" It's that simple. In this context we've described, strategic decision makers must be prepared to create new products and services and adopt state-of-the-art technology if their organizations are to compete successfully and survive. **Creativity,** the ability to combine ideas in a unique way or to make unusual associations between ideas, is an important capability.[17] A creative person or organization develops novel approaches to doing work or unique solutions to problems. But, creativity alone isn't enough. We know from our earlier discussion that innovation is the process of taking a creative idea and turning it into a product or process that can be used or sold. An innovative organization is characterized by its ability to channel creativity into useful outcomes. Both capabilities, being creative and being innovative, are critical to strategic success in this business environment.

Being a World-Class Organization

Given the importance of creating a sustainable competitive advantage in today's business environment, you'd probably agree that ensuring an organization's long-run survival and success isn't easy. One concept with considerable potential for helping strategic decision makers meet that challenge is that of a **world-class organization,** in which strategic decision makers take actions to help it be the best in the world at what it does.[18] Recall our earlier discussion of the business environment with respect to information and knowledge,

FOR YOUR INFORMATION

The DNA of Corporate Innovation

The members of the Innovation Network Inc. **[www.thinksmart.com]** put their heads together and developed The Innovation DNA Model. (You might want to check out all their other interesting creativity-enhancing ideas on the Web site.) This model identifies seven dimensions that need to be in place for organizational innovation to take root. These dimensions include: (1) challenge—the bigger the challenge and the passion behind it, the more energy innovation efforts will need; (2) customer focus—all innovation should be focused on creating value for customers, external or internal; it requires understanding their needs; (3) creativity—everything starts from an idea and the best way to get ideas is to generate a lot of possibilities; (4) communication—open communication of ideas, information, and feelings is the lifeblood of innovation; (5) collaboration—innovation is a group process; (6) completion—innovations require "doing"; that is, decision making, delegating, scheduling, monitoring, and feedback skills; and completed projects should be celebrated; and (7) contemplation—learning from completed projects builds a knowledge base that creates an upward cycle of success. In addition, the organization's culture creates the playing field for all the other elements to happen.

Research a company (Starbucks, Apple, Microsoft, or pick your own) and assess it on these dimensions. Be sure to document your sources, and be prepared to share your findings in class.

Sources: *Innovation Network Inc.*, January 8, 2009; and S. Caudron, "The Economics of Innovation," *Business Finance*, November 1999, pp. 23–27.

Figure 2.4

*Characteristics of
World-Class Organizations*

technology, and increasing globalization, and you can begin to appreciate why being a world-class organization is important. Even if an organization operates in a single geographic location, it should still strive to be the best at what it does in its own little "world" or competitive arena. What characteristics does a world-class organization have? The major ones are shown in Figure 2.4.

Learning Review: Learning Outcome 2.2

- Describe the three major driving forces of the business environment.
- Explain the four major implications of these driving forces.
- Discuss the three critical factors for succeeding in the business environment.

LEARNING OUTCOME 2.3
Discuss Two Organizational Elements That Guide Strategic Decision Makers in Managing Strategically in Today's Context

As strategic decision makers grapple with the challenges of guiding an organization in today's context, two organizational elements are a source of guidance: (1) organizational vision and mission and (2) corporate social responsibility (CSR) and ethics.

Organizational Vision and Mission

It's equally important for an organization to have both an organizational vision *and* a mission. These two concepts are often viewed as the same but we think they're different. An **organizational vision** is a broad comprehensive picture of what a leader wants an organization to become. It's a statement of what the organization stands for, what it believes in, and why it exists. It presents a view beyond what the organization "is" to what the organization "could be."[19] Although it may seem that a vision is simply "fluff"— something that sounds good on paper but does nothing to improve the organization's performance—a clear vision articulated by leaders can motivate organizational members to contribute increased levels of effort.[20]

An effective organizational vision should include four components.[21] One is that the vision *be built on a foundation of the organization's core values and beliefs.* These values and beliefs address what's fundamentally important to the organization, whether it's conducting business ethically and responsibly, satisfying the customer, emphasizing quality in all aspects, or being a technology leader. The vision should stress whatever those core values might be. How important are values? A survey by the American Management Association found that almost 86 percent of the respondents said the values of their organization were specifically stated or written and 64 percent said that the values were linked to performance evaluations and compensation.[22] Although a statement of values doesn't guarantee success, it does provide employees behavioral expectations. For example, if employees know that outstanding customer service is valued by the organization, they can act in ways that champion customer service.

Second, the vision should *elaborate a purpose for the organization.* Every organization has a purpose and that purpose should be specified in the organization's vision. That way, all organizational stakeholders are explicitly aware of why this organization exists.

The third component is that the vision should *include a brief summary of what the organization does.* While it doesn't provide explicit details (that's what the various mission statements do, which we'll discuss shortly), it should explain what's being done to fulfill the purpose. And, this is a good time to say that while they're related, there *is* a difference between an organization's purpose and what it does. For example, there may be several organizations that have the purpose of ecological preservation but the way they carry out that purpose (i.e., what they do) may be different.

The last component of the vision is that it should *specify broad goals.* Goals provide a target that all organizational members work toward meeting. Goals also serve to unify organizational members toward a common end. An organization's vision can and should be a guiding force in every decision.

Although an organizational vision provides an overall picture of where the organization would like to be in the future, a **mission statement** is a statement of what specific organizational units do and what they hope to accomplish. An organization will have a single vision

Strategic Management in Action

Although many old-line manufacturers only dream of transforming themselves into nimble technology companies, Corning Inc. [**www.corning.com**] has actually pulled it off. Maybe you (or older family members or friends) still have Corning baking dishes in your kitchen. The Corning that manufactured those dishes and other glassware still works mostly in glass but in forms that most people would not recognize. The company has shifted its focus to products such as optical fiber and liquid crystal display screens. In fact, the company states that it has a proud history of "enriching people's lives through research and technological innovation."

Go to Corning's Web site, find the company's seven values, and describe them. How will these values affect the way organizational employees manage strategically?

Sources: S. Silver, "Corning's Biggest Bet Yet? Diesel-Filter Technologies," Wall Street Journal, March 7, 2008, pp. B1+; S. M. Mehta, "Bend It Like Corning," Fortune, August 6, 2007, pp. 69–70; S. Silver, "Corning May Offer Window of Opportunity," Wall Street Journal, August 24, 2006, p. C3; Associated Press, "Corning Chairman Houghton Steps Back from Active Duty," Wall Street Journal, May 2, 2006, p. B8; K. Maney, "Corning CEO Insists on Keeping His Eye on Long-Term Ball," USA Today, May 11, 2005, p. 3B; A. Carter, "Reigniting Corning," Money, May 2003 [**www.cnnmoney.com**]; J. Kimelman, "Corning May Be Turning a Corner," New York Times, May 4, 2003, Section 3, p. 6; and T. Aeppel, "Corning's Makeover: From Casseroles to Fiber Optics," Wall Street Journal, July 16, 1999, p. B4.

and potentially several mission statements (divisional, departmental, project work group, etc.) that contribute to the pursuit of the organization's vision. A mission statement provides a focus for employees as they make and implement strategic decisions. Although it's not as broad as the organizational vision, a mission statement provides an overview of each unit's purpose, what it does, and its goals. Each mission statement also aligns with the organizational vision.

The Grey Zone

Are vision and mission statements just a bunch of empty words? A study of several securities firms and investment banks showed that many hours had been spent crafting elegant mission statements that extolled the virtues of teamwork, integrity, and respect for the individual. Yet, the partners at those firms treated their young analysts like second-class citizens. They gave them work that wasn't commensurate with their skills, were openly impolite to them, and, in many instances, were verbally abusive toward them. When these conditions were described to the top decision makers, they said that kind of behavior couldn't be happening—it went against their companies' mission statements. Yet, this type of situation doesn't occur just in securities firms.

Could this situation have been prevented? If so, how? If not, why not? How can strategic decision makers make sure that vision and mission statements are more than empty words?

CSR and Ethics

How much and what type of corporate social responsibility (CSR) business organizations should pursue has been a topic of heated debate for a number of years. **CSR** is the obligation of organizational decision makers to make decisions and act in ways that recognize the interrelatedness of business and society.[23] CSR recognizes the organization's various stakeholders and how they're dealt with. But, it's in the definition of "who" organizations are responsible to that we find a diversity of opinions.

The traditional view was that corporations existed solely to serve the interests of one stakeholder group—the stockholders.[24] The late Milton Friedman, the most outspoken advocate of this view, argued that corporate social programs and actions must be paid for in some way, which adds to the costs of doing business. Those costs must be either passed on to customers in the form of higher prices or absorbed by the organization. In either case, profitability suffers as customers might buy less at higher prices or organizational costs would increase. However, do understand that Friedman didn't say that organizations shouldn't be socially responsible. In fact, he felt they *should* be. But his argument was that the extent of the responsibility was to maximize shareholder returns.

However, the traditional—and purely economic—perspective of CSR has given way to a belief that organizations have a larger societal role to play and a broader constituency to serve than just stockholders alone. Yet, balancing various stakeholder demands is a complicated process as they typically have a wide range of needs and conflicting expectations.[25] What this means for managing strategically is making decisions in ways that will enhance the various stakeholder relationships. **Stakeholders** are individuals or groups who have a stake in or are influenced by an organization's decisions and actions and who, in turn, can

FOR YOUR INFORMATION

Being Green

A number of highly visible global ecological problems and environmental disasters have brought about a new awareness and spirit of environmentalism among strategic decision makers, who increasingly have begun to confront questions about the natural environment and its impact on organizations. The recognition of the close link between an organization's decisions and actions and its impact on the natural environment is referred to as **green management.** As organizations become "greener," we find more of them issuing detailed reports on their environmental performance. The Global Reporting Initiative (GRI) **[www. globalreporting.org]**, launched in 1997 as a joint

initiative of the Coalition for Environmentally Responsible Economies (CERES) and the United Nations Environment Program, has the goal of enhancing the quality, rigor, and utility of sustainability reporting. To that extent, GRI created its Sustainability Reporting Guidelines. Using the Guidelines, hundreds of companies around the globe report their efforts in promoting environmental sustainability.

Check out the GRI Web site. What guidelines does the GRI suggest? Pick out five of the reporting companies and summarize their environmental reports.

Sources: *Global Reporting Initiative Web site* **[www.globalreporting.org]**, *January 8, 2009; M. Connor, "Measuring Sustainability," CRO, Fall 2006, p. 26; and A. Kolk, "Green Reporting," Harvard Business Review, January–February 2000, pp. 15–16.*

influence the organization. Figure 2.5 identifies potential stakeholders with whom an organization may have to contend.

Many organizations believe that strong and socially responsible stakeholder relationships make them more competitive.[26] For instance, every day, General Mills ships three

Figure 2.5

Potential Organizational Stakeholders

FOR YOUR INFORMATION

Ethics in Real Life

An ethics code should be more than great public relations. After all, Enron had a code of ethics, which is ironic considering the unethical behaviors exhibited by many of its top executives. The success—or failure—of corporate ethics programs has less to do with such things as written ethics codes and compliance hotlines, and everything to do with why employees think the programs were established in the first place. For example, George David, CEO of United Technologies Corporation (UTC), believes very deeply in the power of a code of ethics, but the company's ethics program entails much more than that. Although the company has a detailed code of ethics, including 24 standards of conduct, it's not just having the written code that makes ethics work so well. (See the company's code at **http://utc. com/utc/Governance/Code_of_Ethics.html.)** It's the fact that employees know the behavioral expectations,

especially when it comes to ethics. What can strategic decision makers do to make sure their companies' codes of ethics are effective? First, ethics codes should be developed and then communicated regularly and consistently to employees. Second, all levels of management should continually reaffirm the importance of the ethics code and the organization's commitment to it, and consistently discipline those who break it. Finally, top management should set a good example. What they *do* is far more important than what they *say*.

What do you think of these suggestions? Do you agree? Why or why not? What are the implications of these ideas for managing strategically? What did you find at UTC's Web site that might be helpful to other strategic decision makers?

Sources: *UTC Web site [http://utc.com/utc/Governance/Code_of_Ethics.html],* January 8, 2009; J. S. McClenahen, "UTC's Master of Principle," Industry Week, January 2003, pp. 30–36; and "Global Ethics Codes Gain Importance as a Tool to Avoid Litigation and Fines," Wall Street Journal, *August 19, 1999.*

---

semitrailer trucks full of cereal and other packaged goods to food banks around the United States.[27] The message is loud and clear throughout the company that good corporate citizenship "doesn't end with the bottom line." In fact, performance reviews of top executives include an evaluation of community involvement. Although CSR emphasizes the broad picture of an organization's societal interactions, it's also important that these interactions take place in a context of "doing the right thing." That's where the concept of ethics comes in.

The corporate financial scandals in 2001 and 2002 led many people to question how ethical corporate America really is. Thus, it was no wonder that only 18 percent of teens surveyed by Junior Achievement said business leaders were ethical.[28] But it's not just corporate executives who deal with ethical issues. By this time in your life, you've undoubtedly faced numerous ethical dilemmas, both in school and, if you're employed, at your job. For instance, is it ethical to make a copy of inexpensive computer software for a friend who's short of money or to "donate" copies of completed case homework or other assignments to your sorority or fraternity? Or say that you work part-time as a telemarketing representative. Is it ethical for you to pressure customers to purchase a product just so you can win a prize? **Ethics** involves the principles that define right and wrong decisions and behavior. In other words, as we live our lives—attend school, work at a job, engage in hobbies, and so forth—certain decisions and behaviors are ethically "right" and certain decisions and behaviors are ethically "wrong." Ethical considerations should play a role in managing strategically. In fact, some individuals believe that ethics is both a personal and an organizational issue and should be part of the strategic management process.[29]

This means recognizing the ethical implications of the outcomes of strategic decisions and actions. It means considering more than just being in compliance with the law as organizational strategies are formulated and implemented. For example, Avon Products Inc. sells its cosmetics products mainly to women. When Avon asked women what their number-one health concern was, breast cancer was the overwhelming answer. In response, Avon created its Worldwide Fund for Women's Health. This umbrella organization has spread around the globe. The company's biggest women's health program in this fund is the Breast

Cancer Awareness Crusade in the United States. Through this program, the company's sales force educates women about breast cancer by distributing brochures about the disease on their sales visits. In this instance, Avon's strategic decision makers chose to develop and implement a sales strategy that addressed a significant customer concern. Was it the "right" thing to do? Well, Avon's decision makers think so. Not only were they being ethical in their dealings with customers, those customers responded by boosting company sales. Although not every strategic decision will be this broad in scope, the ethical implications for managing strategically are clear: As you're managing strategically, ask yourself, what's the "right" thing to do in making this decision or taking this action? (The Grey Zone ethical dilemmas you'll see in each chapter emphasize the importance of understanding the role of ethics in strategic decision making.)

Learning Review: Learning Outcome 2.3

- Discuss organizational vision and mission statements.
- Define corporate social responsibility.
- Explain who stakeholders are and why they're important to managing strategically.
- Discuss why ethics are important to strategic decision makers.

Learning Outcome 2.1: Describe the different perspectives on competitive advantage.

- ◎ *Managing strategically:* formulating and implementing strategies that allow an organization to develop and maintain a competitive advantage.

- ◎ *Competitive advantage:* what sets an organization apart; its competitive edge; necessary for long-term success and survival of organization.

- ◎ *I/O view:* focuses on structural forces within an industry, the competitive environment of firms, and how these influence competitive advantage; developed by Mike Porter; involves understanding what makes an industry attractive, choosing an attractive industry in which to compete, and choosing an appropriate competitive position within that industry.

- ◎ *RBV:* a firm's unique resources are most important in getting and keeping competitive advantage; *resources* (all of the financial, physical, human, intangible, and structural/cultural assets used by an organization to develop, produce, and deliver products or services to its customers). To be unique, resources must add value (i.e., can be used to exploit positive or buffer against negative external changes), be rare (no other firms have it), be hard to imitate (duplicate) and substitute, and be exploitable .

- ◎ *Guerrilla view:* competitive advantage is temporary; successful organizations must be adept at rapidly and repeatedly disrupting current situation and radically surprising competitors to keep them off balance.

Learning Outcome 2.2: Explain the driving forces, implications, and critical success factors of the business environment.

- ◎ Three driving forces: (1) information revolution—information is the essential resource of production; (2) *technology* (using equipment, materials, knowledge, and experience to perform tasks), which impacts work in three ways: *innovation* (turning a creative idea into a product or process that can be used or sold), bottom-up or mass collaboration capability (customers and individuals have control), and performance (technology can be a powerful tool in helping organizations perform better); and (3) globalization (global marketplace and global competitors).

- ◎ Four major implications of these driving forces: (1) continual change stimulates need for *organizational change* (a structured transition in what organization does and how it does it); (2) reduced need for physical assets—value is found in intangible assets; (3) vanishing distance and compressed time—geography and time no longer play an important role in determining customers and competitors; (4) vulnerability—openness and interconnectedness can leave organization's information, facilities, and employees vulnerable.

- ◎ Three factors critical to success in this new context: (1) ability to embrace change—need *change agents* (someone who initiates and oversees change efforts); (2) *creativity* (ability to combine ideas in a unique way or to make unusual associations between ideas) and innovation capabilities; (3) being a *world-class organization* (an organization in which strategic decision makers are taking actions to help it be the best in the world at what it does).

- ◎ Characteristics include strong customer focus, continual learning and improvement, flexible organization structure, creative human resource management, egalitarian climate, and significant technological support.

Learning Outcome 2.3: Discuss two organizational elements that guide strategic decision makers in managing strategically in today's context.

- Need a single *organizational vision* (broad comprehensive picture of what a leader wants an organization to become), which should (1) be built on a foundation of the organization's core values and beliefs, (2) elaborate a purpose for the organization, (3) include a brief summary of what the organization does, and (4) specify broad goals.

- Also need a *mission statement* (statement of what specific organizational units do and what they hope to accomplish); likely will have several mission statements.

- Vision and mission reflect commitment to *CSR* (obligation of organizational decision makers to make decisions and act in ways that recognize the interrelatedness of business and society), to stakeholders (individuals or groups who have a stake in or are significantly influenced by the organization), and to *ethics* (principles that define right and wrong decisions and behavior).

1. Organizational vision statements can take some interesting directions. Using the Web, find three examples of organizational vision statements and write them down.

   What do you think of these statements? Do they fit the four components of an organizational vision? How might these statements affect the strategic choices made by the company's strategic decision makers?

2. "Technology is fostering a free flow of information." Using a bulleted-list format, write arguments supporting that statement. Then, write arguments against that statement. Be prepared to debate one or both sides in class.

3. To be useful, organizational "knowledge" has to be captured and used. Here are some suggestions for capturing and using it effectively: (a) keep it human; (b) focus on useful knowledge or "know-how"; (c) collect artifacts such as Post-it notes and other documents and make these public; (d) avoid an insular, isolated focus; and (e) keep your knowledge fresh. Explain what you think each of these suggestions means. As you write your explanations, discuss the implications for strategic decision makers.

4. For each of the following quotes, explain what you think they mean and the implications for understanding the context of managing strategically.

   - "To stay ahead, you must have your next idea waiting in the wings." (Rosabeth Moss Kanter, management professor/consultant/author)

   - "Time is a river of passing events, and strong is its current; no sooner is a thing brought to sight than it is swept by and another takes its place, and this too will be swept away." (Marcus Aurelius Antoninus)

5. Every year, *Fortune* publishes lists of America's most admired companies and the global most admired companies. Choose one list. Get the most recent one and answer the following questions.

   - Define the key attributes being used to evaluate companies.

   - What 10 companies are at the top of the list of most admired?

   - Why do you think these companies are at the top of the list? What are they doing differently—that is, how are they managing strategically?

   - What 10 companies are at the bottom of the list? How are they managing strategically?

   - What could strategic decision makers learn from both groups?

6. The total quality management (TQM) movement encouraged organizational managers to *Do it right the first time*. Make it right the first time and you eliminate waste. Finish it right the first time and you save money, time, and customer relationships. Makes sense, doesn't it? However, what if *doing it right the first time* stifles creativity and risk taking? Because breakthrough innovations are rarely well-planned, mistake-free processes, wouldn't an emphasis on *doing it right* suppress going out on a limb to try something different? Maybe *doing it right* isn't as important as *doing it best*. What do you think? Write a paper exploring these concepts.

Strategic Management in Action Cases

CASE #1: Fast Fashion

This Strategic Management in Action case can be found at the beginning of Chapter 2.

Discussion Questions

1. Using Figure 2.3, describe the context facing Zara. Focus especially on describing the driving forces that are affecting the fashion industry and the implications of these driving forces.

2. Again, using Figure 2.3, does Zara have what it takes to succeed in light of this context? Explain.

3. How would proponents of the I/O view analyze this case? How about proponents of the RBV? How about proponents of the guerrilla view?

CASE # 2: Troubles in Toyland?

When my daughters were young, we were so excited when a Toys "R" Us store opened in Springfield! A trip to the Toys "R" Us store was always an adventure . . . usually capped off with the purchase of some new out-fits for their vast collection of Barbie dolls or maybe a new board game. And we weren't the only family (in Springfield or elsewhere) enamored of the vast array of fun toys offered at the stores. Toys "R" Us was where customers went for toys . . . year-round! Its enormous stores were stocked with aisle after aisle of every toy imaginable. As one of those so-called big-box retailers, Toys "R" Us redefined how toys were sold. The company seemed to have everything under control. Its retailing empire encompassed toys, children's clothes, and baby supplies. Its competitive advantages seemed secure.

However, by the end of 1999, the context had begun to change and its competitive advantages started to crumble. That was the year Wal-Mart sur-passed Toys "R" Us in U.S. toy sales. The ruthless competitive pressure from discount retailing giants Wal-Mart and Target ultimately changed the game for Toys "R" Us. It definitely was a grim future for the once-number-one toy retailer in the country.

To cope with this changed environment, the company initially responded by cutting inventory, closing stores to consolidate some distribution and adminis-trative operations, and looking for areas to "beef up," which it did by expanding its online division and acquiring educational toy retailer Imaginarium. But even these strategic changes failed to stem the tide. In a span of five years, the company went through two CEOs. Each tried various options: employee lay-offs,

store remodelings, spin-offs of the baby division, and, eventually, store closings. Finally, in March 2005, three private equity firms bought the retailer and took the company private. In 2006, a new CEO, Jerry Storch, was hired. Storch, who had been vice chair-person of Target, found "an undisciplined company that he believed blamed others for its problems rather than facing its own mistakes. He also found a corpo-rate culture wedded to impulsive strategic forays rather than hard data, a reactive business strategy that he believed would never allow Toys "R" Us to beat its competitors and reinvigorate employees who had given up on the toy industry." As a strategic leader who was more comfortable with crunching numbers and fine-tuning store operations, Storch set about making changes. He replaced more than half of his senior executive team, began testing a wide range of new store concepts, and overhauled the company's marketing efforts.

Storch's strategic efforts have begun to pay off. In 2008, Toys "R" Us was named the Specialty Retailer of the Year. The company has "new financing, new leadership, new vision, new merchandising, new prototypes, new designers and most of all, a renewed sense of purpose." Instead of competing with Wal-Mart and Target on price, Toys "R" Us is pursuing a unique product mix. Storch said, "Differentiation is critical to a specialty retailer. Selling the same prod-ucts at the same price is an empty game. Selling the same products at a higher price than the competition is absolutely a losing hand. The only way for a spe-cialty player to play the game is by selling different products than discounters." Storch recognizes that the context can't be changed, so he is positioning the company to thrive in the context. The newest challenges the company is facing are the federal regulations to eliminate lead-tainted products targeted to children 12 years and younger and the global economic slowdown. Of course, the competitive threats from the discount retailers aren't going to go away. However, the executive team at Toys "R" Us is prepared to face these troubles in toyland just as they have in the past.

Discussion Questions

1. Using Figure 2.3, describe the context facing Toys "R" Us. What driving forces are affecting the specialty retailer industry and the toy industry in particular?

2. How is Toys "R" Us positioning itself to be successful in this context? What do you think of its approaches? Explain.

3. What issues might a company face when it replaces its top leadership in rapid succession? Think both about the benefits and the drawbacks of doing so.

4. What can other companies learn from Toys "R" Us's experiences?

Sources: Based on L. A. Overstreet Allen and C. Carey, "New Rules on Toys Could Spell Doom," *USA Today,* January 9, 2009, p. 3A; "Specialty Retailer of the Year: Toys "R" Us," *Retailing Today,* December 8, 2008, pp. 18–20; "Toys "R" Us CEO on Holiday Shopping," *BusinessWeek Online,* November 26, 2008; M. Bustillo and A. Zimmerman, "Wal-Mart Sparks War Among Big Toy Sellers," *Wall Street Journal,* October 9, 2008, p. B1; and M. Barbaro, "No Playtime at Toy Chain on Its Road to Recovery," *New York Times Online,* November 19, 2006.

CASE #3: Game Not Over, Not Yet

Although their expertise lies in creating games, it's definitely serious business for the video game industry. The computer and video game industry has struggled over the last couple of years as game makers look for new sources of revenues and work to hold down costs. One company, Electronics Arts (EA), exemplifies the challenges of this industry, where customers are fickle and demanding and competition is intense. As one of the world's leading interactive entertainment software companies, EA lives and dies by its innovations. Its product lineup includes over 100 titles such as *Def Jam Vendetta, Madden NFL Football, Lord of the Rings, Rock Band, Need for Speed ProStreet, and The Simpsons.* The company has created over 50 bestsellers (each with more than 1 million copies sold) since 1998. In 2008, revenues were almost $3.7 billion, an increase of 18.6 percent over the previous year. However, the company had a net loss of $454 million. And 2009 doesn't look too promising. The company lowered its sales and profit projections because of changes in the behavior of consumers and retailers.

Paranoia has been a critical part of EA's success. A top game title takes anywhere from 12 to 36 months to produce and costs between $5 million and $10 million. That's a significant investment risk riding on the company's ability to be innovative. John Riccitello (former president and chief operating officer who left the company in 2004 to start a private equity firm but then returned in 2007 as CEO) has guided much of the company's game design accomplishments. He said, "The forgotten aspect of creativity is discipline." The hard part, and the part that EA pursues relentlessly, "is identifying the right idea, assembling the best development team, solving the inevitable technical problems, creating a game that people want to play, getting all of the work done on schedule, getting it to market at the right time, and knowing how to generate buzz about it in an increasingly crowded market." How does EA do it?

It starts with the discipline of understanding ideas. Game designers try to identify the creative center of a game—what they call the "creative x"—so they understand what the game is about. Then, it's the discipline of understanding the customers by using focus groups to pinpoint desires and likes and dislikes. And it's the discipline of sharing best practices and technologies through the company's intranet library. As one employee said, "If somebody develops a better blade of grass in one game, that grass will be in somebody else's game the next day." Then, there's the discipline of developing the next generation of creative leaders. The company's "emerging leaders" program gives participants firsthand experience in departments outside their own. *And* there's the discipline of studying the competition. Employees are encouraged to know the features of competitors' products. Then, it's disciplined project management. Riccitello, known for his strict discipline, said, "If you're working on a game and you miss your deadlines, you won't be working here very long." Although the discipline of creativity is important at EA, you can't overlook the passion of the company's game designers. Nearly everyone at EA grew up playing games. They love what they do and are inspired to look for new and creative challenges not only for the hard-core gamers, but for the casual gamers as well.

Discussion Questions

1. Describe EA's competitive advantage from each of the three perspectives on competitive advantage.

2. Does EA exhibit the critical success factors for the new business context? Explain.

3. Describe the types of resources EA appears to have. Do you think any of these resources might be unique? Explain.

4. What stakeholders might EA have to be concerned with and how might those stakeholders affect EA's strategic decisions and actions?

Sources: Based on B. Charny and Y. I. Kane, "Creator of Sims Games to Leave Electronic Arts," *Wall Street Journal,* April 9, 2009, p. DB4; M. Richtel, "Electronic Arts Forecasts Weaker Profit in 2009," *New York Times Online,* December 10, 2008; T. Burke, "The Hitmakers," *CFO,* November 2008, pp. 43–47; A. LaVallee, "Videogame Makers, States Battle Over Content," *Wall Street Journal,* July 11, 2006, p. D2; R. Levine, "Video Games Struggle to Find the Next Level," *New York Times Online,* May 8, 2006; N. Croal, "He's Got Games," *Newsweek,* December 29, 2003/January 5, 2004, p. 101; P. Lewis, "The Biggest Game in Town," *Fortune,* September 15, 2003, pp. 132–142; C. Salter, "Playing to Win," *Fast Company,* December 2002, pp. 80–91; G. L. Cooper and E. K. Brown, "Video Game Industry Update," *Bank of America Equity Research Brief,* June 7, 2002; and M. Athitakis, "Steve Rechtschaffner, Game Wizard," *Business 2.0,* May 2002, p. 82.

CASE #4: Out of Tune

January 1999 might well be described as the month the music died (to paraphrase a popular song lyric). If the music didn't actually stop then, at the very least, it was the date the music industry changed forever. Why? Shawn Fanning, a student at Northeastern University in Boston, launched Napster, the pioneering Internet file-sharing service that introduced people to "free" music downloading. As the music industry was about to discover, the incredible opportunities offered by the Internet had a dark side.

Music company executives insisted that they weren't caught off guard by the digital distribution revolution. In fact, they believed that it would be a great way to market, promote, and sell directly to fans. However, they weren't prepared for the excruciating efforts of trying to figure out the best ways to adapt to the changed environment.

What the music companies faced was an increasing avalanche of downloading by consumers. Because Internet file sharing offered convenience and anonymity, downloaders saw nothing wrong with it and flocked to Napster's Web site. However, what consumers saw as harmless actions would ultimately have a major negative impact on the music industry as CD and album sales plummeted. The industry decided to fight back the best way it knew how—through the legal system. In December 1999, the Recording Industry Association of America (RIAA)—the trade group representing the U.S. recording industry—sued Napster for contributory copyright infringement. Due to the long appeals process, it was July 2001 before Napster was finally forced out of business. Yet, even with Napster gone, the downloading didn't stop. Other sites such as Grokster (now gone) and KaZaA soon took Napster's place. Obviously, digital distribution was here to stay. Perhaps what the industry needed was a way to work within the changed environment. After all, a report by Forrester Research predicted that by 2008, one-third of all music sales would come from downloads. Another industry report said that what consumers wanted was flexibility, choice, and extras. The challenge for the music companies was to find an acceptable and profitable way to give them what they wanted. How?

Apple's iTunes Store is one example. Open 24/7, the site offers more than 3.5 million songs. As of January 2009, the store had sold 6 billion songs. Most downloaded iTunes files had digital rights management restrictions, but as of April 2009, those restrictions lifted. At that time, iTunes also moved away from its 99 cents pricing strategy and price songs differently. Many dropped to 69 cents, but the biggest hits and newest songs will be priced at $1.29 whereas moderately popular ones will remain at 99 cents. The music companies do receive a royalty percentage for each download. Other online music stores have opened—for example, Microsoft, Wal-Mart, Yahoo, YouTube, and Sony. Even Napster (of which Best Buy now owns 90 percent) is selling music downloads—legally now! Technology also created new markets for music. For instance, sales of master-tones (cell phone ring tones) were a gold mine. However, the total sold in 2008 was down 30 percent from 2007. Growth in this area is unlikely.

In addition to these strategic initiatives, the music industry continued its pursuit of illegal downloading—going after both organizations and individuals. The strategy seemed to work somewhat. According to the CEO of RIAA, "The problem has not been eliminated, but contained. We believe file-trading is flat." However, in mid-December 2008, the recording industry dropped its legal assault—an "abrupt shift of strategy"—and instead focused on more effective ways to combat online music piracy. The industry will now work through the Internet-service providers and use agreements with them to stop customers from illegal file sharing.

Although sales of physical products (CDs, albums, etc.) continue to decline (7 percent in 2008), revenue from digital formats increased 25 percent. Maybe the music companies had finally found the ways to "get in tune" with the realities of this new context.

Discussion Questions

1. Using Figure 2.3, describe the context confronting the music industry.
2. Evaluate the strategic responses used by the music companies in coping with the changed environment.
3. How would proponents of the I/O view analyze this case? How about proponents of the RBV? How about proponents of the guerrilla view?

Sources: Based on E. Pfanner, "Global Music Sales Fell 7% in '08 as CDs Lost Favor," *New York Times Online,* January 17, 2009; E. Smith and Y. I. Kane, "Apple Changes Tune on Music Pricing," *Wall Street Journal,* January 7, 2009, pp. B1+; B. Stone, "Want to Copy iTunes Music? Go Ahead, Apple Says," *New York Times Online,* January 7, 2009; Nielsen SoundScan Press Release, "2008 U.S. Music Purchases Exceed 1.5 Billion, Growth in Overall Music Purchases Exceeds 10%," *Yahoo Finance,* December 31, 2008; S. McBride and E. Smith, "Music Industry to Abandon Mass Suits," *Wall Street Journal,* December 19, 2008, pp. B1+; E. Smith, "Music Industry Changes Its Tune on Podcasting," *Wall Street Journal,* January 2, 2007, p. B2; E. Gundersen, "Mastertones Ring Up Profits," *USA Today,* November 29, 2006, pp. D1+; and J. Graham, USA Today, "Industry Official: Music File-Sharing Contained," *Springfield, Missouri, News-Leader,* June 18, 2006, p. 1E.

CASE #5: Green Footprint

It's a company that sincerely lives its commitment to being socially responsible. Although Timberland is best known for its men's, women's, and kids' footwear, the fact that it champions social responsibility in the ways it does is pretty impressive as well.

Timberland products have a strong and loyal following in the outdoor market. Its signature yellow work boot has become synonymous with outdoor footwear. The company's products are popular globally as shown by its sales revenues, of which 51 percent are international. Like many other companies, 2008 was not kind to Timberland's financial results. Its overall

revenues declined 2.2 percent while sales in the United States declined 8.8 percent, reflecting soft consumer spending. The company's CEO, Jeffrey Swartz, said, "The continued deepening of the global financial crisis, worsening economic conditions, and the impact of these events on consumer confidence have reinforced the importance of financial strength and liquidity access for all companies." But 2008 did have a positive side—in an area that's likely to have a long-lasting impact. Timberland released its new long-term CSR strategy.

The company's CSR strategy has four strategic goals or "pillars." Each pillar is supported by various strategic initiatives with both current and long-term goals. The plan was created with a "rigorous stakeholder engagement process." To demonstrate its commitment and its accountability, Timberland will report quarterly on key CSR performance indicators. As the company stated, "We believe this represents an evolution in our CSR reporting process from static data presentation to dynamic information exchange. In addition, this level of disclosure and reporting will provide invaluable feedback loops to help us achieve the bold goals set forth in our long term CSR strategy."

Discussion Questions

1. How might a company's commitment to being socially responsible affect its strategic management process?

2. Go to Timberland's Web site [www.timberland.com] and locate its CSR strategy. Choose one of the four pillars and explain what strategies the company is pursuing.

3. Do you think a company can be too socially responsible? Explain. What do you think might happen if Timberland's revenues continue to decline? How might a company balance its commitments to being financially responsible and socially responsible? Is that even possible?

Sources: Based on Timberland Web site [**www.timberland.com**], January 6, 2009; "Ford and Timberland Win Ceres-ACCA Awards," *Business & The Environment*, June 2008, pp. 8–9; A. Walker, "Measuring Footprints," *Fast Company*, April 2008, pp. 59–60; E. Clark and R. Tucker, "Proving the Power of Ethical Practices," *Women's Wear Daily*, March 18, 2008, p. 18S; J. Mouawad, "The Greener Guys," *New York Times Online*, May 30, 2006; and J. Reingold, "Walking the Walk," *Fast Company*, November 2005, pp. 80–85.

Endnotes

1. C. Rohwedder, "Zara Grows as Retail Rivals Struggle," *Wall Street Journal,* March 26, 2009, pp. B1+; J. M. Smith, "Fast Fashion," *World Trade,* December 2008, p. 54; R. Murphy, "Inditex Net Creeps Ahead, Sales Rise 11%," *Women's Wear Daily,* December 10, 2008, p. 22; "Fashion Forward," *Foreign Policy,* November/ December 2008, p. 28; S. Edelson and T. Centeno, "Zara Opens New Prototype on Fifth Avenue," *Women's Wear Daily,* December 5, 2008, p. 4; K. Cappell, "Zara Thrives by Breaking All the Rules," *BusinessWeek,* October 20, 2008, p. 66; C. Rohwedder and K. Johnson, "Pace-Setting Zara Seeks More Speed to Fight Its Rising Cheap-Chic Rivals," *Wall Street Journal,* February 20, 2008, pp. B1+; K. Cappell, M. Kamenev, and N. Saminather, "Fashion Conquistador," *BusinessWeek Online,* September 4, 2006; K. Cappell, "Zara's Fast Track to Fashion," *BusinessWeek Online,* September 4, 2006; J. Ewing, "The Winner's Circle," *BusinessWeek Online,* June 26, 2006; "25 Innovators, 6 Industries," *BusinessWeek Online,* April 13, 2006; and R. Tiplady, "Zara: Taking the Lead in Fast-Fashion," *BusinessWeek Online,* April 4, 2006.

2. This discussion of industrial/organization perspective is based on K. R. Conner, "A Historical Comparison of Resource-Based Theory and Five Schools of Thought within Industrial Organization Economics: Do We Have a New Theory of the Firm?" *Journal of Management,* vol. 17, no. 1, 1991, pp. 121–154; M. Porter, *Competitive Advantage: Creating and Sustaining Superior Performance* (New York: Free Press, 1985); and M. Porter, *Competitive Strategy: Techniques for Analyzing Industries and Competitors* (New York: Free Press, 1980).

3. This discussion of RBV is based on C. E. Armstrong and K. Shimizu, "A Review of Approaches to Empirical Research on the Resource-Based View of the Firm," *Journal of Management,* December 2007, pp. 959–986; S. L. Newbert, "Empirical Research on the Resource-Based View of the Firm: An Assessment and Suggestions for Future Research," *Strategic Management Journal,* February 2007, pp. 121–146; D. G. Simon, M. A. Hitt, and R. D. Ireland, "Managing Firm Resources in Dynamic Environments to Create Value: Looking Inside the Black Box," *Academy of Management Review,* January 2007, pp. 273–292; A. A. Lado, N. G. Boyd, P. Wright, and M. Kroll, "Paradox and Theorizing within the Resource-Based View," *Academy of Management Review,* January 2006, pp. 115–131; D. G. Hoopes, T. L. Madsen, and G. Walker, "Guest Editors' Introduction to the Special Issue: Why Is There a Resource-Based View? Toward a Theory of Competitive Heterogeneity," *Strategic Management Journal,* October 2003, pp. 889–902; A. M. Rugman and A. Verbeke, "Edith Penrose's Contribution to the Resource-Based View of Strategic Management," *Strategic Management Journal,* August 2002, pp. 769–780; J. B. Barney, "Looking Inside for Competitive Advantage," *Academy of Management Executive,* November 1995, pp. 49–61; J. B. Barney and E. J. Zajac, "Competitive Organizational Behavior: Toward an Organizationally Based Theory of Competitive Advantage," *Strategic Management Journal,* Winter 1995, pp. 5–9; R. Ashkenas, "Capability: Strategic Tool for a Competitive Edge," *Journal of Business Strategy,* November/December 1995, pp. 13–15; J. B. Black and K. B. Boal, "Strategic Resources: Traits, Configurations, and Paths to Sustainable Competitive Advantage," *Strategic Management Journal,* Summer 1995, pp. 131–138; B. Wernerfelt, "The Resource-Based View of the Firm: Ten Years After," *Strategic Management Journal,* March 1995, pp. 171–174; D. J. Collis, "Research Notes: How Valuable Are Organizational Capabilities," *Strategic Management Journal,* Winter 1994, pp. 143–152; R. Hall, "A Framework Linking Intangible Resources and Capabilities to Sustainable Competitive Advantage," *Academy of Management Journal,* November 1993, pp. 607–618; M. A. Peteraf, "The Cornerstones of Competitive Advantage: A Resource-Based View," *Strategic Management Journal,* March 1993, pp. 179–191; R. Amit and P. J. H. Schoemaker, "Strategic Assets and Organizational Rent," *Strategic Management Journal,* January 1993, pp. 33–46; R. M. Grant, "The Resource-Based Theory of Competitive Advantage: Implications for Strategy Formulation," *California Management Review,* Spring 1991, pp. 114–135; J. B. Barney, "Firm Resources and Sustained Competitive Advantage," *Journal of Management,* vol. 17, no. 1, 1991, pp. 99–120; K. R. Conner, "A Historical-Based Comparison of Resource-Based Theory and Five Schools of Thought within Industrial Organization Economics: Do We Have a New Theory of the Firm?" vol. 35, 1991; J. B. Barney, "Asset Stocks and Sustained Competitive Advantage: A Comment," *Management Science,* December 1989, pp. 1511–1513; I. Dierickx and K. Cool, "Asset Stock Accumulation and Sustainability of Competitive Advantage," *Management Science,* December 1989, pp. 1504–1511; R. P. Rumelt, "Towards a Strategic Theory of the Firm," in R. B. Lamb (ed.), *Competitive Strategic Management* (Upper Saddle River, NJ: Prentice Hall, 1984), pp. 556–570; and B. Wernerfelt, "A Resource-Based View of the Firm," *Strategic Management Journal,* vol. 14, 1984, pp. 4–12.

4. This discussion of the guerrilla view is based on R. R. Wiggins and T. W. Ruefli, "Schumpeter's Ghost: Is Hypercompetition Making the Best of Times Shorter?" *Strategic Management Journal,* October 2005, pp. 887–911; G. Hamel and L. Valikangas, "Zero Trauma—The Essence of Resilience," *Wall Street Journal,* September 16, 2003, p. B2; C. A. Lengnick-Hall and J. A. Wolff, "Similarities and Contradictions in the Core Logic of Three Strategy Research Streams," *Strategic Management Journal,* December 1999, pp. 1109–1132; V. Rindova and C. J. Fombrun, "Constructing Competitive Advantage: The Role of Firm-Constituent Interactions," *Strategic Management Journal,* August 1999, pp. 691–710; K. M. Eisenhardt and S. L. Brown, "Patching: Restitching Business Portfolios in Dynamic Markets," *Harvard Business Review,* May–June 1999, pp. 72–81; B. Chakravarthy, "A New Strategy Framework for Coping With Turbulence," *Sloan Management Review,* Winter 1997, pp. 69–82; R. A. D'Aveni, *Hypercompetition: Managing the Dynamics of Strategic Maneuvering* (New York: Free Press, 1994); D. J. Collis, "Research Note: How Valuable Are Organizational Capabilities?" *Strategic Management Journal,* Winter Special Issue, 1994, pp. 143–152; and K. M. Eisenhardt, "Making Fast Strategic Decisions in High-Velocity Environments," *Academy of Management Journal,* December 1989, pp. 543–576.

5. J. B. Barney, "Looking Inside for Competitive Advantage," *Academy of Management Executive,* November 1995, pp. 49–61.

6. M. Conlin, "Ideas: The Concepts That Are Reshaping the Business World and All of Our Lives," *BusinessWeek,* December 18, 2006,

pp. 96–107; M. Mandel, "Why the Economy Is a Lot Stronger than You Think," *BusinessWeek,* February 13, 2006, pp. 62–70; G. Hitt, "Can President's Plan Keep America Competitive," *Wall Street Journal,* February 2, 2006, pp. A1+; J. Robison, "Is the U.S. Losing Its Competitive Edge?" *Gallup Management Journal Online,* July 14, 2005; "10 Driving Principles of the New Economy," *Business 2.0,* March 2000, pp. 191–284; and M. Mandel, "The New Economy," *BusinessWeek,* January 31, 2000, pp. 73–77.

7. Pui-Wing Tam, "Cutting Files Down to Size," *Wall Street Journal,* May 8, 2007, p. B4; B. Bergstein, "Study: More Data than Space to Hold It," *Springfield, Missouri, News-Leader,* March 11, 2007, pp. 1E+; and R. S. Boyd, "World Choking on a Deluge of Data," *Springfield, Missouri, News Leader,* February 22, 2004, p. 5A.

8. D. Sparks, "An Economy of Change," Miller-McCune, May–June 2009, pp. 18–19; A. Toffler and H. Toffler, *Revolutionary Wealth* (New York: Alfred A. Knopf, 2006); and P. F. Drucker, *Post-Capitalist Society* (New York: HarperBusiness, 1993).

9. J. McGregor, "The World's Most Innovative Companies," *BusinessWeek,* April 24, 2006, p. 64.

10. Ibid.

11. Ibid, p. 76.

12. M. D. Lemonick, "Are We Losing Our Edge?" *Time,* February 13, 2006, pp. 22–33.

13. S. A. Zahra, "The Changing Rules of Global Competitiveness in the 21st Century," *Academy of Management Executive,* February 1999, pp. 36–42; J. A. Petrick, R. F. Shcere, J. D. Brodzinski, J. F. Quinn, and M. F. Ainina, "Global Leadership Skills and Reputational Capital: Intangible Resources for Sustainable Competitive Advantage," *Academy of Management Executive,* February 1999, pp. 58–69; and H. Thomas, T. Pollock, and P. Gorman, "Global Strategic Analyses: Frameworks and Approaches," *Academy of Management Executive,* February 1999, pp. 70–82.

14. "Workplace Security," Special section of *Wall Street Journal,* September 29, 2003, pp. R1–R7; D. Kirkpatrick, "Taking Back the Net," *Fortune,* September 29, 2003, pp. 117–122; T. Purdum, "Preparing for the Worst," *Industry Week,* January 2003, pp. 53–55; and S. Leibs, "Lesson from 9/11: It's Not about Data," *CFO,* September 2002, pp. 31–32.

15. B. C. Reimann, "The New Strategic Leadership: Driving Change, Getting Results!" *Planning Review,* September–October 1994, pp. 6–8.

16. "People Power: Enlisting the Agents of Change," *Chief Executive,* May 1995, pp. 516+.

17. This definition is based on T. M. Amabile, "A Model of Creativity and Innovation in Organizations," in B. M. Staw and L. L. Cummings (eds.), *Research in Organizational Behavior,* vol. 10 (Greenwich, CT: JAI Press, 1988), p. 126.

18. J. B. Quinn, "The Intelligent Enterprise: A New Paradigm," *Academy of Management Executive,* November 2005, pp. 109–121; and R. M. Hodgetts, F. Luthans, and S. M. Lee, "New Paradigm Organizations: From Total Quality to Learning to World Class," *Organizational Dynamics,* Winter 1994, pp. 4–19.

19. S. F. Marino, "Where There Is No Visionary, Companies Falter," *Industry Week,* March 15, 1999, p. 20; D. I. Silvers, "Vision—Not Just for CEOs," *Management Quarterly,* Winter 1994–95, pp. 10–14.

20. L. Larwood, C. M. Falbe, M. P. Kriger, and P. Miesing, "Structure and Meaning of Organizational Vision," *Academy of Management Journal,* June 1995, pp. 740–769; and S. L. Oswald, K. W. Mossholder, and S. G. Harris, "Vision Salience and Strategic Involvement: Implications for Psychological Attachment to Organization and Job," *Strategic Management Journal,* July 1994, pp. 477–489.

21. D. I. Silvers, "Vision—Not Just for CEOs."

22. AMA 2002 Corporate Values Survey, American Management Association Web site [**www.amanet.org**], October 30, 2002.

23. D. J. Wood, "Corporate Social Performance Revisited," *Academy of Management Review,* October 1991, pp. 691–718.

24. M. Friedman, *Capitalism and Freedom* (Chicago: University of Chicago Press, 1962).

25. L. D. Lerner and G. E. Fryxell, "CEO Stakeholder Attitudes and Corporate Social Activity in the *Fortune* 500," *Business and Society,* April 1994, pp. 58–81.

26. E. Laise, "A Few Good Companies," *Smart Money,* January 2004, pp. 25–27; and P. W. Roberts and G. R. Dowling, "Corporate Reputation and Sustained Superior Financial Performance," *Strategic Management Journal,* December 2002, pp. 1077–1093.

27. M. Conlin, J. Hempel, J. Tanzer, and D. Polek, "The Corporate Donors," *BusinessWeek,* December 1, 2003, pp. 92–96.

28. D. Haralson and A. Lewis, "Teens Question Executives' Ethics," *USA Today,* November 11, 2003, p. 1B.

29. L. T. Hosmer, "Strategic Planning as if Ethics Mattered," *Strategic Management Journal,* Summer 1994, pp. 17–34; L. S. Paine, "Managing for Organizational Integrity," *Harvard Business Review,* March–April 1994, pp. 106–117; and A. E. Singer, "Strategy as Moral Philosophy," *Strategic Management Journal,* March 1994, pp. 192–213.

Assessing Opportunities and Threats: Doing an External Analysis

3

LEARNING OUTCOMES

3.1 *Describe what an external analysis is.*

3.2 *Explain how to do an external analysis of an organization's specific and general environments.*

3.3 *Discuss the benefits and challenges of doing an external analysis.*

Not Sold Out

After a couple of years of slight attendance increases, competitors in the movie theater industry had hoped the threats they faced were behind them.[1] Then along came the economy of 2008. Although ticket sales fell less than 1 percent from the previous year, attendance was down 5 percent. The industry pumped up revenue with higher ticket prices and premium 3-D releases. What should industry decision makers do now?

Together, the four largest movie theater chains in the United States have almost 19,000 screens—and a lot of seats to fill. The largest, Regal Entertainment Group (based in Knoxville, Tennessee), has more than 6,400 screens. AMC Entertainment (based in Kansas City, Missouri) has some 5,100 screens. The other two major competitors are Cinemark (based in Plano, Texas—about 4,500 screens) and Carmike Cinemas (based in Columbus, Georgia—about 2,400 screens). The challenge for the big four competitors (and others in the industry) is getting people to come watch movies on all those screens, a decision that encompasses many factors.

One important factor, according to industry analysts, is the uncertainty over how people want their movies delivered, which is largely a trade-off between convenience and quality (or what the experts call fidelity experience). Will consumers choose convenience over quality and use mobile devices such as iPods? Will they trade some quality for convenience and watch at home on surround-sound, flat-screen, high-definition home theater systems? Or will they go to a movie theater with wide screens, high-quality sound systems, and the social experience of being with other movie-goers and enjoy the highest fidelity experience even with the inconveniences? Movie theater competitors believe that mobile devices aren't much of a threat, even though they may be convenient. On the other hand, home theater systems may be more of a threat as they've become more affordable and have "acceptable" quality. Although not likely to replace any of these higher-quality offerings, drive-in theaters, analysts note, are experiencing a resurgence, especially in geographic locations where they can be open year-round.

Another factor strategic decision makers need to wrestle with is the impression consumers have of the movie-going experience. A consumer lifestyle poll showed that the major dislike about going to the movies was the cost, a drawback cited by 36 percent of the respondents. Other factors noted included the noise, uncomfortable seats, the inconvenience, the crowds, and too many previews/commercials before the movie.

A final question facing the movie theater industry *and* the major film studios is how to be proactive in avoiding the problems that the recorded music industry faced with the illegal downloading of songs. The amount of entertainment sold online (which includes both music and video) continues to experience double digit growth. The biggest threat so far has been YouTube, which has become a powerful force in the media world with owner Google's backing. To counter that threat, industry executives have asked for filtering mechanisms to keep unlawful material off the site and to develop some type of licensing arrangements whereby the industry has some protection over its copyrighted film content.

Given these factors, what are the movie theater chains doing? The president of the National Association of Theatre Owners says, "Every decade or so, some new technology is supposed to be the death of movies. Television, video cassettes, the Internet. But, we're still around." However, theater owners aren't just kicking back with a bucket of popcorn. Instead, they're finding ways to make the movie-going experience something special—using such strategies as variable pricing (extending matinee discounts to weeknights or even pricing certain films higher); an all-digital approach with digitized film, satellite delivery of film to theaters, digital keys that "unlock" the film and limit the number of times it can be played, and digital projection (visual and sound); and more and better amenities such as online ticket sales, babysitting, valet parking, alcoholic beverages, and freshly cooked meals. Some movie theaters are even broadcasting live simulcasts of baseball games and rock concerts. As one theater executive said, "We're a little like the drug business. We are the pushers and our customers are the users. Even if business is good, you have to keep giving people more of what they want."

This chapter-opening case illustrates why strategic decision makers must pay attention to changes in the external environment and continue to monitor those changes. As the case points out, external factors can significantly affect companies' strategic decisions and actions. Being alert to changing trends such as customer tastes and habits, what competitors are doing, and even technology is an important step in formulating effective strategies. In this chapter, we'll first describe what an external analysis is. Then, we'll look at how to do one and identify positive and negative aspects of the environment. Finally, we'll discuss why doing an external analysis is important in managing strategically and why managers at all levels of the organization need to analyze and understand what's happening in the external environment.

LEARNING OUTCOME 3.1
Describe What an External Analysis Is

Over the last five years, annual spending on pet services (grooming, birthday parties, spa services, pet sitting, dog walking, etc.) has more than doubled to $3.2 billion.[2] That amount is only a small portion of the more than $43 billion spent annually in the United States by pet owners. Several factors contributing to this increase include the number of households that own a pet (63 percent), passionate pet owners who want to pamper their pets, increasing levels of disposable income, and time pressures. Managers at pet products companies must continue

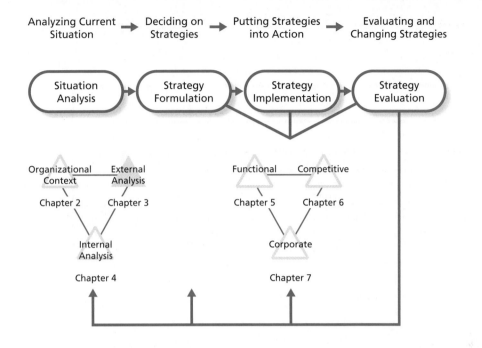

Figure 3.1

Strategic Management in Action

to monitor these trends, especially in light of today's economic climate, with consumers cutting back on nonessential expenditures. However, that's what an external analysis is all about!

An **external analysis** is the process of scanning and evaluating an organization's external environment. It's how strategic managers determine the opportunities and threats facing their organizations. **Opportunities** are positive external trends or changes that may help an organization improve its performance. **Threats** are negative external trends or changes that may hinder an organization's performance. In assessing the current situation, it's important to know what's happening in the external environment so new strategies can be formulated or current strategies changed in response to the opportunities or threats. Figure 3.1 shows how external analysis fits into the overall strategic management process.

Organizations as Open Systems

Organizations are **open systems,** which means they interact with and respond to their environment. As systems, organizations take inputs and process those inputs into outputs. Inputs have to come from somewhere and outputs must be distributed somewhere. That "somewhere" is the external environment. (See Figure 3.2.) In addition, as systems, organizations have interrelated and interdependent parts (departments, units, divisions, etc.) that function as a whole. Any change in any part (or subsystem) can affect the other parts. For instance, if a change is made in marketing, it's likely to affect what happens in manufacturing, accounting, human resources, and so forth. Chester Barnard, an early management theorist, first suggested in 1938 that organizations functioned as systems.[3] However, it took several years for his ideas about organizations as systems to be accepted in mainstream management theory.[4]

Perspectives on Organizational Environments

Because organizations interact with their environment, organizational researchers have looked for ways to describe and understand those environments and their potential impact on organizational performance. These studies can be summarized from two different perspectives: (1) the environment as a source of information and (2) the environment as a source of resources. Let's look at each more closely.

Figure 3.2

Organization as an Open System

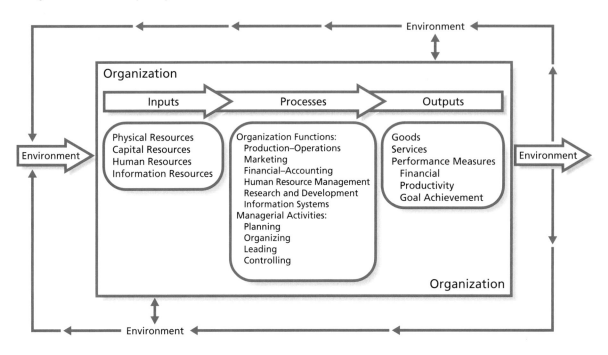

Environment as Information Perspective

In this approach, the environment is viewed as a source of information for decision making.[5] A key element is the idea of **environmental uncertainty,** which is defined as the amount of change and complexity in an organization's environment. The amount of change occurring in an organization's environment can be either dynamic or stable. A more dynamic environment is one that's changing rapidly. If changes are minimal or slow in occurring, the environment is more stable. For instance, the environmental changes taking place in the oil-refining industry are not as rapid as those, say, in the cell phone industry. Therefore, the cell phone industry would be considered more dynamic than the oil-refining industry. Similarly, if decision makers must monitor a number of components in the environment, that environment is complex. If the number of environmental components is few, it's a simple environment. The more complex and dynamic the environment, the more uncertain it is and the more information that decision makers need about the environment to make appropriate decisions. According to this perspective, then, the perceived uncertainty of the environment (amount of change and complexity) dictates the amount and types of information that managers need about that environment. Where do strategic decision makers get that information? They get it from doing an external analysis—in other words, the environment is a source of information.

Environment as Source of Resources Perspective

In this approach, the environment is viewed as a source of scarce and necessary resources that are sought by competing organizations.[6] As the environment becomes more "hostile" (i.e., resources become harder to obtain and control), organizations are subjected to greater uncertainty. Given these uncertain conditions, managers look for ways to acquire and control those critical resources. They do so by monitoring the environment and making

Strategic Management in Action

Indra Nooyi, CEO of PepsiCo, is steering her company through the volatile economic climate by paying close attention to information. For instance, through information analysis, it became clear that the company's beverages division was being hit harder than its snack food division (Frito-Lay). One reason was that consumers who used to not finish an entire soda or water bottle before purchasing a new one are now finishing the beverage. In addition, according to information gathered from convenience-store operators, the housing downturn has led to fewer construc-

tion workers coming in and buying their sodas and snacks. A slowdown like this hadn't been seen in 25 years.

Put yourself in Nooyi's shoes. What other types of external information might you want to look at? How would you classify PepsiCo's environmental uncertainty (i.e., its amount of change and complexity)?

Source: Based on B. Helm, "Blowing Up Pepsi," BusinessWeek, April 27, 2009, pp. 32–36; V. Bauerlein, "Soda-Pop Sales Fall at Faster Rate," Wall Street Journal, March 31, 2009, p. B7; and B. McKay, "PepsiCo CEO Adapts to Tough Climate," Wall Street Journal, September 11, 2008, pp. B1+.

appropriate decisions based on what they see happening, keeping in mind that the environment is the source of those scarce resources. For example, when Toyota wanted to secure its supply of key components for its line of popular hybrid vehicles, it did so by expanding its ownership in a maker of batteries for gasoline–electric hybrid engines.[7]

The main points of each approach are summarized in Table 3.1. Although these two perspectives provide us with a basic understanding of what's involved with an external analysis, how *can* managers determine what's happening in the external environment? That's where environmental scanning comes in.

Environmental Scanning and External Analysis

One impression we get from the previous discussion is that it's important for strategic decision makers to engage in environmental scanning—that is, to know and to evaluate what's happening in the external environment, whether the environment is seen as a source of information, a source of scarce resources, or both. In other words, you need to do an external analysis *and* identify the opportunities and threats facing the organization. For example, look back at the chapter-opening case. Based on their analysis of customer and

---

Environment as Source of Information

- Environment viewed as source of information
- Environments differ in amount of uncertainty
- Uncertainty is determined by complexity and rate of change
- Reducing uncertainty means obtaining information
- Amount of uncertainty determines amount and types of information needed
- Information obtained by analyzing external environment

Environment as Source of Resources

- Environment viewed as source of scarce and valued resources
- Organizations depend on the environment for these resources
- Resources are sought by competing organizations
- Dependency is determined by the difficulty of obtaining and controlling resources
- Reducing dependency means controlling environmental resources
- Controlling environmental resources means knowing about the environment and attempting to change or influence it

Table 3.1

Summary of Two Perspectives on the Environment

Source: Based on Richard A. Bettis and Michael A. Hitt, "The New Competitive Landscape," Strategic Management Journal, Summer 1995, pp. 7–19.

competitor trends, strategic decision makers at the movie theater chains have chosen strategies that they hope will exploit the opportunities and neutralize or avoid the threats in their environment.

- What is an external analysis and what does it show managers?
- How does the concept of an organization as an open system relate to external analysis?
- What does each perspective on organizational environments say?
- What role does environmental uncertainty play in external analysis?
- Why do managers need to do more than just scan the environment?

LEARNING OUTCOME 3.2
Explain How to Do an External Analysis of an Organization's Specific and General Environments

Now that we know *what* an external analysis is, we need to look at *how* you do one. What do managers look at in an external analysis? Where can they find information on the external environment and how do they evaluate this information? How do managers at different organizational levels do an external analysis? We explore these topics in this section. When you've finished reading this material, you'll know how to do an external analysis and to determine an organization's opportunities and threats.

External Environmental Sectors

The external environmental sectors comprise the specific environment and the general environment. The **specific environment** includes customers, competitors, suppliers, and other industry-competitive variables whereas the **general environment** includes economic, demographic, sociocultural, political-legal, and technological sectors. (See Figure 3.3.) Let's look at each.

Specific Environment

Analyzing the specific environment involves looking at industry and competitive variables. An **industry** is a group or groups of organizations producing similar or identical products. These organizations compete for customers to purchase their products and also must secure the necessary resources that are converted into products. We'll use the five-forces model developed by Michael Porter to assess an organization's specific environment.[8] (See Figure 3.4.)

One assumption Porter makes is that some industries are inherently more attractive than others, that is, the profit potential for companies in those industries is higher. For instance, airplane makers Airbus and Boeing have had higher profits than the airlines that buy their planes.[9] The strength and interaction of the five competitive forces are what influence profit potential. A strategic decision maker can determine the opportunities and threats in the specific environment by evaluating these five forces.

Current Rivalry among Existing Firms   The existing firms in your industry are your organization's current competitors. These include the organizations already in the industry that produce and market products similar to yours. For instance, in the soft drink industry,

Figure 3.3

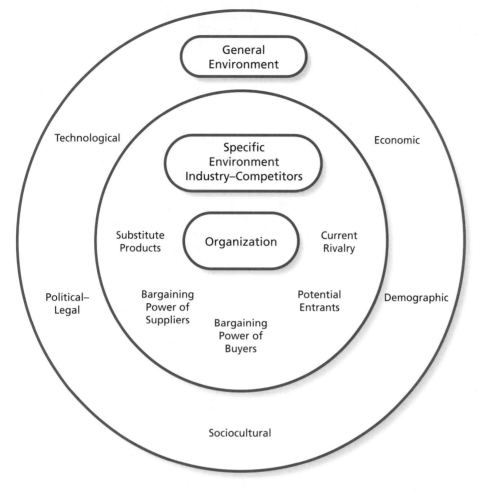

Coca Cola, PepsiCo, Cott, Dr. Pepper Snapple Group, and Wal-Mart (Sam's Choice house brand) would be existing firms. In this part of the five-forces analysis, we determine how intense the rivalry is among these current competitors. Is it intensely competitive or not? Is it "cutthroat" or "polite"? Are competitors constantly trying to take customers away from each other or do competitors seem to get along with each other? The more intense the rivalry among existing firms, the more that the industry's profitability—and thus your company's profitability—is likely to suffer.

What affects the level of rivalry? Porter lists eight conditions that contribute to intense rivalry among existing competitors.

1. *Numerous or equally balanced competitors:* If an industry has a number of competitors, there's a greater likelihood that some firms will think they can take competitive actions and no one will notice, thus keeping the industry in constant competitive turmoil. Or, if competitors are equal in terms of size or resources, they'll constantly be jockeying for position, also creating intense competitive action.

2. *Slow industry growth:* When industry growth has slowed—in other words, consumer demand for the industry's products has leveled off—the "market pie" isn't getting any bigger. For your company to keep growing, you'll have to steal market share away from your competitors. Conditions will be ripe for competitors to battle with each other to maintain or increase market share, making the level of rivalry intense. For example, how many people read a daily newspaper? Not many. Statistics on daily

Figure 3.4

Porter's Five-Forces Model

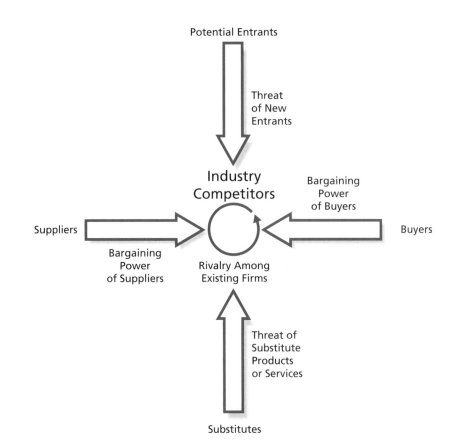

newspaper readership have shown drastically declining numbers over the last 10 years. Newspaper publishers have struggled to find strategies to halt that trend and in the process upped the intensity of competition.[10]

3. *High fixed or storage costs:* If organizations have high fixed costs, they'll do whatever it takes to operate at capacity and thus spread out those fixed costs over a larger volume. This situation often leads to back-and-forth price cutting by competitors in order to attract customers, which increases competitive rivalry. Also, if the industry's products are difficult or costly to store, companies will want to sell their products as quickly as possible (keeping inventory at the lowest possible levels) and often resort to price cutting to do so. In both instances, price cuts by industry competitors keep profits low.

4. *Lack of differentiation or switching costs:* If the industry's product is perceived to be a commodity or like a commodity (i.e., not unique in any way), then customers make their purchase decisions largely because of price and service. Both forms of competition lead to intense rivalry. For instance, you might not think that the casual dining industry would face problems of differentiation. After all, industry competitors such as P. F. Chang's, Romano's Macaroni Grill, Olive Garden, and Chili's have spent significant dollars creating a theme and re-creating it in numerous locations. However, that's exactly what led to this lack of differentiation. Every format—American, Italian, Chinese, or Mexican—that's proved successful has been endlessly copied until it's practically impossible to tell these casual dining "theme" restaurants apart. This has created intense competitive rivalry as each chain attempts to capture consumers' dining-out dollars. Also, if there's no cost (either actual dollars or even the amount of time you'd have to invest to learn about a new product) associated with switching from one competitor's product to another's, then competitive intensity will be high because competitors will be trying to steal customers away from one another.

5. *Addition of capacity in large increments:* In industries where capacity must be added in large increments in order to be economically feasible, these additions by competitors can create competitive disruptions, because the industry will suffer from overcapacity, leading to price cutting and intense competitive rivalry. For instance, in the cruise line industry, a 1,200-passenger boat used to be considered large. Now, cruise ships can carry well over 5,000 passengers and capacity is still being added. For example, in 2009, Royal Caribbean put into service the world's largest (5,400 passengers) and most expensive cruise ship ($1.24 billion) named the *Oasis of the Seas.* This new ship replaces the company's *Freedom of the Seas* as the world's largest cruise ship.[11] If the number of cruise customers decreases, there's intense competitive pressure to keep these boats filled.

6. *Diverse competitors:* When competitors differ in their strategic approaches, philosophies, or circumstances, it's hard to judge how they are going to act and react as they compete. This diversity increases the level of rivalry.

7. *High strategic stakes:* Industry competitors have strong reasons to want to succeed (such as CEO's reputation, large dollar investments, etc.) and will do whatever it takes to do so, even going so far as sacrificing short-run profitability. If industry competitors have this perspective, then rivalry will be high.

8. *High exit barriers:* Porter defines **exit barriers** as "economic, strategic, and emotional factors that keep companies competing in businesses even though they may be earning low or even negative returns on investment."[12] Examples of exit barriers include highly specialized assets that can't be used in other ways or that have low liquidation value; labor agreements that must be honored; or management's unwillingness to leave a business because of pride, fear, or other psychological reasons. If there are high exit barriers, the company is, in a sense, "stuck" in that industry and may use extreme tactics to compete.

● *Strategic Management in Action*

Getting rid of wrinkles is big business, although the economic meltdown did impact the industry. It appears that the economy put a big damper on cosmetics procedures performed. In 2008 (the most current statistics available), cosmetic procedures among Caucasians declined 2 percent while cosmetic procedures among ethnic groups increased 11 percent. Hispanics showed the greatest growth in procedures performed . . . up 18 percent. Many plastic surgeons saw women opting for more minimally invasive procedures such as fillers, Botox, and chemical peels. With an estimated total market value of about $15 billion for drugs, dermal fillers, and other devices used in these procedures, the two largest competitors (Allergan Inc., which makes Botox, and Medicis Pharmaceutical Corporation, which makes Restylane) are locked in a battle to gain even bigger market shares. Allergan markets a product called Juvéderm to compete head-on with Restylane, and Medicis markets a neurotoxin product to compete head-on with Botox. Medicis set up a rewards program (similar to airlines and hotels) for patients who use its product. Then Allergan introduced a Botox customer-benefit program. Each company woos doctors who perform the procedures with educational and research opportunities and other enticements. Even some of the bigger drug companies, such as Johnson & Johnson and Pfizer, have assessed the potential of the industry. As baby boomers continue to age and look for ways to look and feel younger, the "wrinkle wars" are likely to continue.

How would you evaluate the level of current rivalry in this industry?

Sources: *Based on American Society of Plastic Surgeons* **[www.plasticsurgery. org]**, *"Cosmetic Procedures Up in All Ethnic Groups Except Caucasians in 2008,"* Press Release, March 25, 2009; M. Brophy Marcus, *"Faces or Finances? Cosmetic Procedures Dip,"* USA Today, December 1, 2008, p. 4D; American Society of Plastic Surgeons **[www.plasticsurgery.org]**, *"Plastic Surgery Procedures Maintain Steady Growth in 2007,"* Press Release, March 25, 2008; and R. L. Rundle, *"Firms Face Off over Wrinkles,"* Wall Street Journal, January 13–14, 2007, pp. A1+.

One aspect of current rivalry that needs to be clarified is, "*Who* are our current competitors?" Obviously, if an industry includes several firms, you may find that not all those firms are your actual direct competitors or competitors that you'd be concerned with. One answer is to look at only the competitors that are currently in your **strategic group,** which is a group of firms competing within an industry that have similar strategies, resources, and customers. Strategy researchers have proposed that organizations within a strategic group compete more directly than other organizations that also may be in the industry.[13] For instance, even though Mercedes-Benz and General Motors are both in the automobile manufacturing industry, they're not considered direct competitors because they don't have the same customer base, don't have similar resources, and don't use similar strategies. In analyzing current rivalry, it makes sense to look at those organizations whose strategic actions have the most potential to affect your profitability; that means looking at those competitors in the relevant strategic group.

Potential Entrants   Dr. Pepper Snapple Group, the largest beverage marketer after Coke and Pepsi, is going after a share of the fast-growing sports drink market. Under the strategic direction of CEO Larry D. Young, the company introduced Acclerade with an assertive advertising campaign theme "Don't Fade." In seeking to distinguish its product from rivals Gatorade and Powerade, its ads play up test results that show that Acclerade helps endurance. Executives at Gatorade (a product of PepsiCo, which dominates this market) and Powerade (a product of Coca Cola) have indicated that they're not taking the newcomer lightly.[14]

Not only do organizations have to be concerned with the opportunities and threats presented by their current competitors, they also need to be on the lookout for others moving into their industry. Why? Because these organizations bring new capacity to the industry, want to gain customers (market share) and perhaps even possess substantial resources that can be used to launch attacks against current competitors. The threat of entrants depends on the barriers to entry and the reaction by current competitors to entrants. **Barriers to entry** are obstacles to entering an industry. When barriers are high or current competitors can be expected to take significant actions to keep newcomers out, then the threat of entry is low. A low threat of potential entrants is positive for an industry because profitability won't be divided up among more competitors. Porter described seven major entry barriers.

FOR YOUR INFORMATION

The Benefits of Competition

Although we've highlighted the strategic challenges that come from intense competition, are there any benefits? The answer is, of course, there are. An important one is that competitive rivalry forces organizations to be more innovative. Companies want to hold on to their customers and as they look for ways to do that, they must continually innovate their products as well as their work processes. Another benefit is that competition compels companies to be on

their toes: to be effective and efficient at what they do. If they're not, they'll find it difficult to stay competitive and might find any competitive advantage they've been able to develop eroded by more efficient and effective competitors. So, although intense competitive rivalry is a threat, it *can* have some benefits.

Sources: *Based on* D. Moyer, "Don't Fence It In," Harvard Business Review, December 2005, p. 156; L. Kiesling, "Articulating the Benefits of Competition," Knowledge Problem **[www.knowledgeproblem.com]**, June 8, 2005; and S. Davies, H. Coles, M. Olkczak, C. Pike, and C. Wilson, "The Benefits from Competition: Some Illustrative UK Cases," Department of Trade and Industry Economics Paper, no. 8 **[www.dti.gov.uk]**, July 2004.

---

1. *Economies of scale:* Economies of scale refer to the cost savings realized from volume increases. Producing more or doing more can lead to cost savings because fixed costs are spread out over a larger volume, driving the cost per unit down. Potential entrants might think twice because they'd have to come into the industry operating either at a large scale and risk retaliation by current competitors or at a smaller scale and have a cost disadvantage compared to the others.

2. *Cost disadvantages from other than scale:* Established competitors may enjoy cost advantages that potential entrants can't duplicate even if they can operate at a large volume. Such factors include exclusive or protected product technology; favorable access to raw materials; favorable locations; government subsidies; or human resource advantages because of employees' cumulative level of knowledge, learning, and experience. For example, looking back at our chapter-opening case, the top Hollywood studios agreed to a set of technical specifications defining how sharp digital films must be and creating mechanisms to fight illegal piracy.[15] Not only do such technical standards make the industry's products more appealing to customers, they serve as a barrier to others looking to come into the industry because potential entrants would have to adhere to the standards.

3. *Product differentiation:* Current competitors usually have worked hard and spent large sums to establish unique product identification with customers. If it's strong enough, brand identity differentiates an organization and leads to loyal customers. To overcome this brand loyalty, potential entrants have to spend heavily on customer research, advertising, packaging, and other marketing activities, resulting in a significant barrier.

4. *Capital requirements:* If an organization has to invest significant financial resources in order to compete, this makes potential entrants think twice about coming into an industry. Take the ski industry, for example. As customers demanded better amenities at ski sites—good, consistent snow base; groomed trails; comfortable but luxurious accommodations—the capital investment required to satisfy these customer demands rose significantly. Unless potential competitors have that kind of capital, they're shut out of the industry.

5. *Switching costs:* Are you familiar with and do you consistently use one word-processing package? Maybe it's Word or WordPerfect. What keeps you from using another one? For most of us, it's the time and effort we'd have to invest in learning a new set of commands and keyboard shortcuts. That's an example of **switching costs**—the one-time costs facing the buyer who switches from one supplier's product to another's. These costs don't even necessarily have to be monetary costs. They also can be psychological costs associated with change.

6. *Access to distribution channels:* You have a product to sell and you need an outlet or distribution channel for that product. If current competitors have already secured the logical distribution sources, you have to persuade these sources to accept your product. This may mean you have to give the distributor a price break or set up cooperative advertising arrangements, both of which reduce potential profits.

7. *Government policy:* If the government imposes laws and regulations (such as licensing requirements, controlling access to raw materials, air/water pollution standards, product safety standards, product testing time requirements, etc.), it creates a barrier to entry. Potential entrants would have to meet these requirements, which may cost a significant amount. For instance, in the real-estate industry, real-estate agents lobbied state governments to keep discount brokers from coming into their market.[16] If such regulatory or legal protections aren't there, barriers to entry will be lower.

The beverage giants (Coke and Pepsi) are at it again. The bottled water business, once an industry made up of numerous small regional players, continues to be a battleground for the major beverage companies. With a consumption decline in the carbonated soft drink market (from 50 to 45 percent) and with bottled water consumption increasing (from 19 to 24 percent), it's not surprising that Coke and Pepsi want to continue making a big splash in the water market. However, they have to cope with getting their water on the shelves without sacrificing too much of the shelf space of their soft drink products. In addition, small regional water bottlers are vulnerable to the giants' marketing tactics. It's an interesting battle.

Analyze this situation using the seven barriers to entry from the perspective of the current competitors *and* from the perspective of the potential entrants.

Sources: Based on Press Release [**www.beveragemarketing.com**], "U.S. Liquid Refreshment Beverage Market Trends and Developments Assessed in New Beverage Marketing Corporation Report," November 2008; and "Feature Analysis: Soft Drinks Losing Their Fizz," Datamonitor, March 2008.

Bargaining Power of Buyers Your buyers are your customers—those individuals or organizations who purchase your products. How do buyers affect industry profitability? If they have a lot of bargaining power, they can force prices down, bargain for higher quality or more services, or even play competitors against each other trying to see who will give them the best deal. What makes a buyer powerful? One factor is whether the *buyer purchases large volumes of the seller's product.* The implication is that the customer is more important to the seller than the seller is to the customer. This gives that customer a lot of bargaining power. For instance, Wal-Mart can account for a significant part of a manufacturer's revenues. With this much buying power, Wal-Mart can pretty much dictate selling terms. Another factor that influences customers' bargaining power is whether the *products they purchase represent a significant portion of their costs or purchases.* In this situation, customers are going to look for the best price and shop around. Customers will also have significant bargaining power if *the products they purchase are standard or undifferentiated.* Here again, a customer likely will play one supplier against another in an attempt to find the best deal. One more factor that gives buyers greater bargaining power is if they *face little switching costs.* If there are few switching costs or if switching costs are low, then the customer doesn't feel obligated to stay with the original supplier and can shop around. The buyer may also exert bargaining power if *it has low profits or low income levels.* If that's the case, the customer will look for ways to reduce costs, which often means reducing purchasing costs. Another factor that gives customers bargaining power is when *they have the ability and resources themselves to manufacture the products they're purchasing from the industry.* If the customer can make the product it's buying, then it's in a powerful position to ask for concessions from the supplier. For example, some businesses that purchase large quantities of electric power from local utilities have threatened to take their business elsewhere unless they get lower rates. Many of these businesses can do just that by either building their own power-generating plants or persuading a local government to form a municipal system to buy electric power at bulk rates. As customers, these businesses are exerting power. Buyers also have bargaining power if *the industry's product isn't important to the quality of the buyers' products or services.* What this means is that if the buyers don't need the industry's products to get desired quality levels in their products or services, then they have the power to bargain with the industry over prices and services offered. On the other hand, if the industry's product *is* important to the quality of the buyers' products, then the buyers won't have much bargaining power. Lastly, buyers have bargaining power if *they have full information* about product demand, actual market prices, and supplier costs. This information gives the customer good ammunition to get the best possible prices from suppliers. The Internet has played a significant role in customers' access to information. For example, in the car industry, buyers can compare prices and features and bargain for the best deal.

The Grey Zone

Bargaining Power of Suppliers Terex Corporation, a heavy-equipment maker, can't get enough big tires for its mining and other big earth-moving equipment. A shortage of workers at low-cost factories in China is leading to production and shipping delays. Indium—element 49 on the periodic table—plays a small but crucial role in manufacturing LCD screens and it's in short supply. A shortage of a critical chemical used in de-icing runways threatens flight volume at major airports.[17]

If your industry's suppliers have bargaining power, they can raise prices or reduce the number of services provided or the quality of products that your industry purchases. An industry's suppliers include any resource providers: raw materials sources, equipment manufacturers, financial institutions, and even labor sources. How can you tell whether an industry's suppliers are powerful? One thing to look for is *domination by a few companies and more concentration than the industry*. If suppliers are few in number and are selling to an industry that's fragmented (i.e., the buyers are small and not very powerful), then the suppliers will usually be able to exert considerable influence over prices, quality, and sales terms. Another characteristic to look for is *whether there are any substitute products*. If there aren't any good substitutes, then the supplier can exert more power over the industry. But, if the supplier has to compete with possible substitutes, then it doesn't have a lot of bargaining power over the industry. Suppliers can also exert power when *the industry is not an important customer*. If your industry is just one of many that the supplier sells to, then it couldn't care less whether it keeps you as a customer and is more likely to exert bargaining power. On the other hand, if your industry is an important customer, the supplier will want to protect that relationship and won't try to exert bargaining power. Another characteristic to evaluate is whether *the supplier's product is an important input to your industry*. If it is, then the supplier will have more bargaining power. For example, suppliers of silicon wafers have significant power over the semiconductor industry. Even though silicon is one of the most abundant elements on earth, shortfalls in the availability of silicon wafers affect the ability of chipmakers to satisfy demand for their product. This situation gives suppliers a lot of power over computer chip manufacturers. Also, it's important to know whether *the supplier's products are differentiated or whether there are customer switching costs*. If the

New College Nottingham
Learning Centres

supplier's products are differentiated or if your industry would experience switching costs, then the supplier is able to exert more power. The final characteristic for determining supplier power is *the supplier's ability to provide the products that your industry is currently providing.* If the supplier can do what your industry does (i.e., produce or market your industry's products) and do it better or cheaper, then this gives the supplier more bargaining power. In other words, if you don't agree to the supplier's terms and conditions, they could start doing what you do. For instance, apparel conglomerates such as Liz Claiborne, Jones Apparel Group, and Kellwood have "grudgingly tolerated life under the thumb of department stores, tailoring clothing designs to the chains' seasonal whims and paying out markdown money to stores when fashions fail to sell." Now, one supplier, Liz Claiborne, has taken a radical approach. Rather than rely on department stores, the company is building its own retail stores.[18]

Substitute Products   The last industry force we need to discuss is the threat of substitute products. The best way to evaluate this threat is to see whether there are other industries that can satisfy the consumer need that our industry is satisfying. For instance, take a customer's need for something to drink. If your company is in the soft drink industry, substitute products could come from other industries such as fruit drinks, energy drinks, alcoholic beverages, milk or milk-based products, and even bottled water. Any of these industries could fulfill the customer's need for something to drink. (Other soft drink manufacturers would be your competitors and would be evaluated as current rivalry.) If there are no or few substitutes for your industry's product, then this threat isn't very high. However, if there are a few good substitutes or even several not-so-good substitutes for your product, then this isn't favorable for your industry's profitability.

By now, you should have a good grasp of what you examine in an organization's specific environment. Porter's five-forces model provides one framework for determining the opportunities and threats of the industry and competitive environment. A summary of the five forces and what you need to look at as you determine whether they're favorable or unfavorable is shown in Table 3.2.

General Environment

The general environment includes the economic, demographic, sociocultural, political-legal, and technological sectors. The trends in these sectors could have a positive impact (opportunity) or a negative impact (threat) on the organization. However, not everything

● *Strategic Management in Action*

As food manufacturers and fast-food restaurants lower the amount of trans fat in their products, the surging demand for the special soybeans used to produce this valuable alternative to the vegetable oils that are loaded with trans fat has agricultural companies scrambling to convince farmers to grow these beans. One company, the St. Louis–based Monsanto Company, has found it challenging. Despite the demand for the beans, farmers don't seem to think there's enough incentive to grow them especially given the extra work involved and the appeal of planting their fields with high-priced corn needed to supply ethanol demand. But farmers' reluctance is only part of the problem. Monsanto and other competitors haven't been able to create new varieties of trans fat-free soybeans fast enough to meet demand. The situation worsened with New York City's restaurant ban on trans fat.

Analyze this situation using the five-forces model. Where do the opportunities and threats appear to be for Monsanto and other competitors?

Source: *Based on A. Martin, "The Seeds of a Mission," New York Times Online, December 29, 2006.*

| | | Table 3.2 |

Industry-Competitive Forces	Threat	Opportunity
Current Rivalry		
Numerous competitors	✓	
Few competitors		✓
Equally balanced competitors	✓	
One or a few strong competitors		✓
Industry sales growth slowing	✓	
Industry sales growth strong		✓
High fixed or inventory storage costs	✓	
Low fixed or inventory storage costs		✓
No differentiation or no switching costs	✓	
Significant differentiation or significant switching costs		✓
Large capacity increments required	✓	
Minimal capacity increments required		✓
Diverse competitors	✓	
Similar competitors		✓
High strategic stakes	✓	
Low strategic stakes		✓
High exit barriers	✓	
Minimal exit barriers		✓
Potential Entrants		
Significant economies of scale		✓
No or low economies of scale	✓	
Cost disadvantages from other aspects		✓
No other potential cost disadvantages	✓	
Strong product differentiation		✓
Weak product differentiation	✓	
Huge capital requirements		✓
Minimal capital requirements	✓	
Significant switching costs		✓
Minimal switching costs	✓	
Controlled access to distribution channels		✓
Open access to distribution channels	✓	
Government policy protection		✓
No government policy protection	✓	
Bargaining Power of Buyers		
Buyer purchases large volumes	✓	
Buyer purchases small volumes		✓
Products purchased are significant part of buyer's costs	✓	
Products purchased aren't significant part of buyer's costs		✓
Products purchased are standard or undifferentiated	✓	
Products purchased are highly differentiated and unique		✓
Buyer faces few switching costs	✓	
Buyer faces significant switching costs		✓
Buyer's profits are low	✓	
Buyer's profits are strong		✓
Buyer has ability to manufacture products being purchased	✓	
Buyer doesn't have ability to manufacture products		✓
Industry's products aren't important to quality of buyer's products	✓	
Industry's products are important to quality of buyer's products		✓
Buyers have full information	✓	
Buyers have limited information		✓

Evaluating the Five Forces

(continued)

Table 3.2

Continued

Industry-Competitive Forces	Threat	Opportunity
Bargaining Power of Suppliers		
Supplying industry has few companies and is more concentrated	✓	
Supplying industry has many companies and is fragmented		✓
There are no substitute products for supplier's products	✓	
There are substitute products for supplier's products		✓
Industry being supplied is not an important customer	✓	
Industry being supplied is an important customer		✓
Supplier's product is an important input to industry	✓	
Supplier's product is not an important input to industry		✓
Supplier's products are differentiated	✓	
Supplier's products aren't differentiated		✓
There are significant switching costs in supplier's products	✓	
There are minimal switching costs in supplier's products		✓
Supplier has ability to do what buying industry does	✓	
Supplier doesn't have ability to do what buying industry does		✓
Substitute Products		
There are few good substitutes	✓	
There are several not-so-good substitutes	✓	
There are no good substitutes		✓

that happens externally will be an opportunity or threat. Many changes may not even affect an organization. In addition, different industries will be affected differently by external changes. For example, rising interest rates will benefit some industries (i.e., be an opportunity) whereas for other industries, this trend is a threat.

Economic   In today's environment, the opportunities and threats of the economic sector are painfully obvious to many industries. For instance, managers in industries ranging from transportation to banking to retailing recognize the impact that energy and fuel costs have on supplies of raw materials, general business activity, new orders, and order backlogs. Retailers are facing consumers who have lost their appetite for spending, leading strategic decision makers to find strategies to try to get buyers back in the stores. For some retailers—including Circuit City, Linens 'N Things, Sharper Image, Steve and Barry's, among others—the economic threats proved too strong. But for one retailer, Wal-Mart, the economic challenges have provided opportunities to grow revenues as consumers spend more cautiously and look for ways to stretch their dollars.

The economic sector includes macroeconomic data—current statistics and forecasted trends and changes—that reflect what's happening with the overall economy. The major economic data that might be important to scan and evaluate include interest rates; exchange rates and the value of the dollar; budget deficit or surplus; trade deficit or surplus; inflation rates; gross national product (GNP) or gross domestic product (GDP) levels and the resulting stage of the economic cycle; consumer income, spending, and debt levels; employment-unemployment levels; consumer confidence levels; and workforce productivity rates. You want to look at current information as well as forecasted trends when evaluating these economic statistics. What impact, if any, do they have for your organization? For instance, are rising interest rates good or bad—in other words, are they opportunities or threats? If the economy is growing moderately, what does this mean? What if the dollar falls in value against the Chinese yuan or against the euro? Is this good or bad? What if workforce productivity has leveled off and is predicted to stay stagnant? What does this mean? Take consumer debt levels. What industries might be affected positively or negatively by increases in consumer debt levels? These are the types of questions you need to ask as you evaluate the economic sector for opportunities and threats. And keep in mind that industries will be affected differently by these economic trends. For instance, rising interest rates tend to have a favorable impact on the credit card industry but are less favorable for the housing industry. Also, keep in mind that every organization in an industry is faced with the same economic trends and changes. That is, the inflation rate doesn't change just because it's McDonald's, as opposed to Wendy's. So an organization's performance ultimately is determined by how it responds to the various economic opportunities and threats, which is also true for the rest of the general environmental sectors we'll look at.

If your organization does business globally, the economic analysis won't change much. The biggest challenge is likely to be finding available and reliable sources of statistics, although all industrialized and most semi-industrialized countries collect economic data. Also, information is available from the United Nations and other sources such as the CIA *World Factbook.* You can find information on GNP or GDP, which provides clues to the stage of the economic cycle and whether a country's economy is growing or contracting. You also can find information on exchange rates, trade figures, interest rates, and inflation rates. Of these, the most important economic information probably are inflation rates, interest rates, currency exchange rates, and consumer income spending-debt levels. Why? These factors tend to be the most volatile and could significantly affect strategic decisions.

Demographics The year 2007 was a milestone as a record number of babies (some 4,315,000) were born in the United States. The last time births were this high was 1957, right in the middle of the baby boom years. One demographer said, "I suspect this is the beginning of a new kind of baby boom, although it's going to be nowhere near the baby boom of the 1950s or 60s. It will be sort of a boomlet."[19] Also in 2007, the median age at

---

Strategic Management in Action   THE GLOBAL PERSPECTIVE

Reversing a trend that started years ago, many manufacturers are bringing production back to North America and halting plans to send more work overseas. Why? Rising shipping costs. For instance, the retail heating division of DESA LLC (the company best known for making the heaters you see along the sidelines of football fields) saw its cost for shipping one container from China jump from $4,600 to $5,600 over a six-month period. The president of the company said, "My cost of getting a shipping container here from China just keeps going up—and I don't see any end in sight." Economic experts concur, saying that the cost of shipping a container from Asia to the East Coast has tripled since 2000. These experts estimate that transportation costs are now the equivalent of a 9 percent tariff on goods coming into the United States. The higher transportation costs are particularly challenging for lower-value goods and for companies that manufacture heavier and bulkier products.

These circumstances are forcing many manufacturers to reevaluate their production strategies. However, there are some limits to what they can do. For instance, one problem with bringing production back home is that the basic infrastructure needed to support many industries (suppliers who produce parts or repair machines) has declined or disappeared altogether. In addition, many domestic shippers have added a transportation surcharge.

Find and graph the cost of a barrel of oil over the last three years. Why are higher transportation costs particularly challenging for manufacturers of lower-value goods and for heavier and bulkier products? What industries, in addition to the oil industry, might benefit from higher transportation costs?

Source: Based on A. Goel, N. Moussavi, and V. N. Srivatsan, "Time to Rethink Offshoring?" The McKinsey Quarterly [www.mckinseyquarterly.com], September 2008; J. Lahart and C. Dougherty, "U.S. Retools Economy, Curbing Thirst for Oil," Wall Street Journal, August 12, 2008, pp. A1+; D. J. Lynch, "Transport Costs Could Alter World Trade," USA Today, August 12, 2008, pp. 1B+; and T. Aeppel, "Stung by Soaring Transport Costs, Factories Bring Jobs Home Again," Wall Street Journal, June 13, 2008, pp. A1+.

---

first marriage (26 for women and 28 for men) hit its highest peak since the Census Bureau started keeping track in the 1890s.[20] What industries might benefit from or suffer from these trends?

In the demographics sector, you'll evaluate current statistical data and trends in population characteristics. It includes the kinds of information that the U.S. Census Bureau gathers such as gender, age, income levels, ethnic makeup, education, family composition, geographic location, birth rates, employment status, and so forth. Many different organizations—government as well as business—use these data in making strategic decisions. As you look at population statistics, what positive or negative trends do you see that might affect your organization? For instance, census data show that the total U.S. population is over 305.6 million; that there are more Americans over age 30 than under; that the U.S. population is becoming more educated as the number of adults with at least a bachelor's degree increased to 27 percent; that 12.3 percent of the population aged 16 to 64 has a disability; and that Hispanics increased their standing as the largest minority group at 15 percent.[21] What strategic implications might such population changes have for different organizations?

You might find it's also important to examine the interaction of these variables. For instance, which age group has the fastest-growing incomes? Or, in what geographic locations is there a greater concentration of senior citizens? Or, what is the average level of education of Asian Americans? In fact, one particular population group (another term for this is *population cohort*) that you've probably heard a lot about is the baby boomers. This group typically includes individuals who were born between the years 1946 and 1964. A lot is written about the baby boomers because there are so many of them. Through every life stage (going to elementary school, teenage years, climbing the career ladder, and now retirement), they've had an enormous impact simply because of their sheer numbers. Although some experts believe that segmenting markets by age is inappropriate, others say it's a good clue to consumer attitudes and behavior. Other common age cohorts include: the Depression group (born 1912–1921); the World War II group (born 1922–1927); the Postwar group (born 1928–1945); the Generation X or "zoomers" group (born

The nation's fast-growing Hispanic population is attracting the attention of businesses from banks to mobile-phone services to retailers. For instance, Wal-Mart has teamed up with Pollo Campero, a Latin American fried-chicken favorite. In a Supercenter in Rowlett, Texas, you'll find a restaurant with the Guatemalan chain's popular fried chicken. Officials with the new Campero USA Corp. hoped to extend into more than 20 Wal-Mart locations across the United States by the end of 2009. For Wal-Mart, Pollo Campero offers an additional opportunity to capture a diverse range of shoppers and to customize and sell more culturally attuned products in its massive stores.

What potential drawbacks, if any, might there be to these strategies?

Source: Based on News Release, "Now Serving at Wal-Mart: Pollo Campero's Delicious Latin Chicken," [www.campero.com], May 12, 2008; and CNNMoney.com, "Wal-Mart to Serve Fried Chicken," [cnnmoney.com], May 12, 2008.

1965–1977); and Generation Y or echo boomers/millenials (born 1978–1994). This last group also is predicted to be a source of significant demographic opportunities and threats simply because of its size.

As you can probably guess, demographic information is useful for understanding your current customers as well as targeting potential customers. By examining current and forecasted demographic shifts, positive and negative trends can be identified.

The need for demographic information doesn't change if an organization is operating in other countries or is looking to expand globally. It's important to have as much demographic information as possible about current and potential global markets. Most countries collect census information. In developing countries, data collection and statistical analysis might not be as thorough or reliable as that of other nations. However, the United Nations and other organizations do collect a considerable amount of demographic information that could be useful in analyzing this external sector.

Sociocultural   The popularity of iPods and iPhones has many younger office workers demanding Macs instead of the standard-issue PCs that run Microsoft's Windows operating system. For instance, the chief information officer at Juniper Networks stated that, "If we opened it up today, I think 25 percent of our employees would choose Macs." For Apple, the workplace market isn't even one that it has pursued recently. Instead, its "core calling is creating the next cool thing for the world's consumer."[22]

There's more to understanding your current and potential customers than just their demographic characteristics. It's also important to know what's going on with them culturally. In other words, what's a country's culture like and how is it changing? What are the traditions, lifestyles, values, attitudes, beliefs, tastes, patterns of behavior, and how are these changing? These are what the sociocultural sector encompasses. Such trends often aren't as obvious or as easy to determine as the demographic information. Measuring and interpreting people's opinions, values, attitudes, or likes and dislikes tends to be more challenging. However, it's important for strategic decision makers to recognize both the current status and the trends in the sociocultural sector.

How can you determine what's happening in the sociocultural sector? Look at values and attitudes. For instance, some basic cultural values of the United States include individual freedom, strong work ethic, and equality of opportunity. These values influence people's behavior in the way they shop, work, raise their families, and otherwise live their lives. People's attitudes also influence their behavior. Some attitudinal changes over the last few years include (and this list is, by no means, complete) different views of openness versus privacy by the Internet generation, which is more willing to share information online with friends and strangers; most people aged 30 and younger don't follow the news closely at all; middle America volunteers the most; more and more people have to leave for work before

Hallmark Cards always has been quite successful at "reading" social trends and translating those trends into greeting cards. That's why when baby boomers started turning 50 years old, company strategists created a line of cards (birthday, friendship, thinking-of-you, anniversary, etc.) designed to "subtly flatter the aging boomer's flagging middle-aged ego"—a line they called Time of Your Life. They decided to display the line in its own separate section of Hallmark stores and to use advertising displays showing middle-aged people looking youthful in active settings. A Hallmark spokesperson said, "We had done a lot of research showing that baby boomers don't want to get old, but that if it's going to happen, they want to emphasize the positive side of aging." However, what Hallmark failed to understand was that given a choice between shopping in the regular greeting cards section and shopping in a spe-

cial 50-plus section, potential customers, of course, chose the regular cards. After two years of miserable sales, the company scrapped the line.

Go to Hallmark's Web site **[www.hallmark.com]**. Click on About Hallmark and then the Newsroom. In the search box, type in the word "trends." This will bring you to a page describing emerging and evolving trends as perceived by Hallmark.

Which ones are described there? How might these affect strategies at Hallmark? What could other companies learn about sociocultural opportunities and threats from these descriptions?

Source: *Based on Hallmark Web site* **[www.hallmark.com]**, *January 11, 2009; and P. Paul, "Sell It to the Psyche," Inside Business, Time Bonus Section, October 2003, p. A2.*

dawn; eating in (that is, at home) is gaining ground over eating out; a new emphasis on frugality; being "cheap" is cool; willingness to do-it-yourself, especially in home repair, retail transactions, and so forth; more emphasis on religion and spiritual activities, particularly by baby boomers; and increasing use of technology in workplaces, schools, and homes.

In evaluating this sector, you'd also want to look at changes or trends in people's activities, behavior, and purchases. For example, look at how Kraft and other food makers have responded to customers' changing attitudes about food. As consumers demanded healthier versions of their favorite snack foods, companies scaled back calories, sodium, and saturated and trans fats in many products. (Go to any grocery store and check out the number and variety of 100-calorie snacks, products that weren't available five years ago.) Many organizations also have changed their marketing strategies to take advantage of another sociocultural trend—diverse population groups.

The importance of this sector doesn't change if you're in different global locations. However, getting and interpreting this information for different global locations may not be as easy as getting economic and demographic information. That's because there's no standard governmental collection of this type of information. Keep in mind that each country does have its own distinctive culture—generally accepted traditions, lifestyles, values, attitudes, beliefs, tastes, and patterns of behavior. The challenge is to understand that culture. In addition to knowing the current culture, any trends or changes should be analyzed to determine potential opportunities and threats.

Political-Legal   Because of new laws restricting the use of leaf blowers, manufacturers have come out with quieter, more fuel-efficient models. New regulations now require that grocery stores identify the country of origin for meats, produce, and certain nuts. Disabled Americans now have expanded workplace protections under the Americans with Disabilities Act after the passage of a bill by the U.S. Senate.[23]

In this general environmental sector, various laws, regulations, judicial decisions, and political forces currently in effect at the federal, state, and local levels of government are analyzed. (Some of the more significant federal laws and regulations for businesses are shown in Table 3.3.) For instance, new bankruptcy laws have made it harder for consumers to avoid paying their debt and have helped credit card companies, such as American

Table 3.3

Significant Legislation Affecting Businesses

Occupational Safety and Health Act of 1970
Requires employers to provide a working environment free from hazards to health

Consumer Product Safety Act of 1972
Sets standards on selected products, requires warning labels, and orders product recalls

Equal Employment Opportunity Act of 1972
Forbids discrimination in all areas of employer–employee relations

Worker Adjustment and Retraining Notification Act of 1988
Requires employers with 100 or more employees to provide 60 days' notice before a facility closing or mass layoff.

Americans with Disabilities Act of 1990
Prohibits employers from discriminating against individuals with physical or mental disabilities or the chronically ill; also requires organizations to reasonably accommodate these individuals

Civil Rights Act of 1991
Reaffirms and tightens prohibition of discrimination; permits individuals to sue for punitive damages in cases of intentional discrimination

Family and Medical Leave Act of 1993
Grants 12 weeks of unpaid leave each year to employees for the birth or adoption of a child or the care of a spouse, child, or parent with a serious health condition; covers organizations with 50 or more employees

North American Free Trade Agreement of 1993
Creates a free-trade zone between the United States, Canada, and Mexico

U.S. Economic Espionage Act of 1996
Makes theft or misappropriation of trade secrets a federal crime

Sarbanes-Oxley Act of 2002
Holds businesses to higher standards of disclosure and corporate governance

Express Corporation, reduce the number of bankruptcy write-offs they've had to take.[24] This sector might also include analyzing regulations enacted by professional associations (such as the Financial Accounting Standards Board [FASB]). Any legal, regulatory, and political changes or pending judicial decisions also need to be examined. For instance, agreeing with those who complained that existing patent rules stifled innovation, the U.S. Supreme Court issued a ruling making it easier to challenge patents legally.[25] What impact might this ruling have on different industries? Which might find opportunities? Which might face threats? Also, a country's political-legal climate can affect attitudes toward business and how much regulation an industry faces. Other major political-legal concerns include taxation, minimum wage, and product labeling/product safety laws, all of which can have a significant impact on an organization's financial performance. Some areas where businesses might see future laws and regulations include immigration, global warming, and executive compensation.[26]

If an organization does business in other countries, obviously the relevant laws and regulations must be obeyed. In addition, it's important to be aware of political changes as far as who or what political party is in power and the likelihood that new laws and regulations might be enacted. Although political stability is a given in most countries, some do still face volatile and unstable situations.

Strategic Management in Action   THE GLOBAL PERSPECTIVE

Another aspect of the global political environment is the various trade alliances among countries. These alliances—such as the North American Free Trade Agreement (NAFTA), the European Union, the Central America Free Trade Agreement, the Association of Southeast Asian Nations (ASEAN), and the African Union—are easing many of the political and economic restrictions on trade and creating numerous opportunities and threats.

Technological   Seventy percent of Internet users in China are under the age of 30 and like to play online games, download video and music onto their cell phones and MP3 players, and participate in online imaginary worlds. Pony Ma, the CEO of China's hottest Internet company, Tencent, says he "simply wants to let people in China use the Web the way they want."[27] Obviously, he understands the opportunities and threats associated with technological trends and changes, which is the last general environmental sector we want to look at.

Within the technological sector, we look for scientific or technological innovations that create opportunities and threats. The two organizational areas most affected by

Strategic Management in Action

technology are product research and development and organizational work processes. How will changing technology affect your organization's products? Likewise, how will these changes affect the way you produce and deliver your products (your work processes)?

Computerization is one of the most important technological innovations and continues to affect both organizational work processes and product development. For example, retailers directly link to suppliers to replenish inventory as needed. Manufacturers have flexible manufacturing systems that allow them to mass customize products. Airlines have Web pages where customers can arrange flight times, destinations, and fares. Many organizational employees collaborate and communicate online. In addition, innovations in fields such as lasers, robotics, biotechnology, food additives, medicine, consumer electronics, and telecommunications could be opportunities and threats for many different industries. However, keep in mind that the impact of such innovations will be different for different industries. For instance, how might innovations such as smart cards, 3-D printing, and satellite imaging affect different industries?

If your organization is operating globally, a country's level of technological advancement could influence strategies used. Some countries won't have the needed infrastructure to support available technology. For instance, the phone system or telecommunications system may be unreliable or dated. Or, the power (electricity) generation system may be insufficient to support technological requirements. Or a country's highway system may be in poor shape or not conveniently located. Many variables determine whether a given technology will prove to be an opportunity or a threat to your organization in another global location and it's important to assess those variables.

Finding Information on the External Environment and Evaluating It

To find information, look for specific data, statistics, analyses, trends, predictions, forecasts, inferences or statements made by experts, or other types of evidence of what's happening or predicted to happen in the sectors. Then this information needs to be evaluated. Will it help your organization improve its performance currently or in the future, or will it hinder its performance? In other words, does the current external environment present opportunities or threats to your organization? How about the trends? This information about the external environment is used by decision makers to evaluate current strategies and to formulate future strategies.

External information can be found using informal and unscientific observations or by using a more formal, systematic search. For many decision makers, it's enough to talk to customers and suppliers' sales representatives or to read industry trade journals and general news magazines. Such informal, unscientific information-gathering activities often provide sufficient clues to the trends taking place in certain sectors of the external environment, giving strategic decision makers a basis to make effective strategic decisions, even with rather limited information. However, a thorough and comprehensive external analysis requires more of a systematic, deliberate search. In fact, having some type of formal approach is the key to identifying specific opportunities and threats. An **external information system** is an information system that provides managers with needed external information on a regular basis. Again, keep in mind that the whole purpose of the external analysis is to identify potential trends and changes that could positively or negatively impact your organization's performance. How often decision makers need information about external sectors depends on how complex and dynamic an organization's environment is. The more complex and dynamic the environment (i.e., the more environmental uncertainty there is), the more often you'd want information. For some organizations in complex and dynamic industries, this might be as often as once a month. For others,

Spotting Trends

The skill of observing. Do you have it? Can you pick up on what people think is "hot" or popular? Faith Popcorn, an author and well-known trend spotter, actually says that you don't have to be a pro to be good at it. In fact, professionals may be constrained from recognizing emerging trends by rigid organizational structures and their past successes. So, how can *you* become more in tune with what's happening and hone your skills at trend spotting? Here are some suggestions:

1. Remember that valuable information can be found anywhere and everywhere. Read magazines you don't normally read. Watch television shows or movies that you personally might not be interested in. Go places. Do things. Talk to people. Information is the bread and butter of a good trend spotter.

2. File the information away. If your memory isn't as good as it should be, use note cards. What you write down doesn't have to be long and complex. It could be something as simple as "avocado seems to be a hot color,"

"teens seem to be flocking to organized fitness programs," or whatever.

3. Determine whether the fads seem to be part of deeper, wider trends. Do this by assessing whether the fad seems to have staying power, whether the fad is a reflection of a change in people's attitudes or behaviors, and whether you see the fad in more than a few places.

4. Don't expect trends to jump out at you. After all, if they were easy to spot, everyone would be doing it. You have to be alert, be open to new and unusual possibilities, and be willing to work at it.

Spotting trends can be a good skill for strategic decision makers. Such information can provide them with significant insights into potential opportunities and threats. How could trend spotting be part of an external analysis? Are there any drawbacks to trend spotting? Explain.

Sources: Based on B. Snyder Bulik, "Cool Hunting Goes Corporate," Advertising Age, August 1, 2005, pp. 3–26; L. Grossman, "The Quest for Cool," Time, September 8, 2003, pp. 48–54; K. G. Salwen, "Thinking About Tomorrow: An Interview with David Birch," Wall Street Journal, May 24, 1999, p. R30; and R. Furchgott, "Trend-Spotting Anyone Can Play," Business Week Enterprise, March 2, 1998, pp. ENT12–ENT16.

gathering and assessing external information twice or even once a year might be enough. No matter how uncertain the external environment, if current strategies aren't working (getting desired results), decision makers will do something. And that starts with doing an external analysis to determine opportunities and threats.

Doing an external analysis isn't as difficult as it may sound! You may feel that you're going to spend hours locating and interpreting information. Actually, the problem you'll find is not about having *enough* information; it's having *too much* information. To manage this, approach it systematically. For each external sector, ask yourself what information would be important for your organization and industry, keeping in mind that industries differ in terms of the potential impact of external trends. For instance, in the economic sector, you may decide that interest rates are likely to have a significant impact on your industry, so you'd want to find current and forecasted interest rates. If your target customers are teenage girls, you'd probably want to know the demographic and sociocultural trends for this particular group. Thus, you should concentrate on getting the information that's important.

Responsibilities for External Analysis at Different Managerial Levels

In smaller and medium-sized organizations, all employees should monitor changes in the specific (industry-competitive) environment. In fact, in many smaller organizations, frontline employees often have the most direct interactions with customers and supplier representatives, and may have some contact with competitors' employees. These employees, who often hear comments or statements from outsiders, should be educated about the organization's external environment and how important this type of information is to strategic decision making. If they hear comments that possibly indicate changing circumstances, encourage them to share that information. The managers/owners can then determine whether the situation needs further analysis before changing strategies.

In large organizations, doing a single external analysis for the entire organization isn't likely to provide good enough information for making strategic decisions. There are too many and too varied units and levels. In larger organizations, it's the managers who are likely to be responsible for monitoring external trends or changes and identifying potential opportunities or threats. Their responsibilities for the external analysis process will vary somewhat depending on their organizational level.

Just as in smaller organizations, the role of lower-level supervisors in those areas where employees have direct contact with customers and suppliers' sales representatives is to encourage those employees to listen for comments that might indicate emerging trends. The role of mid-level managers is to coordinate any external information provided from the different functional departments or divisional units and to share this information with other organizational units that might benefit. Their role is more of an information gatherer and disseminator. Also, mid-level managers might monitor changes in the general environment that are particularly important to their specific areas of responsibility and to use this information to change strategies. That leaves top-level managers who, because of their broad perspective on situations, see the "whole" picture. These managers will use external information in formulating corporate strategies. In larger organizations where there may be a separate strategy group, an external analysis will be completed as part of a formalized strategic planning process. If there isn't such a group, the information that has been compiled by the various business units and divisions about possible opportunities and threats is what top-level managers will rely on.

No matter at what organizational level you find yourself, you'll be involved in some aspect of external analysis. That reinforces one of this book's premises—that everyone in the organization is involved in managing strategically.

FOR YOUR INFORMATION

Competitor Intelligence

One approach to environmental scanning—**competitor intelligence**—is an information-gathering activity that seeks to identify who competitors are, what they're doing, and how their actions will affect your organization. It's been suggested that 80 percent of what strategic decision makers need to know about competitors can be found out from their own employees, suppliers, and customers. So, competitor intelligence doesn't *have* to involve organizational spying. Advertisements, promotional materials, press releases, reports filed with governmental agencies, annual reports, want ads, newspaper reports, and industry studies are examples of accessible information. Attending trade shows and talking to your company's sales representatives can be other good sources of information on competitors. Many organizations even buy competitors' products and have their engineers break them down (using reverse engineering) to learn about new technical innovations. And the Internet has opened up new sources of competitor intelligence as many corporate Web pages include new product information and other information such as press releases. However, when we hear about companies using unscrupulous methods to get sensitive information, questions and concerns come up regarding ways in which competitor information is gathered. Competitor intelligence becomes illegal corporate spying when it involves the theft of proprietary materials or trade secrets by any means. Often, there's a fine line between what's considered *legal and ethical* and what's considered *legal but unethical*.

Check out the Intelligence Index and CI Tools at **[www.fuld.com]**. What do you think about the information that's discussed there? Do you think competitor intelligence has a place in external analysis? Why or why not?

Sources: Based on M. Orey, "Corporate Snoops," BusinessWeek, October 9, 2006, pp. 46–49; K. Girard, "Snooping on a Shoestring," Business 2.0, May 2003, pp. 64–66; and D. Kinard, "Raising Your Competitive IQ: The Payoff of Paying Attention to Potential Competitors," Association Management, February 2003, pp. 40–44.

- What does the five-forces model look at and how is it used?
- What is examined in each of the five components of the general environment?
- How is an external analysis done for a company that's doing business globally?
- How is information on the external environment found and evaluated?
- Describe the different responsibilities for doing an external analysis.

LEARNING OUTCOME 3.3
Discuss the Benefits and Challenges of Doing an External Analysis

By now, you should have a pretty good feel for what an external analysis is and how one is done, but still may not be convinced why it's important to know what's happening in your organization's external environment. In this section, we're going to look at *why* you need to do an external analysis and at some of the challenges of doing one.

Benefits of Doing an External Analysis

We've already mentioned that the reason for doing an external analysis is to identify potential opportunities and threats facing an organization. By deliberately and systematically analyzing the external environment, a manager can be a **proactive manager**—that is, a manager who anticipates changes and plans for those changes, instead of just simply reacting to them. In fact, proactive managers may, at times, be able to influence various external environmental sectors to the organization's benefit (i.e., encourage changes that would have a positive effect on the organization's performance). For instance, lobbying is one way managers proactively manage their external environment. However, external analysis is important for other reasons as well.

An external analysis provides the information that strategic managers use in planning, decision making, and strategy formulation.[28] Think back to our discussion of the "environment as information" perspective. One real value in studying the external environment is the information it provides. This information is useful to the extent that strategic decision makers can determine ways to take advantage of the positive changes and ways to buffer against, neutralize, or adapt to the negative changes. How? By changing the organization's strategies. These strategies *should be* based on information about markets, customers, technology, and so forth.[29] Because an organization's environment is changing continually, having information about the various external sectors is important in formulating strategies that "align" the organization with its environment.

The "environment as source of resources" perspective also provides another reason for doing an external analysis. An organization's ability to acquire and control needed resources depends on having strategies that take advantage of the environment's abundant resources and strategies that cope with the environment's limited resources.[30] Think back to our description of an organization as an open system. Because the organization depends on the environment as a source of inputs (resources) and as an outlet for outputs, it only makes sense that strategies should be formulated that help the organization get needed resources that then can be converted into desired outputs. Organizations can do that most effectively by understanding what the environment has to offer.

Another reason for doing an external analysis is the realization that today's external environment is increasingly dynamic. Turbulent market conditions, fragmented markets, less brand loyalty, more demanding customers, rapid changes in technology, and intense global competition are just a few of the realities of today's business environment. And these conditions aren't the exception—they're the norm. All sizes and all types of organizations are facing increasingly dynamic environments. In order to effectively cope with these changes, managers need to examine the external environment.[31]

Our final reason for doing an external analysis relates to whether doing so really makes a difference. In other words, does an external analysis really make a difference in an organization's performance? The answer is that it *does* appear to make a difference. Research studies generally have shown that in organizations in which strategic decision makers did external analyses, performance was higher.[32] Performance was typically evaluated using a financial measure such as return on assets or growth in profitability. The fact that doing an external analysis appears to make a difference in performance results is a pretty good reason for wanting to know how to do one and to actually doing it as part of the strategic management process.

Challenges of Doing an External Analysis

There are some challenges associated with doing an external analysis. For one thing, the environment might be changing more rapidly—technology, new competitors, new customers, laws—than realistically can be kept up with. Such rapid change is happening in many industries, not just in high-tech industries. Just keeping track of the current situation *and* changing trends can be a challenge.

Another challenge of doing an external analysis is the amount of time it can consume. Systematically scanning and evaluating the environment is important, yet it takes time, and most strategic decision makers are busy managing and don't feel they have the time. However, external analysis *is* important as part of managing strategically. The key is to make the process as efficient and effective as possible. This may mean doing things such as identifying particularly critical external sectors and monitoring those more frequently and other sectors not as frequently; relying on specialized database searches, news clipping services, or even personalized Internet searches to monitor changes in those significant sectors; or even sharing the responsibilities for analyzing the external sectors with others in the organization.

Finally, you need to understand that while forecasts and trend analyses are a significant part of the external analysis, they aren't perfect. Forecasts aren't facts: they're the best predictions experts have about what they believe is going to happen. For instance, you've probably had the experience of leaving your home without a coat and umbrella after listening to the weather forecast for a sunny, warm day only to be greeted by a cold, pouring rain. Forecasts of business, economic, or attitudinal trends aren't always accurate either. However, strategic decision makers need to be flexible, open, and alert to changing circumstances. Managing strategically is an ongoing process. Strategies don't always succeed, for whatever reason. Results may fall short because of some internal shortcoming or because the predictions we'd made about external opportunities and threats were inaccurate. Whatever the reason, strategies can be changed as needed to take advantage of new information. Even though forecasts, predictions, and trend analyses aren't always 100 percent accurate, they can provide us with a sense of the strategic direction we need to go. Even given the shortcomings, that's a pretty good reason to continue to look at them.

Learning Review: Learning Outcome 3.3

- List some benefits of doing an external analysis.
- Discuss the challenges associated with doing an external analysis.

Learning Outcome 3.1: Describe what an external analysis is.

- *External analysis:* process of scanning and evaluating the external environment in order to identify opportunities and threats.

- *Opportunities:* positive external trends or changes that may help improve the organization's performance; *threats:* negative trends or changes that may hinder the organization's performance.

- Based on the idea that organizations are *open systems,* which means they interact with and respond to their environment.

- Two perspectives on organizational environments: (1) environment as information is based on the idea of *environmental uncertainty:* amount of change and complexity in organization's environment; the more dynamic and complex the environment, the more uncertainty there is and the greater the need for information; (2) environment as a source of resources is based on the idea that as environments become more hostile, the more difficult it is to obtain and control resources; managers monitor environment in order to acquire and control those needed resources.

- Important to scan *and* evaluate external environment.

Learning Outcome 3.2: Explain how to do an external analysis of an organization's specific and general environments.

- External sectors are classified as *specific* (customers, competitors, suppliers, and other industry-competitive variables) and *general* (economic, demographic, sociocultural, political-legal, and technological).

- Specific environment is analyzed using Porter's five-forces model: (1) **current rivalry** is evaluated by eight factors: number of competitors and how balanced their market shares are, rate of industry growth, level of fixed or storage costs, amount of differentiation and switching costs, capacity increments required, diversity of competitors, extent of strategic stakes, and extent of *exit barriers* (those factors that keep companies competing in an industry); current competitors may be determined by *strategic group* (a group of industry firms that have similar strategies, resources, and customers); (2) **potential entrants** is determined by seven factors: *barriers to entry* (obstacles to entering an industry) including economies of scale, cost disadvantages from other than scale, product differentiation, capital requirements, *switching costs* (one-time costs a buyer faces when switching from one competitor's product to another), access to distribution channels, and government policy protection; (3) **bargaining power of buyers** is determined by eight factors: how much the buyer purchases, whether those purchases represent a significant portion of buyer's costs, how much standardization or differentiation products have, whether buyer faces switching costs, level of buyer's profits or income, buyer's ability to manufacture products being purchased, how important products are to buyer, and how much information buyer has; (4) **bargaining power of suppliers** is determined by seven factors: how many suppliers there are, how concentrated they are, whether there are substitute products, how important industry is to supplier, how important supplier's products are to industry, level of differentiation and switching costs, and can industry do what supplier provides; and (5) **threat of substitute products** is determined by whether there is another industry that can satisfy customers' needs.

- The general environment includes five sectors that are evaluated: (1) **economic,** which looks at all the macroeconomic data that reflect what's happening with the overall economy; (2) **demographics,** which looks at current data and trends in population characteristics—census-type information; (3) **sociocultural,** which looks at current data and trends in society and culture—values, attitudes, behavior patterns, and so forth; (4) **political-legal,** which looks at laws, regulations, judicial decisions, and political forces; and (5) **technological,** which looks at scientific or technological innovations.

○ When looking for external information, look for data, statistics, analyses, trends, predictions, forecasts, inferences, or statements made by experts.

○ External analysis can be informal and unscientific or more formal using an *external information system,* an information system that provides managers with needed external information on a regular basis.

○ In smaller and medium-sized organizations, external analysis needs to be done by all employees, especially those on the front line. In larger organizations, external analysis is usually the responsibility of managers.

Learning Outcome 3.3: Discuss the benefits and challenges of doing an external analysis.

○ *Benefits:* (1) makes *managers proactive:* managers who anticipate changes and plan for those changes instead of simply reacting; (2) provides information used in planning, decision making, and formulating strategy; (3) helps organizations get needed resources—environment as source of resources; (4) helps organizations cope with uncertain environments—environment as source of information; and (5) makes a difference in organization's performance.

○ *Challenges:* (1) rapidly changing environment can be hard to keep up with; (2) it's time consuming; and (3) forecasts and trend analyses aren't perfect.

YOU
as
strategic
decision
maker:
building
your
skills

1. Go to the U.S. Census Bureau Web site [**www.census.gov**]. List the major categories and subcategories found there. Choose one of the subcategories and do a more thorough description and analysis of the information in it. How might this information be valuable to strategic decision makers? Evaluate the availability and ease-of-finding information found on the Web site. What "lesson(s)" did you learn from your immersion in the Census Bureau Web site?

2. It has been suggested that one simple way to do an external analysis is by asking these six questions: (a) What is happening in the world today? (b) What does it mean for others? (c) What does it mean for us? (d) What would have to happen first for the results we want to occur? (e) What do we have to do to play a role? and (f) What do we do next? What do you think of this approach to external analysis? What's good about it? Bad?

3. Find three different online sources that report basic economic data. Describe what each of the sources provides. Which would you recommend as a source of economic data? Why?

4. A study for the U.S. Department of Labor completed by the Rand Corporation, a think tank based in Santa Monica, California, showed that the nation's workforce will be smaller and more diverse, more mobile, and more vulnerable to global competition. What implications (positive and negative) do these trends have for organizational strategies?

5. The demographic trend of an aging baby boom generation, combined with struggling financial markets, has forced many people to delay retirement. This has created some interesting strategic scenarios, not only in marketing opportunities and threats, but also in the area of human resources. What opportunities and threats do you see in this convergence of demographic factors? How might these opportunities and threats change for different industries?

6. Two of the major competitors in the fast-food industry—Wendy's and McDonald's—have positioned themselves differently. Wendy's has taken the adult approach, practically ignoring the children's market with its advertising tie-ins and toy giveaways. McDonald's has long pursued the kids' market. Think about demographic and sociocultural trends and changes. How would each organization's interpretation of these trends and changes affect its choice of strategy? Which organization do you think is positioned better? Explain your choice.

7. A survey listing the most important cultural values of the United States included the following (most important listed first): protecting the family, honesty, stable personal relationships, self-esteem, freedom, friendship, and respecting one's ancestors. What do you think are the strategic implications of such findings? Might these implications change for different industries? If so, how? If not, why not?

8. In a survey that asked corporate leaders whether they communicated with their employees about how the economy was impacting their company, 70 percent said no. What do you think of this? Why might they be reluctant to do so? How might more open communication with employees be a benefit?

Strategic Management in Action Cases

CASE #1: Not Sold Out

This Strategic Management in Action case can be found at the beginning of Chapter 3.

1. What external trends do the strategic managers at the movie theater chains have to deal with? What external sectors are these trends part of? Are these external trends of equal importance to the movie theater chains? Explain why or why not.

2. What opportunities and threats do you see in this situation? Describe.

3. How do you think these external trends might affect the strategies used by the movie theater chains? Be specific.

4. If you were a strategic decision maker at the corporate headquarters of one of these movie theater chains, what types of external information would you want? What if you were a manager at a local movie theater: what types of external information would you want?

CASE #2: Going after Generation Y

"We are going to own this generation." These words reflect the not-so-subtle philosophy of Alloy, Inc., which has tried to be a formidable force in Generation Y media and marketing. Despite its claims, the company has never posted a profit since its founding in 1996. Based in New York, Alloy had revenues of over $199 million in 2008 but posted a net loss of $64.4 million.

As a nontraditional media and marketing services company, Alloy focuses on girls and guys between the ages of 10 and 24 using three different outlets: promotions, media, and placement. The promotions and placement business helps marketers place ads and product samples where they will reach teens and young adults. For example, Alloy placed Unilever's Axe Body Spray and Pom Wonderful's Pom Tea at spring-break parties and on college campuses. Says Matthew Diamond, company cofounder and CEO, "We want to be the conduit between corporate America and the youth market." The company also helps customers place advertising in print and broadcast media that's focused on high school and college students and military personnel.

Alloy's media and entertainment division offers diverse products and services. Its Channel One subsidiary, the in-school network, broadcasts 12-minute (including two minutes of advertising) youth-oriented news and public affairs programs in 8,000 public schools. The company's book division churns out books that the teen audience eats up. In fact, at one

point in summer 2008, Alloy had nine books on the *New York Times* best-seller list. One of its books, *The Sisterhood of the Traveling Pants,* was turned into a popular film. And Alloy also has had some of its books turned into TV shows (CW Network's *Gossip Girl* and *Privileged*). Currently, Alloy Entertainment has eight TV pilots in development at Universal and Warner Bros. Other media offerings include Web sites (**[alloy.com]** and **[teen.com]**), print publications, and display boards that are placed on school campuses.

Alloy has not been shy about branching out into various ventures. Since 1999, the company has spent $100 million to acquire 15 companies, not all of which have turned out well for it. For instance, its online social network for high school students (Sconex) never achieved its potential and was shut down in August 2008. In late 2005, it spun off its dELiA*s division (another Generation Y–oriented retailer that it had acquired in 2003). Despite its strategic missteps, the company does have incredible points of contact with large numbers of kids who have significant purchasing power.

Alloy attracts and keeps its target customers in different ways. One thing it does particularly well is tracking what this generation is all about. It extensively studies this age group. One of its collaborative studies (with survey firm Harris Interactive) was an in-depth look at friendships in today's "age of social media."

What they found is that friendships are developed beyond school walls and neighborhoods. Today's teens use e-mail and social networking sites to expand their social connections. Another study it completed (again with Harris Interactive) of college students "painted a definitive picture of modern college students tuned in to digital communications throughout their day." Also, they found that one of the most telling things about this generation is their mobile technology. Another strategy that Alloy uses is not relying on mass-market advertising, which Generation Y consumers tend to distrust. Instead, they get their message out in nontraditional ways that this age group relates to.

The company's goal is to be the leading Generation Y media and marketing services company. Its philosophy is that the business is defined by customers, not by product categories. As their target customer group ages, they intend to follow them by broadening the services and products they offer.

Discussion Questions

1. What general environmental trends, statistics, analyses, and so on might strategic decision makers at Alloy be particularly interested in? Where could they find this information?

2. What do you think is meant by the statement that the business is defined by its customers, not by product categories? What implications does this statement have for assessing external opportunities and threats?

3. What types of competitive information might Alloy's strategic decision makers want? Would the strategic groups concept be useful for such a uniquely positioned company? If so, what other companies might you place in this strategic group? If not, what competitors do you think they might have? How did you choose these competitors?

4. Do some research on Generation Y. What demographic characteristics does this group have? What values and attitudes do they have? Now, check out Alloy's Web site [www.alloy.com]. How is it attempting to appeal to this group? Would you say they're doing a good job of doing so? How might they have to change their strategies as this generation ages?

Sources: Based on E. Steel, "Multimedia Format Makes Alloy a Teen Magnet," *Wall Street Journal*, February 27, 2009, p. B7; Alloy Web site [www.alloy.com], January 12, 2009; H. Coster, "Teen Machine," *Forbes*, November 10, 2008, pp. 86–88; T. Hill, "Big Papers on Campus," *BusinessWeek*, July 9 and 16, 2007, p. 12; and J. A. Briggs, "Hey, Kids, Listen Up," *Forbes*, April 11, 2005, p. 120.

CASE #3: Being the Best

As the nation's leading consumer electronics retailer, Best Buy *is* trying to be the best. But that's not been easy in light of the challenges it's facing in the external environment. Like many other retailers, the economic climate has forced Best Buy to carefully consider its strategic options.

Best Buy was founded under the name Sound of Music in 1966 as a home- and car-stereo store by Dick Schulze (he still remains as board chair), who got tired of working for his father, who would never listen to his ideas on how to improve the family's electronics distribution business. However, while chairing a school board in the early 1980s, Schulze realized that his target customer group—15- to 18-year-old males—was declining sharply. He decided to broaden his product line and target older and more affluent customers by offering appliances and VCRs. In 1981,

a tornado wiped out his entire store (but not the inventory). Schulze decided to spend his entire marketing budget on advertising a huge parking lot sale. The successful sale taught him the importance of strong advertising, wide selection, and low prices—lessons that would serve him well as he built his business. In 1983, Schulze changed the name to Best Buy and began to open larger superstores. The change in store format and the fast-rising popularity of VCRs led to rapid growth. The number of stores grew from 8 to 24 and revenues skyrocketed from $29 million to $240 million.

In 1989, Schulze introduced the warehouse-like store format. By setting up stores so customers could browse where they wanted, the company was able to reduce the number of employees, a real cost saver. Larger store formats were introduced in 1994 and the company kept opening new stores. By 1997, the company realized that it had overextended itself with its expansion efforts, the super-sized stores, and costly consumer financing promotions. In response, the company went through a massive makeover, scaling back expansion plans and doing away with its "no money down, no monthly payments, no interest" program.

In 1999, Best Buy went through another evolutionary change as digital electronics began to flood the market. Store formats now highlighted digital products and featured stations for computer software and DVD demonstrations. They also decided to branch out into audio and video stores by acquiring the Magnolia Hi-Fi chain of stores and The Musicland Group (Sam Goody Stores, Suncoast, On Cue, and Media Play music stores). This strategy turned out to be a mistake and Best Buy sold off the entire Musicland subsidiary in June 2003.

In 2004, the company began focusing on bundling high-end electronics with service and installation, without giving up the low prices. Best Buy's CEO, Brad Anderson, admitted this strategy was risky, stating, "Nobody has been able to do this before. If we can only figure out the puzzle." Why did they start messing with a successful formula? Because Anderson felt there was "trouble" ahead. The company's store base was maturing. Imports were flooding the market and shorter product life cycles were exerting severe price pressures on some of the company's most profitable products—digital TVs, cameras, and home entertainment systems. And then there were Wal-Mart and Costco. These mass merchants and even direct seller Dell had ramped up their consumer electronics offerings. At the time, Anderson reasoned that, "If we do nothing, Wal-Mart will surpass us by the simple fact they're adding more stores than we are each year." There was no way Best Buy could win by "trying to chase the customer out of Wal-Mart." However, even though Best Buy felt that it couldn't compete on merchandise, it could compete with add-on services. Best Buy's acquisition of Geek Squad, a Minneapolis start-up, was an important key to that strategy. In addition, Best Buy began to sell private-label goods. It opened an office in Shanghai in September 2003 that allowed it to source products directly.

Then the company turned to a massive effort to identify and serve its most profitable shoppers (a process called "customer centricity"), an idea based on the belief that not all customers are profitable ones. Some are lucrative, whereas others cost more to sell to than their business is worth. After researching massive amounts of sales and demographics data, Best Buy identified some lucrative consumer segments and gave them the following names: Barry, the affluent tech enthusiast; Jill, a busy suburban mom; Buzz, a young gadget freak; Ray, a price-conscious family guy; Carrie, a young single woman; and others. Each store was oriented toward the segments that most reflected its customer base. Continuing its commitment to this centricity strategy, Best Buy is "getting in touch with its feminine side." As a company vice president said, "We were a boy's toy store designed *for* boys *by* boys." No more. Best Buy has feminized its stores by doing things such as turning down the volume of store music, lowering the bright lights, training salespeople to talk to customers about their lifestyles, and eliminating the flashing lights—all in an attempt to create a softer, more personal atmosphere.

There are risks associated with Best Buy's strategic moves. Economic conditions that are taking a nosedive and consumer confidence that is at its lowest level ever mean that Best Buy must continue to find ways to weather the challenges. Doing nothing isn't a feasible option. It is substantially reducing new store openings and may be forced to lay off employees. Also, in January 2009, after the worst holiday sales season in decades, the company announced CEO Brad Anderson's retirement and the appointment of COO Brian Dunn to the position. In addition, one of Best Buy's major competitors, Circuit City, filed for bankruptcy and closed down all its stores.

Discussion Questions

1. What examples of environmental scanning do you see in this case? What role do you think environmental scanning has played in the company's evolution? What role will it need to play in the company's future?

2. Using Porter's five-forces model and the information in the case, do a brief industry-competitive analysis.

3. What types of information do you think Schulze and Anderson might want from each of the five general environmental sectors? (You don't need to

look up this information. Just indicate what trends they would probably want to keep track of.)

4. What opportunities and threats do you think are facing this industry?

5. Best Buy is not heavily into global sales (it does have stores in Canada). If the company chose to go international, what types of external information might it need to make such a strategic move?

6. Update the information on Best Buy: number of stores, revenues, profits, and employees. Are these numbers increasing or declining?

Sources: Based on Reuters, "Best Buy Names New CEO," *CNNMoney.com,* January 21, 2009; K. Lamiman, "Featured Company: Best Buy Co., Inc.," *Better Investing,* January 2009, pp. 33–34; P. B. Kavilanz, "Best Buy Eyes Layoffs, Slows U.S. Expansion," *CNNMoney.com,* December 16, 2008; L. Zinn Fromm, "In Hard Times, Is Best Buy's Best Good Enough?" *New York Times Online,* December 7, 2008; P. B. Kavilanz, "Best Buy: Most Difficult Climate We've Ever Seen," *CNNMoney.com,* November 12, 2008; M. Fetterman, "Best Buy Gets in Touch with Its Feminine Side," *USA Today,* December 21, 2006, pp. 1B+; N. Maestri, "Best Buy's Geek Squad Steps up Laptop Repair," *Wall Street Journal,* October 23, 2006, p. B6; and M. Boyle, "Best Buy's Giant Gamble," *Fortune,* April 3, 2006, pp. 68–75.

CASE #4: Dressing Up

Even in good times, the department store industry is one of the toughest industries to compete in. Like many of its competitors, Kohl's Corporation is struggling to find a way to continue its successes even when faced with a drastically changed external environment. Based in Menomonee Falls, Wisconsin, Kohl's has more than 1,000 discount department stores in 48 states. The company has aggressively moved into the western and southern United States, although nearly a third of its stores are located in the Midwest. In 2008, the company had revenues of over $16.5 billion (up some 6 percent over 2007) and profits of over $1 billion. One analyst described Kohl's as "the best-positioned department store in this economy and one of the leading retailers with respect to inventory management, technological innovation, and merchandising and marketing execution." To continue its successes, it's important that Kohl's understands the changing needs of its customers.

Over the last few years, customers had become disillusioned with the overall shopping experience at many retail establishments. Long checkout lines, missing or vague product information, out-of-stock products, incorrect price tags, and scarce and often unknowledgeable sales staff have made the shopping experience quite unpleasant. Local shopping malls with their anchor department stores lost much of their popularity with shoppers. Unlike other department stores, Kohl's followed a different path.

Kohl's strategic approach has been built around convenience and price. Its typical store is a box-like structure with one floor of merchandise under inexpensive lighting where shoppers use carts as they browse through the simple racks and shelves of clothing, shoes, and home apparel merchandise. The company is especially selective about its locations. Everything about the way Kohl's does business—who it sells to and how those customers shop—hinges on where it puts its stores. Its goal is to set up shop in the heart of "soccer mom country." It typically avoids malls when looking at store sites, believing that its target customers—young mothers—typically don't have the time for a long drive to a mall location and certainly don't want the parking hassles when they do go shopping. Kohl's approach has been free-standing buildings with smaller parking lots in retailing power centers (a retailing destination where several large, specialty brand retailers often locate together) and other kinds of strip malls. For instance, the Kohl's store in Springfield, Missouri, is located adjacent to a Wal-Mart Super Center, a Home Depot, a McDonald's, a Michael's hobby and crafts store, and other casual dining restaurants. The company's target market is women aged 25 to 54 who have children and whose annual household income is moderate, ranging from $35,000 to $75,000. Even the merchandise selection offered at Kohl's is aimed at this target demographic by selling casual brands (such as Sag Harbor, Villager, Union Bay, Haggar, Jockey, HealthTex, and others) at low prices. To continue attracting this segment, Kohl's added a home furnishings collection called Casa Cristina (named for Cristina Saralegui, the host of a Spanish-language television show on Univision) and its own Food Network brand of dinnerware and cooking tools. In addition, a line of clothing, shoes, and home goods by designer Vera Wang called Simply Vera Vera Wang was introduced in late 2007. In Spring 2009 Kohl's announced that it was adding a casual clothing line for young women designed by Lauren Conrad, the star of the hit MTV show "The Hills." Kohl's believed that its customers wanted to and were willing to purchase more-fashionable merchandise selections. As one retail expert put it, "The chains have decided to design apparel on their own, ensuring that their lower-income customers can buy skinny jeans and satchel bags at the same time as shoppers at higher-end stores."

Although Kohl's has done well in a difficult industry, it is facing some serious challenges. Competitors ranging from J. C. Penney and Sears to Macy's have copied Kohl's approach. Even specialty retailers such as Old Navy (a unit of Gap, Inc.) and American Eagle have shifted from trendy teenage fashion toward clothing that appeals to moms. And on the discount end, Wal-Mart Stores has added national brands and improved the quality of its apparel. However, none has been as aggressive in competing with Kohl's as J. C. Penney has. They also have made their stores easier to navigate and enhanced their selections of casual brands. Most of all, they've lowered their prices to counter the advantage of Kohl's locations, trying to lure back shoppers to malls with better prices. A retail analyst says that J. C. Penney has a distinct advantage over Kohl's in at least two areas: a strong Web presence and big private-label brands that generate strong profits.

Even during the slowing economy, Kohl's made a grab for market share by opening 46 stores. It also was very aggressive on discount pricing. But it did say it was scaling back its plans to have 1,400 stores by 2012. Although Kohl's seems to be on a winning streak, competitor actions and other external trends will keep strategic decision makers on their toes for a while!

Discussion Questions

1. According to the case, what external trends were strategic managers at Kohl's having to deal with? In addition to these, what other external areas might be important to these managers? How might they keep track of changes?

2. If you were a strategic decision maker at the headquarters of Kohl's, what types of external information would you want? What if you were a Kohl's local store manager? What types of external information would you want?

3. Do you think the company's strategic decision makers have done a good job of scanning and assessing the environment? Explain.

4. What conclusion(s) about opportunities and threats can you draw from this case?

Sources: Based on S. Rosenbloom, "The Hills' Star to Design Clothing for Kohls," *New York Times Online,* April 22, 2009; "Kohl's Net Drops 18% Amid Weak Spending," *Wall Street Journal,* February 27, 2009, p. B3; S. Rosenbloom, "Handful of Niche Chains Stay Alive in Retailing," *New York Times Online,* December 20, 2008; WSJ News Roundup, "Nordstrom, Kohl's Earnings Go on Markdown Rack," *Wall Street Journal,* November 14, 2008, p. B3; C. Lu-Lien Tan, "Kohl's Makes Grab for Market Share," *Wall Street Journal,* October 1, 2008, p. B1; C. Coolidge, "Discount Chic," *Forbes,* April 7, 2008, p. 108; V. O'Connell, "How Fashion Makes Its Way from the Runway to the Rack," *Wall Street Journal,* February 8, 2007, pp. D1+; Hoover's Online [www.hoovers.com], February 7, 2007; J. Covert, "Kohl's to Sell Elle-Branded Clothing," *Wall Street Journal,* February 7, 2007, p. B3; R. Dodes and A. Zimmerman, "Cheap Chic: Who Gets It Right?" *Wall Street Journal,* November 25–26, 2006, pp. P1+; D. Koenig and E. Fredrix, "J. C. Penney and Kohl's Battle For Shoppers," *Springfield, Missouri, News-Leader* (Associated Press), November 25, 2006, p. 5B; Bloomberg News, "New Clothing Lines and Rising Profits at Penney and Kohl's," *New York Times Online,* November 10, 2006; M. Barbaro, "Discounters Go on Road to Find New York Style," *New York Times Online,* October 12, 2006; K. Lamiman, "Kohl's Corporation," *Better Investing,* April 2006, pp. 42–43; and G. Creno, "Mall-Shunning Kohl's Fixates on 'Mom Country,'" *Springfield, Missouri, News-Leader,* October 19, 2003, p. 5E.

Endnotes

1. B. Barnes, "Hollywood's Superheroes Save the Day," *New York Times Online,* January 5, 2009; T. Lewan, "Drive-in Theaters Are Making a Comeback," *Springfield, Missouri, News-Leader,* October 11, 2008, p. 5B; M. DeCuir, "Some Food and Alcohol with Your Flick? Cinemas Hope So," *USA Today,* March 27, 2008, p. 3A; B. Barnes, "At Cineplexes, Sports, Opera, Maybe a Movie," *New York Times Online,* March 23, 2008; D. Stuckey and K. Gelles, "Entertainment Sold Online," *USA Today,* February 26, 2008; L. M. Holson, "Hollywood Asks YouTube: Friend or Foe," *New York Times Online,* January 15, 2007; J. Carroll, "Americans Dislike the Cost of Going to the Movies," *Gallup News Service,* December 22, 2006; B. Tedesch, "Online Movie Tickets a Still-Evolving Force," *New York Times Online,* July 10, 2006; S. Bowles, "What, Movies Worry? *USA Today,* March 20, 2006, pp. 1D+; K. Jaworowski, "Seeing DVDs as a Boon to Theaters," *New York Times Online,* March 11, 2006; R. Levine, "Can Theaters Thrive in another Dimension?" *Business 2.0,* March 2006, p. 38; D. Leonhardt, "Changes Ahead for a Theater Near You," *New York Times Online,* February 15, 2006; and K. Kelly, "The Multiplex Under Siege," *Wall Street Journal,* December 24–25, 2005, pp. P1+.

2. Industry Statistics and Trends, report by American Pet Products Manufacturers Association [**www.americanpetproducts.org**], January 11, 2009.

3. C. Barnard, *The Functions of the Executive* (Cambridge, MA: Harvard University Press, 1938).

4. W. R. Dill, "Environment as an Influence on Managerial Autonomy," *Administrative Science Quarterly,* vol. 2, 1958, pp. 409–443; and J. G. March and H. A. Simon, *Organizations* (New York: John Wiley & Sons, 1958).

5. S. F. Matusik and M. B. Heeley, "Absorptive Capacity in the Software Industry: Identifying Dimensions That Affect Knowledge and Knowledge Creation Activities," *Journal of Management,* August 2005, pp. 549–572; R. L. Tung, "Dimensions of Organizational Environments: An Exploratory Study of Their Impact on Organizational Structure," *Academy of Management Journal,* vol. 22, 1979, pp. 672–693; J. R. Galbraith, *Designing Complex Organizations* (Reading, MA: Addison-Wesley, 1973); R. B. Duncan, "Characteristics of Organizational Environments and Perceived Environment Uncertainty," *Administrative Science Quarterly,* vol. 17, 1972, pp. 313–327; and P. R. Lawrence and J. W. Lorsch, "Differentiation and Integration in Complex Organizations," *Administrative Science Quarterly,* vol. 12, 1967, pp. 1–47.

6. C. A. Lengnick-Hall and T. E. Beck, "Adaptive Fit versus Robust Transformation: How Organizations Respond to Environmental Change," *Journal of Management,* October 2005, pp. 738–757; R. Bettis and C. K. Prahalad, "The Visible and the Invisible Hand: Resource Allocation in the Industrial Sector," *Strategic Management Journal,* vol. 4, 1983, pp. 27–43; J. Freeman, "Organizational Life Cycles and Natural Selection Processes," in B. M. Staw and L. L. Cummings (eds.), *Research in Organizational Behavior* (Greenwich, CT: JAI Press, 1982); H. E. Aldrich, *Organizations and Environments* (Englewood Cliffs, NJ: Prentice Hall, 1979); J. Pfeffer and G. R. Salancik, *The External Control of Organizations: A Resource Dependence Perspective* (New York:

Harper & Row, 1978); H. E. Aldrich and J. Pfeffer, "Environments of Organizations," *Annual Review of Sociology,* vol. 2, 1976, pp. 79–105; S. Mindlin, *Organizational Dependence on Environment and Organizational Structure: A Reexamination of the Aston Group,* unpublished master's thesis, Cornell University, Ithaca, NY, 1974; J. Hage and M. Aiken, "Program Change and Organizational Properties," *American Journal of Sociology,* vol. 72, 1973, pp. 503–579; and March & Simon, *Organizations,* 1958.

7. J. Sapsford, "Toyota Moves to Secure Hybrid Parts," *Wall Street Journal,* October 6, 2005, p. A11.

8. M. E. Porter, *Competitive Strategy* (New York: The Free Press, 1980).

9. F. Norris, "Airbus and Boeing Show That Making Planes Beats Flying Them," *New York Times Online,* June 24, 2006.

10. Newspaper Association of America, "Daily Newspaper Readership Trend 1998–2007," [**www.naa.org**], January 11, 2009; and R. Smolkin, "Uncertain Times," *American Journalism Review* [**www.ajr.org**], December/January 2005.

11. "Royal Caribbean Orders Largest, Most Expensive Cruise Ship," *USA Today.com* (The Associated Press), February 7, 2006.

12. Porter, p. 20.

13. J. C. Short, D. J. Ketchen, Jr., T. B. Palmer, G. Hult, and M. Tomas, "Firm, Strategic Group, and Industry Influences on Performance," *Strategic Management Journal,* February 2007, pp. 147–167; G. Leask and D. Parker, "Strategic Group Theory: Review, Examination, and Application in the UK Pharmaceutical Industry," *Journal of Management Development,* vol. 25, no. 4, 2006, pp. 386–408; J. R. Gregg, "Strategic Groups Theory: Past Nuances, Future Frontiers," *Southwest Academy of Management Proceedings,* March 1996, San Antonio, TX, pp. 29–32; J. R. Barney and R. Hoskisson, "Strategic Groups: Untested Assertions and Research Proposals," *Managerial and Decision Economics,* 11, 1990, pp. 187–198; K. Cool and D. Schendel, "Strategic Group Formation and Performance: The Case of the U.S. Pharmaceutical Industry, 1963–1982," *Management Science,* vol. 33, no. 9, 1987, pp. 1101–1124; G. Dess and P. Davis, "Porter's [1980] Generic Strategies as Determinants of Strategic Group Membership and Organizational Performance," *Academy of Management Journal,* vol. 27, no. 3, 1984, pp. 467–488; and M. S. Hunt, *Competition in the Major Home Appliance Industry 1960–1970,* unpublished doctoral dissertation, Harvard University, 1972.

14. S. Elliott, "Cadbury Bets on Protein to Promote Its New Sport Drink," *New York Times Online,* June 29, 2007.

15.. D. Lieberman, "Top Hollywood Studios Agree on Standards for Digital Films," *New York Times Online,* July 28, 2005.

16. N. Knox, "Realtors Fight for Business Model," *USA Today,* July 13, 2006, p. 4B.

17. A. Levin, "De-Icer Shortage Threatens Flights," *USA Today,* December 5, 2008, p. 1A; B. Hindo, "My Kingdom for a Tire," *BusinessWeek,* April 21, 2008, pp. 46–48; T. Aeppel, "Tight Supply Chain Is Good News for Terex," *Wall Street Journal,* August 28, 2006, p. A8; P. B. Kavilanz, "China Labor Pains and Holiday

Woes," *CNNMoney.com,* August 9, 2006; B. Hagenbaugh, "Supplies Fall Short for Tall Tires," *USA Today,* May 17, 2005, p. 4B; and E. Ramstad, "Ever Heard of Indium? Screen Makers Have, and Some Are Worried," *Wall Street Journal,* August 9, 2004, p. B1.

18. M. Barbaro, "At Liz Claiborne, a Bold Fashion Statement," *New York Times Online,* July 31, 2007.

19. S. Jayson, "Is This the Next Baby Boom?" *USA Today,* July 17, 2008, pp. 1A+.

20. S. Jayson, "Waiting for the Right Time," *USA Today,* November 10, 2008, pp. 1D+.

21.. "American FactFinder," U.S. Census Bureau, [**www.census.gov**], January 11, 2009.

22. P. Burrows, "The Mac in the Gray Flannel Suit," *BusinessWeek,* May 12, 2008, pp. 36–42.

23. A. Athavaley, "Lowering the Volume on Leaf Blowers," *Wall Street Journal,* January 7, 2009, p. D8; "Many Foods will Soon Be Labeled by Country of Origin," *New York Times Online,* October 1, 2008; and "Senate Approves Legislation to Expand Workplace Disability Law," *Workforce Management Online,* September 16, 2008.

24. "New Bankruptcy Law Aids American Express," *New York Times Online* (The Associated Press), January 23, 2007.

25. "Businesses Battle Over Patent Laws," *Wall Street Journal,* June 9/10, 2007, p. A7; G. Hitt, "Industries Brace for Tough Battle Over Patent Law," *Wall Street Journal,* June 6, 2007, pp. A1+; J. Bravin and M. Chase, "High Court Eases Way for Patent Challenges," *Wall Street Journal,* January 10, 2007, p. A8; L. Greenhouse, "Supreme Court Weighs the Meaning of 'Obvious,' " *New York Times Online,* November 29, 2006; and J. Bravin, "As Patents Grow More Contentious, Battleground Shifts to High Court," *Wall Street Journal,* November 28, 2006, pp. A1+.

26. "CEOs Want Tough Global-Warming Laws," *CNNMoney.com,* January 22, 2007; and S. Armour, "Crackdown on Hiring of Illegal Workers Shifts to Employers," *USA Today,* May 5, 2006, pp. 1B+.

27. D. Barboza, "Internet Boom in China Is Built on Virtual Fun," *New York Times Online,* February 5, 2007.

28. V. K. Garg, B. A. Walters, and R. L. Priem, "Chief Executive Scanning Emphases, Environmental Dynamism, and Manufacturing Firm Performance," *Strategic Management Journal,* August 2003, pp. 725–744; B. K. Boyd and J. Fulk, "Executive Scanning and Perceived Uncertainty: A Multidimensional Model," *Journal of Management,* vol. 22, no. 1, 1996, pp. 1–21; and R. L. Daft, J. Sormunen, and D. Parks, "Chief Executive Scanning, Environmental Characteristics, and Company Performance: An Empirical Study," *Strategic Management Journal,* March/April 1988, pp. 123–139.

29. P. F. Drucker, "The Information Executives Truly Need," *Harvard Business Review,* January–February 1995, pp. 54–62.

30. C. S. Korberg and G. R. Ungson, "The Effects of Environmental Uncertainty and Dependence on Organizational Structure and Performance: A Comparative Study," *Journal of Management,* Winter 1987, pp. 725–737.

31. R. S. Achrol and L. W. Stern, "Environmental Determinants of Decision-Making Uncertainty in Marketing Channels," *Journal of Marketing,* February 1988, pp. 36–50.

32. Garg, Walters, and Priem, "Chief Executive Scanning Emphases, Environmental Dynamism, and Manufacturing Firm Performance"; S. Kotha and A. Nair, "Strategy and Environment as Determinants of Performance: Evidence from the Japanese Machine Tool Industry," *Strategic Management Journal,* 16, 1995, pp. 497–518; R. Subramanian et al., "An Empirical Examination of the Relationship between Strategy and Scanning," *The Mid-Atlantic Journal of Business,* December 1993, pp. 315–330; and Daft et al., 1988.

Assessing Strengths and Weaknesses: Doing an Internal Analysis

4

LEARNING OUTCOMES

4.1 *Describe what an internal analysis is.*

4.2 *Explain how to do an internal analysis.*

4.3 *Discuss why an internal analysis is important.*

Caring Enough to Be the Very Best

"When you care enough to send the very best." Some of you may recognize this slogan as being that of Hallmark Cards, Inc.[1] Such a boastful slogan can communicate incredible hubris or, in Hallmark's case, reality. Being the best is a business commitment that Hallmark has made since its founding by Joyce Clyde (J. C.) Hall in 1910. The "best" slogan, penned by a Hallmark sales and marketing executive in 1944, was meant to capture the essence of why Hallmark stood head and shoulders above the rest of the greeting-card manufacturers. As Mr. Hall said in his autobiography, "The slogan constantly put pressure on us to make Hallmark cards the very best . . . I somehow feel that without the slogan our products would not have been as good." Today, Hallmark prides itself on and continually strives to uphold its reputation for quality, innovation, and caring.

Based in Kansas City, Missouri, Hallmark is a privately held manufacturer and distributor of greeting cards and personal-expression products. It publishes products in more than 30 languages and sells them through licensing arrangements in more than 100 countries in Latin America, Europe, Africa, and the Asia-Pacific region. The company also licenses designs to other manufacturers in the apparel, domestics, and tabletop (flatware, dinnerware, etc.) industries. Its best-known brands are the Hallmark, Shoebox, and Expressions From Hallmark brands. Some of its brands that you may not even realize belong to Hallmark include Crayola, Silly Putty, Ambassador, Weiner Dog, and Sunrise Greetings. The company's brands can be found on greeting cards, gifts, gift wraps, ornaments, holiday products (cards/gifts/wraps), party products, stationery, memory-keeping products (picture frames, albums, scrapbooks), and special collections.

Hallmark is the largest greeting-card company in the United States. With a little over 50 percent of the market share, it has a strong and enviable industry leadership position. In 2008, the company ranked #93 on *Forbes* magazine's list of largest private companies with revenues of $4.17 billion and over 15,000 employees. The company's stated beliefs and values (see below) guide its strategic decisions and actions.

WE BELIEVE:

That our products and services must enrich people's lives.

That creativity and quality—in our products, services and all that we do—are essential to our success.

That innovation in all areas of our business is essential to attaining and sustaining leadership.

That the people of Hallmark are our company's most valuable resource.

That distinguished financial performance is imperative to accomplish our broader purpose.

That our private ownership must be preserved.

WE VALUE AND ARE COMMITTED TO:

Excellence in all we do.

High standards of ethics and integrity.

Caring and responsible corporate citizenship for Kansas City and for each community in which we operate.

The most important element of Hallmark's success, however, has been its commitment to creativity. "Creativity is our essence." Hallmark employs more creative professionals than any other company in the world and has a strong creative team of more than 800 artists, designers, stylists, writers, editors, and photographers. This team generates more than 19,000 new and redesigned products every year. The company has created an environment that supports its creative team. Resources are committed to the creative process. For instance, the company's creative library provides an ever-changing source of creative inspiration for all. Then there are the corporate fine art collection, renowned visiting speakers, and ongoing education and renewal opportunities. The company also has a culture that nurtures creativity. Some of the creative employees joke that "working at Hallmark is like being paid to go to graduate school." In addition, every job, whether it's marketing, manufacturing, or maintenance, has a clear link to the company's mission of enriching lives.

What factors would you say have contributed to the success of Hallmark Cards? What strengths does it appear to have? How about possible weaknesses? In this chapter, we're going to study the final step in analyzing the current situation—an internal analysis. (See Figure 4.1.) Just as we've done in earlier chapters, we'll first look at *what* an internal analysis is, then at *how* you do one, and finally at *why* an internal analysis is an important part of managing strategically.

LEARNING OUTCOME 4.1
Describe What an Internal Analysis Is

In order to formulate appropriate and effective strategies, it's important to know what an organization can and cannot do particularly well, and what assets it has or doesn't have. As part of managing strategically, an **internal analysis** is the process of evaluating an organization's resources and capabilities. It provides important information about an organization's assets, skills, and work activities—what's good and what's lacking or deficient? The most important part of this analysis involves evaluating the organization's resources, capabilities, and core competencies, all of which we're going to look at next.

A Quick Review of Organizational Resources

We've already discussed resources in relation to the resource-based view of competitive advantage (see Chapter 2). As you'll recall, resources are simply the assets an organization

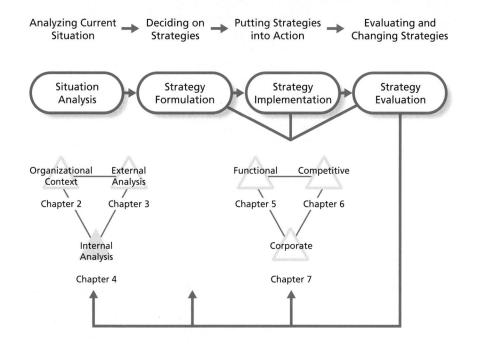

Figure 4.1

Strategic Management in Action

has for doing whatever it's in business to do (making tacos, providing at-home healthcare, or creating and selling greeting cards). These resources (or assets) can be financial, physical, human, intangible, and structural-cultural. Financial resources include debt capacity, credit lines, available equity (stock), cash reserves, and other financial holdings. Physical resources include tangible assets such as buildings, equipment and fixtures, raw materials, office supplies, manufacturing facilities, machines, and so forth. Human resources include the experiences, knowledge, judgment, skills, accumulated wisdom, and competencies of the organization's employees. At Google, for example, employees' programming skills would be part of its human resources. Intangible resources include brand names, patents, trademarks, databases, copyrights, registered designs, and so forth. For instance, Nike's "swoosh" symbol is an intangible resource, as are the Hallmark and Crayola brand names. Finally, structural-cultural resources include such things as organizational history, culture, work systems, policies, relationships, and the organizational structure being used. For example, 3M Corporation's culture stresses employee innovation, which is an important resource because its competitive advantage is based on the ability to continually develop and market innovative products.

Although an organization's resources can be a source of competitive advantage (see Chapter 2), they're also important to the organization's capabilities and core competencies. Figure 4.2 illustrates this relationship.

From Resources to Organizational Capabilities

An organization's resources are the inputs needed to perform its work, whether that's making hamburgers, collecting blood plasma, or producing *High School Musical* at a local community theater. You can view them as the organization's "whats"—what it has or owns. To illustrate, let's use the example of someone who's considered an excellent chef. This person has resources such as pots and pans, spices, cooking skills, equipment, utensils, an efficiently designed kitchen, and other culinary supplies that are used in preparing delicious

Figure 4.2

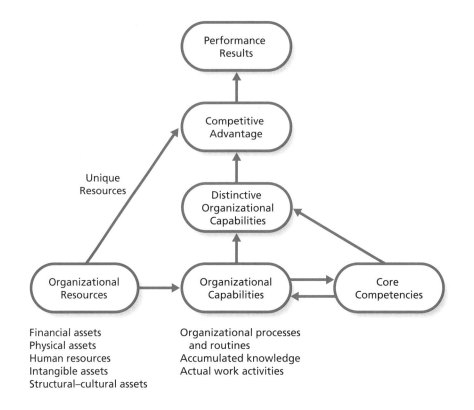

Financial assets
Physical assets
Human resources
Intangible assets
Structural–cultural assets

Organizational processes
 and routines
Accumulated knowledge
Actual work activities

meals. Likewise, an organization has resources that are used by organizational members to do their work and are valuable in helping the organization reach its goals and hopefully contributing to a sustainable competitive advantage. However, by themselves, resources aren't productive—think of the chef who has to rely on his skills and experience to combine the spices and food ingredients using the best equipment to make those gourmet meals. Likewise, organizational resources must be combined and used in some way to get the value out of them. For instance, Travelocity's customer database isn't valuable unless someone uses her knowledge to "mine" the database and find the information needed to make good decisions. As such, resources are the inputs used in **organizational capabilities,** which are the various routines and processes that transform those inputs (resources) into outputs (products including physical goods and services).[2] These **organizational routines and processes** are the regular, predictable, and sequential work activities done by organizational members. An organization is a huge, complex network of these routines and processes encompassing such work activities as procuring raw materials to establishing various product pricing structures to generating end-of-quarter financial and other statistical reports. Think about Hallmark and the various capabilities needed in producing and marketing its products.

As organizational members do their work using organizational resources and routines and processes, they learn how best to capture the value of these resources and turn them into possible core competencies or distinctive organizational capabilities. After all, organizational capabilities don't result from just gathering resources. Instead, capabilities involve interactions between people and between people and other resources.[3] In fact, some organizations never get the hang of it. They're never quite able to develop efficient and effective capabilities and they struggle exhaustively to survive in an increasingly dynamic and competitive marketplace. For instance, look at how Southwest Airlines and Delta Air Lines differ. Both have organizational resources (planes, logos, employees, customer information databases, etc.) and organizational routines and processes (loading and unloading planes, making reservations, doing safety inspections, customer service, etc.), yet Southwest has developed valuable capabilities and competitive advantages while Delta has struggled. However, organizational capabilities can change. Just because they were once the source of competitive advantage doesn't mean that they will continue to be a source of competitive advantage—that is, they don't always lead to a *sustainable* competitive advantage.[4] In today's dynamic and complex environment, capabilities that lead to a competitive advantage now may not do so in the future as conditions and competitors change. Some researchers have proposed that we need to think in terms of **dynamic capabilities**—an organization's ability to build, integrate, and reconfigure capabilities to address rapidly changing environments.[5]

From Capabilities to Core Competencies and Distinctive Capabilities

As we said earlier, every organization has capabilities that enable it to do what it's in business to do. Any major value-creating capabilities organizations have that are essential to their business are known as **core competencies.**[6] For example, executives at Nokia Corporation use their core competencies in product design and customer research to continually look for new applications and services.[7] At Nordstrom's, customer service is a core competency that results from capabilities in sales training and employee recruitment.[8] Although an organization's capabilities are the source of its core competencies, these core competencies also contribute to improving and enhancing other organizational capabilities. (Note the two-directional arrow in Figure 4.2.) So, which comes first? Organizational capabilities do. They're the fundamental building blocks for developing core competencies. Every organization has processes and routines to get work done. Any core competencies an organization has are created out of those routines and processes, accumulated knowledge, and actual work activities. If core competencies *are* established—and not every organization is able to do so—they can, in turn improve and enhance other organizational capabilities and also contribute to developing distinctive capabilities, which as Figure 4.2 shows *is* what leads to a competitive advantage.

Distinctive organizational capabilities are the special and unique capabilities that distinguish an organization from its competitors. For example, Southwest Airlines has developed distinctive organizational capabilities in organizational processes and routines such as gate turnaround, ticketing, and employee–customer interactions. Although every

Figure 4.3

*Characteristics of
Distinctive Organizational
Capabilities*

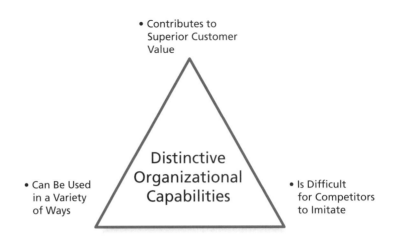

airline has these same organizational processes and routines, Southwest has developed them into distinctive capabilities, leading to a sustainable competitive advantage that has resulted in above-average performance. Even the company from our chapter-opening case, Hallmark, has developed its own set of distinctive capabilities. Distinctive capabilities have three characteristics (see Figure 4.3).[9] First, a distinctive capability contributes to superior customer value and offers real benefits to customers. You need to be good at—that is, have a distinctive capability in—whatever it is that your customers value. For instance, Aristocrat Leisure Limited, an Australian company, recognized that many gamblers at smaller, rural casinos wanted flashy, multiple-line penny, nickel, and dime slots that paid out more frequently than dollar slots. Aristocrat responded and turned these small-coin slots into the gaming industry's hottest product. One analyst said, "Aristocrat got ahead by figuring out what people want."[10] Why be good at something that your customers don't value? For example, Western Union, probably best known for its telegrams, sent the last one on Friday, January 27, 2006. Why? Because nobody sends telegrams anymore. That capability isn't valued by customers in today's world.[11]

The second characteristic of distinctive organizational capabilities is that they should be difficult for competitors to imitate. Think how we described organizational capabilities as the various organizational routines and processes that transform inputs into outputs. Making these capabilities difficult to imitate means balancing a complex array of employee skills and knowledge and harnessing the considerable learning that exists in the organization. It also means recognizing how capabilities span functional areas and how those areas interact with each other. If these complex interactions are strategically managed and exploited, it can be difficult for competitors to imitate even if they have similar resources and organizational processes and routines. For example, Anheuser Busch InBev (AB) has an incredibly accurate approach to finding out what beer drinkers are buying, as well as when, where, and why they're buying.[12] Its data-mining capability—known as BudNet—is AB's little-known "jewel" and the primary reason the company's share of the U.S. beer market edged up to over 50 percent from 48.9 percent, a huge gain in a market where a weak economy, lousy weather, and the threat of tougher drinking laws kept competitors' sales down. AB executives use the data from BudNet to constantly change marketing strategies, to design promotions for particular ethnic groups, and to get early warnings when rivals might have an edge. It's a capability that spans different functional areas, making it hard for competitors to imitate.

Finally, a distinctive organizational capability should be able to be used in a variety of ways. The organizational routines and processes developed in one area should be transferable to other areas of the organization. For example, Honda Corporation's capabilities at developing fuel-efficient, reliable, and responsive engines and drive trains has provided it with access to different markets including automobiles, motorcycles, lawn mowers, snowblowers, tillers, all-terrain vehicles, power generators, marine outboard engines, and now small passenger jets. As a company ad states, "We are first and foremost, an *engineering* company. But we're also the world's largest engine manufacturer."[13] Another example of using a capability in a variety of ways can be seen at United Technologies Corporation, which believes that its capabilities lie in developing technology that conserves energy. By transferring knowledge about the principles of energy conservation among its various business divisions, which include Pratt & Whitney (engines), Otis (elevators), Sikorsky Aviation (helicopters), Hamilton Sunstrand (aircraft systems and other flight controls), and Carrier (heaters and air conditioners), the company has been able to dominate most of its markets.[14] Another example can be seen at W. L. Gore, a company best known for its Gore-Tex fabrics, which are used in a variety of products, especially outdoors apparel. The fact that it's posted a profit every year since it was founded in 1958 confirms that the company has developed significant skills and capabilities in product innovation. More important, the company has shared those critical innovation skills and capabilities across multiple product lines in diverse industries ranging from guitar strings and dental floss to medical devices and filtration equipment. And for at least one of its products—guitar strings—the shared capabilities have led to the number two position in the market in a short span of time.[15]

Now for the two remaining boxes in Figure 4.2, which address competitive advantage and performance results. Competitive advantage, as we know, is what sets an organization apart—its competitive edge. As the figure shows, competitive advantage must come from an organization's unique resources or from its distinctive capabilities. Having a competitive advantage will affect an organization's performance results positively. Although it's possible for an organization to enjoy strong performance results in the short run without a significant competitive advantage, there are limits to how long such results can last. Without a sustainable competitive advantage, long-run success and survival are uncertain. It's important, therefore, that organizational decision makers know where the organization's strengths and weaknesses are in terms of its resources, capabilities, and competencies.

The Role of Strengths and Weaknesses

The whole reason for doing an internal analysis is to assess what the organization has or doesn't have (resources) and what it can and can't do (capabilities)—in other words, its strengths and its weaknesses. **Strengths** are resources that the organization possesses and

Strategic Management in Action

The clothing industry isn't an easy one to compete and be successful in. However, VF Corporation has become one of the world's largest, most profitable clothing conglomerates by doing many things well. One thing the CEO did was buy languishing fashion brands and turn them into winners. How? By using VF's capabilities: state-of-the-art distribution, global buying power, and keen merchandising instincts. For instance, VF bought the North Face brand for a bargain price of $135 million, revamped its sourcing, distribution, and financial operations, and was able to nearly double sales over a five-year period. As one analyst said, "The North Face is a great example of what VF can do. For VF it was easy, and it's not easy for everybody."

Which characteristics of distinctive capabilities does this illustrate? Explain.

Source: *Based on R. Dodes, "VF Dresses Up Its Operations, Bucking Recession," Wall Street Journal, March 30, 2009, p. B3; and M. V. Copeland, "Stitching Together an Apparel Powerhouse," Business 2.0, April 2005, pp. 52–54.*

capabilities that it has developed, both of which can be exploited and developed into a sustainable competitive advantage. Not every strength will lead to a sustainable competitive advantage, but an organization's strengths should be nurtured and reinforced as its main competitive weapons. **Weaknesses,** on the other hand, are resources and capabilities that are lacking or deficient and prevent the organization from developing a sustainable competitive advantage. Organizational weaknesses need to be corrected if they're in critical areas that are preventing the organization from developing a sustainable competitive advantage. However, most organizations have limited resources to correct problems, so strategic decision makers often choose to simply minimize the impact of weaknesses as long as they aren't in areas crucial for developing a sustainable competitive advantage.

Organizational members at all levels of the organization struggle with these types of strategic decisions: What strengths and weaknesses are in my area(s) of responsibility and how can I strategically manage these areas to high levels of performance? Now that we have a good understanding of *what* an internal analysis is, it's time to look at *how* you do one.

Learning Review: Learning Outcome 4.1

- What is an internal analysis and how is it different from an external analysis?
- Describe the relationship between resources, capabilities, and competitive advantage.
- What characteristics do distinctive organizational capabilities have?
- Define strengths and weaknesses.

LEARNING OUTCOME 4.2
Explain How to Do an Internal Analysis

In this section we want to look at three different approaches for doing an internal analysis. The first views the organization's work—what it's in business to do—as a series of value-creating activities. The second is similar to a financial audit, but is used to examine and assess all internal areas of an organization instead of evaluating just financial information. The third focuses on developing a profile of the organization's capabilities. To conclude this section, we'll look at how to determine an organization's strengths and weaknesses.

Value Chain Analysis

Every organization needs customers if it's going to survive. Even not-for-profit organizations must have "customers" who use its services or purchase its products. The premise behind this approach is that customers want (demand) some type of value from the goods and services they purchase or obtain. This value can come from three broad categories: the product is unique and different; the product is low priced; or the product meets the needs of a specific group of customers quickly and efficiently. In order to assess an organization's ability to provide value, strategic decision makers can use an approach developed by Mike Porter called **value chain analysis,** which is a systematic way of examining all the organization's functional activities and how well they create customer value.[16]

As we said earlier, every organization has specific organizational routines and processes—work activities done by organizational members—that allow it to do whatever it's in business to do. Each of these activities creates varying levels of customer value and organizational costs. What strategic decision makers hope is that the customer value

Harley-Davidson (H-D) is best known for its motorcycles and apparel. However, it started selling a "new source of fuel, one that goes into mouths instead of gas tanks and comes in such flavors as teriyaki and pepper." Yes, H-D is selling beef jerky. Joining forces with one of the largest U.S. packaged-foods companies, ConAgra Foods,

H-D has put its familiar name and black-and-orange logo on a food product.

Do you think H-D is creating customer value? Explain.

Source: Based on E. Fredrix, "Harley-Davidson Vrooms Way into Food Business with Jerky," USA Today, October 10, 2006, p. 3B.

created—as evidenced by the products the organization distributes or the services it provides and what customers are willing to "pay" for that value—outweighs the costs of creating that value (the margin). In using the value chain, we're assessing the organization's ability to create customer value through its work activities. In other words, what are the organization's strengths and weaknesses in these areas? Porter believed there were nine activities—five primary and four support—that were important to assess.

The primary activities are those activities that create customer value. These include the organizational routines and processes involved with bringing resources into the business (inbound logistics), processing these resources into the organization's goods or services (operations), physically distributing them to customers (outbound logistics), marketing the goods and services to customers (marketing and sales), and servicing customers (customer service). However, it's not enough to know *what* these activities are; we must judge *how well* the organization is performing these activities. That's the information required to assess strengths and weaknesses. Table 4.1 lists some questions to ask when assessing the primary activities in the value chain.

What about the support activities in the value chain? These activities support the primary activities as well as each other. Although it may seem that the primary activities are the most critical to the organization as they are the ones that create value, keep in mind that doing the primary activities wouldn't be possible without the support activities. For instance, if Hallmark didn't have effective human resources management processes and routines, it wouldn't have employees to design the cards, develop the marketing campaigns, or run the presses that imprint the latest holiday design on gift wrap. And if they can't do these things, they don't create value for the customer, the customer won't be willing to purchase the product, and organizational performance will suffer. How can you assess strengths and weaknesses in the support activities? Table 4.2 (see p. 111) lists some questions to ask in assessing the support activities.

With both assessments, you get a good picture of the resources and capabilities that are strengths and those that are weaknesses. To the extent that the organization performs any of these activities more effectively or efficiently than its competitors, it should be able to achieve a competitive advantage. The advantage of the value chain analysis is that it emphasizes the importance of customer value and how well an organization performs the primary and support activities in creating customer value. However, this approach may not be easy to use because organizational work activities don't always fit nicely and neatly into the primary and support activities framework. Therefore, some strategic decision makers use another approach—an internal audit of organizational functions.

Using an Internal Audit

The internal audit approach starts with the premise that every organization has certain functions that it must perform. In pursuing a sustainable competitive advantage, these

Table 4.1

*Assessing the Primary
Activities in the Value Chain*

Inbound Logistics
- Is there a materials control system? How well does it work?
- What type of inventory control system is there? How well does it work?
- How are raw materials handled and warehoused?
- How efficiently are raw materials handled and warehoused?

Operations
- How productive is our equipment as compared with our competitors?
- What type of plant layout is used? How efficient is it?
- Are production control systems in place to control quality and reduce costs? How efficient and effective are they in doing so?
- Are we using the appropriate level of automation in our production processes?

Outbound Logistics
- Are finished products delivered in a timely fashion to customers?
- Are finished products efficiently delivered to customers?
- Are finished products warehoused efficiently?

Marketing and Sales
- Is marketing research effectively used to identify customer segments and needs?
- Are sales promotions and advertising innovative?
- Have alternative distribution channels been evaluated?
- How competent is the sales force? Is its level of motivation as high as it can be?
- Does our organization present an image of quality to our customers? Does our organization have a favorable reputation?
- How brand loyal are our customers? Does our customer brand loyalty need improvement?
- Do we dominate the various market segments we're in?

Customer Service
- How well do we solicit customer input for product improvements?
- How promptly and effectively are customer complaints handled?
- Are our product warranty and guarantee policies appropriate?
- How effectively do we train employees in customer education and service issues?
- How well do we provide replacement parts and repair services?

Source: *Adapted with the permission of The Free Press, a Division of Simon & Schuster Adult Publishing Group, from* Competitive Advantage: Creating and Sustaining Performance *by Michael E. Porter. Copyright © 1985, 1998 by Michael E. Porter. All rights reserved.*

functions may be performed well or performed poorly. We base our identification of strengths and weaknesses on how well these basic organizational functions are performed. You may be familiar with the concept of a financial audit, which is simply a thorough examination of an organization's financial records and procedures. An **internal audit** is a thorough assessment of an organization's internal areas. It's similar to a financial audit although it obviously focuses on much more than just the financial aspects. Strategic decision makers use the internal audit to assess the organization's resources and capabilities from the perspective of its different functions and organizational elements. Are the necessary resources available so that people can perform their assigned work activities and how well do they perform these work activities (i.e., what are their capabilities)?

An internal audit looks at six organizational functional areas: production–operations, marketing, research and development, financial–accounting, management (which typically includes human resources management and other general management activities), and information systems. Obviously, organizations may have unique functions that don't fit into these categories or they may not call their functions by these names, but these six are

Procurement

- Have we developed alternate sources for obtaining needed resources?
- Are resources procured in a timely fashion? At lowest possible cost? At acceptable quality levels?
- How efficient and effective are our procedures for procuring large capital expenditure resources such as plant, machinery, and buildings?
- Are criteria in place for deciding on lease-versus-purchase decisions?
- Have we established sound long-term relationships with reliable suppliers?

Technological Development

- How successful have our R&D activities been in product and process innovations?
- Is the relationship between R&D employees and other departments strong and reliable?
- Have technology development activities been able to meet critical deadlines?
- What is the quality of our organization's laboratories and other research facilities?
- How qualified and trained are our laboratory technicians and scientists?
- Does our organizational culture encourage creativity and innovation?

Human Resource Management

- How effective are our procedures for recruiting, selecting, orienting, and training employees?
- Are there appropriate employee promotion policies in place and are they used effectively?
- How appropriate are reward systems for motivating and challenging employees?
- Do we have a work environment that minimizes absenteeism and keeps turnover at reasonable levels?
- Are union–organization relations acceptable?
- Do managers and technical personnel actively participate in professional organizations?
- Are levels of employee motivation, job commitment, and job satisfaction acceptable?

Firm Infrastructure

- Is our organization able to identify potential external opportunities and threats?
- Does our strategic planning system facilitate and enhance the accomplishment of organizational goals?
- Are value chain activities coordinated and integrated throughout the organization?
- Can we obtain relatively low-cost funds for capital expenditures and working capital?
- Does our information system support strategic and operational decision making?
- Does our information system provide timely and accurate information on general environmental trends and competitive conditions?
- Do we have good relationships with our stakeholders including public policy makers and interest groups?
- Do we have a good public image of being a responsible corporate citizen?

Source: *Adapted with the permission of The Free Press, a Division of Simon & Schuster Adult Publishing Group, from* Competitive Advantage: Creating and Sustaining Performance *by Michael E. Porter. Copyright © 1985, 1998 by Michael E. Porter. All rights reserved.*

Table 4.2

Assessing the Support Activities in the Value Chain

the most common. Table 4.3 (see p. 113) lists some key questions to use in assessing the strengths and weaknesses of each functional area. This assessment concentrates on the availability or lack of critical resources and the level of capabilities (i.e., how efficiently and effectively work is being done) in each functional area.

In addition to the assessment of the functional areas, an internal audit should look at three other important organizational elements: the strategic managers, the organizational structure, and the organization's culture. Table 4.4 (see p. 115) lists some key questions to use in assessing these areas.

Organizations Need Physicals Too

Have you ever had a physical exam? If you have, you know there's an intense scrutiny of past medical history, current health issues or complaints, and lifestyle factors. This physical exam may point to the need for additional scrutiny with test results compared to normal ranges. Doesn't this seem to be an appropriate analogy for assessing organizations? Could the concept of a "physical exam" be applied to organizations? Here's a guide to giving your organization a physical exam.

Brain function: This would be the organization's strategy and planning function. How well does your organization's "brain" function? Are the strategies and plans getting through to the rest of the organization? Is the "command center" functioning effectively and efficiently?

Nervous system: You need to check your company's reflexes. Are communication and information technology systems responsive as information is gathered and disseminated from the brain?

Eyes, ears, nose, and mouth: These sense organs respond to the outside world. Are the marketing and sales groups "sensing" customers' needs accurately?

Arms, hands, legs, feet, and associated muscle groups: These body parts convert energy into action. What kind of shape are your operations systems in? Do they acquire materials, make things, and deliver them efficiently and effectively?

Lungs and digestive system: In your body, the lungs and digestive system absorb nutrients and filter waste. Are resources being absorbed efficiently? Are you getting rid of waste efficiently?

The heart: You need to have a strong, highly conditioned heart to keep the rest of the body functioning properly. The organization's heart is its culture, its sense of meaning and purpose. How is the flow of culture throughout your organization? Has it cut off circulation or is it sending out strength-giving nutrients?

Source: Based on J. Mariotti, "Give Your Company a Physical," Industry Week, October 5, 1998, p. 74.

Capabilities Assessment Profile

The last approach we're going to discuss is a **capabilities assessment profile,** which is an in-depth evaluation of an organization's capabilities. This approach was developed because strategic decision makers had few guidelines for identifying and evaluating their organization's distinctive capabilities.[17] Assessing capabilities can be rather complex since they arise from the ways that resources are combined in the organization's basic work processes and routines. They're not as easily determined as organizational functions or even the primary and support activities. However, the complex nature of capabilities also makes it harder for competitors to imitate, which makes them excellent sources of sustainable competitive advantage. That's why the capabilities assessment profile can be beneficial: it provides some guidelines for identifying the organization's distinctive capabilities.

A capabilities assessment consists of two phases: (1) identifying distinctive capabilities and (2) developing and leveraging these distinctive capabilities.[18] Because our main interest at this point is analyzing the internal aspects of the organization, we're going to concentrate on the first phase. Phase 2 addresses strategy development issues that are beyond the scope of our discussion of how to do an internal analysis. Figure 4.4 (see p. 115) illustrates the steps in phase 1.

Earlier in the chapter, we described what makes capabilities distinctive—they contribute to superior customer value, they are difficult for competitors to imitate, and they are usable in a variety of ways. These characteristics are important because they reflect the information that's gathered in a capabilities assessment. In fact, the first step in assessing organizational capabilities—*preparing a current product–market profile*—emphasizes

Table 4.3

Internal Audit of Functional Areas

Production–Operations
- Does the organization have reliable and reasonably priced suppliers?
- Are facilities, offices, machinery, and equipment in good working condition?
- Are facilities strategically located close to resources and markets?
- Does the organization have effective inventory control policies and procedures?
- Does the organization utilize quality control procedures? Are these procedures effective?
- How does the organization do on quality assessments?
- Does the organization have an appropriate amount of capacity?
- What is the organization's safety record?
- Does the production-operations process work smoothly and with little disruption?
- Have production-operations goals been established, and are work activities aimed at achieving these goals?
- Do production-operations employees use appropriate operations planning and controlling tools and techniques?
- Has the organization developed any particular competencies in the areas of production-operations?

Marketing
- Does the organization segment markets effectively?
- What is the organization's market position or rank?
- Does the organization position itself well against its competitors?
- What is the organization's market share, and has it been increasing or decreasing?
- Does the organization conduct market research, and is this research effective?
- Is market research information used in making marketing decisions?
- Does the organization have an effective sales force?
- Has the organization priced its products and services appropriately?
- How is product quality and how does it compare with that of competitors?
- Is customer service effective and how does it compare with competitors?
- Is the advertising strategy effective?
- Are promotion and publicity strategies effective?
- Are customer complaints decreasing, increasing, or stable?
- Are customer complaints handled effectively and efficiently?
- Are present channels of distribution reliable and cost effective?
- Are marketing planning and budgeting effective?
- Do marketing employees use appropriate marketing planning and controlling tools and techniques?
- Has the organization developed any particular competencies in any of the marketing areas?

Research and Development
- Does the organization have adequate R&D facilities?
- Are the R&D employees well qualified?
- Does organizational culture encourage creativity and innovation?
- Is communication between R&D and other organizational units effective?
- Are the organization's products technologically competitive?
- If patents are appropriate, are patent applications increasing, decreasing, or stable?
- Is development time from concept to actual product appropriate?
- How many new products have been developed during the last year (or whatever time period is most appropriate)?
- Does the organization commit more, the same, or less to R&D than its competitors do?
- Do R&D employees use appropriate R&D tools and techniques?
- Has the organization developed any particular competencies in the R&D area?

(continued)

Table 4.3

Continued

Financial and Accounting

- Is the organization financially strong or weak according to the financial ratio analyses?
- What are the trends in the organization's financial ratios and how do these compare with industry trends?
- Is the organization able to raise short-term capital?
- Is the organization able to raise long-term capital?
- What is the organization's working capital position? Is it sufficient?
- Are the organization's capital budgeting procedures effective?
- Has the organization established financial goals? Are they appropriate?
- Are dividend payout policies reasonable?
- What type of relationship does the organization have with its creditors and stockholders?
- Is there a match between the organization's sources and uses of funds?
- Do financial-accounting employees use appropriate financial-accounting tools and techniques?
- Has the organization developed any particular competencies in the financial-accounting area?

Management

- Do organization employees manage strategically?
- Are organizational goals clear and measurable? Are they communicated to organizational members?
- Is the organization's structure appropriate?
- What is the organization's culture? Does it support organizational goals and mission?
- Has the organization developed its vision? What about mission(s)?
- Does the organization attract appropriate job applicants?
- Are employee selection procedures effective?
- Does the organization provide employees with appropriate training?
- Are job descriptions and job specifications clear?
- Are jobs effectively designed?
- What is the level of employee morale?
- What is the level of employee turnover?
- Are organizational compensation and reward programs appropriate?
- Are organizational employee discipline and control mechanisms appropriate?
- How does the organization treat its employees?
- What kind of relationships does the organization have with employee groups?
- Does the organization effectively use work teams?
- Are legal guidelines followed in human resource management activities?
- Has the organization developed any competencies in its human resource management activities?
- Has the organization developed any competencies in the management area?

Information Systems–Information Technology

- How does the organization gather and disseminate information? Is it effective and efficient?
- Is the information system used by employees in making decisions?
- Is information updated regularly?
- Is information distributed effectively and efficiently?
- Do employees have access to contribute input to the information system?
- Has the organization made an investment in information technology that's greater than, equal to, or less than competitors?
- Is information technology used effectively and efficiently in all areas of the organization?
- Is the organization's information system secure?
- Is the organization's information system user friendly?
- Are training workshops or seminars provided for users of the information system?
- Are employees in the information systems–information technology area well qualified?
- Has the organization developed any competencies in the information systems–information technology area?

organization–customer interactions. In this step, we identify what we're selling, who we're selling to, and whether we're providing superior customer value and offering the customer desirable benefits. To do this, we need information about specific products and markets; principal competitors in each of these product-market segments; and performance measures, such as sales growth rates, market share, competitive position, contributions to sales and earnings—for each product-market segment.

Once we have a current (and thorough) product-market profile, the next step in the capabilities assessment is *identifying sources of competitive advantage and disadvantage in the main product-market segments.* We want to know why customers choose our products instead of our competitors. This assessment would involve identifying specific cost, product, and service attributes. When customers purchase a product (a good or a service), what they're actually purchasing is a bundle of attributes that they believe will satisfy their needs.[19] These attributes vary by product and market. For example, camera customers may

Figure 4.4

Identifying Distinctive Organizational Capabilities

Step 1 Prepare current product–market profile.

Step 2 Identify sources of competitive advantage and disadvantage in the main product–market segments.

Step 3 Describe all the organizational capabilities and competencies.

Step 4 Sort the core capabilities and competencies according to strategic importance.

Step 5 Identify and agree on the key capabilities and competencies.

be interested in product attributes such as picture clarity, camera speeds, camera size, or price. Airline customers might choose a particular airline based on attributes such as safety record, close adherence to arrival-departure schedules, customer service, meal availability, convenience of arrival-departure times, and price. Community arts customers might choose a live theater performance on the basis of attributes such as familiarity with the play, actors starring in the play, or ticket price. Again, in this step we're attempting to identify those attributes that our customers value in our products and what competitive advantages or disadvantages these attributes provide us.

With this information, then, we're ready to pinpoint the organizational capabilities that lead to those sources of competitive advantage and disadvantage. Step 3 involves *describing organizational capabilities and competencies.* To identify those capabilities, you need to closely examine the resources, skills, and abilities of the organization's various divisions. Let's look at an example to help explain this. Suppose that you're a strategic manager at one of the nation's airlines. Your analysis of sources of competitive advantage and disadvantage (step 2) showed that one reason customers choose your airline over competitors is because scheduled flights left on time consistently. In step 3, you need to uncover what resources and capabilities led to this competitive advantage. You might find, for example, that consistent departures were the result of a well-trained ground crew who loaded baggage efficiently and effectively; appropriate numbers of customer service representatives who processed passengers quickly; a system of paperless ticketing and boarding passes; and experienced pilots who knew the ins and outs of getting quick control tower clearance for takeoff. This intense analysis of the organizational resources and the routines and processes behind the capabilities is an important step. It forces strategic decision makers to really understand what has to happen in order to deliver superior customer value and benefits. Even strategic decision makers in not-for-profit organizations should assess what resources and routines and processes lead to customers' willingness to support, sponsor, and advocate their products and programs. This is probably the most difficult step in the capabilities profile. Yet, it's also the one that yields the most important information because it gets to the heart of the matter—the most basic aspects of organizational work and the important interactions that take place as this work is performed by organizational members.

What's next? Step 4 involves *sorting these core capabilities and competencies according to their strategic importance.* In other words, which capabilities are most important for building the organization's future? Judging which capabilities are strategically important is a matter of evaluating each according to three criteria: (1) Does the capability provide tangible customer benefits? (2) Is the capability difficult for competitors to imitate? (3) Can the

Strategic Management in Action

Kimberly-Clark's Kleenex still faces intense marketplace battles even though it's an established brand—over 85 years old! One challenge: people use its name to describe any type of tissue. Another challenge: cheap generic brands flooding store shelves. Protecting and nurturing the brand is important, however, because it's part of Kimberly-Clark's consumer tissue division, which contributes more than one-third to the company's annual sales. Company executives have decided on a "high-stakes bet—Kleenex laced with a mild pesticide to fight cold and flu viruses." They had tried such a product back in 1984,

with little luck. Of course, the name they used for the product—Avert Virucidal—may have played a role in that failed strategy. However, in the late 1990s, as consumers began snatching up hand sanitizers and antibacterial soaps, the company decided it was time to reexamine the antiviral idea.

What organizational functional areas do you think would play a role in getting such a product up and running?

Sources: Based on J. L. Yang, "The Bottom Line," Fortune, September 1, 2008, pp. 107–112; and E. Byron, "Can a Re-Engineered Kleenex Cure a Brand's Sniffles?" Wall Street Journal, January 22, 2007, pp. A1+.

Yves Guillemot has made his Ubisoft game studios some of the most efficient and creative in the videogame industry. (Note: The company's name is a combination of "ubiquity" and "software.") Although bigger competitors, like Electronic Arts, have spent millions building glitzy studios in southern California, Guillemot took a different approach. He chose to save costs by opening game studios in low-cost locations such as Morocco, China, Romania, and Canada. Today, the company has studios in more than 20 countries (including its newest ones opened in 2008 in China,

Singapore, Ukraine, and India) and their average operating cost per employee is about a third less than the industry average. Recruiting and managing its young, talented, computer-savvy game designers is crucial to Ubisoft's strategy.

What do you think of Ubisoft's approach? What are the implications for the resources and capabilities the company needs?

Sources: *Based on Hoover's Online* [**www.hoovers.com**], *January 19, 2009; and G. Keighley, "Massively Multinational Player,"* **Business 2.0**, *March 2005, pp. 64–66.*

capability provide wide access to a number of different markets? If these criteria sound familiar, it's because we described them earlier as the characteristics of a distinctive capability. This analysis will show you how organizational capabilities differ in their strategic importance. Those that are most important strategically should be placed at the top of the list and on down. By sorting organizational capabilities according to level of strategic importance, strategic decision makers gain an understanding of their organization's critical strengths and weaknesses. But, there's one more step in a capabilities assessment profile.

The final step involves *identifying and agreeing on the key competencies and capabilities.* Based on the ranking of strategic importance, decision makers can easily identify the organization's key competencies and capabilities. What's difficult is agreeing that these *are* the key ones. Obviously, when certain organizational capabilities are selected as more critical to competitive advantage than others, it's likely to affect future resource allocation and organizational support for various departments, units, or divisions. Therefore, even though organizational members may be impacted differently, getting agreement on the organization's key capabilities is an important step in capabilities assessment. Without agreement on these critical capabilities, managing strategically for a sustainable competitive advantage will be extremely difficult.

Although the capabilities assessment approach provides a thorough analysis of the organization's important strategic capabilities, it's a complicated process. It's an approach probably most useful to upper-level strategic managers because it requires assessing a vast number of underlying organizational capabilities that don't always fit nicely and neatly into narrowly defined specific functional areas.

Determining Strengths and Weaknesses

Each internal analysis approach can be used to identify an organization's resources and capabilities. Whether it's from the perspective of analyzing customer value created by an organization's primary and support activities, from the perspective of auditing an organization's various functional areas, or from the perspective of identifying distinctive capabilities, we get a broad picture of an organization's resources and work routines and processes. However, that's only half the picture. We have to do more than just *identify* these factors. We also need to *determine* the organization's strengths and weaknesses in each of these areas. What are its strong points? What are its weak points? What resources and capabilities can be enhanced and exploited for a sustainable competitive advantage? What resources and capabilities are lacking or not used effectively? Strategic decision makers can determine

Figure 4.5

Criteria to Judge Organizational Strengths and Weakness

Past Performance Trends

Comparison Against Competitors

Are organizational resources and capabilities strengths or weaknesses?

Specific Goals or Targets

Personal Opinions of Strategic Decision Makers or Consultants

this as they analyze the various internal organizational areas and measure them against some criteria.[20] Figure 4.5 identifies four such criteria.

One criterion that could be used to determine strengths or weaknesses is past performance trends. This criterion could include any performance measures such as financial ratios, operational efficiency statistics, employee productivity statistics, or quality control data. Any organizational area that's measurable could be assessed by looking at the trends. For instance, is market share increasing or decreasing? Are liquidity ratios going up or down? Is the number of product returns increasing or decreasing? Are employee-training expenditures reducing product reject rates? For example, think about what organizational performance trends Hallmark's CEO might assess when making strategic decisions. Such quantitative measures could be used as indicators of organizational strengths and weaknesses. Although performance trends show important information about the organization's use of resources and capabilities, it doesn't show us whether performance is up to standards.

FOR YOUR INFORMATION

Market Share Myth

One commonly used measure in comparing against competitors is market share. Is it an appropriate measure? Nearly every business is mesmerized by market share—keeping it or increasing it. Conventional wisdom about the importance of market share was that the biggest market share would give a company the biggest revenues and the lowest cost per unit. That approach may have worked in the past. However, the reality of today's environment is that increasing market share may not be the route to continued competitive advantage and profitability. Having the most customers doesn't automatically translate into having the most profits. In fact, one study found that 70 percent of the time, the company with the largest market share didn't

have the highest rate of return. Strategic decision makers need to address how customers' needs are changing and how they can best meet those changing needs. Maybe *that's* how companies need to measure themselves against their competitors—by how well they're meeting customers' changing needs.

What do you think? Do you agree with the premises of this argument regarding the decreased importance of market share? What are the implications for doing an internal analysis? Are there customers an organization might not want? Explain.

Sources: Based on "The Myth of Market Share: Can Focusing Too Much on the Competition Harm Profitability?" Knowledge@Wharton **[knowledge.wharton. upenn.edu]***, January 24, 2007; L. Selden and G. Colvin, "Will This Customer Sink Your Stock?" Fortune, September 30, 2002, pp. 127–130; and R. Brooks, "Alienating Customers Isn't Always a Bad Idea, Many Firms Discover," Wall Street Journal, January 7, 1999, pp. A1+.*

Therefore, another criterion to use in assessing organizational strengths and weaknesses is how actual performance measures up against specific performance goals. **Organizational goals** are statements of desired outcomes. Every organization needs goals in all functional areas and at all levels that state *what* it hopes to accomplish by *when*. Such goals provide direction by specifying what and how organizational resources and capabilities are used in carrying out the organizational vision and missions. By comparing actual performance in the various functional areas against stated goals, strengths and weaknesses can be assessed. However, just looking at performance trends or how organizational performance measures up to the goals isn't enough to help us determine whether these strengths or weaknesses can be used to influence the development of potential sustainable competitive advantage. To do this, competitor comparisons are needed, which is another criterion we can use to measure strengths and weaknesses.

By comparing resources and capabilities against competitors, an organization can see how it stacks up. Remember from Chapter 3 that we looked at competitors as part of our external analysis. In an internal analysis, the focus needs to be on *how* competitors are doing. This information could include surveys and rankings published in external information sources. For instance, *Fortune* publishes an annual corporate reputation survey that ranks industry competitors according to what companies are most admired. *BusinessWeek* publishes annual rankings of research and development expenditures. We also might find competitor information in articles in business or general news magazines, other types of public documents such as annual reports or Securities and Exchange Commission filings, industry association newsletters, networking at professional meetings, customer contacts, and even the competitor's Web home page. A key consideration for gathering this information is whether competitive-intelligence methods are legal and ethical. (See *The Grey Zone* ethical issue.) The legal aspect is fairly clear—competitor intelligence becomes illegal corporate spying when it involves stealing proprietary materials or trade secrets by any means.[21] However, deciding whether something is ethical may not be as easy. For example, there's nothing unethical about scouring published sources for competitor information but ethical issues might arise if you decide to rummage through a competitor's trash bins for information or pretend to be a job applicant. These difficult decisions about competitive intelligence arise because often there's a fine line between what's considered *legal and ethical* and what's considered *legal but unethical*. For instance, at Procter & Gamble (P&G), executives hired competitive-intelligence firms to gather information on its competitors in the hair-care business. At least one of these firms

The Grey Zone

Some techniques that have been suggested for gathering competitor information include: (1) Pretend to be a journalist writing a story. Call up competitors' offices and interview them. (2) Dig through a competitor's trash. (3) Sit outside a competitor's place of business and count how many customers go in. (4) Get copies of your competitors' in-house newsletters and read them. (5) Call the Better Business Bureau and ask whether competitors have had any complaints filed against them and if so, what kind of complaints. (6) Have friends call competitors for price lists, brochures, or other marketing information. Do you think these methods are ethical or unethical? Why? What ethical guidelines might you propose for strategic decision makers when doing competitor intelligence?

misrepresented itself to competitor Unilever's employees, trespassed at Unilever's hair-care headquarters in Chicago, and went through trash dumpsters to gain information. In P&G's defense, when the CEO found out, he immediately fired the individuals responsible and apologized to Unilever.[22] Although there are no easy answers in these ethical dilemmas, be alert to the perceived "rightness" or "wrongness" of competitive-intelligence gathering methods.[23]

The last criterion for judging organizational strengths and weaknesses is personal or subjective opinions of strategic decision makers or consultants. Sometimes the best assessment is the personal opinion of those who are directly involved in the activity, as it may not be possible to quantitatively measure every resource or capability. And quantitative measures—such as trends or comparisons against standards—don't always capture what's really going on in a particular functional area, so qualitative opinions or assessments of organizational members can be useful in determining strengths or weaknesses. Also, if outside consultants are working with an organization's departments or divisions, what's their opinion? What do they see as strengths or weaknesses? Although this particular criterion can't be used to do case analysis for this class (unless you're studying a local organization), it's likely to be useful in assessing strengths and weaknesses when you're actually working in an organization.

By now, you should have a fairly good idea of what's involved in *doing* an internal analysis and identifying strengths and weaknesses. It's more than simply identifying an organization's internal resources and capabilities. It's also assessing whether those resources and capabilities are sufficient and can be sources of sustainable competitive advantage. Although we've discussed what internal analysis is and how to do one, we haven't yet addressed *why* it's an important part of managing strategically.

Learning Review: Learning Outcome 4.2

- How would the value chain approach to internal analysis be used?
- What does an organizational internal audit evaluate?
- How do you judge which organizational capabilities are strategically important?
- Describe the criteria that can be used to judge organizational resources and capabilities as either strengths or weaknesses.

LEARNING OUTCOME 4.3
Discuss Why an Internal Analysis Is Important

Doing an internal analysis is important for two reasons: (1) it's the only way to identify an organization's strengths and weaknesses, and (2) it's needed for making good strategic decisions. Let's explain.

As we stated at the beginning of the chapter, an internal analysis is a process of identifying and evaluating an organization's resources and capabilities. The outcome from an internal analysis is information about those resources, skills, and work routines and processes. What strengths do we have because of our specific resources and capabilities? What weaknesses do we have? If we didn't do this analysis, this critical strategic information wouldn't be available. But, this information in and of itself isn't useful. It's how strategic decision makers *use* this information that's important.

With the information from an internal analysis, strategic decision makers can make intelligent judgments about what competitive advantages the organization might currently have, what might potentially be developed into competitive advantages, and what might be preventing competitive advantages from being developed. This internal information, coupled with the information from the external analysis and information about the organizational context, provides the basis for deciding what strategic actions are necessary for sustainable competitive advantage.

Learning Review: Learning Outcome 4.3

- Why is an internal analysis an important part of managing strategically?

Learning Outcome 4.1: Describe what an internal analysis is.

- ○ *Internal analysis:* process of evaluating an organization's resources and capabilities.
- ○ *Resources (financial, physical, human, intangible, and structural-cultural):* can be a source of competitive advantage but are also important as the inputs needed for organization's capabilities and core competencies.
- ○ *Organizational capabilities:* various routines and processes that transform inputs into outputs. This doesn't happen just by gathering together resources. Instead, the resources have to be used and combined. *Organizational routines and processes:* the regular, predictable, and sequential work activities done by organizational members.
- ○ As organizational members do their work using resources and routines and processes, they learn how best to capture the value out of those resources and turn them into possible core competencies or distinctive capabilities. The capabilities that lead to a competitive advantage may change so organizations need to think in terms of *dynamic capabilities:* an organization's ability to build, integrate, and reconfigure capabilities to address changing environments.
- ○ *Core competencies:* major value-creating capabilities that are essential to an organization's business. They are not sources of competitive advantage themselves but can contribute to developing distinctive capabilities and improving other organizational capabilities.
- ○ *Distinctive organizational capabilities:* the special and unique capabilities that distinguish an organization from its competitors. They have three characteristics: they (1) contribute to superior customer value, (2) are difficult for competitors to imitate, and (3) can be used in a variety of ways. Distinctive capabilities can lead to a competitive advantage.
- ○ Main reason for doing internal analysis is to identify *strengths* (resources an organization possesses and capabilities an organization has developed, both of which can be developed into sustainable competitive advantage) and *weaknesses* (resources and capabilities that are lacking or deficient and prevent the organization from developing a sustainable competitive advantage).

Learning Outcome 4.2: Explain how to do an internal analysis.

- ○ There are three different techniques to do an internal analysis: value chain, internal audit, and capabilities assessment profile.
- ○ *Value chain:* a systematic way of examining all the organization's functional activities and how well they create customer value. The value chain was developed by Mike Porter and focuses on assessing the five primary and four support work activities. The five primary activities include inbound logistics, operations, marketing and sales, outbound logistics, and customer service. The four support work activities include procurement, technological development, human resource management, and firm infrastructure.
- ○ *Internal audit:* a thorough assessment of an organization's internal functional areas. It looks at six organizational functions: production–operations, marketing, research and development, financial–accounting, management, and information systems. In addition, the internal audit looks at three other organizational elements: the strategic managers, the organizational structure, and the organization's culture.
- ○ The capabilities assessment profile is an in-depth evaluation of an organization's capabilities. It consists of two phases: (1) identifying distinctive capabilities and (2) developing and leveraging these distinctive capabilities. The five steps include

(1) preparing a current product-market profile, (2) identifying sources of competitive advantage and disadvantage in the main product-market segments, (3) describing organizational capabilities and competencies, (4) sorting these core capabilities and competencies according to their strategic importance, and (5) identifying and agreeing on the key competencies and capabilities.

○ An organization's strengths and weaknesses can be assessed according to four criteria: (1) past performance trends, (2) *organizational goals:* statements of desired outcomes, (3) competitor comparisons, and (4) personal opinions of strategic decision makers or consultants.

○ Competitor comparisons can introduce legal and ethical issues.

Learning Outcome 4.3: Discuss why an internal analysis is important.

○ Important for two reasons: (1) only way to identify an organization's strengths and weaknesses and (2) needed for making good strategic decisions.

YOU
as
strategic
decision
maker:
building
your
skills

1. The conventional view that leading brands maintain their market leadership for long periods of time may be inaccurate. Strategic decision makers can no longer assume that they will be able to retain their companies' brand leadership over decades. In fact, studies of brands show that consumers are finding it harder to distinguish among competing products. With this in mind, answer the following questions: (a) What type of resources are brands? (b) What are the implications of these statements for internal analysis? (c) Could brands ever be the ultimate competitive weapon? Why or why not? (d) Could a brand ever be a weakness? Explain.

2. Customer loyalty can be a powerful competitive advantage. And customer loyalty is more than repeat purchasing. Customers who are loyal tend to buy more over time and, most important, tend to tell others about a company to their family, friends, and colleagues. Enterprise Rent-A-Car figured this out early on and rather than having a complicated and sophisticated customer research program, they focus on two simple questions—one about the quality of the customer's rental experience, and the second, the likelihood that they would rent from the company again. What do you think about this view? What organizational capabilities would be necessary to develop customer loyalty? Check out Enterprise's Web site [**www.enterprise.com**]. Look at the statements of the company's mission, culture, and founding values. How do these relate to customer loyalty?

3. A study by Fuld & Company, a competitive-intelligence firm, found that companies fail to use as much as 70 percent of the online business data they buy.[24] Why do you think strategic decision makers might not look at business data? Why are such actions a problem? What recommendations might you have for strategic decision makers regarding business data?

4. Asking the right questions is an important skill for strategic decision makers. Here are some questions that might be useful:

   • How can we do that? (Don't ask "why can't we do that?")

   • How else can we do that? What else could we do?

   • Will you help me? Can you explain that to me again?

   • Who, what, why, where, when, how, and how much?

   • Who will do what and by when?

   Would these types of questions be useful in doing an internal analysis? Why or why not?

5. In the cosmetics industry, knowing what and how the various competitors are doing could be important strategic information in developing a sustainable competitive advantage. Suppose that you're a manager at the Estée Lauder Companies. What types of competitive-intelligence information would you want, and where would you find it? Create a table showing what you've come up with. Be prepared to support your ideas in class. (You'll probably need to do some outside research—library, Internet, or otherwise—to complete this assignment.)

6. Find five examples of companies' goals. List these goals on a sheet of paper. Then, do some reverse thinking here and list what organizational resources and capabilities would be needed to accomplish those goals.

7. Studies of companies that are leaders in achieving exceptional customer profitability show that there are six steps they have taken to do so: (1) figure out the needs of your most profitable customers; (2) get creative by imagining competitively superior ways to deliver value to customers; (3) test and verify your hypotheses; (4) tell customers

how great your value propositions are; (5) apply the best approaches on a large scale; and (6) start over, as even the most successful initiatives need to be revised over time. What do you think of these suggestions? What are the implications for developing core competencies and distinctive capabilities? How could an internal analysis help an organization in this process?

CASE #1: Caring Enough to Be the Very Best

This Strategic Management in Action case can be found at the beginning of Chapter 4.

Discussion Questions

1. What resources and capabilities does Hallmark Cards seem to have? Does the company have any distinctive capability(ies)? Explain. Now, take a look at the Greeting Card Association Web site [www.greetingcard.org]. What information might be useful to Hallmark's strategic decision makers in assessing any company strengths and weaknesses?

2. What would it take to be "the very best" in this industry? Does Hallmark seem to be doing what it takes?

3. Check out the careers section on the company's Web site [corporate.hallmark.com]. What are the company's main divisions and departments and what is each responsible for? If you were to assess these areas as part of an internal analysis, what resources and capabilities might you look for?

4. Brand licensing has been important to Hallmark's business. What is brand licensing? What do you think strategic decision makers would need to know about brand licensing before deciding whether it's an appropriate strategy to pursue?

CASE # 2: New Flight Plan

February 14, 2007 (now known inside the company as 2/14), is a date that JetBlue Airways executives—and many of its passengers—won't soon forget. A devastating East Coast winter storm slowed operations at JetBlue's home base at New York's Kennedy Airport, leaving passengers stuck in planes on airport runways for up to 10 hours. Although that scenario alone was bad enough, the situation only got worse when attempts to recover from that fiasco led to a "six-day saga of more than 1,100 canceled flights"—an airline operations *and* customer service nightmare. In fact, this "extraordinary stumble" led *BusinessWeek* magazine to remove JetBlue from the number four spot in its first-ever ranking of Customer Service Champs, a ranking based on customer input. The impact of this situation on JetBlue's operations and reputation were felt for a long time. Although the company made an all-out effort to address problems, one analyst said, "What matters most is execution—doing the deep, hard, organizational work to ensure this never happens again."

JetBlue, founded in 1999, was the third airline that David Neeleman, an aviation industry veteran and former Southwest Airlines employee, had a hand in creating. (The other two: Morris Air, which was bought by Southwest in 1993, and WestJet Airlines, a Canadian-based discount carrier). In many ways, JetBlue resembled a smaller, younger version of Southwest, another airline many in the industry cite as a success story. From the beginning, JetBlue's goal was to "bring humanity back to air travel" and Neeleman had a vision for a different kind of airline—one that emphasized low fares, a sophisticated style, *and* a new concept of customer service. Analysts described the airline as "hip and sassy," but also said it was focused on "taking care of business by being hyper-efficient and keeping costs low." And JetBlue's approach obviously struck a chord with consumers as it has ranked number one or two on the Airline Quality Rating List since 2003 and ranked high in every measured category in the airline satisfaction ratings by J. D. Power & Associates. Neeleman said his past experiences had taught him six things: (1) do more for customers, (2) only the paranoid survive, (3) actions speak louder than words, (4) the best culture polices itself, (5) competition is the ultimate motivation, and (6) employees have to understand the business.

The ice storm aftermath hadn't been JetBlue's only slip-up, probably just its most publicized. Such functional challenges aren't uncommon for growing companies. For instance, in the company's early years, newly promoted managers with no time to be trained had to learn on the job how to be leaders, a situation that didn't go over too well with employees. However, Neeleman responded quickly to this problem by instituting mandatory leadership training programs, a move that resulted in happier workers and ultimately, happier customers. Two other problems were the "slow upward creep in company operating costs" and the erosion of its competitive advantage as traditional, older, and larger airlines sharply cut their labor costs.

JetBlue responded to these challenges by cutting back its aggressive growth rate. It sold five jets in its fleet and deferred delivery of 21 Airbus jets and 10 Embraer jets. It also removed one row of seats from its Airbus planes, which meant the plane could fly with three flight attendants instead of four and save fuel because the plane was carrying less weight—passengers, crew, and baggage. JetBlue had determined that this change alone would save about $6 million a year, even after taking into account revenues lost because of fewer seats.

In response to the post–Valentine's Day fiasco, Neeleman took full responsibility and said it was obvious that the company's "systems to deal with the consequences of bad weather did not keep up with the growth." He vowed to get the problems fixed and announced a "customer bill of rights" that would "compensate passengers for slip-ups and ensure that they don't find themselves trapped for hours on airplanes waiting to take off or trying to return to a gate." In a further attempt to bounce back from the troubles, Russell Chew, formerly the head of operations for the Federal Aviation Administration, was hired as the company's chief operating officer. Despite these actions, JetBlue's board of directors removed Neeleman from the CEO position in May 2007 and replaced him with Dave Barger, one of JetBlue's original senior managers. Barger has implemented a more conservative atmosphere. The company sold a stake to Germany's Lufthansa and slowed plans to add more planes and cities. And like the other airlines struggling with the challenging economic situation, JetBlue sought additional revenue sources to offset rising fuel prices including charging for extra legroom and selling blankets and pillows. Meanwhile, Neeleman stepped down from his role as nonexecutive chairperson and announced plans to start a new airline based in São Paulo, Brazil.

Discussion Questions

1. What resources and capabilities does JetBlue appear to have? Could any of these be considered distinctive? Explain. What would it take to make capabilities distinctive?

2. How might Neeleman's six lessons from his past experiences affect the resources and capabilities that were developed by JetBlue?

3. JetBlue's ice storm "stumble" led one analyst to say that what matters most is "execution" and that JetBlue was going to have to do the "deep, hard, organizational work to ensure this never happens again." What are the implications for JetBlue's resources and capabilities? What could other companies learn from this?

4. What strengths and weaknesses does JetBlue appear to have? Do you think a one-time event, like an ice storm, will have a long-term impact on a company's fundamental strengths? Explain. How can it prevent those strengths from becoming weaknesses?

5. What approach to internal analysis would you suggest that CEO David Barger use in assessing his organization's strengths and weaknesses? Why?

Sources: Based on M. Maynard, "At JetBlue, Growing Up Is Hard to Do," *New York Times Online*, October 5, 2008; M. Maynard, "JetBlue Starts Selling Blankets and Pillows," *New York Times Online*, August 5, 2008; "JetBlue Delays Buying 21 Airliners," *New York Times Online* (The Associated Press), May 28, 2008; Reuters, "JetBlue's Chairman Will Be Stepping Down," *New York Times Online*, April 10, 2008; G. Stoller, "JetBlue Joins Other Airlines in Charging for Extra Legroom," *USA Today*, March 24, 2008; B. D. Bowen and D. E. Headley, "Airline Quality Rating 2008," AQR Aero, Inc. **[http://www.aqr.aero/aqrreports/2008aqr.pdf]**; D. Reed, "JetBlue Tries to Bounce Back from Storm of Trouble," *USA Today*, June 7, 2007, pp. 1B+; J. McGregor, "An Extraordinary Stumble at JetBlue," *BusinessWeek*, March 5, 2007, pp. 58–59; S. Carey and D. Everson, "Lessons on the Fly: JetBlue's New Tactics," *Wall Street Journal*, February 27, 2007, p. B1+; S. Carey and D. Aalund, "JetBlue Plans Overhaul As Snafus Irk Customers," *Wall Street Journal*, February 20, 2007, p. A11; J. Bailey, "JetBlue's CEO Is 'Mortified' After Fliers Are Stranded," *New York Times Online*, February 19, 2007; and J. Bailey, "JetBlue Adding Some Legroom by Removing Seats from Airbus 320 Planes," *New York Times Online*, December 14, 2006.

CASE #3: Shooting for Success

Using an exceptionally well-executed game plan, the National Basketball Association (NBA) has emerged as a truly global brand. The transformation of a once-faltering domestic sport into a global commercial success reflects a keen understanding of resources and capabilities. And much of the credit goes to NBA commissioner David Stern, who has been with the league since 1984, and has deliberately built the NBA into a global brand. He says, "Basketball is a universal language, and it's going to bloom on a global basis."

Professional basketball sparked the interest of fans and players around the globe in the mid-1990s, and the NBA cashed in on the game's universal appeal. At one time, if you had asked someone in China what the most popular basketball team was, the answer would have been the "Red Oxen" from Chicago (the Bulls). Today, NBA is the third most googled word in China and the center of attention *comes* from China. Yao Ming, the 7'6" all-star centerpiece of the Houston Rockets, has a personality that appeals to fans around the world. But he's not the only global player in the league. NBA team rosters feature 78 international players from 31 countries. Some of these players included the Dallas Mavericks' Dirk Nowitzki, a seven-footer from Germany; Pau Gasol of the Los Angeles Lakers, a native of Spain and also seven feet tall; San Antonio Spurs' guard Tony Parker from France; Denver Nuggets' forward Nenê from Brazil; Utah Jazz guard Gordan Giricek from Croatia; and Darko Milicic, a seven-footer from Serbia, now playing for the Toronto Raptors. A trend that started as a trickle in the 1980s with occasional foreign stars like Hakeem Olajuwon (Nigeria) and the late Drazen Petrovic (Croatia) turned into a flood.

In addition to the global players now in the U.S. league, the NBA has taken its game global. The league holds several preseason games in Europe, Latin America, and Asia. And developers are building modern arenas in Europe to help promote expansion of the game. Attendance at Euroleague, the region's top professional basketball organization, has been steady. Even India is interested in growing its national game with the NBA's help. But today's global appeal didn't come easily.

The brutal player contract negotiations during the 1998–1999 season forced the cancellation of more than one-third of the league's games. The resulting lockout frustrated and angered fans and delayed many of the league's promising global business initiatives. Then, there were the not one, not two, but three retirements of one of the NBA's most popular players ever, Michael Jordan (1993, 1999, and 2003), that took away one of the league's key draws, both as a player and as a global celebrity. However, even with these struggles, Stern didn't throw in the towel. To address the strategic challenges facing the NBA, he looked at what the league had to offer: consumer familiarity with basketball both domestically and globally, talented young players, and a recognized image and track record. He felt that if those things could be exploited, the NBA might be able to turn its game around.

One thing Stern did was expand the NBA's global network of offices. He explained, "The model is the rock concert. Sell lots of records. Tour occasionally." Another thing he did was enhance the league's global presence through its Web site and through its broadcasting deals. Today, over 30 percent of the visitors to the NBA Web site are from China, although there are sites also in Spanish, Japanese, French, and German. This allows the NBA to push its games and merchandise to fans around the world via their computers. And coverage of the league from both the Internet and broadcasting now reaches 215 countries in 41 different languages. The NBA recently teamed with Hewlett-Packard to create new technology that will provide real-time statistics to improve the game and enrich the experiences of fans on, and off, the court. As Stern said, "It's the best reality programming that plays around the world."

Such global appeal and technology exploitation is filling the league's coffers. The NBA makes about $300 million (out of total revenues of about $4.4 billion) from overseas and China is the biggest contributor toward that figure. In early 2008, the Walt Disney Company and four Chinese investment firms took an 11 percent stake in the NBA's subsidiary in China. NBA China will have the right to create teams in China and will own all broadcasting rights and merchandising. Says Stern, "This is globalization." Stern and his executive team at the NBA are continuing to take actions to enhance their resources and capabilities globally.

Discussion Questions

1. From this abbreviated description, what resources and capabilities do you think the NBA has? Does the fact that an organization is striving for global success make it more difficult to develop unique resources and distinctive capabilities? Explain.

2. Take each of the three approaches to internal analysis and describe how each could be used in analyzing the strengths and weaknesses of the NBA. Which one do you think is most appropriate for an organization like the NBA? Support your choice.

3. Look at each of the strategic initiatives implemented by Stern. Are they exploiting the NBA's strengths and minimizing its weaknesses? Explain.

Sources: Based on National Basketball Association [www.nba.com], January 20, 2009; "Technology Tipoff," *Wall Street Journal*, October 30, 2008, p. A8; M. J. de la Merced, "Disney and 4 Chinese Investment Firms to Buy Stake in NBA's China Subsidiary," *New York Times Online*, January 14, 2008; R. Nance, "Back on the Ball," *USA Today*, October 30, 2007, pp. 1C+; E. Pells, "Leagues Try to Cash In on China," *Springfield, Missouri, News-Leader* (The Associated Press), August 5, 2007, p. 8D; R. Adams and A. Thompson, "Basketball Challenge," *Wall Street Journal*, January 17, 2007, pp. B1+; and D. Eisenberg, "The NBA's Global Game Plan," *Time*, March 17, 2003, pp. 59–63.)

CASE #4: New Recipe

From the publication of her first book on entertaining back in 1982 to what is now the media empire called Martha Stewart Living Omnimedia (MSLO), Martha Stewart has capitalized on what she does best—helping people create a lifestyle in which the ultimate in cooking, decorating, entertaining, and other home-making arts are emphasized and celebrated. What exactly does MSLO do? The company has two primary strategic goals: to provide original "how-to" content and information to as many consumers as possible and to turn customers into "doers" by offering them the information and products they need for do-it-yourself projects. The business is built around core subject areas including cooking, entertaining, weddings, crafts, gardening, home, holidays, babies and children, and keeping and preserving (clothes, mementos, decorative artifacts, etc.). From these different subject areas, content is developed for different media including magazines, books, network television, cable television, newspapers and radio, and the Web. In addition, the core subject areas have evolved into merchandise lines (sheets, towels, table linens, paints, etc.) at Kmart, Sherwin Williams, Macy's, and Wal-Mart. Martha Stewart herself personified the Martha Stewart brand. It appeared that the company had positioned its resources and capabilities well to exploit sociocultural and demographic trends. However, when Stewart was convicted in March 2004 of obstructing justice and making false statements related to the timing of a sale of ImClone stock and sentenced to a five-month prison term, her namesake company braced for some serious challenges in maintaining its competitive advantage. And they did endure some serious challenges. While Stewart served out her sentence, her namesake TV show was put on hold and company executives tried to "carefully de-emphasize the 'Martha-ness' of its products." The company was not profitable from 2002 through 2006, but had a small profit ($10 million) in 2007. In 2008, which was a challenging year for many companies, MSLO saw its revenues decline by 13.3 percent and suffered a $15.7 million loss. Despite all this, Stewart was not about to let go of the company that so personified her. Not surprisingly, she planned "her comeback with her signature painstaking precision." Although she no longer serves as CEO or chairperson of the company (her title is simply "Founder"), Stewart's personal imprint is still obvious.

Today, MSLO is organized into four business divisions: publishing, broadcasting, merchandising, and Internet. The publishing division includes its magazines and books. The flagship magazine, *Martha Stewart Living*, is the "significant generator of content for our asset library." It was named by *Adweek* as number 8 on the 2008 Hot List of Top 10 Magazines. Other publications include *Everyday Food, Martha Stewart Weddings, Body & Soul Blueprint: Design Your Life* (a lifestyle publication for women aged 25–45 that was shut down in early 2008), and numerous books on subjects ranging from housekeeping to baking to weddings. The broadcasting division includes company activities related to television programming, distribution of that programming domestically and internationally, and satellite radio. The cornerstone of this division is *The Martha Stewart Show,* a daily how-to series that's filmed in front of a studio audience. The merchandising division is responsible for selling Martha Stewart–branded products at "multiple price points through several distribution channels." These partnerships include the Martha Stewart Collection at Macy's, Martha Stewart Colors at Lowe's, Martha Stewart at Costco, Martha Stewart Everyday at Kmart, and Martha Stewart craft products at Wal-Mart. The fourth business segment, Internet, consists of "advertiser-supported, free content, the direct-to-consumer floral business, and the new line of Martha Stewart–branded digital photography products with Kodak." MSLO's Web site has content related to "how-to" information for customers, including the ever-popular recipe finder. The Web site has been completely revamped with a new look for easier search and navigation.

In mid-2008, MSLO's CEO, Susan Lyne, who was described by many as "strong and media savvy," stepped down. Her job was split between two co-CEOs, Wendy Harris Millard (who was the president of media) and Robin Marino (who was president of merchandising). This arrangement didn't last long! After only one year and "numerous clashes with Ms. Stewart," Millard announced that she would leave the company in June 2009. The company's independent board is chaired by entertainment veteran Charles A. Koppelman, a man described as so "un-Martha-like that he refers to flowers as 'some pink things.'" The company is forming an advisory committee to focus on the strategic direction of the company. The company does face some challenges. One woman still defines the brand. What happens when Martha is no longer able to serve in all the capacities she currently does? And is Martha, the personality, overused and overexposed in the marketplace? In an attempt to extend the company's brands, negotiations with two prominent tastemakers—fashion designer Cynthia Rowley and home-decorating guru Jonathan Adler—were started but broken off before any deals were signed. And the company faces intense competition from new faces such as

Rachel Ray (whose show averages 46 percent more viewers than Stewart's), Paula Deen, and Giada De Laurentiis. Finally, the economic climate is having an impact on advertising revenues and on consumer expenditures. The fourth quarter of 2008 was especially difficult as the company had an $8 million loss as a result of a write-down of the value of its magazine business and a fall-off in revenues from its Kmart deal.

Discussion Questions

1. What resources and capabilities did MSLO appear to have? Do those resources and capabilities need to change? Why or why not?

2. Go to the company's Web site **[www.marthastewart.com]** and find the information on the company's business divisions. (Hint: Start your search by looking at Investor Relations.) Pick one of the divisions and describe and evaluate the strategies being implemented.

3. Do some research on co-CEOs. What other companies have such an arrangement? What benefits and challenges does such an arrangement entail?

4. How could MSLO's strategic decision makers use value chain analysis in assessing the company's strengths and weaknesses? How about an internal audit? How about a capabilities assessment profile?

Sources: Based on S. Ovide and S. Vranica, "Martha Stewart Shakes Up Ranks," *Wall Street Journal,* April 22, 2009, p. B6; S. J. Adler, "Martha Stewart's Managing Tips," *BusinessWeek,* March 9, 2009, pp. 60–61; K. E. Grace and S. Ovide, "Martha Stewart Swings to Loss on Write-Down," *Wall Street Journal,* February 26, 2009, p. B7; Martha Stewart Living Omnimedia **[www.marthastewart.com]**, January 20, 2009; "Questions for Martha Stewart," *Fortune,* December 8, 2008, pp. 32–34; S. Ovide, "Martha Stewart Products Hit Shelves at Wal-Mart," *Wall Street Journal,* July 10, 2008, p. B7; A. D'Innocenzio, "Martha Stewart CEO Calls It Quits," *USA Today* (The Associated Press), June 12, 2008, p. 4B; "Martha Stewart CEO Steps Down," *CNNMoney.com,* June 11, 2008; AdWeek 2008 Hot List **[www.mediaweek.com]**, March 31, 2008; S. Kapner, "Martha Stewart Seeks New Stars," *CNNMoney.com,* January 16, 2008; D. Brady, "The Reinvention of Martha Stewart," *BusinessWeek,* November 6, 2006, pp. 76–79; J. Schlosser, "Macromanaging at Martha Stewart Living," *CNNMoney.com,* September 13, 2006; K. Naughton, "Renovating Martha Inc.," *Newsweek,* February 27, 2006, p. 46; and Interview with Martha Stewart, "I Consider Myself the Visionary Still," *BusinessWeek,* December 19, 2006, pp. 54–56.

CASE #5: Higher and Higher

You may not be familiar with the Haier Group Company (sounds like "higher"), but if you've ever shopped for a refrigerator, microwave, or air conditioner at Wal-Mart, Best Buy, Bed Bath & Beyond, Target, or Lowe's, you've undoubtedly seen, if not purchased, the company's products. Haier Group is China's largest home appliance maker and its best-known global company. In 2007, it was number two on the list of most admired companies in Asia, and in 2006 was named the number one most admired company in China in the *Wall Street Journal Asia's* reader survey. It enjoys enviable prestige in its home country (a survey of "young, fashionable" Chinese ranked Haier as the country's third most popular brand, behind Shanghai Volkswagen and Motorola, with Coca-Cola fourth). And the company's brands have begun to gain even wider worldwide recognition. In 2006, for the third consecutive year, Haier was named one of the world's most recognizable brands. Despite these accomplishments, CEO Zhang Ruimin still has ambitious goals for the company. He wants to make Haier into a strong global competitor comparable to companies such as General Electric in the United States, Mercedes-Benz in Germany, and Toyota in Japan. Ruimin is considered by many to be China's leading corporate executive. In 2002, he became the first businessman ever elected to the Chinese Communist Party's Central Committee, a major political triumph for the 54-year-old with an M.B.A. from China's University of Science and Technology. Ruimin has been described as "a very charismatic business leader and not just in the Chinese perspective. He's emerging as a global business leader."

The Haier Group started as the Qingdao Refrigerator Company. When Ruimin took charge of the government-controlled company in 1984, his first action as CEO was to take a hammer and smash 76 refrigerators because of their poor quality. Why? To drive home the point that product quality was going to improve. At that time, the company had only one product and 800 workers. Today, some 50,000 employees in more than 30 factories worldwide manufacture and assemble products in some 96 different categories from air conditioners to mobile phones to vacuums and refrigerators and more. The Haier Group exports its products to more than 100 countries and regions and has established more than 58,000 global sales outlets. Its annual revenues are around $6.5 billion. Although Haier is the number-one domestic appliance producer in China, it's one of the world's top four largest home appliance makers. Major competitors include Electrolux, LG Electronics, Whirlpool, and General Electric.

Overseas growth is important for Haier because the company's core products in China have slim profit margins due to increasing foreign competition. An important division for the Haier Group is Haier America, its U.S. sales and marketing arm. From its headquarters in New York to its state-of-the-art refrigerator manufacturing facility in South Carolina, Haier America has tried to establish itself as a powerful U.S. brand known for original products. And in some ways, they've succeeded. For instance, one of its most innovative and popular products was a frog-shaped television console, which also doubled as a night-light and asked kids to answer math problems before switching itself on. Other popular products include its compact refrigerators, wine coolers, and office refrigerators. Now, Haier America is working to change the perception of Chinese brands as low-end, lower quality. To accomplish this, it recently unveiled a line of eco-friendly, technology-laden appliances in the mid-price range ($600–$1,500), as compared to the $200–$300 range it's known for. One analyst commented that, "They won't be able to transform their image quickly, but it can be done." But so far, that goal hasn't been achieved. Haier's U.S. ambitions have run up against hurdles. The new refrigerator cost 10 times to make what it would have cost the company to make in China. In addition, the collapsing U.S. economy stifled consumer demand just as Haier's U.S.-made products came on the market. Another problem it has struggled with at its U.S. factory has been that the rigid, top-down management structure so suited to the Chinese workforce has not worked well with its American workers, who are accustomed to a less authoritarian style. Said one analyst, "Haier is at a crossroads as it attempts to build a dynamic global company out of a bureaucratic, formerly state-owned enterprise."

Ruimin's plans for pushing his company "higher and higher" rests on its ability to exploit its resources and capabilities as they pursue their goal of becoming (and remaining) a powerful global brand. Will it happen?

Discussion Questions

1. What resources and capabilities does the Haier Group appear to have? Are any of these capabilities distinctive? Explain. What will it take to make its capabilities distinctive?

2. What strengths and weaknesses does the Haier Group appear to have? How could it prevent its strengths from becoming weaknesses?

3. What approach to internal analysis would you suggest that CEO Zhang Ruimin use in assessing his organization's strengths and weaknesses? Why?

4. What do you think of Zhang's goals for his company? What must the company do to exploit its resources and capabilities in order to reach these goals?

Sources: Based on M. Fong, "Chinese Refrigerator Maker Finds U.S. Chilly," *Wall Street Journal,* March 18, 2008, pp. B1+; R. Flannery, "Watch Your Back," *Forbes,* April 23, 2007, pp. 104–105; Z. Ruimin, "Raising Haier," *Harvard Business Review,* February 2007, pp. 141–146; T. W. Lin, "Lessons from China," *Strategic Finance,* October 2006, pp. 48–55; P. Engardio, "Haier: Taking a Brand Name Higher," *BusinessWeek Online,* July 31, 2006; M. Omar and R. L. Williams, "Managing and Maintaining Corporate Reputation and Brand Identity: Haier Group Logo," *Brand Management,* April–June, 2006, pp. 268–275; G. Khermouch, B. Einhorn, and D. Roberts, "Breaking into the Name Game," *BusinessWeek,* April 7, 2003, p. 54; and D. J. Lynch, "CEO Pushes China's Haier as Global Brand," *USA Today,* January 3, 2003, pp. 1B+.

Endnotes

1. Hallmark Web site [**www.hallmark.com**], January 15, 2009; E. Byron, "Happy Holidays! But Don't Expect Too Much from Santa Claus," *Wall Street Journal,* December 6/7, 2008, pp. A1+; S. Elliott, "Thinking of You (Especially the Media Buyers)," *New York Times Online,* August 26, 2008; D. Twiddy, "Hallmark Says Farewell to Some Greeting-Card Plants in U.S., Canada," *Springfield, Missouri, News-Leader,* (The Associated Press), June 5, 2008, p. 6A; P. J. Sauer, "I Just IM'd To Say I Love You," *Fast Company,* May 2008, p. 52; E. Olson, "To Compete with E-Mail Greetings, Funny Cards Try to be Topical," *New York Times Online,* August 20, 2007; and M. Sedensky, "Greeting Card Graveyard," *Springfield, Missouri, News-Leader* (The Associated Press), March 28, 2006, p. 5B.

2. S. K. Ethiraj, P. Kale, M. S. Krishnan, and J. V. Singh, "Where Do Capabilities Come From and How Do They Matter? A Study in the Software Services Industry," *Strategic Management Journal,* January 2005, pp. 25–45; and D. J. Collis, "Research Note: How Valuable Are Organizational Capabilities," *Strategic Management Journal,* Winter 1994, pp. 143–152.

3. R. M. Grant, "The Resource-Based Theory of Competitive Advantage: Implications for Strategy Formulation," *California Management Review,* Spring 1991, pp. 114–135.

4. Collis, *Strategic Management Journal,* pp. 143–152.

5. S. G. Winter, "Understanding Dynamic Capabilities," *Strategic Management Journal,* October 2003, pp. 991–995; C. E. Helfat and M. A. Peteraf, "The Dynamic Resource-Based View: Capability Lifecycles," *Strategic Management Journal,* October 2003, pp. 997–1010; S. A. Zahra and G. George, "Absorptive Capacity: A Review, Reconceptualization, and Extension," *Academy of Management Review,* April 2002, pp. 185–203; G. S. Day, "The Capabilities of Market-Driven Organizations," *Journal of Marketing,* October 1994, pp. 37–52; and C. K. Prahalad and G. Hamel, "The Core Competence of the Corporation," *Harvard Business Review,* May–June 1990, pp. 79–91.

6. Prahalad and Hamel, pp. 79–91.

7. C. Bryan-Low, "Nokia Maps Plan for GPS Handsets," *Wall Street Journal,* March 1, 2007, p. B4.

8. K. P. Coyne, S. J. D. Hall, and P. G. Clifford, "Is Your Core Competence a Mirage? *The McKinsey Quarterly,* no. 1, 1997 [**www.mckinseyquarterly.com**].

9. G. S. Day, *Journal of Marketing,* p. 39.

10. S. Hamner, "Heaven from Pennies," *Business 2.0,* August 2005, p. 54.

11. S. Freierman, "Telegram Falls Silent Stop Era Ends Stop," *New York Times Online,* February 6, 2006.

12. K. Kelleher, "66,207,897 Bottles of Beer on the Wall," *Business 2.0,* January–February 2004, pp. 47–49.

13. B. Vlasic, "Honda Stays True to Efficient Driving," *New York Times Online,* August 26, 2008; M. Maynard, "Honda Adding a Jet, a Six-Passenger Model, to its Lineup," *New York Times Online,* July 26, 2006; and Honda Ad, front inside cover of *Forbes,* July 7, 2003.

14. B. Nelson, "The Thinker," *Forbes,* March 3, 2003, pp. 62–64.

15. D. Sacks, "The Gore-Tex of Guitar Strings," *Fast Company,* December 2003, p. 46; and A. Harrington, "Who's Afraid of a New Product" *Fortune,* November 10, 2003, pp. 189–192.

16. See M. E. Porter, *Competitive Advantage: Creating and Sustaining Superior Performance,* chap. 2 (New York: The Free Press, 1985).

17. D. Ulrich and N. Smallwood, "Capitalizing on Capabilities," *Harvard Business Review,* June 2004, pp. 119–127; and K. E. Marino, "Developing Consensus on Firm Competencies and Capabilities," *Academy of Management Executive,* August 1996, pp. 40–51.

18. This discussion of the capabilities assessment profile is based on K. E. Marino, *Academy of Management Executive.*

19. P. Kotler, *Marketing Management,* 8th ed. (Upper Saddle River, NJ: Prentice Hall, 1996), p. 195.

20. H. H. Stevenson, "Defining Corporate Strengths and Weaknesses," *Sloan Management Review,* Spring 1967, pp. 51–68.

21. B. Rosner, "HR Should Get a Clue: Corporate Spying Is Real," *Workforce,* April 2001, pp. 72–75.

22. A. Serwer, "P&G's Covert Operation," *Fortune,* September 17, 2001, pp. 42–44.

23. K. Western, "Ethical Spying," *Business Ethics,* September–October 1995, pp. 22–23.

24. "Expensive Unused Data are Clogging up Budgets and Decision-Making," *Wall Street Journal,* July 1, 1999, p. A1.

Functional Strategies

5

LEARNING OUTCOMES

5.1 *Explain how the functional strategies are part of the strategic management process.*

5.2 *Describe the functional strategies an organization needs.*

5.3 *Discuss how functional strategies are implemented and evaluated.*

Driving for Success

Strategic Management in Action

Case #1

What a difference the passage of time makes. Toyota Motor Corporation's first U.S. import in the late 1950s flopped miserably.[1] That car—called the Toyopet Crown—overheated, vibrated when its speed went over 60 miles per hour, and looked ridiculous. Despite that dreadful product launch in the all-important U.S. car market, Toyota has vastly improved its business. Although it's now number one in worldwide sales (it surpassed General Motors [G.M.] in 2008), Toyota, too, is suffering from the global economic crisis, having lost money in fiscal year 2008 for the first time in seven decades. Despite the challenging times, Toyota continues to do many things exceptionally well.

Evaluations of Toyota's work methods and processes consistently conclude that the company's successes are due to a well-coordinated mix of functional strategies. The company leaves nothing to chance. Four management principles (the 4P model) guide employees: problem solving, people and partners, process, and philosophy. The idea behind these principles is that "Good Thinking Means Good Product." And that's where the scientific process—a significant part of Toyota's culture—plays a role. The scientific process is based on the idea that any change requires a rigorous problem-solving process with a detailed assessment of the current state of affairs and a plan for improvement. This approach is so ingrained at Toyota that the system actually inspires workers and managers to engage in the kinds of experimentation that are the hallmarks of an innovative organization.

The 4P model guides the Toyota Production System (TPS). In Toyota's highly efficient and effective manufacturing area, its work activities and production flows are rigidly scripted, yet exceedingly flexible. As the company has discovered, those rigid but flexible specifications encourage creativity. Also, the company uses just-in-time production, which means that "each process produces only what is needed by the next process in a continuous flow." This approach (well-known worldwide and often referred to as lean manufacturing) helps ensure that quality products are produced efficiently through completely eliminating waste, inconsistencies, and unreasonable requirements on the production line. The TPS also relies on the idea of *jikoda*, which has historical significance to Toyota because Sakichi Toyoda, the founder of the Toyota Group, invented Japan's first self-powered or automatic loom. As used in the TPS, *jikoda* refers to "automation with a human touch." What this means is that an automated machine can be stopped by the operator if a problem arises. Assembly line employees use a problem display board called an "andon" that allows them to identify problems in the production line at a glance. If they see a problem, they know what to do and how to improve. When the company announced product recalls, the obsession with details helped resolve the underlying problems. The individual in charge of quality said, "My responsibility is to tell all Toyota employees the quality aspect of their jobs," and he is doing that. It's not just the production strategies that have been the keys to Toyota's success, however; all its functional strategies contribute.

What about Toyota's marketing strategies? Although its advertising has never been cutting edge (like some other Japanese car companies), it does showcase the unique features of its cars. And Toyota recognizes how important marketing research is. It has a marketing research group in California that keeps tabs on demographic and economic developments and uses this information to predict consumer trends and to create products to capitalize on them. The company's human resource (HR) strategies emphasize education and training. For instance, Toyota recognized that as cars became more complex, mechanics needed training to maintain and repair those technology-laden vehicles. It established the U.S. Toyota Technical Education Network (T-TEN), a partnership with select vocational and community colleges, to train highly skilled technicians to work on Toyota products. The program was so successful that it's now done globally. In research and development (R&D), Toyota is a master. For instance, when Toyota wanted to find a way to make a custom car in five days (something unheard of in the car industry), it relied on R&D to help make that happen. Also, the company's Prius was the first commercially viable and profitable hybrid car. And now Toyota is going after Chevrolet's Volt with its own plug-in hybrid electric vehicle. It is introducing this vehicle at least one year before G.M. As one analyst said, "If Toyota stays on schedule, it will win at least a psychological advantage over G.M." Toyota epitomizes a company that recognizes the importance of functional strategies to organizational success.

As our chapter-opening case illustrates, when an organization's functional strategies are managed strategically, it's able to exploit the resources, capabilities, and core competencies found in its various functions. In this chapter, we'll be discussing the role of the functional strategies in managing strategically.

LEARNING OUTCOME 5.1
Explain How the Functional Strategies Are Part of the Strategic Management Process

In this chapter, we begin to look at *how* strategic decision makers formulate and implement organizational strategies. We're approaching this step in strategic management by looking at functional strategies first.

Strategic Management in Action: Process

Although we've studied several aspects of strategic management in action, the process still may seem confusing. (See Figure 5.1.) It's like trying to complete a large three-dimensional jigsaw puzzle and you're not quite sure how you're going to do it. You decide to start at the bottom, assembling puzzle pieces using the picture of the completed puzzle shown on the box lid as a guide. That's also the best way to think about an organization's strategies. Using

Figure 5.1

Strategic Management in Action

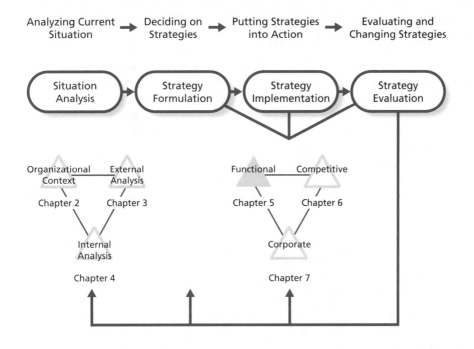

this analogy, the "completed puzzle" would be the overall corporate direction and goals set by the organization's top managers. The puzzle pieces represent the organization's functional strategies. Achieving that "completed puzzle" requires using the functional strategies to help move the organization in the desired direction toward the established goals. That's why we want to look at the functional strategies first. But do remember that the functional strategies *are* developed taking into account the organization's overall vision, mission(s), and corporate and competitive strategies.

One situation in which corporate strategies are addressed immediately is when an organization is first founded. Here, the overall strategic goal(s) and direction are formulated by the CEO and the top management team, thus establishing what work activities organizational employees must do. Over time, as the organization does what it's in business to do and as employees in the various functional areas do their jobs, organizational resources are used, capabilities and core competencies are developed, and distinctive capabilities may begin to emerge that eventually become sources of sustainable competitive advantage. At that point, the specific functional strategies should be supporting the business-level (competitive) and corporate-level strategies. Because you'll most likely encounter situations in which an organization or its divisions are *not* new, it makes sense to look at the functional strategies first as we look at the process of deciding the most appropriate strategies—that is, the ones that will lead to a sustainable competitive advantage.

What happens if the corporate or competitive strategies aren't working and need to be revised to accommodate changes in either the external or internal environments? What if there is no sustainable competitive advantage? Again, strategic decision makers look at the organization's various functional units to see what is and isn't working.

What Happens After the SWOT Analysis?

After completing the SWOT analysis, decision makers have information about the positive and negative aspects of both the external and internal environments. If the organization's strengths in the various functional units can be exploited as competitive advantages, particularly in light of any relevant external opportunities, the organization may well be on its way to achieving high levels of performance. In addition, if the SWOT analysis points to

Super Bowl Sunday. It's the second highest food consumption day of the year, behind Thanksgiving. And the food of choice? Pizza. More pizza is sold on Super Bowl Sunday than any other day of the year. For the 2009 Super Bowl, Pizza Hut expected to sell 2.5 million pizzas and Domino's expected to deliver more than 1.1 million pizzas. Why the increased demand on that one day? Pizza is the one food that seems to meet game-day criteria: It's cheap. It's easy. And it's social. The challenge for the pizza companies is making sure they can meet customers' demands. What are the implications for an organization's functional areas? How might a SWOT analysis help?

Sources: Based on E. Bryson York, "Super Bowl Sunday's Other Contest: Pizza Delivery," Advertising Age [adage.com], January 29, 2009; R. Slawsky, "Pizzerias Prep For Big Day," Pizza Marketplace [**www.pizzamarketplace.com**], January 29, 2009; and T. Perry, Gannett News Service, "Pizza Tops Super Bowl Sunday Menu," Pensacola News Journal [**www.pnj.com**], January 21, 2009.

threats in any of the organization's external areas or weaknesses in the internal areas, changes in functional strategies might be needed to counteract them.

The SWOT analysis points to strategic issues organizational decision makers must address in their pursuit of sustainable competitive advantage and high levels of performance. Many strategic issues concern good or bad performance in the various functional areas. Even if it's evident from the SWOT analysis that the organization's corporate or competitive strategies need to be changed, strategists base their decisions on the resources, capabilities, and core competencies found in the functional areas—lending more support as to why we look at functional strategies first.

Learning Review: Learning Outcome 5.1

- How do the functional strategies fit into the strategic management in action process?
- How does the work done in the functional areas support the creation of a competitive advantage?
- What happens after the SWOT analysis is completed?

LEARNING OUTCOME 5.2
Describe the Functional Strategies an Organization Needs

In Chapter 1, we defined an organization's **functional** (or **operational**) **strategies** as the goal-directed plans and actions of the organization's functional areas. We're going to look at these strategies with the assumption that all organizations must acquire and transform resources (inputs) into outputs (products), which then are made available to the organization's customers or clients. The functional strategies help ensure that the resources and capabilities found in the functional areas are used efficiently and effectively in doing the organization's business. In doing this, organizations have three functional concerns: the product, the people, and the support processes. Figure 5.2 illustrates this relationship.

Functional Strategies—The Product

It takes more than seven years to make the world's largest and most complicated warship— a nuclear-powered, Nimitz-class U.S. Navy aircraft carrier.[2] "Putting together an aircraft carrier is like no other manufacturing task in the world. It is the most technologically

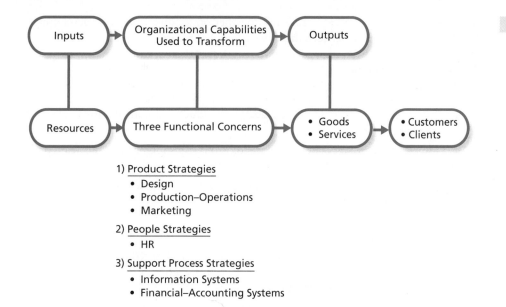

Figure 5.2

The Three Functional
Concerns of Organizations

1) Product Strategies
   - Design
   - Production–Operations
   - Marketing

2) People Strategies
   - HR

3) Support Process Strategies
   - Information Systems
   - Financial–Accounting Systems

challenging and toughest product to manufacture." Each ship costs more than $4 billion and involves more than 47,000 tons of precision-welded steel, more than 1 million distinct parts, 900 miles of wire and cable, around 40 million skilled-worker hours, and massive numbers of engineers. Not many products are this complex, yet even organizations with a simple product must produce that product. Before this can happen, however, the product must be designed. And once the product is designed and produced, it must be marketed to appropriate customers. Design, production-operations, and marketing are the three main tasks associated with the product. Let's look at each of these tasks and the strategies for completing them. But first, remember that products can refer to goods *or* services.

Product Design and Development Strategies

These strategies are usually part of the organization's R&D functional area, where one strategic choice concerns timing. Does the organization intend to be the first to introduce or use innovations or is it going to follow or mimic others' innovations? An organization that's first to bring a new product or innovation to the marketplace is called a **first mover.** The strategic advantages and disadvantages of being a first mover are shown in Table 5.1.

Other important strategic choices in R&D involve who will do it and how it will take place. The *who* choice determines who will be responsible for developing new ideas and designing new products. Will it be a separate R&D department of product designers, scientists, or engineers? Will it be a **cross-functional team,** which is a group of individuals from

Advantages	Disadvantages
• Reputation for being innovative and an industry leader	• Uncertainty over exact direction technology and market will go
• Cost and learning benefits resulting from moving along experience curve first	• Risk of competitors imitating innovations (free-rider effect)
• Control over scarce assets preventing competitors from having access to them	• Financial and strategic risks
• Opportunity to begin building customer relationships and customer loyalty	• High development costs

Table 5.1

First Mover
Advantages–Disadvantages

various functional departments who work together on product or process development? Or, will it be something in between those two options? The *how* of R&D involves the actual sequence of activities from idea generation to product design, which can involve several strategic choices including:

- Will there be a formal or informal process for generating ideas?
- What type of and how much research (product and market-industry) will be needed?
- Will there be extensive or limited use of product prototypes, product tests, design reviews, and test markets?

Once products have been designed, they're ready to be produced, which involves an organization's production-operations strategies.

Production-Operations Strategies

As our chapter-opening case illustrates, production-operations strategies are important because organizations can create a sustainable competitive advantage when those strategies are well integrated with the other functional areas of the organization and when they support the overall company goals.[3] **Production-operations** refers to the process of creating and providing goods and services. The process used to create and provide physical (tangible) goods is fairly obvious; the process to create and provide services isn't quite so easy to see.

What do we know about the production-operations process? We know that different organizations will use different approaches. For instance, the process Toyota uses for producing its vehicles isn't the same as the process Google uses in creating a new feature on its Web site. Both, however, will use whatever organizational resources and capabilities are needed and available to produce their product. The goal of the production-operations strategies is to ensure that products are available when, where, and how needed by customers or clients.

The main strategic choices in the production-operations function include how products will be produced and where they will be produced. These decisions encompass strategies for (1) designing the production-operations process including capacity, layout, location, and so forth and (2) managing the production-operations process including managing the supply chain, quality, inventory, planning and scheduling, maintenance, and so forth.

Strategic Management in Action

Loading an airplane is part of the production-operations process for airlines. After all, "producing" the "service" that customers have paid for means the planes have to be back in the air as quickly as possible to get to the next destination. Also, airlines don't make money with their planes sitting on the ground. Even a few extra minutes to get a plane loaded can throw a day's schedule off. So the airlines have tried a variety of techniques to find the best way to get people on and off planes. From a simple back-to-front approach that's still used by most airlines to more complicated approaches such as the reverse pyramid system, the outside-in technique, and the "nonsystem system" pioneered by Southwest Airlines in which passengers board in the order they arrive with no assigned seats. (Check out this Southwest video at **[http://www.blogsouthwest. com/2007/09/19/to-assign-or-not-to-assign-that-is-the-question/]**.) The variable that keeps airlines carefully planning their production-operations is the "unpredictability of human behavior." Because that behavior is so hard to predict, some experts believe that other tactics, such as limiting carry-on baggage, is likely to be more effective in faster gate turnaround than some complicated loading system. Can you think of some other production-operations strategies that might be important to airlines?

Source: Based on P. B. Finney, "Loading an Airliner Is Rocket Science," New York Times Online, November 14, 2006.

Employees at Japanese eyeglasses retailer Meganesuper are required to wear glasses at work even if they don't need them to see properly. The company's head of advertising and investor relations has 60 pairs. Why have this requirement? "Putting themselves in customers' shoes can elicit information that surveys can't." It also helps them critique the company's products and sales process. For instance, when employees wore the company's molded-plastic glasses and found that the frames kept slipping down their noses, they suggested adding the nose pads commonly found in wire-frame glasses. The feature became an instant hit with customers.

Source: Based on P. Dvorak, "Seeing Through Buyers' Eyes," Wall Street Journal, January 29, 2007, p. B4.

Marketing Strategies

Once products are produced, the next step is to efficiently and effectively get those products to the customers when, where, and how they want them.[4] That's the role of **marketing,** which is defined as a process of assessing and meeting the wants and needs of individuals or groups by creating, offering, and exchanging products of value. An organization's marketing strategies are directed at effectively and efficiently managing the two "Cs"—customers and competitors. Organizations do this through the strategic choices they make in terms of segmentation or target market, differentiation, positioning, and marketing mix (commonly known as the 4 Ps: product, pricing, promotion, and place). Other potential marketing strategies include connecting with customers (current and potential, domestic and global), gathering marketing insights (customers and competitors), building strong brands, designing effective marketing communications, and efficiently and effectively managing the marketing function.

Functional Strategies—The People

"At L'Oreal, success starts with people. Our people are our most precious asset. Respect for people, their ideas and differences, is the only path to our sustainable long-term growth."[5] How often have you heard a statement like "Our people are our most important asset"? More important, can an organization's people strategies (that is, the human resources or HR strategies) help it establish a sustainable competitive advantage? The answer seems to be "yes," as shown by various studies.[6] And if HR strategies can contribute to getting competitive advantage, can they affect performance? Other studies that have looked at the link between performance and HR policies and practices have shown that certain ones *can* have a positive impact on performance.[7] These **high-performance work practices** are ones that lead to both high individual and high organizational performance. Table 5.2 lists some of these practices. These types of HR practices can improve the knowledge, skills, and abilities of an organization's current and potential employees, increase their motivation, reduce loafing on the job, and help retain quality employees while encouraging nonperformers to leave the organization.

		Table 5.2
• Self-directed work teams	• Job rotation	
• Problem-solving groups	• Total Quality Management programs	*Examples of High-Performance Work Practices*
• Contingent pay	• Information sharing	
• Attitude surveys	• Employee suggestions implemented.	

Source: Based on Brian Becker and Barry Gerhort, "The Impact of Human Resource Management on Organizational Performance: Progress and Prospects," Academy of Management Journal, August 1996, pp. 779–801.

The strategic challenge facing many organizations in today's uncertain and daunting economic environment is how to maintain a balance of showing employees that they are valued while trying to control costs. In such difficult times, painful decisions often have to be made in the HR area. A survey by consulting firm Watson Wyatt in December 2008 showed that the most common strategic responses have been restricting company travel, hiring freezes, layoffs, and downgrading or canceling holiday parties. An even more troubling finding was that while 39 percent of companies had already made layoffs, an additional 23 percent expected to do so in 2009.[8] The U.S. job loss in 2008 was the worst since 1945—2.8 million jobs gone, 1.9 million of those in the last four months of the year. And companies not only eliminated jobs but cut the wages of surviving employees.[9] Some companies, however, are bucking that trend as explained in the FYI box, "To Layoff or Not to Layoff."

An organization's HR strategies reflect its commitment to and treatment of its employees. Because an organization's people are the ones who do the work involved in implementing the other strategies, the HR strategies must closely align with those other

FOR YOUR INFORMATION

To Layoff or Not to Layoff

Monday, January 26, 2009. On that one day alone, Home Depot, Caterpillar, Sprint Nextel, and Pfizer combined to announce more than 70,000 job cuts. In January 2009, more than 50 major companies cut a total of over 200,000 jobs. Are mass layoffs the answer to an intensifying economic downturn? Some experts say no and some companies are bucking the trend. The reason for layoffs is clear. Payrolls are one of the first places businesses look to cut expenses. However, layoffs may be a short-sighted fix. The increasing number of people looking for work means even more consumers are likely to spend less and foreclosures and credit card delinquencies might increase, leading to even weaker demand for products and more problems. And though some might think that the surviving employees might be more motivated to work harder—I have a job and I want to be sure I keep it—that's not necessarily what happens. Employee morale and productivity often decline. "No one wins when people spend more time worrying about whether they're going to be the next to go than they do actually working." If employees aren't productive, customers will eventually notice and a company could start losing business because of unsatisfactory customer service. In addition, deep HR cuts makes it that much tougher to meet consumer demand once it does bounce back.

Some companies have taken a different approach. They've vowed to not lay off any workers, even during times of financial hardships. Companies such as Lincoln Electric and Nucor had "no layoff" policies in place long before this economic downturn and have no plans to change them. Other companies, including Southwest Airlines, FedEx, Aflac, and Erie Insurance, don't have a formal policy barring layoffs but say that "there is no history of layoffs and no plans to lay off workers going forward." Although they're not using extensive layoffs to control labor costs, they often resort to other, less drastic measures such as four-day workweeks, unpaid vacations, unpaid furloughs of short duration, wage freezes, pension cuts, no bonuses paid, and flexible work schedules. The HR director at a Pennsylvania-based manufacturer said, "We have a very skilled and competent workforce and the last thing we want to do is lose them when we're assuming this economy is going to come back." But there can be a downside to the sacrifices made by employees. Workers may grow frustrated, want their full compensation back, or may even prefer a layoff that at least provides a sense of permanence. Do some research on employee layoffs. What are companies doing to make it easier for those being laid off? What about for the survivors? What do you think of a company asking employees to take a pay cut or work fewer hours so that no one has to be laid off? How willing would you be to do something like that?

Sources: Based on L. Petrecca, "More Companies Turn to Furloughs to Save Money, Jobs," USA Today, March 5, 2009, pp. 1B+; P. R. La Monica, "Layoffs Aren't the Answer," CNNMoney.com, January 27, 2009; "No Layoffs—Ever!" CNNMoney.com, January 23, 2009; W. J. McEwen, "Who's Caring for the Customers?" Gallup Management Journal [gmj.gallup.com], January 8, 2009; M. Richtel, "More Companies Cut Labor Costs without Layoffs," New York Times Online, December 22, 2008; and J. Dickler, "Employers: No Layoffs Here," CNNMoney.com, December 11, 2008.

strategies in order to assure that the right numbers of the appropriately skilled people are in the right place at the right time and that the organization's workforce is being used effectively and efficiently.[10] Strategic choices in the HR area involve getting people into the organization (HR planning, recruiting, and staffing), making sure they have the knowledge and skills necessary to do their jobs and helping them do those jobs better (orientation and training), assessing how well they do those jobs and making needed corrections (performance appraisal and disciplinary actions), and motivating high levels of effort and compensating them fairly and appropriately (compensation and benefits). Other potential strategies may address HR issues such as employee relations, job design, diversity efforts, workplace safety and health, and workplace misbehavior.

We've discussed the first two of an organization's functional concerns: the product and the people. That leaves the third functional concern—the support processes.

Functional Strategies—The Support Processes

As organizations acquire and transform resources into products by doing what they're in business to do, they need information about the activities taking place and they need to account for the transactions and exchanges between the organization and its suppliers and customers. This is done through the organization's two main support processes— information systems and financial-accounting systems. Just like the other functional areas, these areas also involve certain strategies that help the organization efficiently and effectively do its work and, it is hoped, contribute to creating a sustainable competitive advantage. Let's look first at the information systems.

Information Systems

How would you like to do your job as a student (study, write papers, take tests, etc.) without information? It would be pretty tough, wouldn't it? Information affects how effectively and efficiently organizational members can do their work. Without information, the payroll clerk doesn't know what deductions to make from paychecks; the sales representative doesn't know what prices to quote a potential customer; or the plant manager doesn't know how this month's product quality levels compared to last month's. It's essential to have information to make decisions and to carry out work duties. How do organizational members get information? Through an **information system,** which is a system for collecting, processing, storing, and disseminating any and all information that managers need to operate a business.

The Grey Zone

Corporate blogs are becoming more popular. Because anyone can visit the site and read the message, companies have become concerned about messages that may include sensitive data, criticize managers or competitors, use inflammatory language, or contain misrepresentations. Companies also worry about the reactions of stakeholders who may disagree with or be offended by blog postings. Many companies have developed blog policies for employees to follow. (For an example, see the policy developed by Sun Microsystems at **[www.sun.com/communities/guidelines.jsp]**.) What do you think of this? Should corporate blogs be allowed? Why or why not? What ethical issues might arise? What guidelines might you suggest for corporate blogs?

⬤ Strategic Management in Action

Harrah's Entertainment, the Las Vegas–based gaming company, is fanatical about customer service, and for good reason. Company research showed that customers who were satisfied with the service they received at a Harrah's casino increased their gaming expenditures by 10 percent and those who were extremely satisfied increased their gaming expenditures by 24 percent. Harrah's was able to discover this important customer service–expenditures connection because of its incredibly sophisticated information system and because all employees were made aware of this information so they truly understood their vital role in providing outstanding customer service. Now, Harrah's is taking its knowledge management to a new level by developing a pilot project in which casino staff will forecast customer spending, which they hope will help boost revenue.

Sources: Based on J. Hagel and J. S. Brown, "Harrah's New Twist on Prediction Markets," BusinessWeek Online, December 23, 2008; J. Barsky, "Elite Rewards Programs Score High with Hotel Guests," Hotel and Motel Management, November 3, 2008, p. 27; J. L. Heskett, T. O. Jones, G. W. Loveman, W. E. Sasser, and L. A. Schlesinger, "Putting the Service-Profit Chain to Work," Harvard Business Review, July–August 2008, pp. 118–129; D. Greenfield, "From Idea to Innovation: Companies Are Using Online Voting Tools and Prediction Markets to Conceive New Products," November 10, 2008, p. 26; M. Millstein, "Customer Relationships Make Playing the Odds Easy," Chain Store Age, December 2007, p. 22A; and G. Loveman, "Diamonds in the Data Mine," Harvard Business Review, May 2003, pp. 109–113.

What role do information and information systems play in managing strategically?[11] It depends on how important it is to have the right types of information when, where, and how organizational members need it. Two strategic decisions most associated with the organization's information system are the choice of system technology and the choice of types of information systems needed. These decisions will depend on how important information is to developing a sustainable competitive advantage. Also, it's unlikely that a single information system can provide all the information needed. Instead, an organization probably will have many different types of information systems serving different organizational levels and functions.

Financial-Accounting Systems

The final organizational support process we're going to look at involves the organization's financial-accounting systems, which provide strategic decision makers with information about the organization's financial transactions, accounts, and standing. This information is critical in planning the organization's future strategies. In designing the financial-accounting systems, we must make sure that we have the information we need, when we need it, and in the form needed. Strategic decisions in this functional area would involve choices about collecting and using financial and accounting data, evaluating financial performance (what types and how often), doing financial forecasting and budgeting (what types and how often), determining the optimum financing mix (equity or debt, short-term or long-term), and effectively and efficiently managing the financial-accounting functional area.

Learning Review: Learning Outcome 5.2

- What are the three functional concerns of organizations?
- What are the three main tasks associated with the product?
- What strategic choices are there in product design and development, production-operations, and marketing?
- What types of HR strategies are there and what are they designed to do?
- What types of support strategies are there and what are they designed to do?

LEARNING OUTCOME 5.3
Discuss How Functional Strategies Are Implemented and Evaluated

There are a couple of issues we still need to address regarding an organization's functional strategies. First, what's involved with implementing these strategies? Next, how do we evaluate the functional strategies and what do we do if they aren't working as well as we'd planned? Finally, how do we coordinate these strategies with the other organizational strategies?

Implementing the Various Functional Strategies

Implementing these strategies very simply means *doing* them. What comes to mind is Nike's marketing slogan, "Just Do It." Implementing the functional strategies involves deciding what work processes and work activities will need to be done in the functional area, making sure those processes and activities have the necessary resources to complete the work, and then just doing it. At the functional level, the work that needs to be done is relatively narrow in scope and definition because each functional area has its own specific responsibilities in contributing to the overall organizational goals. This doesn't mean, however, that the various functional areas don't coordinate with each other. Quite the contrary! Coordinating these areas is one of the keys to managing strategically at this level.[12] What does this mean for implementation?

Managing the organization's various functional areas as separate "chimneys" or "silos" might keep an organization from exploiting its key resources and capabilities and being able to develop them into a sustainable competitive advantage. And as the functional strategies are implemented through the various work processes and activities unique to each functional area, it's important to foster an environment in which all areas work together to accomplish the organization's vision, missions, and goals. What happens if organizations don't do this is that a strategy implemented in one functional area has the potential to impact other functional areas.

Evaluating Strategies and Making Changes

Retailers excited about the prospect of lower labor costs have been rapidly adding customer self-checkout lanes but the downside is that these self-checkout counters are killing impulse buys. For instance, one study found that impulse purchases dropped by 45 percent.[13] Was this functional strategy a good decision? What should retailers do now? This example illustrates the importance of strategy evaluation.

How do we know whether an organization's functional strategies are working and what do we do if they're not? If you go back and look at Figure 5.1 on p. 137, you'll see that evaluating and changing strategies are part of the strategic management in action process. Strategy evaluation at the functional level involves using specific performance measures—quantitative *and* qualitative—for each functional area. For instance, how many product coupons were redeemed from the seasonal sales promotion program? How many and what types of problems have been encountered since the new management information system was put in place? Or, what's the manufacturing product reject rate? Like any evaluation process, the actual performance measures must be compared against some standard. These standards are the strategic goals established in each functional area. For instance, if the goal of a new employee safety awareness program was to decrease employee disability claims, did this happen? Was that HR strategy successful? If the rate of employee disability claims didn't go down, then we'd try to determine what happened and why. Maybe the safety information wasn't communicated clearly or maybe the manufacturing unit was behind in its work and employees were being rushed to complete the work and ended up being care-less. Strategy evaluation involves looking at what *was* done, what was *supposed* to be done, assessing any variances, and trying to determine what happened.

If actual performance doesn't measure up to standards and if we think a change in a functional strategy is needed, then what? It depends on how critical the strategy is to the accomplishment of other organizational goals and whether it's something we can control and change. If we determine that the functional strategy is important and controllable, we'd look once again to the first steps in strategic management in action—that is, analyzing the current situation and then formulating appropriate strategies. Any changes in functional strategies would then be implemented and after a certain period of time, evaluated, and changed, if necessary.

Coordinating with Other Organizational Strategies

Not only is it important for functional strategies to be coordinated with each other, it's important that they be coordinated with the other organizational strategies. Each organizational level—functional, business, corporate—needs to coordinate with and support the other levels in order to develop sustainable competitive advantages.[14] Strategic choices made at the business (competitive) and corporate levels do affect and are affected by the functional strategies being implemented. Depending on what corporate and competitive strategies are being pursued, certain functional areas might be more important in carrying out those strategies. Then, it would be important for the resources, capabilities, and core competencies in those areas to be developed and exploited. This strategic coordination and interdependency reflects the fact that an organization is a *system* with interrelated and interdependent parts.

In addition, if strategic changes are made at the other levels, changes in functional strategies might be warranted. For example, say that the organization decides to start selling its products in a foreign market. What's it going to take to implement this major strategy? It means formulating and implementing numerous functional strategies—marketing, HR, production-operations, and so forth—to implement this change.

As you can see, the functional strategies play an important role in executing the vision, missions, and goals of the organization. That's why they need to be coordinated with the other levels of strategies and modified to accommodate changes in those strategies. As we stated at the beginning of this chapter, it's important for an organization's functional strategies to be managed strategically so that its resources, capabilities, and core competencies can be developed into sustainable competitive advantage. Think back to the chapter-opening case. The strategic decision makers at Toyota have created a system in which the functional-level strategies have been finely tuned and are contributing to the company's success. The

● *Strategic Management in Action*

The *Wall Street Journal* is a giant in the business-reporting industry. And that description used to pertain not only to its acclaimed content but its physical size. In a cost-saving move, the newspaper's publisher, Dow Jones, cut the width of the paper. The main savings—about $18 million a year—came from using less newsprint. However, that change also impacted other functional areas. What changes do you think the editorial, production, marketing, HR, and information systems areas might have had to make?

Sources: Based on S. Sutel, The Associated Press, "Wall Street Journal to Change Its Looks," Springfield, Missouri, News-Leader, December 4, 2006, p. 5B; K. Q. Seelye, "In Tough Times, a Redesigned Journal," New York Times Online, December 4, 2006; and The Associated Press, "Dow Jones to Shrink 'Wall Street Journal,' Cut Some Data," USA Today Online, October 12, 2005.

effectiveness and efficiency of the strategies implemented at the functional levels have had a significant impact on the success of the corporate and business strategies as well as on current and future revenues.

Learning Review: Learning Outcome 5.3

- How are the functional strategies implemented?
- Why do the functional strategies need to be evaluated?
- Why is it important for the functional strategies to be (a) coordinated with each other, and (b) coordinated with the other organizational strategies?

Learning Outcome 5.1: Explain how the functional strategies are part of the strategic management process.

- The functional strategies help move the organization in the desired direction toward the established goals but are developed taking into account the organization's vision, missions, and corporate and competitive strategies.

- With the information from the SWOT analysis, strategic decision makers decide whether to change the corporate or competitive strategies based on the resources, capabilities, and core competencies found in the functional areas.

Learning Outcome 5.2: Describe the functional strategies an organization needs.

- *Functional strategies:* short-term, goal-directed decisions and actions of the organization's various functional areas.

- All organizations must acquire and transform resources (inputs) into outputs (products), which are then made available to the organization's customers or clients.

- Organizations have three functional concerns: the product, the people, and the support processes.

- The Product: product functional strategies include product design, production-operations, and marketing.

- Product design and development strategies are part of the R&D functional area. Strategic choices include timing (*first mover:* organization that's first to bring a new product or innovation to the marketplace); who will do design and development (separate R&D department, *cross-functional team:* a group of individuals from various departments who work together on product or process development, or some combination); and how design and development process will take place (formal or informal process, type of and how much research, and extensive or limited use of various R&D tasks).

- *Production-operations:* process of creating and providing goods and services. Strategic choices include how and where products will be produced. These choices encompass the design and management of the production-operations process.

- *Marketing:* process of assessing and meeting the wants and needs of individuals or groups by creating, offering, and exchanging products of value. Marketing strategies are directed at managing the two Cs: customers and competitors. Strategic choices involve segmentation or target market, differentiation, positioning, marketing mix, connecting with customers, gaining marketing insights, building strong brands, designing effective marketing communications, and managing the marketing functional area.

- The People: people (HR) functional strategies reflect an organization's commitment to and its treatment of its employees. HR strategies can be a significant source of competitive advantage and can have a positive impact on performance (*high-performance work practices:* HR practices that lead to both high individual and high organizational performance). Strategic choices involve getting people into the organization, making sure they have the necessary knowledge and skills to do their jobs and helping them do those jobs better, assessing how well they do those jobs and making needed corrections, and motivating high levels of effort and compensating them fairly. May also address other HR issues such as employee relations, diversity efforts, and so on.

- The Support Processes: support processes support the organization as it does its work. The two main ones include information systems and financial-accounting systems.

- *Information system:* a system for collecting, processing, storing, and disseminating information that managers need to operate a business. Strategic choices involve the choice of system technology and the choice of types of information systems desired.

- Financial-accounting systems provide strategic decision makers with information about the organization's financial accounts and financial position. Strategic choices include collecting and using financial-accounting data, evaluating financial performance, doing financial forecasting and budgeting, determining the optimum financing mix, and effectively and efficiently managing the financial-accounting area.

Learning Outcome 5.3: Discuss how functional strategies are implemented and evaluated.

- Implementing the functional strategies involves deciding what work processes and activities need to be done, making sure the resources are available to do the work, and then just doing it.

- Evaluating the functional strategies involves using specific performance measures, both quantitative and qualitative. Any needed changes to the strategies would take place after an analysis of the situation to see what happened.

- Strategies in the functional areas need to be coordinated with each other *and* with other organizational strategies.

**YOU
as
strategic
decision
maker:
building
your
skills**

1. Although the styles and details may have changed, the shirts, skirts, and jackets we wear today aren't a whole lot different than what was worn a decade ago. However, the ways they're produced have been transformed by a forced infusion of information technology. When American apparel makers learned to view their product not as pieces of fabric sewn together but as a process of harnessing information along a chain that runs from the factory floor to the retail counter, they were able to improve their performance. Strategic factors such as bar coding, computer systems and software, high-tech distribution centers, and uniformity standards have played a role in this reinvention of the clothing industry. How would each of these factors affect a clothing manufacturer's functional strategies in R&D, production-operations, marketing, HR management, information systems, and financial-accounting systems?

2. Jack Welch, former CEO of General Electric, was noted for his managerial skills and abilities. The secret to his success was described as not a series of brilliant insights or bold gambles but a fanatical attention to detail. What do you think this statement means? What are the implications for strategically managing an organization's functional strategies?

3. There's a federal law called the Economic Espionage Act of 1996 that protects businesses from having their highly confidential product information stolen. Theft of intellectual property by trusted insiders (employees or contractors) happens frequently. One study estimated that intellectual property loss worldwide amounted to between $500 and $600 billion annually. Many types of organizations in many types of industries are vulnerable. What are the implications for the way an organization's functional strategies are formulated and implemented? Think about each functional area that might be affected and how it would be affected.

4. Many organizations are putting customer service activities online and making them available 24/7. What would be the advantages of this strategic approach? What disadvantages might there be? How could strategic decision makers address the disadvantages?

5. Corporate sponsorships of special events and programs (sports programs, entertainment attractions, festivals and fairs, medical-education-social causes, and the arts) are a unique type of marketing strategy. The number of such sponsorships is slowing down. Do some research on corporate sponsorships. Find five examples of companies using corporate sponsorships. Describe these examples in a brief paper. What types of corporate sponsorships are these companies doing? Given the nature of the company's industry, why do you think they chose the sponsorship they did? Do you think these corporate sponsorships are an effective and efficient marketing strategy? Why or why not?

6. How important is a fun workplace to employees? Many experts say that being recognized as a fun place to work can be an important competitive edge when recruiting in a tight labor market. Fun-loving firms indicate that incorporating humor and fun in the workplace reduces stress, increases job satisfaction, stimulates creativity, and increases productivity. Research the topic of fun and humor in the workplace. What are the pros and cons of this strategic choice? Make a bulleted list of your findings. Be prepared to debate the topic (from either side) in class.

7. "Why do companies spend billions of dollars on information technology systems that fail to respond to the needs of those who run them?" This complaint isn't unique. What are the implications for designing effective information systems strategies? Be specific.

8. Revenue management (also called yield management) is proposed as a strategic tool that can help strategists make better decisions. Drawing from the fields of operations research, economics, finance, and marketing, revenue management uses a disciplined approach to forecasting demand for products or services, figuring out how to most efficiently provide them, and using price as a lever to influence demand and generate as much revenue as possible. Research the topic of revenue management. Make a bulleted list of its key points.

9. Customer service would appear to be an important strategic goal of any organization. Yet, surveys of customer satisfaction by the University of Michigan conclude that customer service could be improved. Research the topic of customer service. Then, in a short paper, describe which functional strategies might have to change and how they need to change to improve customer service.

10. Every year, *Fortune* magazine honors the 100 best companies to work for. Get the latest list. (The list is published in January.) What are the top 10 companies on the list? Select three of these companies to research. What types of functional strategies are these three companies using? What could other companies learn from the strategies being used by these companies?

Strategic Management in Action Cases

CASE #1: Driving for Success

This Strategic Management in Action case can be found at the beginning of Chapter 5.

Discussion Questions

1. What do you think are the keys to Toyota's success?

2. Do you think production or marketing would be most important to Toyota? Support your choice.

3. Is strategy coordination important to Toyota? Explain.

4. Go to the company's Web site **[www.toyota. co.jp/en]**. Identify and describe three examples of functional strategies you find there.

CASE #2: Casting a Wider Net

One of the most popular tourist destinations in Missouri isn't what you might expect. You'd find it in the southwest corner of the state in Springfield. It's Bass Pro Shops Outdoor World. Some 4 million people visit this one store annually. (Over 90 million people visit all its stores annually.) Although most visitors are hunting, fishing, and outdoors enthusiasts, many come just to see the sights and to experience the retail atmosphere of the store. There's a four-story cascading waterfall, rifle and archery ranges, a putting green, and an indoor driving range. Visitors can get their hair cut at the barbershop and then arrange to have a lure made from their hair clippings. They can grab a latté at the coffee shop or eat a full meal at Hemingway's Blue Water Café, whose showpiece is a 30,000-gallon saltwater aquarium. And then there are the incredible wildlife displays throughout—many of which have become popular photo spots for visitors. Despite all of these fascinating attractions, the heart (and soul) of the store is still the row after row of guns, decoys, tents, rods, reels, lures, campers, clothing, and other sports and outdoors equipment and apparel. There's even one enormous store wing that showcases boats—speedboats, houseboats, pontoon boats, fiberglass boats, and aluminum boats. There's something for everyone to experience and enjoy.

Johnny Morris, founder of Bass Pro, was born and raised in Springfield. In 1971, he opened a bait shop in a small corner of his father's liquor store. From that humble beginning, the company has grown to be a dominant player in the outdoors and sporting goods market. Morris's operating philosophy is to never allow the customer to have a dull moment. His retailing approach has been one of excitement and entertainment. The design of the flagship (the "granddaddy") store—and ultimately, all the other stores—was developed after trips to other popular retailing destinations to understand their appeal. One visit to L. L. Bean in Freeport, Maine, was particularly memorable. Morris felt that if that store could draw well over 3.5 million visitors a year to the middle of nowhere, then he could do that, and better, in Springfield. The retailing success that is Bass Pro Shops has been duplicated now in 50 different locations from Islamorada, Florida, to Oklahoma City, and from Baltimore to Las Vegas. The company has additional stores planned (including one in The Pyramid in Memphis) and continues to look for new opportunities.

Although the stores are a vital part of Bass Pro's strategies, they aren't the only way that customers can purchase Bass Pro's goods. The company's catalogs and Internet sales are important parts of its operations, as well. Bass Pro's catalog, first launched in 1974, was the first step in the company's national recognition. These two marketing tools have played a significant role in helping develop the fierce brand loyalty of Bass Pro's many customers. In addition to these retailing strategies, Bass Pro also sponsors several TV and radio programs and runs a luxurious resort in the Ozark Mountains. The company's mission statement reads: "To be the leading merchant of outdoor recreational products, inspiring people to love, enjoy, and conserve the great outdoors." And that's exactly what Bass Pro has done and continues to do.

Discussion Questions

1. What examples of functional strategies do you see in this case? Label your examples and be specific in describing them.

2. As a company grows, what challenges might it face in replicating in different locations what's made it successful? How might these challenges be addressed?

3. How might a company's mission statement affect how it does its business? How does Bass Pro Shop's mission statement affect the way it does its business?

Sources: Based on Bass Pro [www.basspro.com], January 30, 2009; *Springfield Business Journal* Staff, "Shelby County Approves Bass Pro for Memphis Pyramid," *SBJ.net*, November 24, 2008; A. M. Heher, The Associated Press, "Destination Stores Struggle," *Springfield, Missouri, News-Leader*, July 26, 2008, p. 2G; C. Smith, "Luring Bass Pro," *Springfield Business Journal*, March 17–23, 2008, pp. 1+; D. Tang, "Bass Pro Casts a Wider Net," *Springfield, Missouri, News-Leader*, October 22, 2006, pp. 1E+; B. Saporito, "Riding the Bass Boom," *Time Inside Business*, November 2005, pp. A21–A28; K. Culp, "Bass Pro 'Granddaddy' Spawns New Generation," *Springfield, Missouri, News-Leader*, March 14, 2004, pp. 1A+; E. McDowell, "Adventures in Retailing," *New York Times*, March 20, 1999, p. B1; and author's personal experiences visiting the "granddaddy" store in Springfield.

CASE #3: Diamonds Are a Guy's Best Friend

Buying a diamond ring for that all-important moment of "popping the question" can be a frightening experience. After all, most people (and guys, in particular) don't have much experience in purchasing the product. And it's an expensive product . . . one you want to make sure is an intelligent and affordable purchase. When Mark Vadon, a 28-year-old management consultant, walked into a Tiffany store to buy an engagement ring in 1998, he left empty-handed, intimidated and frustrated by the experience. With thousands of dollars at stake, his own lack of knowledge about the product meant he didn't know whether the salespersons were being honest about the diamonds they were selling. He eventually found a ring online at a site named Internet Diamonds. A few weeks after purchasing the ring, Vadon happened to be in Seattle and found the store front of Internet Diamonds. After discussions with the owner, Vadon recognized the potential opportunity that this online diamond shop offered. It was clearing $250,000 a month in revenue despite no advertising budget and a bare-bones design. He offered the owner $5 million for an 85 percent stake in the company. At the end of 1999, Vadon changed the name to the more exotic Blue Nile. Vadon's goal was to develop a user-friendly site that would demystify diamond purchasing by educating consumers about diamonds and offering a vast selection of products in different price ranges. Blue Nile capitalizes on a man's common fear that jewelry stores will exploit his ignorance.

At the end of 2000, the company had $44 million in revenue, but managed to lose $30 million, largely because it had spent $40 million on television advertising. This was also the time when many dot-coms were going bust. However, some shrewd business decisions kept Blue Nile afloat. It cut its workforce before many others did and the company's investors put another $7 million into the company. It also eliminated the advertising budget. The company's marketing officer said, "Either we were going to build this thing through word of mouth or we were going to see revenues collapse and we would all go home." Although 2001 was a tough year, sales rose 10 percent. Since that time, sales have grown 30 to 50 percent annually and stand at over $319 million. Now, in an ironic twist of fate, as the largest online retailer of certified diamonds, Blue Nile ranks behind only Tiffany & Company in diamond ring sales. How has it been able to do this?

The company's philosophy, as stated on its Web site, is: "Offer high-quality diamonds and fine jewelry at outstanding prices." When selling products on the Internet, you don't see your customers. Thus, living up to that promise of quality becomes even more critical. Blue Nile has done this by setting high quality standards. It starts with selecting the finest loose diamonds and jewelry and evaluating them on a standardized grading scale. In addition, each loose diamond has a grading report from an independent diamond grading lab (either the Gemological Institute of America or the

American Gem Society Laboratories). Other aspects of the "Blue Nile Advantage" include being recognized for excellence, taking care of the details, being there to help, providing customers information about more than the Four Cs, and helping customers find the perfect jewelry. Oh . . . and one other thing. Mark Vadon believes that one of his most important roles is understanding what customers are experiencing, especially because they aren't in stores having face-to-face interactions with salespersons. So every morning he goes through electronic reports that show all incoming orders. He opens up 20 or so of those orders and reads any that are above $50,000. In addition, Vadon's phone has something called a service observer button, which allows him to listen in on customer service calls, something he usually does when he's doing e-mail. Here's what he says about that practice, "I do this for two reasons: It helps me understand how well our call center's working and it allows me to hear the customers, which is so critical."

Discussion Questions

1. What functional strategies do you see described in this case?

2. Go to the company's Web site [**www.bluenile. com**] and find the description of The Blue Nile Advantage. Describe what it says about the company's advantages. For each, describe which functional areas might be involved and how.

3. Being a total e-business (refer back to Chapter 1 for definition), Blue Nile's production-operations function probably has some interesting challenges. What do you think those challenges might be? How would you prepare the company for those challenges?

4. Mark Vadon says that Starbucks is his corporate role model. What do you think an online diamond retailer could learn from a company such as Starbucks?

Sources: Based on Blue Nile Web site [**www.bluenile.com**], January 30, 2009; "I Like Innovative, Disruptive Businesses: Interview with Marc Stolzman, CFO of Blue Nile," *CFO*, February 2009, pp. 38–40; J. Werdigier, "Diamond Sales, and Prices, Plunge," *New York Times Online*, February 21, 2009; J. Greene, "Blue Nile: A Guy's Best Friend," *BusinessWeek*, June 9, 2008, pp. 39–40; M. Vadon, "Engaging With the Customer," *Fortune*, May 14, 2007, p. 28; and G. Rivlin, "When Buying a Diamond Starts With a Mouse," *New York Times Online*, January 7, 2007.

CASE #4: Super Store

The Pacific Northwest is home to a third corporate giant that might not be as familiar as the other two (Microsoft and Starbucks), and that's Costco Wholesale Corporation. Costco operates an international chain of membership warehouses that carry quality, brand-name merchandise at substantially lower prices than those found at other wholesale or retail sources. Shoppers can find products ranging from groceries and jewelry to furniture and office equipment. Whereas a grocery store typically might stock 40,000 items and a Wal-Mart might stock 100,000 items, Costco stocks only the 4,000 most popular items it can find. And Costco's approach has been very popular with its shoppers. Why? The country manager of Costco Canada says, "They do it because there's value here. And despite the simplicity (cement floors, steel racks, pallets of goods, and no decorations), you walk in and you say 'wow.'" The company's CEO and president, Jim Sinegal, says,

"Costco is able to offer lower prices and better values by eliminating virtually all the frills and costs historically associated with conventional wholesalers and retailers, including salespeople, fancy buildings, delivery, billing and accounts receivable. We run a tight operation with extremely low overhead which enables us to pass on dramatic savings to our members." Costco has some 53 million cardholders and those members have been loyal as shown by the 87 percent renewal rate.

At the end of 2008, Costco had almost 545 warehouses operating around the globe. New stores continue to be added each year and the CEO said that store count could top 1,000 by the year 2017 if the company continued to expand at its current rate. Some of its newest projects include installing solar panels on some of its stores in California, which have already reduced electricity bills by 20 percent. The company is exploring installing the fixtures in stores in other similarly sunny locations. And it recently tightened its policy on the return of electronics products. Costco had allowed its customers—who pay annual membership fees of $50 to $100 to shop at its warehouses—an unlimited grace period to return purchases for a full refund. The one exception had been a six-month deadline for returning desktop and laptop computers. However, because of the "squeeze" being put on its profit margins, Costco had to put a 90-day limit for a full refund on returns of electronics such as televisions, cameras, iPods, cell phones, and so forth. Prior to implementing this new policy, Costco had tried other methods such as introducing a 1-800 number that customers could call to get answers to technical questions and offering on a limited scale a third-party service for installing high-definition TVs in homes. Although the company had hoped these methods would resolve the financial strains, the company's chief financial officer said, "These actions are improving the numbers, but they're not fixing the entire thing."

Another issue the company faced was a lawsuit filed on behalf of more than 700 female workers who claimed that the "retailer had systematically discriminated against women seeking jobs as managers." Women represent 45 percent of the chain's employees, but only 12.9 percent of store managers and 16.6 percent of assistant managers. In January 2007, a federal judge granted class-action status to that lawsuit. This meant that the plaintiffs in the case "should consist of all current and former female employees nationwide who have been denied store manager or assistant store manager positions since January 3, 2002." In the past, Costco has denied any discrimination but this lawsuit is forcing them to take a look at how they choose potential managers. "Unlike most competitors, Costco neither posts openings for such positions nor accepts applications for them. Instead, a largely male group of senior executives handpicks managers." There's an office inside headquarters called the "Green Room" that only senior executives can access where the photos of up-and-coming leaders are posted. Despite Costco's popularity with its customers, company executives face significant functional challenges that have to be addressed.

Discussion Questions

1. Describe examples of different functional strategies you see in this case. Be specific and be sure to label what type of functional strategy you think it is. What positive things do you see about these strategies? Negative things?

2. What impact might the company's functional strategies have on how the company competes and on its future growth plans?

3. How should Costco evaluate whether changes are needed in its functional strategies? Be specific in describing what strategies might need to be changed and how you would evaluate this.

4. Do you think the company needs to make strategic changes? Why or why not?

Sources: Based on Costco Web site [www.costco.com], January 30, 2009; D. J. Boyle, "Stock to Study: Costco Wholesale Corporation," *Better Investing*, December 2008, p. 31; J. Chu and K. Rockwood, "Thinking Outside the Box," *Fast Company*, November 2008, pp. 128–132; J. McGregor, "Costco's Artful Discounts," *BusinessWeek*, October 20, 2008, pp. 58–60; K. Hudson, "Costco Tightens Policy on Returning Electronics," *Wall Street Journal*, February 27, 2007, p. B4; D. Desjardins, "Costco CEO: Store Count Could Top 1,000 by End of Decade," *Retailing Today*, February 12, 2007, p. 3; J. Bick, "24 Rolls of Toilet Paper, a Tub of Salsa, and Plasma TV," *New York Times Online*, January 28, 2007; S. Greenhouse and M. Barbaro, "Costco Bias Suit Is Given Class-Action Status," *New York Times Online*, January 12, 2007; M. Shalfi, "Costco Commitment," *Retail Merchandiser*, January 2007, pp. 8–11; and M. Boyle, "Why Costco Is So Addictive," *Fortune*, October 30, 2006, pp. 126–132.

Endnotes

1. L. Linebaugh and J. Murphy, "Toyota Bets on Upgraded Prius to Bolster Global Sales," *Wall Street Journal,* January 13, 2009, p. B6; M. Maynard, "Toyota Plans to Leapfrog G.M. With a Plug-In," *New York Times Online,* January 12, 2009; B. Vlasic and M. Fackler, "Car Slump Jolts Toyota, Halting 70 Years of Gain," *New York Times Online,* December 23, 2008; J. Murphy, "Toyota's Global Woes Start to Hit Home in Japan," *Wall Street Journal,* November 4, 2008, p. A10; book review of "Toyota Culture: The Heart and Soul of the Toyota Way," by J. Liker and Michael Hoseus, in *Industry Week,* October 2008, p. 18; H. Takeuchi, E. Osono, and N. Shimizu, "The Contradictions That Drive Toyota's Success," *Harvard Business Review,* June 2008, pp. 96–103; A. Taylor III, "America's Best Car Company," *CNNMoney.com,* March 7, 2007; M. Spector and G. Chon, "Toyota University Opens Admission to Outsiders," *Wall Street Journal,* March 5, 2007, pp. B1+; M. Fackler, "The 'Toyota Way' Is Translated for a New Generation of Foreign Managers," *New York Times Online,* February 15, 2007; I. Rowley, "Even Toyota Isn't Perfect," *BusinessWeek,* January 22, 2007, p. 54; B. Bremner and C. Dawson, "Can Anything Stop Toyota?" *BusinessWeek,* November 17, 2003, pp. 114–122; S. Spear and H. K. Bowen, "Decoding the DNA of the Toyota Production System," *Harvard Business Review,* September–October, 1999, pp. 96–106; and R. L. Simison, "Toyota Finds Way to Make a Custom Car in 5 Days," *Wall Street Journal,* August 6, 1999.

2. P. Siekman, "Build to Order: One Aircraft Carrier," *Fortune,* July 22, 2002, pp. 180[B]–180[J].

3. Information for this section on production-operations is based on J. Heizer and B. Render, *Operations Management,* 8th ed. (Upper Saddle River, NJ: Prentice Hall, 2007).

4. Information for this section on marketing is based on P. Kotler and G. Armstrong, *Principles of Marketing,* 12th ed. (Upper Saddle River, NJ: Prentice Hall, 2008); P. Kotler and K. L. Keller, *Marketing Management,* 12th ed. (Upper Saddle River, NJ: Prentice Hall, 2006); and P. Doyle and P. Stern, *Marketing Management and Strategy,* 4th ed. (Upper Saddle River, NJ: Prentice Hall, 2006).

5. L'Oreal advertisement, *Diversity Inc.,* November 2006, p. 9.

6. A. Carmeli and J. Schaubroeck, "How Leveraging Human Resource Capital With Its Competitive Distinctiveness Enhances the Performance of Commercial and Public Organizations," *Human Resource Management,* Winter 2005, pp. 391–412; R. Batt, "Managing Customer Services: Human Resource Practices, Quit Rates, and Sales Growth," *Academy of Management Journal,* June 2002, pp. 587–597; J. Pfeffer, *The Human Equation: Building Profits By Putting People First* (Boston: Harvard Business School Press, 1998); A. A. Lado and M. C. Wilson, "Human Resource Systems and Sustained Competitive Advantage: A Competency-Based Perspective," *Academy of Management Review,* October 1994, pp. 699–727; J. Pfeffer, *Competitive Advantage Through People* (Boston: Harvard Business School Press, 1994); and P. M. Wright and G. C. McMahan, "Theoretical Perspectives for Strategic Human Resource Management," *Journal of Management,* 1991, pp. 295–320.

7. "Human Capital: A Key to Higher Market Value," *Business Finance,* December 1999, p. 15; M. A. Huselid, "The Impact of Human Resource Management Practices on Turnover, Productivity, and Corporate Financial Performance," *Academy of Management Journal,* June 1995, pp. 635–672.

8. "Effect of the Economic Crisis on HR Programs," Watson Wyatt Worldwide [**www.watsonwyatt.com**], December 2008.

9. C. Dougherty, "Big Firms Deepen Job, Wage Cuts," *Wall Street Journal,* January 17/18, 2009, pp. A1+; K. Evans and K. Maher, "Yearly Job Loss Worst Since 1945," *Wall Street Journal,* January 10, 2009, p. A1+; and D. Goldman, "Worst Year for Jobs Since '45," *CNNMoney.com,* January 9, 2009.

10. Information for this section was based primarily on L. R. Gomez-Mejia, D. B. Balkin, and R. Cardy, *Managing Human Resources,* 5th ed. (Upper Saddle River, NJ: Prentice Hall, 2007).

11. Information for this section was based primarily on J. Laudon and K. Laudon, *Management Information Systems: Managing the Digital Firm,* 10th ed. (Upper Saddle River, NJ: Prentice Hall, 2007).

12. Strategic Management at Wharton, "A New Tool for Resurrecting an Old Theory of the Firm," *Knowledge@Wharton* [**knowledge.wharton.upenn.edu**], May 17, 2006.

13. J. McGregor, "Check Those Impulses," *BusinessWeek,* August 21/28, 2006, p. 16.

14. D. Nath and D. Sudharshan, "Measuring Strategy Coherence Through Patterns of Strategic Choice," *Strategic Management Journal,* January 1994, pp. 43–61.

Competitive Strategies

LEARNING OUTCOMES

6.1 *Explain what competitive advantage is and what it implies.*

6.2 *Describe the different competitive strategies.*

6.3 *Discuss how competitive strategies are implemented and evaluated.*

There's no doubt that people like to watch movies but how they watch those movies is changing. Although many people still prefer going to an actual movie theater, more and more are settling back in their easy chairs in front of home entertainment systems, especially now that technology has improved to the point where those systems are affordable and offer many of the same features as those found in movie theaters. Along with the changes in *where* people watch movies, *how* people get those movies has changed. For many, the weekend used to start with a trip to the video rental store to search the racks for something good to watch, an approach Blockbuster built its business on. Today's consumers are more likely to choose a movie by going to their computer and visiting an online DVD subscription and delivery site where the movies come to the customers—a model invented by Netflix.[1]

Launched in 1999, Netflix's subscriber base grew rapidly. It now has more than 9 million subscribers and more than 100,000 movie titles from which to choose. "The company's appeal and success are built on providing the most expansive selection of DVDs, an easy way to choose movies, and fast, free delivery." A company milestone was reached in late February 2007, when Netflix delivered its one billionth DVD, a goal that took about seven-and-a-half years to accomplish—"about seven months less than it took McDonald's Corporation to sell one billion hamburgers after opening its first restaurant." To commemorate the occasion, one customer in Texas received a lifetime subscription.

Netflix founder and CEO Reed Hastings believes in the approach he pioneered and has set some ambitious goals for his company: build the world's best Internet movie service and grow earnings per share (EPS) and subscribers every year. However, success ultimately attracts competition. Other companies want a piece of the market. Trying to gain an edge in how customers get the movies they want, when and where they want them, has led to an all-out competitive war. Now, what Netflix did to Blockbuster, Blockbuster and other competitors are doing to Netflix. Hastings said he has learned never to underestimate the competition. He says, "We erroneously concluded that Blockbuster probably wasn't going to launch a competitive effort when they hadn't by 2003. Then, in 2004, they did. We thought . . . well they won't put much money behind it. Over the past four years, they've invested more than $500 million against us."

The in-home filmed entertainment industry is intensely competitive and continually changing. Many customers have multiple providers (e.g., HBO, renting a DVD from Blockbuster or Red Box, buying a DVD, downloading a movie from Apple) and may use any or all of those services in the same month. Netflix also sees video-on-demand and movie delivery over the Internet becoming a more competitive distribution channel. In many metropolitan areas, video-on-demand is currently available and Internet delivery of movies is available from providers such as iTunes, Hulu, Vongo, Movielink, and CinemaNow. Wanting to maintain its competitive position, Netflix announced in early 2009 agreements with LG Electronics and Vizio that let viewers get Netflix service through those companies' television sets.

To counter such competitive challenges, Hastings is focusing the company's competitive strengths on a number of initiatives including: continually developing a comprehensive library of titles; personalizing merchandising efforts to each and every customer; keeping costs low even as the subscriber base expands; and emphasizing convenience, selection, and fast delivery. With both large and smaller companies hoping to get established in the market, the competition is intense. Does Netflix have the script it needs to be a dominant player? CEO Hastings says, "If it's true that you should be judged by the quality of your competitors, we must be doing pretty well."

As this chapter-opening case illustrates, competition is a given for all organizations, regardless of size, type, geographic location, or even reputation. Even not-for-profit organizations compete for resources and customers. A small, local community theater faces competition from other entertainment options—both local and global—just as Google faces competition from Yahoo, MSN, Ask, and other Internet search services. How can organizations deal with competition and still achieve strategic goals? By formulating and implementing appropriate competitive strategies. For instance, when Netflix established agreements with television makers for delivering Netflix service, it was betting that its approach to the video download market would be a smart competitive move leading to increased sales and profits and an even more enviable competitive position. In this chapter, we're going to look at the various competitive strategies—what they are and how they're implemented, evaluated, and changed. (Figure 6.1 illustrates how competitive strategies

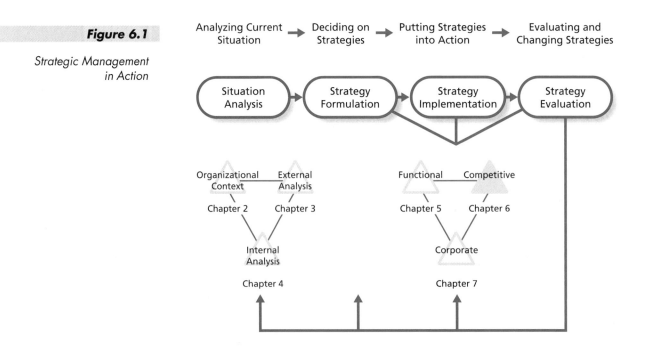

Figure 6.1

Strategic Management in Action

fit into the overall strategic management in action process.) We're going to start by reviewing competitive advantage and then discussing the competitive environment.

LEARNING OUTCOME 6.1
Explain What Competitive Advantage Is and What It Implies

As we've said numerous times, competitive advantage is a key concept in strategic management. Getting it and keeping it is what managing strategically is all about. Remember that **competitive advantage** is what sets an organization apart. In other words, an organization does something that others can't or does it better than others do (distinctive capability). Or, an organization has something that other competitors don't (unique resource). An organization's competitive strategies are designed to exploit its competitive advantage. However, other organizations also are attempting to develop competitive advantage and their competitive actions can easily (and often quickly) erode your own competitive advantage. Because competitive advantage implies there are competitors, let's look at the competitive environment to better understand the conditions under which competitive advantage is sought.

Understanding the Competitive Environment

Competition is everywhere. Most industries and organizations have experienced some competition at some point. To understand the competitive environment, we first have to understand *what* competition is and then look at *who* our competitors are.

What Is Competition?

In the United States alone, there are 102 LCD television brands, 66 more than in 2002.[2] Do you think there's competition in that market? Absolutely! **Competition** is when organizations battle or vie for some desired object or outcome. For business organizations, that's typically customers, market share, survey ranking, or needed resources. Although individuals and teams also compete for desired objects or outcomes, our primary interest is competition as it relates to organizations. What competition might an organization face? We can answer this by looking at *who* competitors are.

Who Are Competitors?

There are three approaches to defining an organization's competitors. (See Figure 6.2.) Let's look at each.[3]

➤ ● *Strategic Management in Action*

You can find competition in the most unlikely of situations and places. For instance, two of the nation's biggest nurses' unions are battling over workers. Each has tried to disrupt the other's organizing drives by using tactics such as ad campaigns, lawsuits, and breaking into Web job sites.

Competition also has erupted among cities in emerging economies that are vying to be known as the world's next great financial center even as existing centers (London, New York, Berlin, and Zurich) fight to maintain their status as pillars of capitalism. For instance, the Shanghai World Financial Center is one of the world's tallest skyscrapers but also symbolizes Shanghai's bid to become a major financial center. In Taipei, the Financial Center Corp.'s Taipei 101 skyscraper is a symbol of Taiwan's financial aspirations. Did you ever think that competition could happen like this? Can you think of other situations like this, outside business and athletics, where competition is taking place?

Sources: Based on K. Maher, "Nurses Unions Square Off Over Workers," Wall Street Journal, May 19, 2008, p. A3; and A. Rappeport, "If You Build It, Will They Come?" CFO, October 2007, pp. 33–35.

Figure 6.2 *Three Approaches to Defining Competition*

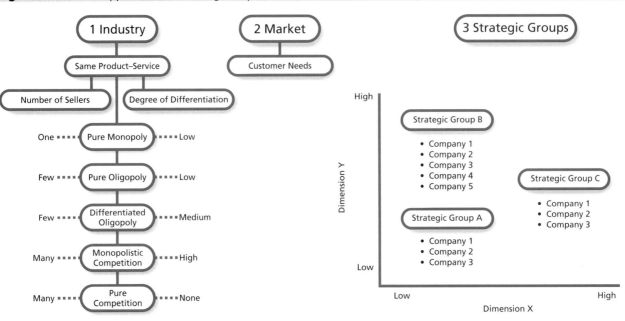

The industry perspective identifies competitors as organizations that are making and selling the same or very similar goods or services. Examples are the video rental industry, the supermarket industry, the automobile industry, the credit card industry, or the spa industry. As Figure 6.2 shows, these industries can be described according to the number of sellers and the degree of differentiation, both of which affect the intensity of competition.

The second approach, the market perspective, says competitors are organizations that satisfy the same customer need. So, for example, if the customer need is entertainment, competitors might range from video game companies to theme parks to movie theaters to the local community symphony orchestra to online video downloading. The intensity of competition in the market perspective depends on how well customers' needs are understood or defined and how well different organizations are able to meet those needs.

The third and final approach, the strategic groups concept introduced in Chapter 3, is based on the idea that there are groups of firms competing in an industry with similar strategies, resources, and customers.[4] In a single industry, you might find few or several strategic groups, depending on what strategic factors are important to customers. For instance, two factors that could be used to group competitors are price and quality. However, the dimensions used to group competitors can be different for every industry and even for different industry segments. Table 6.1 lists some dimensions that might be used to distinguish strategic groups. An example of grouping competitors in the cosmetics industry is shown in Figure 6.3. Note that the strategic factors used to group these competitors aren't price and quality, but price and distribution strategy, two factors important to that industry.

The strategic groups approach is a good way to define *who* competitors are because your most relevant competitors are those in your strategic group. Although competition might come from organizations in other strategic groups, your main competitive concern is those organizations in your own strategic group. How intense the competition is will depend on how effectively each competitor has developed its competitive advantage and on the competitive strategies each uses.

- Price
- Quality
- Level of vertical integration
- Geographic scope
- Product line breadth-depth
- Level of diversification

- R&D expenditures
- Market share
- Profits
- Product characteristics
- Any other relevant strategic factor

Table 6.1

Possible Dimensions for Identifying Strategic Groups

Although the strategic groups approach is frequently used to define an industry's competitors, there is some controversy about whether specific, identifiable strategic groups even exist.[5] These questions generally concern the factors used to define a strategic group and how those factors are chosen and used to establish specific and identifiable groups. Despite these questions, the strategic groups concept is useful in determining an organization's competitors and in explaining the components of organizational performance.[6]

No matter which approach is used to define competitors, it's clear that there are other organizations struggling to secure customers, resources, and other desired outcomes. Each of these competitors has resources and capabilities it's attempting to exploit. That's what we want to look at next—the role that resources and capabilities play in competitive advantage.

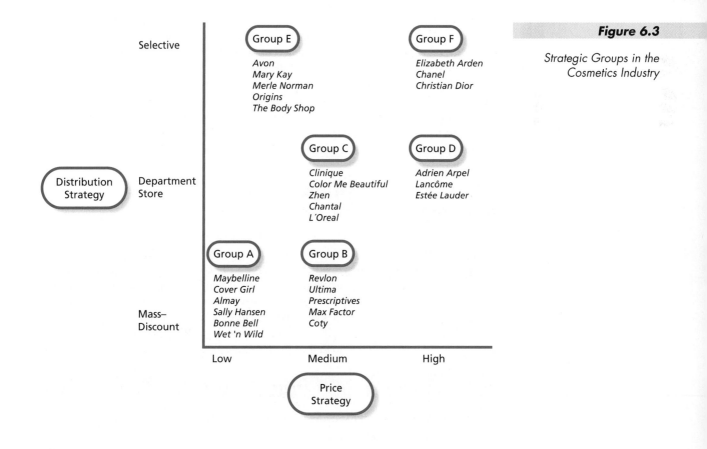

Figure 6.3

Strategic Groups in the Cosmetics Industry

Strategic Management in Action

The smartphone market has become intensely competitive. "In the decade since [founder] Mike Lazaridis first traveled the U.S. handing out BlackBerrys to corporate information officers, Canadian-based Research in Motion (RIM) has dominated this market." However, the company is finding its dominant market share (50 percent) now being attacked by Apple, Palm, Samsung, and Motorola, especially in the consumer market, which is the fastest-growing market for these products. Of all these "new" competitors, Apple's iPhone seems to be the biggest threat because of the wide array of popular applications that have been created by independent developers. In response, RIM held its first developers' conference in October 2008. What other actions might RIM need to do to protect its competitive position?

Sources: Based on M. Richtel, "Can the Cellphone Industry Keep Growing?" New York Times Online, February 4, 2009; and J. Hempel, "BlackBerry Battles Back," Fortune, November 24, 2008, pp. 45–50.

The Role of Resources and Distinctive Capabilities in Gaining Competitive Advantage

What makes some organizations more successful than others—however success is measured? Why do some professional basketball teams consistently win championships or draw large crowds? Why do some organizations have consistent and continuous growth in revenues and profits? Why do some colleges, universities, or departmental majors experience continually increasing enrollments? Why do some organizations appear consistently on lists ranking "the best," "most admired," or "most innovative?" Every organization has resources and capabilities to do whatever it's in business to do; however, not every organization effectively exploits the resources or capabilities it has or obtains the resources or capabilities it needs but doesn't have. Some organizations are able to put it all together and develop those distinctive organizational capabilities that provide them with a sustainable competitive advantage. Other organizations never get it done.

Organizations develop strategies to exploit their current resources and capabilities or to vie for needed resources and capabilities so they can get desired outcomes (customers, market share, resources, etc.). And other organizations are doing exactly the same thing. Competitive advantage, by its very nature, implies trying to gain the edge on others. As organizations fight for competitive advantage, the stage for competition—intense, moderate, or mild—is set.

From Competitive Advantage to Competitive Strategies

As organizations attempt to create a sustainable competitive advantage, they're looking for ways to set themselves apart and to compete. An organization or business unit does this using its **competitive strategy,** which is based on the competitive advantage(s) that the organization has been able to develop. For example, Netflix's competitive strategy is based on what it saw as its competitive advantage—its unique DVD rental and distribution service. As an organization refines and sharpens its competitive advantage (whether found in unique resources or distinctive capabilities), the basis for its competitive strategy is established. What we're going to look at next, then, are the various competitive strategies.

Learning Review: Learning Outcome 6.1

- Is competition an issue for all organizations? Discuss.
- What is competitive advantage?

When you think of Russian aircraft, you might picture Tom Cruise in *Top Gun* battling MiG fighter jets. Russia has a strong reputation in military aircraft. However, it's not as well known for commercial aviation. One Russian manufacturer, Ilyushin, couldn't keep pace with Boeing and Airbus and left the passenger aircraft business. Now, another manufacturer, the Sukhoi Holding Company, is staging a comeback with its Sukhoi Superjet 100, a regional jet designed to compete with the likes of Bombardier of Canada and Embraer of Brazil. Mikhail Pogosyan, chief executive of Sukhoi, says, "Our strategic goal is to be a world player in aviation. Our company is to be a winner. We are not to get a silver medal. We are to be first. By

2024, we hope to control 15 percent of the world's regional passenger plane market." The company is likely to find it tough going in this industry where the market is shrinking. "The world market for regional jets has contracted in recent years, and that trend is not expected to reverse, in part because so many regional jets have already been sold." To compete, Sukhoi will have to find something (resources and capabilities) that will set it apart.

Source: *Based on News Release, "Sukhoi Aims to Control 15% of Regional Plane Market by 2024,"* [**www.sukhoi.org/eng/news/company**], *June 7, 2008;* A. Osborn, *"Russia's $800 Million Airliner Bet Has High Stakes," Wall Street Journal, June 26, 2007, p. A6; and L. Wayne, "Russians Re-entering Passenger Jet Market," New York Times Online, July 20, 2006.*

- Compare and contrast the three approaches to defining competitors.
- What role do resources and distinctive capabilities play in gaining competitive advantage?
- Define competitive strategy. What's the connection between competitive advantage and competitive strategy?

LEARNING OUTCOME 6.2
Describe the Different Competitive Strategies

Although it may seem there are numerous ways an organization competes, the number of competitive strategies is actually few. In this section, we want to look at some specific competitive strategies; first the traditional approaches and then some contemporary perspectives.

Traditional Approaches to Defining Competitive Strategy

Two popular approaches to defining competitive strategies include Miles and Snow's adaptive strategies and Porter's generic competitive strategies.[7]

Miles and Snow's Adaptive Strategies

Miles and Snow's approach is based on the strategies organizations use to adapt to their uncertain competitive environments. They identified four strategic postures: prospector, defender, analyzer, and reactor. Research using the Miles and Snow typology generally has supported the appropriateness of these strategies' descriptions of how organizations are competing.[8] Table 6.2 summarizes the characteristics of each.

The **prospector strategy** is one in which an organization continually innovates by finding and exploiting new product and market opportunities. A prospector's competitive strength is its ability to survey a wide range of rapidly changing environmental conditions, trends, and situations and to create new products and services to fit this dynamic environment. The prospector's competitive strategy is to continually innovate, develop, and test new products. They're constantly prospecting—on the lookout—for new directions to pursue. This continual search for innovation creates uncertainties for the prospector's competitors; they never know what's

Table 6.2

*Miles and Snow's
Adaptive Strategies*

Strategy	Characteristics
Prospector	Organization seeks innovation Demonstrated ability to survey dynamic environment and develop new products-services to fit the changing environment Frequently and continually innovating, developing, and testing new products-services Competitors are uncertain about prospector's future strategic decisions and actions
Defender	Searches for market stability Produces only a limited product line Seeks to protect (defend) its well-established business Does whatever is necessary to aggressively prevent competitors from entering its turf Can carve out and maintain niches within its industry that competitors find difficult to penetrate
Analyzer	Strategy of analysis and imitation Thoroughly analyzes new business ideas (products, services, markets) before deciding to jump in Watches for and copies the promising and successful ideas of prospectors
Reactor	Lacks coherent strategic plan Simply reacts to environmental changes Makes strategic adjustments only when finally forced to do so Unable to respond quickly to environmental changes because resources-capabilities are lacking or are not developed or exploited properly

Source: *Based on R. E. Miles and C. C. Snow,* Organizational Strategy, Structure, and Process *(New York: McGraw-Hill, 1978).*

going to happen next or what to expect from the prospector. If the prospector can develop new products that the market desires and is willing to pay for, it will have a competitive advantage. Examples of organizations using this strategy would be Fox Broadcasting Network and MTV in the broadcast television industry. Both are noted for their innovative television network programming and willingness to pursue new directions. They're able to tap into changing societal attitudes and interests (think *The Hills* and *American Idol*) and develop TV programs that appeal to these new audiences. And they're willing to constantly push the envelope in developing new products. Their competitive advantage stems from their ability to assess environmental trends and continually create innovative programs.

The **defender strategy** is used by organizations to protect current market share by emphasizing existing products and producing only a limited product line. Defenders have well-established businesses that they're seeking to safeguard. They'll do whatever it takes to aggressively prevent competitors from coming into their turf.[9] Large companies with dominant market share, such as Anheuser-Busch InBev or IBM, may use a defender strategy to aggressively protect their crucial markets. Another example of a company using a defender strategy is Cleveland-based Lincoln Electric Holdings. As a leading manufacturer of welding products, it vigorously protects its product lines and market share against competitors by providing outstanding customer service and aggressively matching price cuts. It's also common to find small or medium-sized companies using this strategy. (See The Grey Zone box for an example.) A defender succeeds with this strategy as long as its primary technology and narrow product line remain competitive. Over time, defenders can carve out and maintain niches within their industries that competitors find difficult to penetrate.

Constantino de Oliveira Jr. has built a profitable airline—Brazil's Gol Linhas Aéreas Inteligentes (Gol Intelligent Airlines)—by "stealing ideas" from JetBlue and Southwest

The Grey Zone

What if you were a regional business and your industry's global dominant player decided to publicly boast in *your* location that its products were better than yours? That's exactly what happened to Utz Foods, a Pennsylvania snack foods manufacturer. PepsiCo's Frito-Lay unit conducted taste tests and then erected a billboard not far from where Utz Foods is based that blared, "The Harrisburg area prefers the taste of Lay's over Utz." Frito-Lay used the same tactic in Chicago, home of Jays Foods Inc., posting a billboard at a busy downtown intersection making the same type of boast. The "little guys" decided to fight back and a federal judge ordered Frito-Lay to remove the sign in downtown Chicago after concluding that the company "failed to weed out non-Chicago residents from its chip test." What do you think of this situation? Did Frito-Lay do something wrong? Does competition mean "all's fair in love and war?" Or should there be some ethical dimensions to such decisions? What if you were a strategic decision maker at Frito-Lay? Would you have done anything differently? How might you deal with this ethical dilemma of wanting to "do the right thing" in an intensely competitive industry?

Source: Based on C. Terhune, "Snack Giant's Boasts Sting Regional Rivals," Wall Street Journal, July 29, 2004, p. B1+.

Airlines.[10] He's using the **analyzer strategy,** which is a strategy of analysis and imitation. Analyzers watch for and copy the successful ideas of prospectors. They compete by following the direction that prospectors pioneer. Organizations using this strategy also thoroughly analyze new business ideas before jumping in. They'll systematically assess and evaluate whether this move is appropriate for them. For example, consumer products company Unilever uses the analyzer strategy for its Suave shampoo and skin care product line. Suave markets its lines by matching the packaging, smell, and feel of rival's products. Another example is COSMI Corporation, which makes and mass markets inexpensive education, entertainment, and business software. Its chief corporate officer describes the company as an "imitator, not an innovator" and says that he'd rather leave being first in the market to the "Microsofts of the software world and come out with simpler versions of whatever proves successful."[11]

Finally, the **reactor strategy** is characterized by the lack of a coherent strategic plan or apparent means of competing. Reactors simply react to environmental changes and make adjustments only when finally forced to do so by environmental pressures. Oftentimes, reactors are unable to respond quickly to perceived environmental changes because either they

---

➤ ● Strategic Management in Action   THE GLOBAL PERSPECTIVE

Kouta Matsuda, who successfully took on Starbucks in Tokyo, is now challenging them again, "this time in its own backyard" by opening the first U.S. store of his Koots Green Tea chain in Bellevue, Washington. Mr. Matsuda is betting that the novelty of his drinks and the increasing interest in the health benefits attributed to tea will entice customers, "even in the nation's most coffee-crazy city." According to the trade group Tea Association of the USA, American sales of tea have quadrupled over the last decade although much of that growth was in chilled beverages such as iced tea. But coffee is still the most popular hot drink. Mr. Matsuda said he would try to overcome this "by making his stores look and feel like specialty coffee stores."

Sources: Based on J. P. Simrany, "The State of the U.S. Tea Industry," Tea Association of the United States [www.teausa.org], February 12, 2009; and M. Fackler, "Sushi Is to Mrs. Paul's as Green Tea Lattes Are to . . . ?" New York Times Online, October 28, 2006.

lack the needed resources or capabilities or they're not able to exploit their current resources and capabilities. Obviously, this is *not* a recommended competitive strategy for developing a competitive advantage. In fact, the reactor strategy can be thought of as a "default" strategy, almost a nonstrategy position. Some examples of organizations that have used the reactor strategy—intentionally or not—include Sears, Sizzler International Inc. (the steakhouse chain), and Digital Equipment Corporation. In each of these instances, the organization lagged significantly behind its competitors in products offered and had no consistent strategic direction. Without significant strategic changes, a reactor will always be in a weak competitive position.

Porter's Generic Competitive Strategies

In addition to his five forces model (external analysis) and value chain (internal analysis), Porter also suggested that it's important for organizations to have an appropriate competitive strategy.

What is an "appropriate" competitive strategy? It's one based on an organization's competitive advantage, which Porter says can come from only one of two sources: having the lowest costs in the industry or possessing significant and desirable differences from competitors.[12] Another important strategic factor is the scope of the product market in which the organization wishes to compete—that is, broad (competing in all or most market segments) or narrow (competing in only one segment or a few segments). The mix of these factors provides the basis for his generic competitive strategies—cost leadership, differentiation, and focus.

You may be wondering why Porter called these strategies "generic." The term simply refers to the fact that they can be pursued by any type or size organization in any type or size industry. We're going to provide more detail on his strategies because they're so well known.

Cost Leadership Strategy   The **cost leadership strategy** (or low-cost strategy) is one in which an organization strives to have the lowest costs in its industry and produces products for a broad customer base. The main goal of the cost leader is to have *the* lowest costs in the industry. Notice that the emphasis here is on *costs*, not *prices*. In other words, the cost leader is striving to have the lowest total unit costs in the industry. Because the cost leader does have the lowest costs in the industry, it can potentially charge the lowest prices and still earn

---

FOR YOUR INFORMATION

The Copycat Economy

Have you seen the Swiffer WetJet? How about ReadyMop? When Procter & Gamble brought out its Swiffer WetJet mop, they thought they had a breakthrough winner product and charged a premium price for it. But not long after Swiffer's debut, Clorox Company brought out its copycat product, ReadyMop, an action that forced P&G to cut its price in half. And this scenario has been repeated continuously in other industries with other products. The situation has been described as the "copycat economy." Whereas a hot new idea used to mean years of fat profits, rivals now move into markets almost instantaneously. The question for strategic decision makers is "How do you make money in such an environment, especially when demand is flat?" And, unfortunately, there are no easy answers. For some industries, product upgrades are the answer. In other industries, companies have to continuously pump out cutting-edge products that fetch premium prices, no matter for how short a time. Others are finding that they have to continually fine-tune product formulas and designs. And finally, some companies have gone the opposite way by focusing research on fewer products, tenaciously defending patents, and vigorously promoting well-established brands with heavy marketing. Find other examples of copycat products (goods or services). How has the initial player responded to the competitive challenge? What strategies is the copycat using? Can you think of other possible strategic responses that either player might use?

Source: *Based on P. Engardio and F. Keenan, "The Copycat Economy," BusinessWeek, August 26, 2002, pp. 94–96.*

Strategic Management in Action

profits. Although every organization should attempt to keep costs low—that's just smart business—the cost leader is choosing to *compete* on the basis of having the lowest costs. What are the advantages of having the lowest costs? Having the lowest costs means that the cost leader can charge a lower price than its competitors and still earn significant profits. It also means that when competitive rivalry heats up and a price war breaks out, the cost leader is in a better position to withstand it and continue earning profits.

What does it take to successfully pursue the cost leadership strategy? Everything the cost leader does is aimed at keeping costs as low as possible. Efficiency in all areas is critical, and all resources, distinctive capabilities, and functional strategies are directed at that. The cost leader isn't going to have deep and wide product lines. That's too expensive, and the cost leader has chosen to compete on the basis of low costs, not on being different from competitors. The cost leader will market products aimed at the "average" customer. Little or no product frills or variations will be available. The cost leader organization isn't going to have fancy artwork on the walls or plush office furniture at corporate headquarters. It's unlikely that you'll see a cost leader with an elaborate high-tech, multimedia interactive Web site *unless* it was determined that this would be a cost-effective and efficient way to reach masses of potential customers. In fact, being a cost leader doesn't mean ignoring the latest advances in technology. Quite the opposite. If new and improved technology can pave the way to further lowering costs, the cost leader will jump on it. For instance, Collective Brands, Inc., a shoe retailer with over $3 billion in annual sales, has a modern automated warehouse at corporate headquarters in Topeka, Kansas. Out of this warehouse, which spans 17 acres under one roof, the company's 4,900 stores can be restocked with styles and sizes with about a day's notice.[13] Another example of a company using the low-cost strategy is steel manufacturer Nucor Corporation. After three years of testing, it began using a "radical new process known as 'strip casting' . . . which should give the company a huge cost advantage over traditional steelmakers."[14] Then there's the ultimate low-cost leader—Wal-Mart. As the world's largest retailer, you'd expect business operations befitting such a corporate icon, but you'd be wrong. At Wal-Mart's headquarters, office furnishings are modern but plain. Employees take out their own trash. There's no free coffee or soda. And the bathrooms on corporate jets have curtains, not doors.[15] By focusing on efficient, cost-effective performance rather than on image, Wal-Mart has been able to prosper in a competitive industry. Other characteristics of cost leaders include strict attention to production controls; rigorous use of budgets; little product differentiation—just enough to satisfy what the mass market might demand; limited market segmentation; emphasis on productivity improvements; and resources, distinctive capabilities, and core competencies found in production-operations and materials management.

What are the drawbacks of this strategy? The main danger is that competitors might find ways of lowering costs even further, taking away the cost leader's cost advantage. The cost leader's competitive strategy is successful as long as it can maintain its cost advantage. Another drawback of this strategy is that competitors might be able to easily imitate what the cost leader is doing and erode the cost advantage. Finally, a drawback of the cost leadership strategy is that the cost leader, in its all-out pursuit of lowering costs, might lose sight of changing customer tastes and needs. In other words, it doesn't matter how cost efficiently you can produce or market a product or service if no one is willing to purchase it even at rock-bottom prices.

Differentiation Strategy   The Hastens Vividus ultraluxe bed sells for over $49,000. A 12-piece box of Noka chocolates costs $39. For that amount, you get a total of 0.9 ounce of chocolate in the black and silver box. That comes to $693 a pound.[16] These companies are using a **differentiation strategy,** in which an organization competes by providing unique (different) products with features that customers value, perceive as different, and are willing to pay a premium price for. The main goal of the differentiator is competing by providing goods or services that are truly unique and different in the eyes of customers. If the differentiator can do this, it can charge a premium price because customers perceive that the product or service is different and that it uniquely meets their needs. This premium price provides the profit incentive to compete on the basis of differentiation.

What does it take to be a successful differentiator? All its capabilities, resources, and functional strategies are aimed at isolating and understanding specific market segments and developing product features that are valued by customers in those segments. The differentiator will have broad and wide product lines—that is, many different models, features, price ranges, and so forth. In fact, *how* the differentiator chooses to differentiate is practically endless. There are countless variations of market segments and product features that a differentiator might use. What's important to the differentiator is that the customer *perceives* the product or service as different and unique and worth the extra price. Because the differentiation strategy can be expensive, the differentiator also needs to control costs to protect profits, but not to the extent that it loses its source of differentiation. Remember that the differentiator is competing on the basis of being unique, not on the basis of having the lowest costs.

Other characteristics of differentiators often include differentiating themselves along as many dimensions as possible and segmenting the market into many niches. In addition, the differentiator works hard to establish **brand loyalty,** when customers consistently and repeatedly seek out, purchase, and use a particular brand. Brand loyalty can be a very powerful competitive weapon for the differentiator. Not surprisingly, the differentiator's unique resources and distinctive capabilities tend to be in marketing and research and development.

What are the drawbacks of the differentiation strategy? One is that the organization must remain unique in customers' eyes, which may be difficult depending on competitors' abilities to imitate and copy successful differentiation features. If the product loses its uniqueness in customers' eyes, they won't be willing to pay the premium price just to have the differentiated product. For example, Pottery Barn used to be one-of-a-kind in a fragmented home-furnishings industry. Its products were unique and had a style all their own. However, Pottery Barn lost some of that uniqueness as competitors such as Restoration Hardware, Target, and even Wal-Mart started offering similar but cheaper products.[17] Another drawback is that customers might become more price sensitive and the product differences might become less important. In this instance, also, the organization might find that its competitive advantage based on being different and unique no longer works.

FOR YOUR INFORMATION

Selling Luxury

In today's economic climate, luxury products are difficult to sell. A late 2008 Gallup poll showed that 49 percent of people making $90,000 or more a year said they believed that economic conditions were "poor," a 23-point increase in a couple months' time. Other government reports from late 2008 showed that consumers cut their spending and increased their personal savings. The chief economist at global economic consulting firm MFR said, "Consumers are rational. They respond to incentives and conditions, and right now the conditions and incentives are: spend as little as you can, and pay down as much as you can. You hunker down. That's what they're doing." Under such conditions, what's a differentiator to do? Companies that sell luxury goods are using rational, logical, left-brain appeal-ing approaches—special deals, useful features, long-term savings. For instance, Lexus ads promote "Lowest Cost of Ownership," stressing its cars' decent fuel economy, durability, and resale value. In pitching its new high-end Profile washer-and-dryer set, General Electric focuses on the technology that measures the optimal amount of soap and water per load. And Swiss skin-care company La Prairie is making an intellectual pitch to consumers for its $145 anti-aging eye cream by pointing out that the cream contains ingredients usually only available in pricey prescription ointments. Find other examples of luxury marketers trying new approaches to selling their products. What do you think of these pitches? Is the differentiation strategy one that's appropriate only in good economic times? Explain.

Sources: Based on J. Healy, "Consumers Are Saving More and Spending Less," New York Times Online, February 3, 2009; B. Helm and D. Kiley, "How to Sell Luxury to Penny-Pinchers," BusinessWeek, November 10, 2008, p. 60; and S. Hamm, "The New Age of Frugality," BusinessWeek, pp. 54–58.

Focus Strategy   The **focus strategy** is when an organization pursues either a cost or differentiation advantage but within a limited (narrow) customer group or segment. A focuser concentrates on serving a specific market niche. As Figure 6.4 shows, there are three broad ways to segment specialized market niches: (1) geographical, (2) type of customer, or (3) product line segment. A geographical niche can be defined in terms of region or locality. For example, Midwest Air Group serves more than 30 Midwestern destinations. By focusing on this particular geographic area, the company has built a substantial and loyal customer base, so loyal in fact that another airline wanted to acquire the company, an offer Midwest rejected. A customer niche focuses on a specific group of customers. In this specialized niche, customers can find products tailored to their unique needs. For instance, Christine Columbus is a mail-order catalog that offers items specifically for women travelers. Finally, a product line niche would focus on a specific and specialized product line. Rhino Entertainment Company, for example, has built a successful business specializing in anthologies, compilations, and reissues of popular music and TV shows. The company's collections created a new market niche. All these organizations have chosen to compete on the basis of some specific and narrow niche.

What's involved with the focus strategy? As stated earlier, a focuser can pursue either a cost or differentiation advantage. A cost focuser competes by having lower costs than the overall industry cost leader in specific and narrow niches. For example, U.K.–based Megabus offers a "discount airline" approach to bus service in about 30 destinations. Passengers can ride for as little as $1.50. To keep prices low, Megabus cuts costs by using online booking and sidewalk stops, instead of bus stations.[18] The cost focus strategy also can be successful if an organization can produce complex or custom-built products that don't lend themselves easily to cost efficiencies by the industry's overall cost leaders.

The differentiation focuser can use whatever forms of differentiation the broad differentiator might use—product features, product innovations, product quality, customer responsiveness, or whatever. The only difference, however, is that the focuser is specializing in one or a few segments instead of all market segments. For example, a Chicago company called Intelligentsia Coffee doesn't intend to follow the buy-low, sell-high business model. Instead, "they buy high and sell high." They pay above Fair Trade rates (50 to 200 percent over) for coffee beans they say are so good that "customers will pay $20 and more a pound retail." The company's green coffee buyer says, "On the grower side and the consumer side, we're trying to create a culture of quality."[19]

What are the advantages of the focus strategy? One distinct advantage is that the focuser knows its market niche well. The focuser can stay close to customers and respond quickly to their changing needs—often much quicker than organizations pursuing a broad market. By effectively and efficiently responding to customers' needs, the focuser can, in turn, develop strong brand loyalty. This brand loyalty can be hard for other competitors to overcome. Also, if the focuser can provide products or services that the broad competitors can't or won't, then it will have the niche all to itself.

What are the drawbacks of the focus strategy? One drawback is that the focuser often operates at a small scale, making it difficult to lower costs significantly. However, with technological advancements such as flexible manufacturing systems, this drawback isn't as

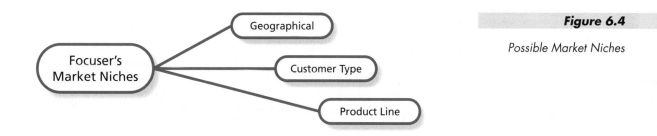

Figure 6.4

Possible Market Niches

Arif Masood Naqvi, the chief executive of private equity firm Abraaj Capital, wants to "create a one-stop financial services shop, serving up everything that companies and investors need, from lending to investment banking to brokerage." An ambitious plan indeed. However, Mr. Naqvi wants to focus on serving the Middle East and Southeast Asia and to beat the large global banks that are establishing business in those fast-growing markets. Mr. Naqvi says, "The only way we can compete is to add scale and mass." Do you think a cost focus or a differentiation focus strategy might be more appropriate? Explain.

Sources: Based on Abraaj Capital Web site [**www.abraaj.com**], February 12, 2009; and H. Timmons, "A Middle East Equity Giant with a Small Global Footprint," New York Times Online, December 8, 2006.

critical as it once was. In other words, as information and computer technology have become more affordable, focusers have discovered that economies (cost efficiencies) don't necessarily have to come from large-scale production runs. Many times, the focuser can be just as efficient running small batches as the large-scale competitor can be running large batches. Another drawback is that the niche customers might change their tastes or needs. As it's often difficult for a focuser to change niches easily and quickly, this could be a serious problem. In addition, any technological changes that might impact the niche can have a similar effect. Finally, there's always the threat of a broad-based differentiator taking notice of the focuser's market niche, especially if the focuser is enjoying a significant level of success, and moving in to offer products to those customers. In other words, the focuser is subject to being "outfocused" by its competitors—large and small.

The final aspect of Porter's generic competitive strategies we need to discuss is the concept of being **stuck in the middle,** which happens when an organization hasn't developed a low cost or a differentiation competitive advantage. An organization becomes stuck in the middle when its costs are too high to compete with the low-cost leader or when its products and services aren't differentiated enough to compete with the differentiator. As you can imagine, stuck in the middle isn't a good place to be. Getting unstuck means choosing which competitive advantage to pursue and then doing so by aligning resources, distinctive capabilities, and core competencies.

Contemporary Views on Competitive Strategy

Although the traditional approaches to describing an organization's competitive strategies are widely used, the contemporary views provide an expanded and more realistic description of the competitive strategies organizations are using. In this section, we want to look at two of these.

Integrated Low Cost–Differentiation Strategy

Porter's original work on competitive advantage and competitive strategies maintained that an organization could not simultaneously pursue a low cost and a differentiation advantage. To do so meant the risk of being stuck in the middle and not successfully developing or exploiting either competitive advantage. You had to do one or the other.[20] Despite strong empirical support for Porter's strategy framework,[21] several strategy researchers began to question this "mutual exclusivity" of the low cost and differentiation strategies.[22] Instead of having to pursue *either* low cost *or* differentiation, was it possible that organizations could pursue both strategies simultaneously and successfully? Strategy research evidence has shown that organizations *can* successfully pursue an **integrated low cost–differentiation strategy,** a strategy that involves simultaneously achieving low costs and high levels of differentiation.[23]

This strategy is not an easy one to pursue because an organization pretty much has to be good at everything it does. What are some examples of organizations that have successfully implemented such a strategy? One is McDonald's, which has succeeded in an intensely competitive market by continually innovating new products and by emphasizing efficiency and standardization to keep its costs low. Other organizations such as Southwest Airlines, Google, and Toyota also have been able to successfully pursue this hybrid competitive strategy. What makes an integrated low cost–differentiation strategy possible?

The answer is technology. Successfully establishing sources of differentiation can be expensive. When creating, manufacturing, and marketing a wide range of quality products or services, it's often difficult to keep costs as low as possible. Yet, the widespread availability and increasing affordability of information technology has made it easier for organizations to pursue product and service differentiation and still keep their costs low. Technological advancements such as flexible manufacturing systems, just-in-time inventory systems, and integrated information systems have opened the door for competing on the basis of having low costs *and* being unique. However, keep in mind that just because technology is available doesn't mean that every organization that uses it will be able to successfully pursue an integrated low cost–differentiation strategy. It still takes strict attention to keeping costs as low as possible and providing products with enough desirable features for the marketplace.

Mintzberg's Generic Competitive Strategies

Henry Mintzberg has developed an alternative typology of competitive strategies that he felt better reflected the increasing complexity of the competitive environment.[24] He proposed six possible competitive strategies as shown in Figure 6.5.

Differentiation by price is a modification of Porter's cost leadership strategy. Mintzberg argued that having the lowest costs didn't provide a competitive advantage by itself, but that the advantage came from the fact it allowed the organization to charge below-average market prices. Therefore, an organization pursuing this strategy was instead differentiating on the basis of price. Differentiation by marketing image describes a strategy in which an organization attempts to create a certain image in customers' minds and uses that marketing image as a potent competitive weapon. The competitive strategy of differentiation by product design can be used to describe organizations that compete on the basis of providing desirable product features and design configurations. An organization that followed this strategy would attempt to give customers a wide selection of product features and different designs. Differentiation by quality described a strategy in which organizations compete by delivering higher reliability and performance at a comparable price. In this strategy, superior product quality was pursued as the organization's competitive advantage. The competitive strategy of differentiation by product support emphasized the customer support services provided by the organization. In this strategy, competitive advantage would be sought through providing an all-encompassing bundle of desired customer support services.

Strategic Management in Action

Dell once was a shining example of the integrated low cost–differentiation strategy. It had succeeded in an intensely competitive market by providing high-quality products and services while holding down costs so it could undercut Gateway, Hewlett-Packard, IBM, and other PC makers in price. The secret? Dell was able to keep its costs low and its level of differentiation high by developing and exploiting a competitive advantage based on a disciplined, extremely low-cost corporate culture, while still providing high-quality products and services. However, as they discovered, maintaining the resources and distinctive capabilities so necessary to being successful at this strategy isn't easy. The company struggled during 2006 and 2007 with disappointing earnings and an SEC investigation into its finances. After undergoing some serious changes, it's trying to regain the competitive edge it once held.

Figure 6.5

*Mintzberg's Generic
Competitive Strategies*

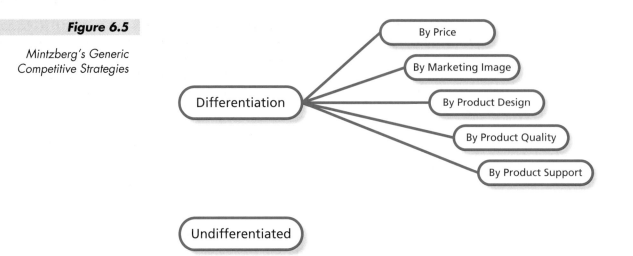

Finally, the undifferentiated strategy described situations in which an organization had no basis for differentiation or when it deliberately followed a copycat strategy.

What's the verdict on Mintzberg's alternative generic competitive strategies typology? It appears that his approach may have merit.[25] Research shows it has strong conceptual clarity and descriptive power. Although it will probably never replace the popularity of Porter's competitive strategies or Miles and Snow's adaptive strategies, Mintzberg's typology does seem to capture the essence of competitive strategies being used by organizations in today's complex and dynamic competitive climate. As such, it provides an alternative way to describe organizations' competitive strategies.

No matter how you describe competitive strategies, the main thing to remember about them is that they should exploit the competitive advantage(s) the organization has developed. Without a competitive advantage that's been developed from its unique resources or distinctive capabilities, it will be extremely difficult for an organization to compete successfully in any given situation, no matter what competitive strategy it might be using.

Learning Review: Learning Outcome 6.2

- Describe each of Miles and Snow's four adaptive strategies.
- According to Porter, what are the two types of competitive advantage?
- Describe each of Porter's generic competitive strategies.
- What does it mean to be "stuck in the middle"?
- What is the integrated low cost–differentiation strategy and how does it contradict the concept behind Porter's generic competitive strategies?
- Describe each of the competitive strategies in Mintzberg's generic strategy typology.

LEARNING OUTCOME 6.3
Discuss How Competitive Strategies Are Implemented and Evaluated

Look back at the chapter-opening case. What type of competitive strategy did Netflix appear to be pursuing? How can you tell? You'll probably note such things as its competitive culture, marketing expertise, and its willingness to move into new markets. The competitive

FOR YOUR INFORMATION

New Strategies for Achieving—and Keeping—Market Domination

"Having a market stronghold has never been more important since the best strongholds create power." Is it possible for an organization to dominate its market today? Yes, but it's not easy to achieve. A company that dominates "is so powerful in a geographic, product, or customer segment that it sets the standard for all others in terms of price, performance, reliability, and other characteristics." According to Richard A. D'Aveni, there are five ways to acquire and preserve a stronghold. He calls them the Five S's: securing, separating, surrounding, storming, and shape-shifting. Let's look at each:

Securing: The idea of securing is similar to any entity, such as a country, that wants to secure its borders from attack, which they do by erecting strong walls or barriers. Or think of a business that secures its information network through firewalls and encryption mechanisms. In the strategy context of market domination, securing refers to barriers that block competitors from entering a market.

Separating: The idea of separating refers to a strategy in which companies "make tacit alliances with competitors that allow a peaceful coexistence of nonoverlapping strongholds in the same market." For instance, Home Depot and Lowe's initially coexisted by dividing up the home improvement market with Home Depot focused on do-it-yourselfers and professionals and Lowe's focused more on women and on secondary cities mainly in the Southeastern United States.

Surrounding: In the surround strategy, a company surrounds rivals' strongholds in order to contain them. In effect, you're "locking in" your competitors to the strategic choices they've made. For instance, Panera Bread Company has succeeded in part because it recognized that the "big three" fast-food companies (McDonald's, Wendy's, and Burger King) were "locked in" to their powerful brand images of low prices and the family-with-kids market. Panera and other similar fast-food or casual restaurants have been able to attract less price-sensitive customers.

Storming: This strategy involves "storming a rival's stronghold by breaking through, going around, or neutralizing its entry barriers." D'Aveni uses Sears as an example of being stormed, as it was by Wal-Mart in all kinds of consumer products, by Circuit City in appliances and electronics, and by specialty catalogs in its Sears Catalog division.

Shape-Shifting: This strategy "changes the borders—and size—of strongholds by changing the competitive landscape." D'Aveni identifies three ways to do this: convergence (redrawing boundaries between industries—think Apple's introduction of the iPhone), reinventing strongholds (identifying new types of customers and products within existing industry definitions), and recombining existing segments (think Microsoft's move from desktop operating systems to word processing, spreadsheets, Internet browser, etc.).

Source: *Based on R. A. D'Aveni, "Mapping Your Competitive Position,"* Harvard Business Review, *November 2007, pp. 110–120; R. A. D'Aveni, "Leaders of the Pack,"* Wall Street Journal, *March 3–4, 2007, p. R9; and R. A. D'Aveni,* Hypercompetition: Managing the Dynamics of Strategic Maneuvering *(New York: Free Press, 1994).*

strategy an organization is using can be seen by what's actually being done or implemented. Strategy implementation is critical. If a strategy is not implemented, then it's nothing more than an idea. And, if you remember the entire strategic management process model, once a strategy is implemented, it must be assessed or evaluated, and modified if needed. In this section we want to look at how organizations' competitive strategies are implemented, evaluated, and changed.

Implementing Competitive Strategy

How does Abercrombie & Fitch keep current styles in its stores? How does Collective Brands Inc. restock its stores within a day's notice? Obviously, employees, facilities and equipment, work activities, and work systems have to be in place to facilitate such accomplishments. (Think in terms of resources, distinctive capabilities, and core competencies.) That's what implementation is all about. An organization's resources and capabilities are developed and used within its various functional areas, so it shouldn't come as a surprise that the organization's functional strategies play a significant role in implementing competitive strategy. That's what we're going to look at first. We'll then discuss the competitive actions an organization might take as it implements its overall competitive strategy.

The Role of Functional Strategies

The challenge in implementing competitive strategy is to create and exploit a sustainable competitive advantage. As we've said many times, competitive advantage comes from an organization's ability to use its resources to develop capabilities that, in turn, may become distinctive. All of this happens through the functional strategies being used.

The functional strategies play a dual role in implementing competitive strategy. First, the initial choice of an appropriate competitive strategy depends on the organizational resources and capabilities currently available or being acquired and developed through the functional strategies. Each competitive strategy requires certain skills, resources, and capabilities in order to successfully attain a sustainable competitive advantage. For instance, in the cost leadership strategy, tight cost controls are critical, which means strategic decision makers want to develop skills, resources, and capabilities (e.g., engineering skills, low-cost distribution systems, products designed for efficient manufacturing) that do just that. In the differentiation strategy, it's critical to understand customers and what they value, which means developing skills, resources, and capabilities in marketing, product design, market research, and so forth. (See Table 6.3.)

The functional strategies also play another role. Once the organization's competitive strategy is determined, the resources, capabilities, and competencies found in the various functional areas are *how* the competitive strategy is implemented.

The functional strategies being used should support whatever competitive advantage—and, of course, competitive strategy—is being pursued. This means that, for instance, if we've chosen to compete on the basis of having the lowest costs, then the functional strategies should support and reinforce that strategy. Cost efficiencies would be pursued in all operational areas but particularly in production-operations. Also, financial strategies could support operational efficiency by determining what technology investments would best contribute to lowering costs. In fact, all an organization's resources, distinctive capabilities, and core competencies would be directed at attaining the goal of having the lowest costs. Likewise, if an organization chose to compete on the basis of differentiation or even on both low costs and differentiation, then its functional strategies should support those choices or it

---

● Strategic Management in Action   **THE GLOBAL PERSPECTIVE**

Singapore Airlines (SIA) has long been a favorite of business travelers because of its amazing customer service and special amenities. Chief executive Chew Choon Seng is well aware of new rivals, the most "threatening" probably being Emirates, an airline based out of Dubai, United Arab Emirates, which is positioning itself as offering premium service but low prices. However, Chew continues to emphasize what has made SIA successful—its focus on the details. It's those details that help it keep its strong customer appeal and yet be able to with-stand the extreme cost-pricing pressures in the airline industry. For instance, to improve its food, the company invested $1 million in a simulator that mimics the air pressure and humidity found inside a plane. One thing it discovered—use less spices. How has SIA recognized the importance of functional strategies to its ability to compete?

Source: Based on S. McCartney, "The Middle Seat: Cooking Up Ways to Improve Steaks on a Plane," Wall Street Journal, January 20, 2009, p. B9; and J. Doebele, "The Engineer," Forbes, January 9, 2006, pp. 122–123.

Table 6.3 Requirements for Porter's Competitive Strategies

Generic Strategy	Commonly Required Skills and Resources	Common Organizational Requirements
Overall Cost Leadership	Sustained capital investment Process engineering skills Intense supervision of labor Products designed for ease of manufacture Low-cost distribution system	Tight cost control Frequent, detailed control reports Structured organization and responsibilities Incentives based on meeting strict quantitative targets
Differentiation	Strong marketing abilities Product engineering Creative flair Strong capability in basic research Corporate reputation for quality or technological leadership Long tradition in the industry or unique combination of skills drawn from other businesses Strong cooperation from channels	Strong coordination among functions in R&D, product development, and marketing Subjective measurement and incentives instead of quantitative measures Amenities to attract highly skilled labor, scientists, or creative people
Focus	Combination of the above policies directed at the particular strategic target	Combination of the above policies directed at the particular strategic target

Source: *Adapted with permission of The Free Press, a Division of Simon & Schuster Adult Publishing Group from* Competitive Strategy: Techniques for Analyzing Industries and Competitors *by Michael E. Porter. Copyright © 1980, 1998 by The Free Press. All rights reserved.*

will never develop a competitive advantage. To summarize, the functional strategies—that is, how the organization develops and exploits its resources, core competencies, and distinctive capabilities—influence both *what* competitive strategy is most appropriate and *how* that strategy is implemented.

It should be fairly obvious by now that an organization's functional strategies play a critical role in the implementation of its competitive strategy. Without developing and exploiting the organization's resources, capabilities, and core competencies—which is done through the functional strategies being used—there will be no hope of developing a competitive advantage. If the organization doesn't have or can't develop a sustainable competitive advantage, it's going to have a tough time competing and staying in business. Let's now look at the types of competitive actions an organization might use as it implements its competitive strategy.

Competitive Actions

Once an organization's competitive strategy is implemented through specific functional decisions and actions, the real fun begins! The very notion of "competitive" strategy means that the organization is going to be competing "against" other organizations—vying for customers, market share, or other desired objects or outcomes. What happens in this competitive "dance" is that organizations use certain tactics in the ongoing battle to acquire or keep whatever object or outcome they're after.

The competitive actions taken by organizations typically are described using a military or sports analogy—offensive and defensive moves. Why? Because that's what organizations are doing when they compete: they're going after competitors' positions or they're defending their own position. **Offensive moves** are an organization's attempts to exploit and strengthen its competitive position through attacks on a competitor's position. What are some offensive moves an organization might use?[26] A frontal assault is when the attacking firm goes head-to-head with its competitor and matches the competitor in every possible category such as price, promotion, product features, and distribution channel. This competitive move can be an effective way to gain market share from weaker competitors. It's also a good way to slice away rivals' competitive advantages. Another offensive tactic is to attack competitors' weaknesses. How? An organization might concentrate on geographic areas where its competitor is weak. Or it might begin serving customer segments that a competitor is ignoring or in which the competitors' offerings are weak. The organization might introduce new product models or product features to fill gaps its competitors aren't serving. What this offensive tactic entails is attacking wherever the competitor has specific weaknesses. Another offensive tactic is to use an all-out attack on competitors by hitting them from both the product *and* the market segment side. Needless to say, this all-out competitive attack requires significant resources and capabilities. Another type of offensive move is to avoid direct, head-on competitive challenges by maneuvering around competitors and subtly changing the rules of the game. How? The most typical way is that the organization attempts to create new market segments that competitors aren't serving by introducing products with different features. This competitive action cuts the market out from under the competitor and forces the competitor to play catch-up. Finally, another possible offensive tactic is to use "guerrilla" attacks—small, intermittent, seemingly random assaults on competitors' markets. For instance, an organization might use special promotions, price incentives, or advertising campaigns to lure away competitors' customers.

Offensive moves are good ways to attack competitors and strengthen your own competitive position. What happens when *your* organization is the one being attacked or threatened with attack? That's where the defensive competitive moves come in.

Defensive moves are an organization's attempts to protect its competitive advantage and turf. Defensive moves don't increase an organization's competitive advantage but can make that competitive advantage more sustainable.[27] Let's look at some defensive moves an organization might use. One is to prevent challengers from attacking by not giving them any areas to attack. For instance, an organization could offer a full line of products in every profitable market segment, keep prices low on products that most closely match competitors' offerings, use exclusive agreements with dealers to block competitors from using them, protect technologies through patents or licenses, or use any other number of possible preventive strategic actions. Again, the intent of this particular defensive move is to make sure competitors don't have any holes or weaknesses to attack. Another possible defensive move is to increase competitors' beliefs that significant retaliation can be expected if competitive attacks are initiated. How could an organization signal the market that it's serious about retaliating if attacked? Public announcements by managers to "protect" market share are important, as are strong responses to competitors' moves. Doing things such as matching price cuts or matching promotion incentives signals competitors that you aren't going to sit back and let them steal away your customers. Competitive counterattacks are particularly critical if the markets or segments being attacked are crucial to the organization. These types of retaliatory actions should be approached cautiously, however, particularly in instances in which the attacker is a new entrant to the market. Why? Research has shown that the typical *new* entrant doesn't pose a serious threat and aggressive retaliation can be expensive.[28] The final type of defensive move involves lowering the incentive for a competitor to attack. If a potential attacker is led to believe that the expectations of future profits are minimal, chances are it won't want to challenge the current leader. For instance, an organization might use media announcements to highlight problems in the industry or it might deliberately keep prices low and continually invest in cost-lowering actions. All these moves make it less attractive for a competitor to launch an attack.

Evaluating and Changing Competitive Strategy

The organization's competitive actions and responses being implemented through the various functional strategies must be monitored and evaluated for performance effectiveness and efficiency. What are the results of the various strategies? Are they having the intended effect? Are we successfully exploiting our competitive advantage? Why or why not? These are the types of questions to be asked when evaluating the competitive strategy. Because most organizations' competitive strategies are targeted at increasing sales revenues, market share, or profitability, data on these particular performance areas would be needed in order to determine the impact of the competitive strategies. Likewise, not-for-profit organizations should assess the results of their competitive strategies even though they're not focused on revenues, market share, or profitability. For instance, strategy evaluation might address such areas as: Did the number of plasma and blood donors increase? Did the number of contributors to the church building fund go up or did the average donation amount increase? Did governmental funding of the community drug outreach program increase? No matter what type of organization or type of competitive strategy being used, it's important to measure its impact.

It's not enough, however, to look at only the results of the competitive strategy. What if results aren't as high as expected, or what if they're better than expected? Then what? Part of the evaluation of the competitive strategy is also to determine what happened and why. We do this by trying to pinpoint areas of competitive weakness. Has the market changed and we haven't? Are the organization's numerous resources and capabilities being used effectively and efficiently so that the needed and crucial competitive advantage is being developed and exploited? Which ones are and which ones aren't? As you can see, evaluating competitive strategy turns out to be an assessment of the organization's various functional areas and the activities being performed there. If that evaluation shows that the intended impact or desired levels of performance haven't been reached, changes may be necessary. However, changing an organization's competitive strategy isn't something that it wants to do frequently. Why? Because each competitive strategy entails the development of specific resources, distinctive capabilities, and core competencies. To change the competitive strategy would mean modifying or redeveloping those strategic elements, which is both difficult and expensive. This doesn't, and shouldn't, mean that an organization would *never* change its basic competitive approach; what it does mean, though, is that this type of major strategic change should be approached cautiously, realistically, and intelligently.

Although changing an organization's basic competitive strategy may not be common, modifying its competitive actions *is*. The popular business press frequently reports on organizations changing their competitive actions. As competitors battle for desired outcomes or objects, they'll try one thing. If that doesn't work, they'll try something else. That's the reality of the competitive struggle that's taking place. As we stated at the beginning of the chapter, competition is a given for all sizes and types of organizations. It's a game that the players are trying to win. Organizations improve their chances of doing so if they choose a competitive strategy that supports and exploits their competitive advantage.

Learning Review: Learning Outcome 6.3

- Why is strategy implementation critical?
- Describe the role(s) that functional strategies play in implementing the organization's competitive strategy.
- Describe the offensive and defensive competitive actions an organization might use.
- How should an organization's competitive strategy be evaluated?

the bottom line

Learning Outcome 6.1: Explain what competitive advantage is and what it implies.

- *Competitive advantage:* what sets an organization apart, which can come from distinctive capabilities or unique resources. It implies there are other competitors.

- *Competition:* when organizations battle or vie for some desired object or outcome. The types of competition an organization might face can be understood by looking at who competitors are.

- Three approaches to defining an organization's competitors include: (1) industry perspective, which identifies competitors as organizations that are making and selling the same or highly similar goods or services; (2) market perspective, which says competitors are organizations that satisfy the same customer need; and (3) strategic groups concept, which is based on the idea there are groups of firms competing within an industry that have similar strategies, resources, and customers.

- Organizations develop strategies that exploit resources and capabilities to get a competitive advantage, thus setting the stage for competition.

- *Competitive strategy:* strategy for how an organization or business unit is going to compete.

Learning Outcome 6.2: Describe the different competitive strategies.

- The traditional approaches to defining competitive strategies are Miles and Snow's adaptive strategies and Porter's generic competitive strategies.

- Miles and Snow's four adaptive strategies include: (1) *prospector:* a strategy in which an organization continually innovates by finding and exploiting new product and market opportunities; (2) *defender:* a strategy used by an organization to protect its current market share by emphasizing existing products and producing a limited product line; (3) *analyzer:* a strategy of analysis and imitation; and (4) *reactor:* a strategy characterized by the lack of a coherent strategic plan or apparent means of competing.

- Porter's generic competitive strategies are based on competitive advantage (either low costs or unique and desirable differences) and product-market scope (broad or narrow). He identifies three strategies: (1) *cost leadership:* a strategy in which an organization strives to have the lowest costs in its industry and produces or provides products for a broad customer base; (2) *differentiation:* a strategy in which an organization competes by providing unique (different) products in the broad market that customers value, perceive as different, and are willing to pay a premium price for; the differentiator works hard to establish *brand loyalty,* which is when customers consistently and repeatedly seek out, purchase, and use a particular brand; (3) *focus:* a strategy in which an organization pursues either a cost or differentiation advantage in a limited customer segment.

- Porter also identifies a strategy of *stuck in the middle,* which happens when an organization can't develop a low cost or a differentiation advantage.

- There are two contemporary views on competitive strategy. The first is the *integrated low cost–differentiation strategy,* which involves simultaneously achieving low costs and high differentiation. Some organizations have been able to do this because of technology.

- The second contemporary view is Mintzberg's generic competitive strategies. He proposes that an organization's strategy is either differentiation or being undifferentiated. If it chooses differentiation, it does so by price, marketing image, product design, product quality, or product support.

Learning Outcome 6.3: Discuss how competitive strategies are implemented and evaluated.

○ Competitive strategies are implemented through the functional strategies; that is, the resources and distinctive capabilities found in the functional areas influence which competitive strategy is most feasible. In addition, the functional strategies support the organization's competitive advantage and strategy.

○ Competitive strategies are also implemented through competitive actions, which include: (1) *offensive moves:* an organization's attempts to exploit and strengthen its competitive position through attacks on a competitor's position, and (2) *defensive moves:* an organization's attempts to protect its competitive advantage and turf.

○ Competitive strategies are evaluated by the performance results obtained. What competitive weaknesses and strengths does the organization have?

○ Changing the competitive strategy isn't something that organizations do frequently because it's based on specific resources, distinctive capabilities, and core competencies developed in the functional areas. Changing would mean modifying or redeveloping those. What is likely to be changed are the organization's competitive actions.

YOU
as
strategic
decision
maker:
building
your
skills

1. A patent is a legal property that allows its holder to prevent others from employing this property for their own use for a specified period of time. A patent protects an invention and is valid for up to 20 years from the date of filing a patent application. Research patents and the patent application process. (You might want to access the U.S. Patent & Trademark Office Web site at [**www.uspto.gov**].) How many types of patents are there? What other interesting information about patents did you find? Would patents play any role in an organization's choice of competitive strategy? Explain.

2. A survey by consulting firm McKinsey found that managers are satisfied to respond to competitors' actions in a less active way. The survey asked executives how their companies responded to a competitor's significant price change or significant innovation. A majority said they found out about the competitive move too late to do anything about it. How would you interpret these results? What would be your suggestions to managers about competitive actions?[29]

3. Product comebacks. Long-established brand names are finding it necessary to update their competitive strategies in order to keep up with a continually and rapidly changing economy. For instance, Volvo moved away from emphasizing safety to advertisements that appeal to younger customers. Find three examples of brands or products that have been "shocked" back to life. Describe what each company has done (is doing) to implement the product comeback. What are the implications for competitive strategy?

4. Competition is a whole lot like war. What can strategic decision makers learn from military strategists? Sun-Tzu, the great Chinese military strategist, wrote *The Art of War* sometime between 480 and 221 B.C. Could his warfare strategies be used in battling competitors? Here's one interpretation of some of these strategies:

   - Don't start what you shouldn't begin.
   - The impossible is impossible.
   - Don't attack a tank with a peashooter.
   - Attack what isn't defended.
   - If you can't attack, defend.
   - Illusion creates confusion.
   - Do what they don't expect.
   - Rather than assuming they won't attack, position yourself so they can't attack.
   - The unprepared can be defeated.
   - The unknowing can be outsmarted.
   - Do not challenge unless you have the means to win.
   - Do not fight unless you're determined to win.

   What do you think of these "strategies?" What implications do you see for an organization's competitive strategy?

5. Henry Ford once said, "Competition whose motive is merely to compete, to drive some other fellow out, never carries very far. The competitor to be feared is one who never bothers about you at all, but goes on making his own business better all the time. Businesses that grow by development and improvement do not die. But when a business ceases to be creative, when it believes it has reached perfection and needs to do nothing but produce—no improvement, no development—it is done."[30] Are his thoughts still valid in today's environment? Explain.

6. Most organizations face an intensely competitive environment. With this type of competitive pressure, strategic managers might be tempted to engage in unethical competitive actions and activities in order to keep ahead of competitors. Do some research to find four examples of what you think are unfair competitive moves. Write a short paper explaining the examples you've found, why you think they're unfair, and what you'd do about it.

7. Select an industry that you know about or that you're interested in. (You might want to select an industry where you're concentrating your postgraduation job search.) Do a strategic groups analysis, covering as many of the potential competitors as you can. Determine what strategic dimensions would be most appropriate for grouping competitors. Then, group competitors according to your strategic dimensions. Be sure to put your analysis on a chart showing the strategic dimensions and the various strategic groups. Write up a brief explanation (1 to 2 pages) of what you did, how you did it, and why you did what you did.

8. "Perception in the marketplace is a significant factor to success." Do you agree? Why or why not? What implications does it have for competitive strategy?

9. Interbrand Corporation is a global design and marketing consultant known for its brand surveys. Go to the company's Web site [**www.interbrand.com**] and check out the latest global brand survey. Pick three companies from the top ten global brands. Research those companies and describe their competitive strategies (using any of the approaches we've discussed). Do you think the value of those companies' brands contribute to their ability to create a sustainable competitive advantage? Explain.

Strategic Management in Action Cases

CASE #1: Scripting the Future

This Strategic Management in Action case can be found at the beginning of Chapter 6.

Discussion Questions

1. Describe what you think Netflix's competitive strategy is using Miles and Snow's and Porter's framework. Explain each of your choices.

2. What competitive advantage(s) do you think Netflix has? Have its resources, capabilities, or core competencies contributed to its competitive advantage(s)? Explain.

3. Do Netflix's functional strategies support its competitive strategy? Explain.

4. What do you think Netflix is going to have to do to maintain its competitive position, especially as its industry changes?

CASE #2: Thinking Outside the Box

The package delivery industry is an all-out war between two main competitors, UPS and FedEx. Right now, the advantage appears to be tilting toward UPS. Smaller, flashier FedEx has been described as a "collection of marketers with trucks and planes" whereas UPS has been described as "industrial engineers with a collection of trucks and planes." In 2008, which was a tough year for most companies, UPS earned $3.0 billion on sales of $51.4 billion. FedEx, on the other hand, earned $1.1 billion on sales of $37.9 billion. Founded in 1907, UPS practically owns the business of economical ground delivery of packages to any address in the United States and is striving to do the same around the world.

UPS once considered itself a trucking company with technology. Now it's eyeing a future beyond just simple package delivery and considers itself more a technology company with trucks. For example, in one building at the company's sprawling mega-facility at Louisville (Kentucky) International Airport, repair technicians work on faulty laptops, cell phones, printers, and digital projectors. In another building, workers pack sports apparel for distribution. And in yet another building, UPS employees pack digital cameras with CD-ROMs, straps, and operating instructions. This work is all part of the company division known as UPS Supply Chain Solutions, which offers services such as logistics and freight forwarding, and represents UPS's aggressive moves for new business and deeper, more lucrative relationships with companies. But UPS isn't ignoring its roots as a deliverer of packages. At that same facility, itself a modern marvel of automation and technology, "countless cameras, scales, and scanners photograph, weigh, and monitor every package while belts, tracks, and chutes miraculously pilot the lot of them—with no package getting closer than 18 inches to the next—to their outgoing gates." And that's just the first step in the process of delivering more than 15.7 million packages and documents per business day globally.

To efficiently and effectively run this part of the business, UPS has a fleet of about 101,000 motor vehicles and more than 600 aircraft. But it takes more than resources to do what UPS does. Over the years, UPS had developed a successful business model in which uniformity and efficiency are the strategic factors behind the precise methods of correct package delivery. For instance, the company's legendary operations training encompassed everything from training drivers to hold their keys on a pinky finger so they didn't waste time fumbling in their pockets for the keys to asking employees to clean off their desks at the end of the day so they could have an efficient start in the morning. These strategic factors weren't changing. Instead, the company began looking at how to build on its key resources, capabilities, and competencies using a new tool—technology. The company's vast electronic tracking system is anchored by the smart label found on every package. This label contains exhaustive details about the parcel from its class of service to its destination and can be scanned from any angle, a plus for people and packages on the go.

Other technology includes the Delivery Information Acquisition Device, the brown tablet PDA that customers sign when receiving a delivery. All UPS drivers carry one for capturing and transmitting parcel pickup and delivery data. And once that package gets to the warehouse, the information flow doesn't stop. UPS loaders scan labels on the incoming packages with a wearable scanner device. A Bluetooth transmitter sends the tracking information to a terminal, which is then transmitted via a Wi-Fi network to the company's database. The goal? To get information from the customer to the driver to the warehouse to the Web and back to the customer as quickly as possible.

As UPS declares on its Web site, it's not just in the delivery business, it's in the customer satisfaction business. Meeting and exceeding customer needs will continue to be the company's driving force.

Discussion Questions

1. Describe UPS's competitive strategy using Miles and Snow's framework and Porter's framework. Explain each choice.

2. What competitive advantage(s) do you think UPS has? Have its resources, capabilities, and core competencies contributed to its competitive advantage(s)? Explain.

3. Do UPS's functional strategies support its competitive strategy? Explain.

4. What do you think UPS is going to have to do to maintain its strong competitive position?

Sources: Based on Company Press Release, "UPS Reports Results for 4th Quarter, Full Year," [www.ups.com], February 3, 2009; M. Boyle, "UPS and FedEx Think Outside the Box," *BusinessWeek*, September 15, 2008, p. 64; S. B. Donnelly, "Out of the Box," *Time Inside Business*, December 2004, pp. A1–A8; and D. Foust, "Big Brown's New Bag," *BusinessWeek*, July 19, 2004, pp. 54–56.

CASE #3: Fizz Factor

As one of the world's largest manufacturers, distributors, and marketers of nonalcoholic beverages, the Coca-Cola Company (Coke) knows all about competition. The company's flagship brand, Coca-Cola, competes directly with Pepsi Cola, the flagship brand of PepsiCo. And the competition doesn't stop there! From bottled water to diet soda to energy drinks, market supremacy is the goal. However, Coke has something unique and valuable that Pepsi does not . . . an iconic global brand.

Each year, global brand consulting firm Interbrand, in conjunction with *BusinessWeek,* identifies the best global brands. For the last eight years, Coke has been number one on the list. (PepsiCo ranked in the twenties on these lists.) Having the "best" global brand, at least according to this ranking, means that the brand has value, just like any other asset. In another ranking of the Top 100 Brands done by consulting group Millward Brown, Coke was one of the top four companies for the last three years. (PepsiCo ranked in the forties and thirties on these lists.) Despite its market-leading brand, Coke cannot take anything for granted especially in today's harsh economic climate and in such an intensely competitive industry. What's Coke serving up now?

In late December 2008, the U.S. Food and Drug Administration okayed a natural, zero-calorie sweetener for soft drinks derived from the herb stevia. Using its branded name for the sugar substitute, Truvia, Coke immediately launched three flavors of a juice drink in its Odwalla line. However, PepsiCo also launched several drinks with the sweetener using its branded name, PureVia.

Starting in late January 2009, 24 years after one of the most famous marketing blunders ever, Coke began quietly dropping the word "Classic" from its labels. That single word designation was added to the labels in 1985 to distinguish the original formula from a sweeter and vastly unpopular version of its flagship product. The new-Coke product introduction was called one of "the more noteworthy debacles in marketing history." When the company introduced the new product, it failed to realize how passionately people felt about the original Coke. One branding expert said, "They failed to understand the emotional significance to people that messing with Coke would have." However, enough time had passed that Coke felt it was time to change. And the timing coincided with the introduction of its new global advertising campaign called "Open Happiness."

Finally, Coke is taking steps to revamp its design strategy. Although it has a rich design heritage—from the shape of its bottle to the lettering and curves on that bottle—company executives felt it was time to step it up and do a total top-to-bottom redesign. When David Butler was hired as vice president of design in 2003, he was told, "We need to do more with design. Go figure it out." In his review of design at Coke, he found that "Coke had 450 brands, more than 300 different models of vending machines, innumerable bottling and retail partners, and no consistent global design standards." Initial design changes have included the aluminum contour bottle, which has been called a "sexy update of the glass bottle" and which feels more modern but is less expensive to produce. In addition, Coke introduced a new sleeker, sculptural cooler, which uses 30 to 40 percent less energy. Realizing that its vendors might not want to invest in the new coolers when they had ones that were still working, Butler's team designed inexpensive modular panels that could be attached to those still-functional coolers. But both sides "won"—the retailer got a new fresh look and Coke got consistency in its brand message. Butler's team is now reviewing all 450 brands in the company's portfolio.

Discussion Questions

1. Which competitive strategy does Coke appear to be using according to Miles and Snow's framework? Porter's framework? Explain each choice.

2. What do you think has contributed to Coke's ability to compete in this market? Be specific and be descriptive.

3. Competitive strategy is a choice of how an organization is going to compete in its industry or market so that it can develop a sustainable competitive advantage. Given the nature of this industry, what competitive strategy would be most likely to allow an organization to develop a sustainable competitive advantage? Explain your choice. Is this what Coke is doing? Explain.

4. What do you think Coke is going to have to do to maintain its strong competitive position?

Sources: Based on C. Palmeri and N. Byrnes, "Coke and Pepsi Try Reinventing Water," *BusinessWeek,* March 2, 2009, p. 58; D. Machan, "Putting the Fizz Back in Coke," *SmartMoney,* January 2009, pp. 24–25; S. Clifford, "Coca-Cola Deleting 'Classic' From Coke Label," *New York Times Online,* January 31, 2009; Best Global Brands Ranking, Interbrand [www.interbrand.com], January 28, 2009; Top 100 Brand Ranking, Millward Brown [www.millwardbrown.com], January 28, 2009; S. Rubenstein, "Coke and Pepsi Stoked for Stevia After FDA Green Light," *WSJ.com,* December 18, 2008; B. McKay, "Coke Set to Unveil Natural Diet Drink," *Wall Street Journal,* December 15, 2008, p. B1; and J. Scanlon, "The Shape of a New Coke," *BusinessWeek,* September 8, 2008, p. 72.

CASE #4: They've Got Game

With one of the world's most recognizable slogans (Just Do It) and brand logos (the swoosh), you wouldn't think that Nike would have to worry about the competition. However, in the athletic apparel industry where consumer tastes are fickle and the intensity of rivalry high, even Nike needs effective competitive strategies.

Nike, the company, reflects the brash confidence of its founder and board chairperson, Phil Knight. He still believes, as one of his company's most controversial Olympic ads once stated, "You don't win silver. You lose gold." With that type of attitude, it's no wonder that its shoes are consistently top sellers and that Nike is the innovator and industry leader as the world's number one athletic apparel company with 40 percent of the U.S. athletic footwear market. How does Nike play the game?

One thing that Nike understands well is the power of a competitive spirit, which continues to be a guiding force in the way the company does business. This competitive spirit, instilled by the late Bill Bowerman, Knight's mentor and track coach at the University of Oregon, has characterized the company's culture from the early days. The company (then called Blue Ribbon Sports) began with a handshake between Knight and Bowerman as they decided to import cheap, high-tech Japanese "Tiger" shoes to challenge Adidas, the industry leader. Even then, Knight was not afraid to go after someone, even the industry leader. And this competitive spirit influences strategic actions in other areas. For instance, when Foot Locker (one of Nike's biggest retailers), upset by Nike's hard-nosed marketing tactics, trimmed orders and slashed prices, Nike struck back by cutting shipments to the company on some of its top sellers. The move had serious consequences (Nike's U.S. sales fell 5 percent and its stock price plummeted), but it also brought Foot Locker back to the bargaining table. Later, an analyst said, "Nike knew its actions were going to have a negative impact, but they did it anyway" because they knew they'd prevail at the end. Even the company's name reflects this competitive spirit: Nike is the name of the Greek goddess of victory.

Another thing that Nike understands well is marketing. Knight has been called the "most powerful person in sports" even though he's never played pro sports or owned a pro sports team. What he's done, though, is rewrite the rules of sports marketing. When he signed a young basketball player by the name of Michael Jordan, an endorsement relationship began that even today remains the gold standard. And Nike continues to go after the new sports geniuses. For instance, Nike consistently beats rivals to sign top athletes to endorsement contracts. And you can't discuss Nike's marketing prowess without mentioning the company's legendary ads. Nike has always taken chances in its advertising by sounding off on social and political issues in sports. Knight says he knows that he risks offending people but believes "the publicity and notoriety are worth it." CEO Mark Parker says that the company is making major changes at the retail level. He says, "We're grabbing the opportunity to take Nike and our industry to someplace new, where consumers have experiences that are physical and digital and mobile." In addition, the company acquired Umbro, one of the world's great football brands.

Not only is the company on the cutting edge in its marketing, but it continues to take risks in its products. It's gone after more specialized markets such as skateboarding and golf. And it's developed a new collection of casual and sporty street apparel. Whether the company can exploit its brand power in these new markets remains to be seen. But one thing is for sure . . . this company's got game!

Discussion Questions

1. Describe Nike's competitive strategy using Miles and Snow's framework and Porter's framework. Explain each choice.

2. What competitive advantage(s) do you think Nike has? Have its resources, capabilities, or core competencies contributed to its competitive advantage? Explain.

3. Do Nike's functional strategies support its competitive strategy? Explain.

4. What do you think Nike has to do to maintain its strong competitive position?

Sources: Based on Nike 2008 Annual Report, [www.nike.com], February 13, 2009; E. Levenson, "Citizen Nike," *Fortune*, November 24, 2008, pp. 165–170; J. Greene, "This Social Network is Up and Running," *BusinessWeek*, November 17, 2008, pp. 74–76; S. Skidmore, "Nike to Change Shopping Experience," *Centre Daily Times Online*, March 23, 2007; S. Holmes, "Changing the Game on Nike," *BusinessWeek*, January 22, 2007, p. 80; and S. Elliott, "Nike Reaches Deeper Into New Media to Find Young Buyers," *New York Times Online*, October 31, 2006.

CASE #5: Fashion Forward

It's a store that most 18 to 24 year-olds have probably never set foot in . . . unless accompanied by a parent or older female. However, specialty retailer Chico's FAS has succeeded in an intensely competitive market as a designer and seller of sophisticated, casual-to-dressy clothing and accessories. Its Chico's brand is targeted at moderate-to-high income, fashion conscious baby boomer women. Chico's clothing features colorful designs in unique patterns that can be accessorized in various ways. The company's White House|Black Market brand focuses on moderate-to-high income young women (ages 25 and up). As the name suggests, these stores offer fashion only in the classic and timeless colors of black and white and related shades. The company's Soma brand sells exclusively designed private branded intimate apparel, sleepwear, and active wear. Given its target markets, Chico's competes with the likes of Dillard's,

Macy's, Bloomingdale's, Talbot's, Nordstrom, and Neiman Marcus—all heavy hitters in the fashion retail industry.

During the 2008 Olympics in Beijing, Chico's got an unexpected boost from an unlikely source. As U.S. swimmer Michael Phelps collected gold medal after gold medal in the Water Cube, his mom, Debbie Phelps, was stylishly attired from head-to-toe in Chico's clothing. She said, "Before I left for Beijing, I went to my Chico's store and picked out my entire wardrobe for the trip. I knew I was going to need to be prepared for a variety of events, activities, and climates so I picked key pieces that I could mix and match, dress up, and dress down. That's what I love about Chico's. Their clothes aren't only well made but also great for travel . . . It's fun. I love Chico's!"

During the Olympic telecasts, hundreds of Chico's customers called and e-mailed the company's headquarters in Fort Myers, Florida, to say that they had noticed that Ms. Phelps was wearing the company's clothes. Recognizing a possible marketing opportunity with a woman who was a prime example of its targeted demographic, Chico's soon signed an endorsement deal with Debbie Phelps. Ms. Phelps said she was surprised and flattered by the offer. "How great an honor it is to be able to represent a company that you believe in, that you really love." This arrangement reflects what marketing experts describe as attempts by fashion companies to capitalize on real people in the public eye who wear their clothes. This move toward "authentic endorsers" is a shift away from clothes and jewelry being given to celebrities and socialites to wear. In another instance, Michelle Obama wore a dress from the company's White House | Black Market chain during an interview in June 2008 on ABC's *The View*.

Despite the positive exposure its brands have received, Chico's, like most other retailers, has struggled during the economic downturn. However, the company plans to continue doing what it does best by offering women fun fashions and great styles.

Discussion Questions

1. What do you think it's likely to take to be a successful competitor in the specialty retail industry? Does Chico's seem to be doing those things? Explain.

2. What do you think of the concept of authentic endorsers? Is it likely to be appealing to customers? Explain.

3. What advantages are there to companies having endorsement contracts? Disadvantages? In what ways might a company's competitive advantage be affected?

Sources: Based on J. Saranow and R. A. Smith, "Olympic Mom Fits Bill for Chico's," *Wall Street Journal,* September 3, 2008, p. B8; L. Petrecca, "Chico's Basks in Golden Glow Through Phelps' Mom," *USA Today,* August 22, 2008, p. 1B; and PR Newswire, "Chico's: Debbie Phelps' Lucky Charm!" **[www.prnewswire.com]**, August 19, 2008.

Endnotes

1. A. Abkowitz, "The Movie Man," *Fortune*, February 2, 2009, p. 24; J. Hoyt, "Netflix Posts 45% Jump in Quarterly Profit As Firm Adds New Customers, Trims Costs," *Wall Street Journal*, January 27, 2009, p. B4; B. Stone, "LG Adds a Direct Internet Link to a Line of HDTVs," *New York Times Online*, January 5, 2009; S. H. Wildstrom, "Turning Your Xbox Into a Box Office," *BusinessWeek*, December 8, 2008, p. 80; Reuters, "Blockbuster Eyes Movielink in $50M Deal," *CNNMoney.com*, March 1, 2007; G. Gentile, Associated Press, "BitTorrent to Launch Movie, TV Downloads," *BusinessWeek.com*, February 26, 2007; M. Liedtke, The Associated Press, "Netflix Delivers 1 Billionth DVD," *BusinessWeek Online*, February 25, 2007; The Associated Press, "Netflix Names New Interim COO," *BusinessWeek Online*, February 20, 2007; P. Gogoi, "Wal-Mart Enters the Movie Download Wars," *BusinessWeek.com*, February 6, 2007; A. Hesseldahl, "More Movies than iTunes," *BusinessWeek.com*, February 2, 2007; Stocks in the News, "Netflix Delivers Upbeat News," *BusinessWeek Online*, January 25, 2007; J. Jones, "Blockbuster Marries Stores to Internet," *New York Times Online*, January 20, 2007; M. Liedtke, "Netflix Offers Instant Access," *USA Today*, January 16, 2007, p. 5B; M. Helft, "Netflix to Deliver Movies to the PC," *New York Times Online*, January 16, 2007; P. B. Kavilanz, "Wal-Mart Launches Digital Movie Downloads," *CNNMoney.com*, November 28, 2006; Knowledge@Wharton, "What's Next for Netflix?" *Knowledge@Wharton*, November 1, 2006; T. J. Mullaney, "Coming Soon to a Netflix Near You," *BusinessWeek Online*, June 9, 2006; P. Lewis, "Two Thumbs Down for UnBox," *CNNMoney.com*, October 3, 2006; C. Holahan, "Don't Nix Netflix Just Yet," *BusinessWeek Online*, September 11, 2006; T. J. Mullaney, "Coming Soon to a Netflix Near You," *BusinessWeek Online*, June 9, 2006; T. J. Mullaney, "Netflix: The Mail-Order Movie House that Clobbered Blockbuster," *BusinessWeek*, June 5, 2006, pp. 56–57; and J. Heileman, "Showtime for Netflix," *Business 2.0*, March 2005, pp. 36–38.

2. P. Engardio, "Flat Panels, Thin Margins," *BusinessWeek*, February 26, 2007; and D. Darlin, "The No-Name Brand Behind the Latest Flat-Panel Price War," *New York Times Online*, February 12, 2007.

3. P. Kotler, *Marketing Management*, 5th ed. (Upper Saddle River, NJ: Prentice Hall, 2000), pp. 220–223.

4. See Michael E. Porter, *Competitive Strategy* (New York: Free Press, 1980), Chapter 7.

5. D. J. Ketchen, Jr., C. C. Snow, and V. L. Hoover, "Research on Competitive Dynamics: Recent Accomplishments and Future Challenges," *Journal of Management*, vol. 30, no. 6, 2004, pp. 779–804; and D. Dranove, M. Peteraf, and M. Shanley, "Do Strategic Groups Exist? An Economic Framework for Analysis," *Strategic Management Journal*, November 1998, pp. 1029–1044; and J. B. Barney and R. E. Hoskisson, "Strategic Groups: Untested Assertions and Research Proposals," *Managerial and Decision Economics*, vol. 11, 1990, pp. 187–198.

6. J. C. Short, D. Ketchen Jr., T. B. Palmer, and G. T. M. Hult, "Firm, Strategic Group, and Industry Influences on Performance," *Strategic Management Journal*, February 2007, pp. 147–167.

7. D. J. Ketchen, Jr., "An Interview with Raymond E. Miles and Charles C. Snow," *Academy of Management Executive*, November 2003, pp. 95–118; D. E. Abell, *Defining the Business: The Starting Point of Strategic Planning* (Englewood Cliffs, NJ: Prentice Hall, 1980); M. E. Porter, *Competitive Strategy: Techniques for Analyzing Industries and Competitors* (New York: Free Press, 1980); and R. E. Miles and C. C. Snow, *Organizational Strategy, Structure, and Process* (New York: McGraw-Hill Book Company, 1978).

8. B. Kabanoff and S. Brown, "Knowledge Structures of Prospectors, Analyzers, and Defenders: Content, Structure, Stability, and Performance," *Strategic Management Journal*, February 2008, pp. 149–171; W. S. Desarbo, C. A. Di Benedetto, M. Song, and I. Sinha, "Revisiting the Miles and Snow Strategic Framework: Uncovering Interrelationships between Strategic Types, Capabilities, Environmental Uncertainty, and Firm Performance," *Strategic Management Journal*, January 2005, pp. 47–74; D. F. Jennings and S. L. Seaman, "High and Low Levels of Organizational Adaptation: An Empirical Analysis of Strategy, Structure, and Performance," *Strategic Management Journal*, July 1995, pp. 459–475; J. Tan and R. J. Litschert, "Environment-Strategy Relationship and Its Performance Implications: An Empirical Study of the Chinese Electronics Industry," *Strategic Management Journal*, January 1994, pp. 1–20; D. H. Doty, W. H. Glick, and G. P. Huber, "Fit, Equifinality, and Organizational Effectiveness: A Test of Two Configurational Theories," *Academy of Management Journal*, December 1993, pp. 1196–1250; D. Dvir, E. Segev, and A. Shenhar, "Technology's Varying Impact on the Success of Strategic Business Units Within the Miles and Snow Typology," *Strategic Management Journal*, February 1993, pp. 155–162; S. M. Shortell and E. J. Zajac, "Perceptual and Archival Measures of Miles and Snow's Strategic Types: A Comprehensive Assessment of Reliability and Validity," *Academy of Management Journal*, December 1990, pp. 817–832; S. A. Zahra and J. A. Pearce II, "Research Evidence on the Miles-Snow Typology," *Journal of Management*, December 1990, pp. 751–768; and D. C. Hambrick, "Some Tests of the Effectiveness and Functional Attributes of Miles and Snow's Strategic Types," *Academy of Management Journal*, March 1983, pp. 5–26.

9. J. H. Roberts, "Defensive Marketing: How a Strong Incumbent Can Protect Its Position," *Harvard Business Review*, November 2005, pp. 150–157.

10. K. A. Dolan, "From Buses to Planes," *Forbes*, October 31, 2005, pp. 118–120.

11. D. Fenn, "Money Rules," *Inc.*, April 2001, p. 94.

12. M. E. Porter, *Competitive Advantage* (New York: Free Press, 1985); and M. E. Porter, *Competitive Strategy* (New York: Free Press, 1980).

13. Hoover's Online [**www.hoovers.com**], February 11, 2009; and M. B. Grover, "The Odd Couple," *Forbes*, November 18, 1996, pp. 178–181.

14. D. Foust, "Soaring on Wings of Steel," *BusinessWeek*, April 4, 2005, p. 70.

15. "The Frugal Life of the Wal-Mart Muckety-Muck," *Business 2.0*, May 2002, p. 22.

16. A. M. Heher, The Associated Press, "Ultra-Luxe Bed Promises Good Nights for a High Price," *Springfield, Missouri, News-Leader*, March 9, 2007, p. 2A; and D. Darlin, "Figuring Out Gift

Giving in the Age of $2,000-a-Pound Chocolate," *New York Times Online,* February 10, 2007.

17. M. E. Lloyd, "That Pottery Barn Look Isn't So Unique Anymore," *Wall Street Journal,* March 21, 2007, pp. B1+.

18. T. Kim, The Indianapolis Star, "Company Takes Southwest Approach to Bus Service," *USA Today,* May 30, 2006, p. 7B; and T. W. Martin, "Where $1.50 Buys You a 300-Mile Journey," *Wall Street Journal,* July 6, 2006, pp. D1+.

19. M. Weissman, "A Coffee Connoisseur on a Mission: Buy High and Sell High," *New York Times Online,* June 22, 2006.

20. Porter, *Competitive Advantage,* p. 17.

21. C. Campbell-Hunt, "What Have We Learned About Generic Competitive Strategy? A Meta-Analysis," *Strategic Management Journal,* March 2000, pp. 127–154; R. B. Robinson and J. B. Pearce, "Planned Patterns of Strategic Behavior and Their Relationship to Business Unit Performance," *Strategic Management Journal,* vol. 9, no. 1, 1988, pp. 43–60; D. Miller and P. H. Friesen, "Porter's Generic Strategies and Performance: An Empirical Examination with American Data," *Organization Studies,* vol. 7, 1986, pp. 37–55; G. G. Dess and P. S. Davis, "Porter's Generic Strategies as Determinants of Strategic Group Membership and Organizational Performance," *Academy of Management Review,* vol. 21, 1984, pp. 467–488; and D. Hambrick, "An Empirical Typology of Mature Industrial Product Environments," *Academy of Management Journal,* vol. 26, 1983, pp. 213–230.

22. E. Kim, D. Nam, and J. L. Stimpert, "The Applicability of Porter's Generic Strategies in the Digital Age: Assumptions, Conjectures, and Suggestions," *Journal of Management,* vol. 30, no. 5, 2004, pp. 569–589; S. Kotha and B. L. Vadlamani, "Assessing Generic Strategies: An Empirical Investigation of Two Competing Typologies in Discrete Manufacturing Industries," *Strategic Management Journal,* January 1995, pp. 75–83; H. Mintzberg, "Generic Strategies: Toward a Comprehensive Framework," *Advances in Strategic Management,* vol. 5 (Greenwich, CT: JAI Press, 1988), pp. 1–67; C. W. L. Hill, "Differentiation versus Low Cost or Differentiation and Low Cost," *Academy of Management Review,* July 1988, pp. 401–412; J. J. Chrisman, C. W. Hofer, and W. R. Boulton, "Toward a System for Classifying Business Strategies," *Academy of Management Review,* July 1988, pp. 413–428; and P. Wright, "A Refinement of Porter's Generic Strategies," *Strategic Management Journal,* vol. 8, no. 1, 1987, pp. 93–101.

23. C. W. L. Hill and G. R. Jones, *Strategic Management Theory,* 3rd ed. (Boston: Houghton Mifflin Company, 1995), pp. 178–179; S. Cappel, P. Wright, M. Kroll, and D. Wyld, "Competitive Strategies and Business Performance: An Empirical Study of Select Service Businesses," *International Journal of Management,* March 1992, pp. 1–11; D. Miller, "The Generic Strategy Trap," *Journal of Business Strategy,* January–February 1991, pp. 37–41; and R. E. White, "Organizing to Make Business Unit Strategies Work," *Handbook of Business Strategy,* 2nd ed., edited by H. E. Glass (Boston: Warren, Gorham, and Lamont, 1991), pp. 24.1–24.14.

24. Mintzberg, 1988.

25. Kotha and Vadlamani, 1995.

26. The information in this section is based on various articles in L. Fahey in L. Fahey, ed., *The Strategic Management Reader* (Englewood Cliffs, NJ: Prentice Hall, 1989), pp. 178–205.

27. The information on this section is based on Porter, *Competitive Advantage,* pp. 482–512.

28. W. T. Robinson, "Marketing Mix Reactions to New Business Ventures," The PIMSletter on Business Strategy, no. 42 (Cambridge, MA: Strategic Planning Institute), 1988, p. 9.

29. K. Coyne and J. Horn, "How Companies Respond to Competitors: A McKinsey Global Survey," *The McKinsey Quarterly,* May 2008 [**www.mckinseyquarterly.com**].

30. "Newsworthy Quotes," *Strategy & Business,* 1st quarter 1999, p. 155.

Corporate Strategies

LEARNING OUTCOMES

7.1 *Explain what corporate strategy is.*

7.2 *Discuss organizational growth strategies.*

7.3 *Describe the organizational stability strategy.*

7.4 *Describe organizational renewal strategies.*

7.5 *Discuss how corporate strategy is evaluated and changed.*

Changing the Menu

"How do you spell cheese? K-R-A-F-T." Although that slogan may say what many people think Kraft Foods is about, that impression would be wrong. As the world's second-largest food company in revenues behind Switzerland-based Nestlé, Kraft is so much more than cheese.[1] And Kraft's history is a fascinating digest of a company that's used many different aspects of corporate strategy.

From its beginning in 1903 to today, Kraft has looked for ways to grow its business. It has continually developed new products—Miracle Whip, macaroni and cheese dinners, Parkay margarine, Tang powdered beverages, Velveeta, and most recently, its Oscar Mayer Deli Creations flatbread sandwiches. In 1980, Kraft diversified its businesses by merging with Dart Industries, although each business continued to operate separately. This combination lasted six years. In 1988, Kraft was acquired by Philip Morris Companies (the tobacco company), which merged it with another of its units, General Foods, in 1989. This combination created the largest U.S. food maker, Kraft General Foods, although both businesses continued to run independently. During the 1990s, other global competitors became more powerful and Kraft General Foods struggled. To cut costs, the two businesses discontinued almost 300 food items. In 1995, corporate parent Philip Morris integrated both businesses into Kraft Foods. It immediately sold some businesses (Lender's bagels, Log Cabin, the bakery unit, and others) and bought others (Del Monte's pudding business, Taco Bell's grocery line, Boca Burger, and Balance Bar). In 2000, parent company Philip Morris purchased Nabisco Holdings and folded it into Kraft Foods. In 2001, Kraft Foods went public and sold several business divisions. In 2002, a corporate restructuring eliminated several thousand jobs. The company also sold some brands—primarily its candy brands—that didn't fit its portfolio. In 2003, the company announced it was reducing the fat and sugar content and portion sizes of its products, a strategy abandoned a year later after research showed that consumers didn't like it. Also, in 2004, the chairman of corporate parent Altria (Philip Morris Company's new name) announced a complete spin-off of Kraft Foods, which officially happened on March 30, 2007. With Altria's 88.6 percent stake in Kraft distributed to its shareholders, Kraft Foods was now independent, with all the performance expectations associated with being a publicly traded company. As one analyst said, "Altria may have been okay with an underachiever, but outside stockholders generally want to see quick results." CEO Irene Rosenfeld has "crafted" a corporate direction for the company that exploits its competitive advantage in light of the changes taking place in the food industry. After assuming the CEO job at Kraft in June 2006 (leaving her position as chairman and CEO of PepsiCo's Frito-Lay division), Rosenfeld "spent months talking to employees and peeking inside consumers' kitchens—from suburban Chicago to the capital of China." Her conclusion? Kraft Foods "had lost sight of how its offerings fit into consumers' lives. Deep cost cutting had affected product quality, eroding the strength of some brands and causing the company to lose market share. Workers were afraid to speak up when they saw problems." Her solution: a new strategy to reignite growth by expanding into developing countries, cutting costs without hurting quality, and empowering local managers to make decisions. She says, "We are about to take this great portfolio of ours in a new direction that's more consistent with the reality of consumers' lives today. We have all kinds of capabilities in terms of manufacturing and selling and distribution. We've got complementary products that go together. Our challenge is how do we leverage those assets to accelerate our growth?" Will Kraft Foods's new corporate menu be what it needs?

Deciding the optimal mix of businesses and the overall direction of the organization are key parts of corporate strategy. Examples of corporate strategy in the chapter-opening case can be seen in the decisions that strategic managers at Kraft and corporate parent Philip Morris/Altria made as they moved into and out of various businesses. They didn't, and couldn't, know how those strategic actions would turn out, but they *did* know that the convergence of certain environmental threats and opportunities coupled with their organization's strengths and weaknesses had to be addressed. Although not every organization faces the challenges that Kraft did, all strategic decision makers must look at the broad and long-term strategic issues facing their organizations and decide what corporate strategies best address those issues.

In this chapter, we'll first look at how corporate strategy differs for single- and multiple-business organizations. In addition, we'll explore how corporate strategy is related to the other organizational strategies we've discussed in previous chapters. Then, we'll discuss the various types of corporate strategies that organizations might choose to implement. Finally, we'll look at what's involved with evaluating and changing corporate strategies.

LEARNING OUTCOME 7.1
Explain What Corporate Strategy Is

The struggling U.S. economy is challenging many companies in industries from retail and travel to banking and automobiles. The challenges have proved to be too much for some. For instance, Steve and Barry's LLC, once one of the country's fastest-growing store chains and billed as "the future of discount retailing," filed for Chapter 11 bankruptcy protection.[2] In a short span of six months, the company went from a national retail phenomenon to collapse. Such are the realities and challenges associated with corporate strategy, the last type of organizational strategy we need to study.

We defined **corporate strategy** in Chapter 1 as a strategy concerned with the choices of what business(es) to be in and what to do with those businesses. One thing we need to know in relation to an organization's corporate strategy is whether it's a single- or multiple-business organization.

Single- and Multiple-Business Organizations

A **single-business organization** is primarily in one industry. A **multiple-business organization** is in more than one industry. For instance, Coca-Cola can be considered a single-business organization because it competes primarily in the beverage industry. Even though it's a large company with multiple products, multiple markets, and multiple outlets, it is still primarily a beverage company. On the other hand, Coke's biggest competitor, PepsiCo, is a multiple-business organization because it's in different industries. Its business units include its snack food business (Frito-Lay), its beverage business (Pepsi, Diet Pepsi, and its other beverages), its prepared foods business (Quaker Foods North America), and its international business (PepsiCo International). Just like Altria (Kraft Foods's parent company in our chapter-opening case), PepsiCo also spun off a business—its restaurant unit, which included Taco Bell, Pizza Hut, and KFC and which is now known as YUM! Brands. Why is this distinction between single- and multiple-business organizations important? Because it influences an organization's overall strategic direction, what corporate strategy is used, and how that strategy is implemented and managed.

Another aspect we need to consider is how corporate strategy relates to the other organizational strategies. What role does corporate strategy play and how does it relate to the functional and competitive strategies?

Relating Corporate Strategy to Other Organizational Strategies

The corporate strategy establishes the overall direction that the organization hopes to go and the other organizational strategies—functional and competitive—provide the means for making sure the organization gets there. As discussed in earlier chapters, those "means" are the resources, distinctive capabilities, core competencies, and competitive advantage(s) found in the organization's functional and competitive strategies. For example, suppose an organization, such as Kraft Foods, has a goal of expanding into developing countries. It uses appropriate functional and competitive strategies to help realize that goal. Figure 7.1 shows how corporate strategy fits into the overall strategic management in action process.

Each type of strategy—corporate, competitive, and functional—is important to whether the organization does what it's in business to do and whether it achieves its strategic goals. Coordinating these strategies is critical to managing strategically. The corporate

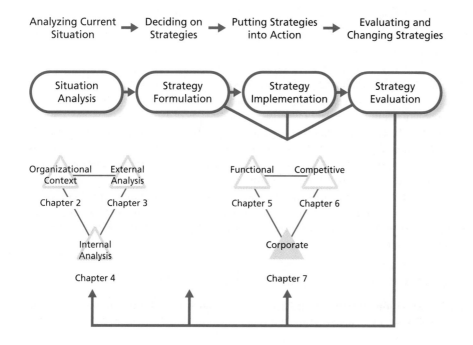

Figure 7.1

Strategic Management in Action

strategy can't be implemented effectively or efficiently without the resources, capabilities, and competencies being developed and used in the competitive and functional strategies. And, the competitive and functional strategies that are implemented must support the overall strategic direction and corporate strategy. Next, we're going to look at the overall direction an organization might go.

What Are the Corporate Strategic Directions?

Strategic decision makers can choose from three corporate strategic directions: (1) moving an organization forward, (2) keeping an organization as is, or (3) reversing an organization's decline. What does each mean?

Moving forward means an organization's strategic managers hope to expand the organization's activities or operations—that is, to grow. How? By choosing a growth strategy (or strategies) that is appropriate given the situation. Keeping an organization as is means it's not growing, but also isn't falling behind. This is a stability strategy. Finally, reversing a decline describes situations in which an organization has problems and may be seeing declines in one or more performance areas. These situations are typically addressed with a renewal strategy.

Now you know the three main types of corporate strategies: growth, stability, and renewal. In the rest of this chapter, we're going to discuss these strategies—what they are and how they're implemented, evaluated, and changed.

Learning Review: Learning Outcome 7.1

- What is corporate strategy?
- Contrast single-business and multiple-business organizations.
- How is corporate strategy related to the other organizational strategies?
- Describe each of the three corporate strategic directions.

LEARNING OUTCOME 7.2
Discuss Organizational Growth Strategies

Growth is an appealing goal to business and not-for-profit organizations alike. For instance, a university develops new degree programs or changes old ones in order to attract more customers (students) and resources (funding, alumni donations, books, buildings, equipment, etc.). Kraft Foods adds brands to its portfolio. Or, McDonald's opens additional outlets in various cities throughout Southeast Asia. All these strategic actions illustrate different ways for an organization to grow.

A **growth strategy** is one that expands the products offered or markets served by an organization or expands its activities or operations either through current business(es) or through new business(es). Organizations use growth strategies to meet performance goals they may have. Typical goals for business organizations include increasing revenues, profits, or other financial/performance measures. Not-for-profit organizations might have goals such as increasing the number of clients served or patrons attracted, broadening the geographic area of coverage, or even perhaps increasing the number of programs offered. What specific growth strategies might organizations use in pursuing such goals?

Types of Growth Strategies

If an organization's strategic managers decide that growth is the direction they want to go, they have different ways to do this as shown in Figure 7.2.

Figure 7.2

Possible Growth Strategies

Concentration

Concentration is a growth strategy in which an organization concentrates on its primary line of business and looks for ways to meet its growth goals by expanding its core business. When an organization grows by adding products or opening new locations, it's using the concentration strategy. As long as growth goals can be achieved with this strategy, most organizations will continue it.

Three concentration options are shown in Figure 7.3 and reflect various combinations of current product(s) and market(s), and new product(s) and market(s).[3]

Product–market exploitation describes attempts by the organization to increase sales of its current product(s) in its current market(s). How? It might use incentives to get current customers to buy more of the current product. For example, anytime that Kraft uses a "buy 2, get 1 free" coupon for any of its brands, that's a strategy to increase revenues by getting customers to buy more of the current product. Or an organization might advertise other uses for a product as Church and Dwight Company did to increase sales of its Arm & Hammer baking soda. Just think of the numerous ways, beyond its original use in baking, that consumers are encouraged to use baking soda—air freshener, cleaner, deodorant, and so forth. There are numerous other ways an organization can try to get customers to use more of its current products.

Using the *product development* option, organizations create new products to sell to its current market (customers). What is a "new" product? It might be new products with new features (options, sizes, and ingredients) that often are aimed at current customers. In

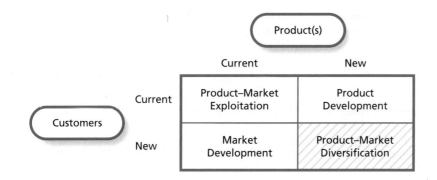

Figure 7.3

Concentration Strategy Options

addition, it can include improved or modified versions of existing products. Kraft used this strategy when it turned Oreo cookies into Oreo ice-cream cones, pie crusts, miniature Oreos, and seasonal Oreos with different-colored filling. Apple's iPod is another example of different product variations (color, size, storage capability, etc.) to extend its sales reach. Another example is World Wrestling Entertainment's introduction of a new lifestyle magazine aimed at the same young, male fans watching its cable TV programming. In each example, product development was intended to encourage sales of new or improved products to current customers.

The *market development* option describes when an organization sells its current products in new markets. What are "new" markets? It might be additional geographic areas or it might be other market segments not currently served. For instance, Ocean Spray Cranberries Inc. was faced with the challenge of how to grow the market for its cranberry products.[4] CEO Randy Papadellis said, "We need to find ways to introduce the cranberry to a whole new generation of consumers." The company added recipes to its Web site for a cranberry Cosmotini and cranberry bruschetta. It also showed customers how to use Craisins (dried cranberries) in products such as trail mix and salsa. Many skin care companies are going after an important untapped market—males. Although department stores have sold expensive men's skin care products for years, skin care companies are now going mainstream with these products by selling them at drugstores and discount retailers. These are examples of market development—current products aimed at a new market.

To summarize the concentration strategy, an organization looks for ways to grow its core business using different combinations of product(s) and market(s). The focus is on finding ways to meet growth goals by concentrating on its core business.

The remaining option shown in Figure 7.3—product–market diversification—isn't usually viewed as a concentration option as it involves expanding into new products and new markets. This strategic move usually involves diversifying, which we'll discuss in a later chapter section.

The advantage of the concentration strategy is that an organization becomes very good at what it does. Strategic managers know the industry and their competitors well. The organization's functional and competitive strategies can be fine-tuned to ensure that a sustainable competitive advantage is developed because strategic managers know what customers want and know how to provide it. Everyone in the organization can concentrate on the primary business and on developing and exploiting the unique resources, distinctive capabilities, and core competencies critical to success in this market.

The main drawback of the concentration strategy is that the organization is vulnerable to both industry and other external changes. This risk can be minimized by noticing significant

---

Strategic Management in Action **THE GLOBAL PERSPECTIVE**

Kuka Robotics is Europe's largest manufacturer of automated industrial machines (robots). The century-old German manufacturing equipment supplier found its profits disappearing because it relied too much on the automobile industry. As that industry slumped, Kuka's CEO, Berndt Liepert, began looking for new markets. Company engineers began to wonder whether its robotic equipment could be used in different industries. One said, "We could attach a chair to the end of it and make a fun ride." And that's just what they did! Kuka found lucrative markets in a variety of new industries and turned Kuka's robots into "the stars of internationally renowned action movies and theme parks." Its Robocoaster is "capable of 1.4 million combinations of programmable twists, swirls, and loops." One key to Kuka's success with this market development strategy was making sure its robots didn't look like industrial equipment.

Source: Based on S. Schubert, "Taking Robots for a Ride," Business 2.0, August 2005, pp. 46–47.

Maybe you've never heard of Navteq Corporation, but it has been recognized as a "hot growth company." The Chicago-based tech company, which was acquired by mobile-phone maker Nokia, is a digital map-maker that made its reputation selling maps for navigation systems in luxury cars. However, problems in the luxury car market dragged down Navteq's sales as well. CEO Judson C. Green needed to point his company in a new direction. He didn't abandon the car-based navigation market but instead looked at the growing opportunities in handheld devices. He says, "I'm imagining [location services] for tomorrow's household on both cars, all their cell phones, and even on their digital cameras, iPods, and games." This move is reflected in the company's financials. Its revenue from navigation-equipped vehicles has slipped to about 50 percent. Meanwhile, revenue growth from handhelds is expected to double.

Source: Based on R. O. Crockett, "Location, Location, Location," BusinessWeek, November 6, 2006, pp. 90–94.

trends, but strategic managers need to be willing to adjust the organization's direction, should that become necessary. For example, the Royal Typewriter Company unwisely chose to continue producing typewriters even as personal computers became standard office equipment and demand for typewriters plummeted. The result—it's no longer in business. If an organization implements its concentration strategy blindly without understanding the opportunities and threats facing the industry, *not* achieving its growth goals may be the least of its problems!

Although the concentration strategy may seem ideal for small organizations, it isn't used exclusively by them. In fact, most large businesses started off using the concentration strategy and many continue to use it to pursue growth. For example, Beckman Coulter, Inc., a Fullerton, California-based organization with annual revenues of almost $3.1 billion, has successfully used the concentration strategy to become one of the world's largest medical diagnostics equipment companies.[5] The company has grown by continually innovating new products and processes in this industry. Another example is Bose Corporation of Framingham, Massachusetts. The company's innovative audio products have helped make it the world's number one audio equipment manufacturer with annual sales of more than $2.1 billion.[6] Again, this organization has grown because of product innovations concentrated in its primary industry.

If an organization can't meet its growth goals by concentrating on its core business, it may begin to look at other growth strategies.

Vertical Integration

The **vertical integration strategy** is one in which an organization grows by gaining control of its inputs (backward), its outputs (forward), or both. In backward vertical integration, the organization gains controls of its inputs or resources by becoming its own supplier. For example, eBay owns an online payment business that helps it provide more secure transactions and helps it gain control over one of its most critical work processes. Another example is CVS Pharmacy, the U.S. drug chain with the most outlets, which acquired Caremark RX, the number two company in pharmacy-benefits management, creating "the nation's premier integrated pharmacy services provider."[7]

In forward vertical integration, the organization gains control of its outputs (products or services) by becoming its own distributor such as through an outlet store or maybe through franchising. For example, Apple Computer has over 200 retail stores worldwide to distribute its products. De Beers, the South African diamond mining company, has a few select retail locations around the globe. Even Coach, which was the first fashion manufacturer to open its own retail store in 1981, now gets about 75 percent of its revenue from its own outlets.

The vertical integration strategy is a growth strategy because an organization expands its activities and operations by becoming a source of supply or a source of distribution. However, because it's expanding into industries connected to its primary business, it's still considered a single-business organization. It's simply taking another path to meeting growth goals by controlling different parts of the value chain.

Studies of vertical integration strategies have shown mixed results in terms of whether the strategy helped or hurt performance. Generally speaking, the benefits of vertical integration seem to slightly outweigh the costs.[8]

Horizontal Integration

Live Nation, the largest concert promoter in the United States, combined operations with competitor HOB Entertainment, the operator of the House of Blues Clubs. Some critics "warned the deal would provide Live Nation excessive power in determining how much performers are paid and where they play."[9] French cosmetics giant L'Oreal acquired London-based retailer The Body Shop for $1.1 billion. Colgate-Palmolive acquired the all-natural personal care products manufacturer Tom's of Maine for $100 million. Each of these is an example of the **horizontal integration strategy,** which is a strategy in which an organization grows by combining operations with its competitors.

This growth strategy keeps an organization in the same industry and provides a way to expand market share and strengthen competitive position, but the big question with horizontal integration is, is it legal? The U.S. Federal Trade Commission and Department of Justice assess the impact of such combinations on the industry competition and evaluate whether antitrust laws might be violated. Even globally, the European Union has been quite active in approving or rejecting proposed horizontal growth strategies, especially those with a potential impact on its member countries. If government regulators perceive that competition is likely to decrease or that the end consumer would be unfairly impacted, the combined business probably will not be allowed. Despite this potential problem, however, many organizations have successfully used this strategy to grow.

Horizontal integration can be an appropriate corporate growth strategy as long as (1) it enables the company to meet its growth goals, (2) it can be strategically managed to attain a sustainable competitive advantage, *and* (3) it satisfies legal and regulatory guidelines.

Diversification

The **diversification strategy** is a strategy in which an organization grows by moving into a different industry. There are two major types of diversification—related and unrelated. **Related (concentric) diversification** is diversifying into a different industry but one that's

---

● Strategic Management in Action   THE GLOBAL PERSPECTIVE

Horizontal integration knows no borders! Wanting to get into fast-growing niches, the Coca-Cola Company proposed purchasing one of China's largest beverage makers, the Huiyuan Juice Group Ltd., for $2.3 billion. The deal would have been one of the biggest foreign takeovers of a Chinese company and given Coke a strong presence in that market. But as we've said, horizontal integration efforts have to meet legal and regulatory requirements. In this instance, China's Ministry of Commerce rejected Coca-Cola Company's proposal because the deal "could hurt competition in the local market."

However, in the intensely competitive airline market, American Airlines and its two main European partners, British Airways and Spain's Iberia, are cooperating internationally on pricing, scheduling, and marketing.

Source: Based on Dow Jones Newswire, "China Ministry: Coca-Cola, Huiyuan Deal to Hurt Competition," CNNMoney.com, March 18, 2009; "Coca-Cola Seeks Anti-Trust Nod for Huiyuan Deal," China Daily, December 3, 2008, p. 14; B. McKay, S. Canaves, and G. A. Fowler, "Coke Deal Juices Its China Business," Wall Street Journal, September 4, 2008, pp. B1+; and D. Michaels and S. Carey, "American, BA, Iberia Seek Closer Ties," Wall Street Journal, August 11, 2008, pp. B1+.

---

related in some way to the organization's current business. **Unrelated (conglomerate) diversification** is diversifying into a completely different industry not related to the organization's current business. Either strategy results in a multiple-business organization because it's no longer in just one industry. Let's look more closely at these two types of diversification.

How can diversification—which means "different"—ever be related? In other words, how is a different industry "related" to the one an organization is currently in? An organization using related diversification to achieve its growth goals is looking for some type of strategic "fit" where it can transfer its resources, distinctive capabilities, and core competencies to the new industry and apply those in such a way that a sustainable competitive advantage results. This search for strategic "synergy" is the idea that the performance of combined operations will be much greater than the performance of each unit separately. How does synergy happen? Through the interactions that occur as operations are combined and resources, capabilities, and core competencies are shared. A statement made by Steve Perry (lead singer of the 1980s rock group Journey) when the band got back together in 1996, describes synergy perfectly: "Individually, none of us made the music as magically as we collectively make it together."[10] That's what synergy is all about—the combined operations are more "magical" than what each unit could do separately. Figure 7.4 illustrates ways an organization might transfer resources, capabilities, and core competencies in achieving synergy.

What businesses have used a related diversification strategy? One is Apple, which is in a variety of businesses from music (iTunes Store and iPod) and cellphones (iPhone) to retail shops (Apple Stores) and, of course, its personal computers. Another is eBay, which acquired Skype Technologies for $2.6 billion. Although each industry (Internet auction and Internet phone) is different, they obviously have common characteristics, thus allowing eBay to share resources, capabilities, and competencies. As with any strategy, there's no guarantee that related diversification will always help an organization reach its strategic goals. Here's one example that *didn't* work. When Anheuser-Busch entered the snack food industry with its Eagle Snacks business unit, it felt it could exploit certain marketing synergies (distribution channels, customer use, product similarities) developed as the market leader in the beer business and transfer those resources and capabilities to the snack food industry. However, it was never able to develop a competitive advantage against industry leader Frito-Lay (a business unit of PepsiCo) in this intensely competitive market. As a result, the company shut Eagle Snacks down.

What about unrelated diversification? This growth strategy involves an organization moving into industries in which there is no strategic fit. Why would an organization choose

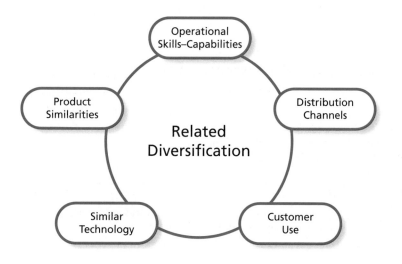

Figure 7.4

Types of Related Diversification

to be in industries with no possible strategic relationships or potential synergies? Most often, it will use this approach when its core industry and related industries don't offer enough growth potential. For an organization to pursue and achieve its growth goals, it has to look elsewhere. Also, some organizations might choose unrelated diversification if their specialized resources, capabilities, and core competencies can't be easily applied to other industries outside its core business. This obviously would limit the options for growth.

Because of the challenges of strategically managing such different businesses, there aren't many companies that use this growth strategy, although some do. For instance, Fortune Brands is a crazy quilt of businesses that produces market-leading products such as Jim Beam bourbon, Courvoisier cognac, Möen faucets, Aristokraft and Schrock cabinets, DeKuyper cordials, Titleist golf balls, and Master Lock padlocks. Another example is Lancaster Colony Corporation, which makes and markets Marzetti salad dressing, Dee Zee truck running boards and Protecta truck bed liners, Colony and Fostoria glassware, and Candle-lite candles and potpourri. Finally, another example from the global arena is none other than Toyota, which, in addition to its automobiles, is into prefabricated houses, advertising, roof gardens, and consulting, among other businesses.[11]

Is diversification an effective growth strategy? Research studies have shown that, for the most part, related diversification is superior to unrelated diversification.[12] If an organization can develop and exploit the potential synergies in the resources, capabilities, and core competencies of its diversified operations, then it's likely to create a sustainable competitive advantage. However, doing that isn't easy, by any means. The ability to strategically manage diverse businesses and develop a sustainable competitive advantage—no matter how related the different industries might be—is crucial. Also, although performance results from unrelated diversification haven't fared as well according to certain research, the strategy probably can be valuable at times. Once again, it depends on how effectively the diverse operations are managed as a sustainable competitive advantage is sought.[13]

International

According to Figure 7.2 on p. 193, another growth strategy is international. An organization's corporate strategies might involve looking for ways to grow by taking advantage of the potential opportunities offered by global markets or by protecting the organization's core operations from global competitors.[14] The international strategies are so important that we're devoting the majority of Chapter 8 to discussing them. We need to point out, however, that it is possible for an organization to "go international" as it pursues growth using any of the other strategies. That is, if an organization chooses to vertically integrate, it could do so globally as well as domestically. If a related diversification strategy is being implemented, it could involve combining the operations of organizations in different countries as well as those in the home market.

Implementing the Growth Strategies

As we've just seen, organizations have specific corporate strategy alternatives they can use to pursue growth goals. As we've discussed in previous chapters, however, choosing a strategy is only part of the picture. That strategy must be implemented. For the growth strategies, implementation options include (1) mergers–acquisitions, (2) internal development, and (3) strategic partnering.

Mergers–Acquisitions

One way an organization can implement its growth strategies is to "purchase" what it needs. Such purchases are done through mergers and acquisitions, both of which describe situations in which an organization combines its operations with another's, but is done differently. A **merger** is a legal transaction in which two or more organizations combine operations through an exchange of stock and create a third entity. Mergers usually take place between organizations that are similar in size and are usually "friendly"—that is, a merger is usually acceptable to all the concerned parties. On the other hand, an **acquisition** is an outright purchase of an organization by another. The purchased organization is absorbed by the purchasing organization. Acquisitions usually are between organizations of unequal sizes and can be friendly or hostile. Friendly acquisitions are ones in which the combination is desired by the respective organizations. When an organization being acquired doesn't want to be acquired, it's often referred to as a **hostile takeover.** In fact, the target of a hostile takeover often will take steps to prevent the acquisition.

The popularity of mergers and acquisitions seems to go in cycles.[15] Keep in mind that a merger or acquisition could be used by an organization when implementing *any* of the growth strategies—concentration, vertical integration, horizontal integration, or diversification. The main feature of mergers–acquisitions as a way to implement growth strategies is that the organization is "buying" its expanded product lines, markets, activities, or operations. We want to look next at another alternative for implementing the growth strategies.

Internal Development

In **internal development,** an organization grows by creating and developing new business activities itself. In this approach, strategic decision makers believe they have the necessary resources, distinctive capabilities, and core competencies to do it themselves. Using internal development, strategic managers choose to acquire needed resources and develop crucial capabilities to meet desired growth goals rather than deal with the risks, aggravations, and challenges of combining two or more different organizations. This doesn't mean, though, that internal development doesn't face the same types of challenges.

When would mergers or acquisitions be preferable and when would internal development be preferable? The choice depends on: (1) the new industry's barriers to entry, (2) the relatedness of the new business to the existing one, (3) the speed and development costs associated with each approach, (4) the risks associated with each approach, and (5) the stage of the industry life cycle.[16] These factors are summarized in Table 7.1.

Although both merger–acquisition and internal development continue to be popular, organizations are using other approaches, which fall under the category of strategic partnering.

Strategic Partnering

Is it possible for an organization to exploit the benefits of combining operations with other organization(s) in order to pursue growth while also minimizing the challenges and risks of buying a business or developing one from the ground up? Welcome to the world of **strategic partnering,** in which two or more organizations establish a legitimate relationship (partnership) by combining their resources, distinctive capabilities, and core competencies for some business purpose. It's an umbrella term that covers a variety of situations from loose relationships among partnering organizations to formal legal arrangements. These cooperative arrangements can be used to implement any of the growth strategies. For instance, an organization may decide to strategically partner with one of its suppliers or distributors (vertical integration), or it might develop a strategic partnership with a competitor (horizontal integration) or with an organization in a related industry (related diversification). Rather than growing by acquisition or internal development, an organization's strategic decision makers choose to develop a strategic partnership. The three main types of strategic partnerships are: (1) joint ventures, (2) long-term contracts, and (3) strategic alliances.

In a **joint venture,** two or more separate organizations form a separate independent organization for strategic purposes. In this cooperative arrangement, the strategic partners typically own equal shares of the new joint venture. A joint venture is often used when the partners do not want to or cannot legally join together permanently. Instead, the partners

Table 7.1

Mergers–Acquisitions or Internal Development

Use Merger–Acquisition When:	Use Internal Development When:
• Maturity stage of industry life cycle • High barriers to entry • New industry not closely related to existing one • Unwilling to accept time frame and development costs of starting new business • Unwilling to accept risks of starting new business	• Embryonic or growth stage of industry life cycle • Low barriers to entry • New industry closely related to existing one • Willing to accept time frame and development costs of starting new business • Willing to accept risks of starting new business

create this separate entity to do whatever business activity they're joining together to do. These business activities range from product development to manufacturing or marketing a product. Also, a joint venture is a popular partnering method in international growth because it minimizes the financial and political–legal constraints that accompany mergers–acquisitions and internal development. For example, a long-running joint venture is the New United Motor Manufacturing Company (NUMMI) formed by General Motors and Toyota in 1984. (Check it out at [**www.nummi.com**].) This joint venture was created to help introduce a new automobile production system into the United States and is still in operation.[17] Another example is the strategic partnership between French hair care and cosmetics group L'Oreal SA and Swiss food group Nestlé SA to develop cosmetic nutritional supplements. The new company, called Laboratoires Inneov, is headquartered in France and makes products aimed at improving the quality of skin, hair, and nails by supplying nutrients essential to their care.[18] Finally, Clorox Company and Procter & Gamble entered a joint venture to develop products such as garbage bags and plastic wraps. Both companies provided employees and manufacturing equipment to the venture.[19]

Another type of strategic partnership is a **long-term contract,** a legal contract between organizations covering a specific business purpose. Long-term contracts typically have been used between an organization and its suppliers. They're often viewed as a variation of vertical integration without an organization having to buy the supplier or internally develop its own supply source. Instead, it locks a supplier into a long-term relationship in which both partners understand the importance of developing resources, capabilities, and core competencies for a sustainable competitive advantage. The organization benefits by having an assured supplier that meets its cost and quality expectations. The supplier benefits by having an assured outlet for its products. The partners in a long-term contract often find that it's in their best interests to share resources, capabilities, and core competencies so that both can capture potential benefits. Again, that's the attraction of the long-term contract as a strategic partnership. The partners recognize and accept that they must work together in order for both to profit.

The last type of strategic partnership we're going to discuss is the **strategic alliance,** in which two or more organizations share resources, capabilities, or competencies to pursue some business purpose. You might be thinking that this sounds very similar to a joint venture. In the case of a strategic alliance, however, there's no separate entity formed. Instead, the partnering organizations simply share whatever they need to in order to do whatever

FOR YOUR INFORMATION

Why Alliances Make Sense

Companies worldwide are finding ways to build bridges to each other. Although these resulting alliances may not always work, they often make more sense than acquisitions. Here are some reasons why alliances make sense: flexibility and informality of arrangements promote efficiencies; provide access to new markets and technologies; entail less paperwork when creating and disbanding projects; risks and expenses are shared by multiple parties; independent brand identification is kept and can be exploited; working with partners possessing multiple skills can create major synergies; rivals can often work together harmoniously; alliances can take on varied forms from simple to complex; dozens of participants can be accommodated in alliance arrangements; and antitrust laws can protect R&D activities. Do alliances make strategic sense? One expert says, "The future of business is that fewer companies will succeed by going it alone." What do you think?

Sources: *Based on D. Durfee, "Try Before You Buy," CFO, May 2006, pp. 48–54; B. McEvily and A. Marcus, "Embedded Ties and the Acquisition of Competitive Capabilities," Strategic Management Journal, November 2005, pp. 1033–1055; R. D. Ireland, M. A. Hitt, and D. Vaidyanath, "Alliance Management as a Source of Competitive Advantage," Journal of Management, 2002, Vol. 28, No. 3, pp. 413–446; E. Krell, "The Alliance Advantage," Business Finance, July 2002, pp. 16–23; D. Sparks, "Partners," BusinessWeek, October 25, 1999, pp. 106–112; and D. Brady, "When Is Cozy Too Cozy?" BusinessWeek, October 25, 1999, pp. 127–130.*

Not all alliances work out. When Amazon.com and Toys "R" Us (TRU) signed an agreement in 2000, it seemed like a dream alliance. The agreement—which said for 10 years, Amazon would devote part of its Web site to baby and toy products of TRU—was "widely heralded as an example of how young Internet companies like Amazon would soon be tying up with 'bricks and mortar' retailers to mutual benefit." After about a year, however, the "dream" alliance turned ugly. The disagreement eventually ended up in court with each party claiming it had been deceived by the other. TRU believed that "Amazon violated its promise that it would be the sole seller of toys, games, and baby products on Amazon's Web site. Amazon claimed that TRU failed to deliver on its promise to maintain a certain selection of toys." This toy story ended with a judge ruling against Amazon, stating that "Amazon had breached the agreement and damaged its partner's unique position and ability to plan or craft strategies."

Sources: Based on M. S. Ouchi, "Toy Story Winds Up Leaving Amazon Grim," Seattle Times Online, March 3, 2006; Bloomberg News, "Toys 'R' Us Wins Suit Against Amazon," Boston Globe Online, March 3, 2006; and M. Mangalindan, "Game Over," Wall Street Journal, January 23, 2006, pp. A1+.

they want to do. Most often, strategic alliances are pursued in order to encourage product innovation, bring stability to cyclical businesses, expand product line offerings, or to cement relationships with suppliers, distributors, or competitors. For example, Yahoo and eBay joined together in an alliance to boost each other's strengths in online advertising, payments, and communications.[20] PepsiCo and Lipton joined together to sell canned iced tea beverages. PepsiCo brought its marketing strengths in canned beverages and Lipton brought its recognized tea brand and customer base. Although each organization could have attempted this on its own, the hurdles to developing a sustainable competitive advantage would have been much higher. By combining their strengths, the two partners have dominated this product line. Another example of a strategic alliance would be the arrangement between industrial giants Honda Motor and GE. The two teamed up to produce an engine to power a new generation of smaller, lower-cost business jets.[21] As you can see, each partner in a strategic alliance can reap the benefits of growth by contributing to the alliance its unique resources, capabilities, or core competencies.

Strategic partnering arrangements are growing in popularity.[22] Keep in mind that the intent of all strategic partnerships is to gain the benefits of growth while minimizing the drawbacks of buying or internally developing. Strategic partnerships should be approached with the same careful preparation and diligence as an acquisition–merger or an internally developed business. There's no guarantee that the hoped-for strategic benefits will be achieved using these arrangements. Trust among all strategic partners is a critical component to making these arrangements successful.[23]

Learning Review: Learning Outcome 7.2

- Define growth strategy.
- Describe the various corporate growth strategies
- Discuss how the corporate growth strategies can be implemented.

LEARNING OUTCOME 7.3
Describe the Organizational Stability Strategy

Although it may seem odd that an organization might want to stay as it is, there are times when its resources, distinctive capabilities, and core competencies are stretched to their limits and growing might risk the organization's competitive advantage. It's times like these when strategic managers may decide it's best for the organization to stay as is. The **stability strategy** is one in which an organization maintains its current size and current activities.

When Is Stability an Appropriate Strategic Choice?

There are times when strategic managers might decide that the stability strategy is most appropriate. One might be when an industry is in a period of rapid upheaval with several key industry and general external forces drastically changing, making the future highly uncertain. At times like this, strategic managers might decide that the prudent course of action is to sit tight and wait to see what happens. This doesn't mean that organizational resources and capabilities are allowed to deteriorate. Quite the contrary! In order to stabilize and maintain the organization's current position, it's important to maintain investments in the various businesses or functions. The stability strategy doesn't mean slipping backward, but it also doesn't mean moving ahead. It's simply stabilizing at the current level of operations.

Another time when strategic managers might pursue the stability strategy is if an industry is facing slow or no growth opportunities. In this instance, strategic managers might decide to keep the organization operating at current levels before making any strategic moves into new industries. This period of stability allows them time to analyze their strategic options—diversification, vertical integration, or horizontal integration—to address the disadvantages of being in a low- or no-growth industry. Given the current economic conditions in the United States and around the globe, many companies have decided to pursue stability until conditions improve.

An organization's strategic managers also might choose a stability strategy if it has been growing rapidly and needs some "down" time in order to build up its resources and capabilities again. For instance, Staples Inc., the office-supply retailer, believed it was important to open as many stores as possible and proceeded to open 1,500 stores in the United States over a fifteen-year period. However, it pulled back on store expansion plans in order to better manage activities and operations at the current level. Once managers felt they had made current stores as competitive as possible, they started adding stores once again.

Stability also might be an appropriate strategy for large firms in an industry that's in the maturity stage of the industry life cycle. In this situation, if profits and other performance results are satisfactory *and* if strategic decision makers are relatively risk averse, they may choose to "stay as they are" rather than pursuing growth.

Finally, although most strategic managers in large organizations prefer pursuing growth (and often are rewarded for doing so), many small business owners may follow a stability strategy indefinitely. Why? Because they may feel that their business is successful enough just as it is and that it adequately meets their personal goals.

Although there may be other times when a stability strategy is appropriate, these are the most common examples. Keep in mind that the stability strategy is typically a short-run strategy. Because industry and competitive conditions continue to change while an organization stays as is, it's important for strategic managers to strengthen the organization's resources, capabilities, and core competencies, so it doesn't lose its competitive position or competitive advantage.

Implementing the Stability Strategy

There's not much to implementing the stability strategy. Primarily, it involves *not* growing, but also *not* allowing the organization to decline. In other words, during stability, the organization won't be doing such things as putting new products out on the market, developing new programs, or adding production capacity. This doesn't mean that organizational resources, capabilities, and core competencies don't change during periods of stability. In fact, organizations often use this time to assess operations and activities, and strengthen and reinforce those that need it. The stability period essentially gives the organization an opportunity to "take a breather" and prepare itself for pursuing growth.

Although stability can be an appropriate corporate strategy for an organization, it's important to remember that, for most organizations, it should be a short-run strategy. If an organization becomes too complacent, it's susceptible to losing its competitive position. And, if an organization finds during the period of stability that significant organizational weaknesses exist or that performance is declining, then it may be necessary to look at a different strategic direction altogether—organizational renewal, and that's the final corporate strategy we need to discuss.

Learning Review: Learning Outcome 7.3

- What is a stability strategy?
- Why might an organization choose a stability strategy?
- Describe how a stability strategy is implemented.

LEARNING OUTCOME 7.4
Describe Organizational Renewal Strategies

Business periodicals frequently report on organizations that aren't meeting their strategic objectives or whose performance is declining. It's obvious that strategic managers in these organizations have *not* done an effective job of managing strategically and have been *not* been able to develop or exploit a sustainable competitive advantage. The organization is in trouble and something needs to be done. It can't achieve financial success or, in the worst-case scenario, might not survive. Given these circumstances, the organization's situation can be described as declining and it's important for strategic managers to implement strategies that reverse the decline and put the organization back on a more appropriate path to successfully achieving its strategic goals. The strategies used to do this are called **renewal strategies.** In this section, we'll discuss two organizational renewal strategies—retrenchment and turnaround—and how these strategies are implemented. Before we get into a discussion of these specific strategies, we need to look at some possible causes and indicators of performance declines.

What Leads to Performance Declines?

We can say that, generally speaking, an organization's strategic managers don't deliberately make bad strategic decisions thus causing an organization's performance to decline. However, strategic decisions they do make or strategies they do implement may create conditions that keep the organization from developing or exploiting a sustainable competitive advantage. Without this competitive advantage, it's going to be difficult for an organization to meet its strategic goals and have desirable performance outcomes. What leads to this situation? Figure 7.5 shows the main causes of performance decline that researchers have identified.[24] As you can see, the primary cause of corporate decline is poor management as all other causes can be traced to it. If strategic managers are inept, incompetent, or incapable of strategically managing all aspects of the organization, then organizational performance is likely to suffer. Strategic decisions to overexpand or expand too rapidly indicate poor

Figure 7.5

Possible Causes of Corporate Decline

management judgment. In addition, if an organization has inadequate financial controls or if costs are out-of-control or too high to be competitive, then its strategic managers aren't doing their job. Likewise, there's no excuse for not anticipating new competitors or shifts in consumer demand. Although strategic managers don't have all the answers, they should—as we discussed in Chapter 3—systematically scan and evaluate the external environment for significant trends. There's simply no excuse for strategic managers not to be aware of what's happening in their external environment. That's poor management! Finally, managers who are slow to respond or who never respond to significant changes in their external and internal situations are doing a poor job of managing strategically. Inertia can be a kiss of death in today's environment!

Can strategic managers tell when performance declines might be imminent? Some of the signs are listed in Table 7.2.[25] Again, if everyone in the organization is managing strategically and focused on developing and exploiting the organization's competitive advantage, then performance declines shouldn't happen. However, we know that doing a perfect job of managing strategically isn't likely or probably even realistic. Even the best-managed organizations sometimes find that performance results aren't what was expected and goals aren't being met. If an organization's overall performance is declining, then organizational renewal strategies may need to be implemented.

- Excess number of personnel
- Unnecessary and cumbersome administrative procedures
- Fear of conflict or taking risks
- Tolerating work incompetence at any level or in any area of the organization
- Lack of clear vision, mission, or goals
- Ineffective or poor communication within various units and between various units

Table 7.2

Signs of Declining Performance

Renewal Strategies

The two main renewal strategies are retrenchment and turnaround. Both are designed to halt declining performance and to return an organization to more desirable performance levels.

Retrenchment

The **retrenchment strategy** is a short-run renewal strategy designed to address organizational weaknesses that are leading to performance declines. In a retrenchment situation, an organization doesn't necessarily have negative financial returns. Although it may have had some time periods when revenues didn't cover expenses, this isn't the typical sign that an organization needs to retrench. Instead, the usual situation in retrenchment is that the organization hasn't been able to meet its strategic goals. Revenues and profits aren't negative but may be declining and the organization needs to do something to reverse the slide or it soon may face significant performance declines leading to severe financial problems.

Retrenchment is a military term that describes when a military unit "goes back to the trenches" in order to stabilize, revitalize, and prepare for entering battle again. That's pretty descriptive of what organizations must do, as well, in retrenching. Strategic managers must stabilize operations, replenish or revitalize organizational resources and capabilities, and prepare to compete once again. At a later point, we'll discuss how retrenchment strategies are implemented.

What happens if the organization's circumstances are more serious? What if the organization's profits aren't just declining, but instead there *aren't* any profits, only losses? And, what if other performance results are also significantly low or negative? Such a situation calls for a more drastic strategic response.

Turnaround

The **turnaround strategy** is a renewal strategy that's designed for situations in which the organization's performance problems are more serious. An organization has to be "turned around" or its very survival may be in jeopardy. Some well-known companies that have had to use a turnaround strategy include Sears, Delta Airlines, Kmart, Chrysler, General Motors, Ford Motor, Motorola, Mitsubishi, Cray, Intuit, and Apple, among many others. In each instance, the organization faced severe external and internal pressures and had to make strategic changes in order to remain a viable entity. There's no guarantee that a turnaround strategy will accomplish the desired results and make the organization a strong competitor once again, but without it, the organization is doomed to fail.

Implementing Renewal Strategies

Implementing the renewal strategies involves two actions: cutting costs and restructuring. A retrenchment strategy typically does not involve as extensive a use of these actions as a turnaround strategy does.

Cost Cutting

In Chapter 6 we discussed the concept of having low costs or even having the *lowest* costs in the industry as a source of competitive advantage. Cost cutting alone as a response to declining performance has little to do with developing a sustainable competitive advantage. Instead, the need to cut costs is approached as a way to bring an organization's performance results back in line with expectations. Strategic managers want to avoid severely cutting costs in those areas they feel are critical for the organization to retain or to exploit a competitive advantage, however weak that advantage may be. What strategic managers should try to do as they cut costs is revitalize the organization's performance (retrenchment) or save the organization (turnaround).

Cost cutting can be across-the-board (implemented in all areas of the organization) or selective (implemented in selected areas). Obviously, in a turnaround strategy, the cuts need to be more extensive and comprehensive.

How do organizations try to cut costs? Strategic decision makers evaluate whether there are any redundancies, inefficiencies, or waste in work activities (i.e., in the organization's capabilities) that could be eliminated. They'll also evaluate whether there are resources that could be eliminated or used more efficiently. For example, UPS found that it could cut costs by over $200,000 annually by changing the light bulbs in the "Exit" signs in its buildings to a lower wattage. Although that might not seem like a significant amount to an organization whose revenues are in the billions of dollars, keep in mind that this is just one small cost cut with savings that could be redirected to other resources or capabilities that UPS needs for a sustainable competitive advantage, or savings that could be applied directly to the bottom line. Either way, the company comes out ahead!

Generally, if additional cuts are needed to keep performance from declining further, strategic managers may have to look at reducing or eliminating certain work activities or even entire departments, units, or divisions. We'll discuss the more severe cost cutting when we get into the restructuring section and look at downsizing as an implementation option.

Restructuring

Other strategic actions an organization might take as it implements a retrenchment or turnaround strategy involve restructuring its operations. There are a number of ways that an organization can restructure. In many instances, it includes refocusing on the organization's primary business(es) as it sells off, spins off, liquidates, or downsizes. In fact, research has shown organizational refocusing to be the most beneficial form of restructuring an organization can do.[26] Let's look at the various ways an organization can restructure and refocus itself.

One possible strategic action an organization might take is to sell off one or more of its business units. Frequently, when an organization finds that a business unit isn't performing up to expectations or doesn't fit in with the organization's long-run direction, strategic managers will choose to sell it. The process of selling a business to another organization where it will continue as an ongoing business is called **divestment.** To whom might an organization sell a business unit? Possible buyers include independent investors, other companies, or the management of the business unit being divested. Remember our earlier discussion of ways to implement corporate growth strategies that one way for organizations to grow is through acquisition. Those acquisitions have to come from somewhere. When one company is acquiring, that means another company has to be selling.

Another possibility for restructuring is to remove a business unit through a **spin-off,** which typically involves setting up a business unit as a separate, independent business by distributing its shares of stock. We saw this in our chapter-opening case when Altria completed the spin-off of Kraft Foods.

What happens if there's no buyer for a business unit or if there's no possibility of spinning off the business unit? The only strategic option at that point might be **liquidation,** which is shutting down a business completely. A business unit that's liquidated will not continue as an ongoing business. There may be ways to sell the business's assets but that's the only revenue an organization could see from liquidating a business unit. As you can well imagine, liquidation is often a strategic action of last resort, but it may be the only option if a turnaround strategy hasn't worked.

Part of an organization's cost-cutting or restructuring efforts might involve **downsizing,** which is an organizational restructuring in which individuals are laid off from their jobs. Although downsizing can be a quick way to cut costs, simply cutting the number of employees without some type of strategic analysis of where employee cuts might be most beneficial is dangerous.[27] For the organization to be competitive when it eventually

After 20-plus years of acquisitions, Todd Stitzer, CEO of Cadbury Schweppes, the U.K.–based company, was about to make his biggest deal yet—splitting up the company. The maker of popular consumer products including Dr Pepper, 7Up, Snapple, YooHoo, Bubbalicious, Chiclets, Trident, Sour Patch Kids, and, of course, Cadbury chocolates, was splitting off its American beverage unit from its candy businesses. The strategic move had long been pushed by company shareholders who felt that separating the businesses would

"help the company focus on improving and expanding its confectionary unit, which analysts consider to be the core of the company." Even Cadbury's chairman said, "Now is the moment to separate and give both management teams the opportunity to extract the full potential of the business."

Sources: Based on J. Werdigier, "Cadbury to Separate Drinks and Candy Businesses," New York Times Online, March 16, 2007; and D. Ball and B. McKay, "In Breakup, CEO of Cadbury Faces His Biggest Deal," Wall Street Journal, March 16, 2007, pp. A1+.

emerges from retrenchment or turnaround—if and when that happens—it's important that downsizing be done for the right reasons. In fact, research has shown that downsizing efforts can improve stockholder wealth when they're done for strategic purposes.[28] How can strategic managers make downsizing effective? Table 7.3 lists some recommendations.

The final option for restructuring the organization is one of last resort. **Bankruptcy** is the failure of a business, a process in which it's dissolved or reorganized under the protection of bankruptcy legislation. It's often the outcome of years of significant performance declines after other restructuring or cost-cutting actions have had little effect or have not been implemented effectively. What happens when an organization "goes bankrupt?"

The act of going bankrupt by a business dramatically changed with the Bankruptcy Reform Act of 1979.[29] This legislation encouraged firms to reorganize (Chapter 11 bankruptcy) rather than liquidate their assets (Chapter 7 bankruptcy). Thus, the aftermath of bankruptcy depends on which type of bankruptcy filing is used. An organization in Chapter 7 bankruptcy will have its assets liquidated by the court with the proceeds used to pay off as many outstanding debts as possible. An organization in Chapter 11 bankruptcy reorganizes its debts and is protected from creditors collecting on debts until such time as it can emerge from bankruptcy. Although bankruptcy may not be a preferred strategic action, when an organization's turnaround strategy hasn't been effective, it may be the *only* option open to the organization.

We need to clarify a couple of things regarding the alternatives for implementing organizational renewal strategies. One is that these strategic actions typically aren't used only one at a time or by themselves. Instead, it's often necessary to use a combination of these alternatives as an organization struggles to regain or develop a sustainable competitive advantage. In fact, most organizations faced with the need to retrench or to do serious restructuring (needed for a turnaround) will look at a coordinated long-run program of strategic actions. Another is that while we discuss restructuring and cost-cutting actions in

Table 7.3 *Making Downsizing Effective*	• Communicate openly and honestly about needed actions • Clarify goals and expectations before, during, and after downsizing • Eliminate unnecessary work *activities* rather than making across-the-board cuts in *people* • Outsource work if it can be done more inexpensively and more effectively elsewhere • Provide whatever assistance is appropriate to downsized individuals • Counsel, communicate with, and seek input from those employees not downsized • Ensure that those individuals remaining after downsizing know they are a valuable and much-needed organizational resource

relation to retrenchment and turnaround strategies, the fact is that organizations don't have to be pursuing *only* these strategies to implement these actions. Strategic managers may use selected cost-cutting or restructuring actions (such as divesting selected business units) even during periods of organizational growth if these strategic actions are viewed as contributing to the organization's development or exploitation of a competitive advantage. That's the important key—is the organization's competitive advantage(s) enhanced and strengthened by these actions?

Learning Review: Learning Outcome 7.4

- Discuss the causes of corporate decline.
- Describe the two organizational renewal strategies.
- What two strategic actions are used in implementing the renewal strategies?
- Describe organizational restructuring actions.
- Why are most organizational renewal strategies used in combination?

LEARNING OUTCOME 7.5
Discuss How Corporate Strategy Is Evaluated and Changed

An organization's corporate strategy has been implemented. The competitive strategy and various functional strategies are aligned with the overall direction that strategic managers have chosen for the organization and are being implemented. How do you know it's all working as it should? How do you know whether the corporate strategy has been successful? How could the corporate strategy be evaluated? That's what we need to discuss in this section.

Evaluating Corporate Strategies

Evaluation is an important part of the entire strategic management process. Without evaluation, strategic managers wouldn't have a clue as to whether the implemented strategies—at any level of the organization—were working. We've discussed the specifics of evaluating the functional and competitive strategies in earlier chapters. Now we need to look at how the corporate strategy is evaluated. It shouldn't come as a surprise that the tools used in evaluating corporate strategy tend to be broad and encompass the overall performance of the organization rather than just focusing on narrow functional areas. We will look at four main evaluation techniques: (1) corporate goals; (2) efficiency, effectiveness, and productivity measures; (3) benchmarking; and (4) portfolio analysis.

Corporate Goals

The corporate goals indicate the desired end results or targets that strategic managers have established. Although each functional area and each business unit also have goals that are being pursued, corporate goals tend to be broader, more comprehensive, and longer-term than these others. However, remember that success in meeting the goals at the functional and competitive (business) levels determines whether corporate goals are met. In other words, attaining functional and competitive goals is how an organization achieves its corporate goals. If the functional and competitive goals aren't reached, an organization can't meet its corporate goals. Again, this simply reflects the interactions and interdependence among the various types or strategies.

Figure 7.6

Types of Corporate Goals

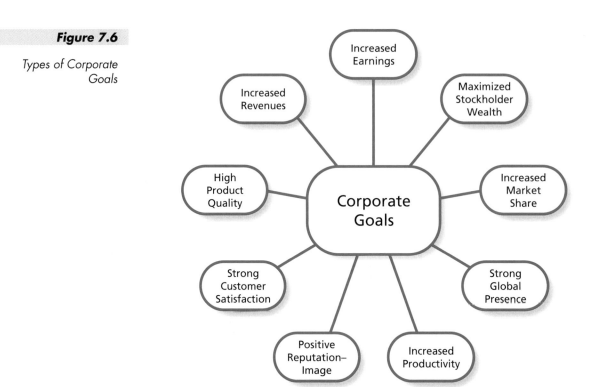

What types of corporate goals might an organization have? Figure 7.6 lists some of common ones. For a publicly held corporation, maximizing stockholder wealth is an important goal. Why? As the organization's legal owners, stockholders expect an appropriate return on their investment in exchange for providing capital. However, even not-for-profit, government, and privately held organizations need corporate goals to guide decision making. Remember that the goals should reflect the organization's vision, missions, and the overall direction it intends to go.

In evaluating corporate strategy, goals become the standards against which actual performance is measured. Say, for instance, that a corporate goal is to increase the organization's market share by 1 percent. Strategic managers would evaluate to see whether this happened. It's helpful for corporate goals to be quantified but that may not always be possible. Nonquantifiable areas shouldn't be ignored, however; sometimes a qualitative (subjective) assessment can be just as useful in evaluating corporate performance as can a quantitative one. Also, remember that not every organization is pursuing growth. Organizations using the stability strategy or renewal strategies will have goals that reflect those organizational directions. In these situations, the attainment of those goals should be evaluated.

Efficiency, Effectiveness, and Productivity Measures

Three specific organizational measures that can be used in evaluating an organization's corporate strategy are efficiency, effectiveness, and productivity. These measures represent its ability to use its limited resources strategically in achieving high levels of corporate performance.

Efficiency is an organization's ability to minimize resource use in achieving organizational goals. **Effectiveness** is an organization's ability to reach its goals. **Productivity** is a specific measure of how many inputs it took to produce outputs and is typically used in the production–operations area. It's measured by taking the overall output of goods and services produced, divided by the inputs used in generating that output.

The Grey Zone

Although these organizational measures may not be easy to calculate, strategic decision makers should attempt to gauge how efficient, effective, and productive the organization is. They should be concerned with getting activities completed so that goals are attained (effectiveness) efficiently and productively. Total organizational performance is a result of the interaction of a vast array of work activities at many different levels and in different areas of the organization; therefore, these three measures are appropriate assessments of how well the organization works *and* how well it's doing at moving in the desired corporate direction (growth, stability, or renewal).

Benchmarking

Benchmarking is the search for best practices inside or outside an organization. The actual process of benchmarking may be useful for implementing strategy, whereas the specific "benchmarks" or best practices can be a standard against which to measure corporate strategy performance. In Chapter 2 we observed that a world-class organization strives to be the best in the world at what it does. Using the benchmarks, strategic managers can evaluate whether the organization is being strategically managed as a world-class organization and where improvements are needed. Is overall organizational performance up to the standards of the best in the world? For example, Southwest Airlines studied Indy 500 pit crews, who can change a race car's tire in under 15 seconds, to see how their gate crews could make their gate turnaround times even faster. Why benchmark against Indy pit crews? Southwest felt they were the best in the world at incredibly fast turnaround and, as Southwest's strategic managers reasoned, you don't make money sitting on the ground. You've got to have quick ground turnaround time and get the planes back in the air flying passengers to the next location. The benchmark or best practice was a standard against which to measure one aspect of corporate performance.

Portfolio Analysis

The last approach to evaluating corporate performance we're going to discuss is portfolio analysis. What's in an organization's "portfolio"? The answer would be an organization's various business units. If it has only one business unit, then portfolio analysis would be useless because there's no evaluation or comparison of specific businesses. (We should mention that single-business organizations with multiple brands may use portfolio analysis to evaluate those brands but that's not our focus here.) However, if the organization has multiple business units—in the same or different industries—then portfolio analysis can be used to evaluate corporate performance.

Portfolio analysis is done with two-dimensional matrices that summarize internal and external factors. We're going to focus on three main portfolio analysis approaches: (1) the BCG matrix, (2) the McKinsey–GE stoplight matrix, and (3) the product–market evolution matrix.

The *BCG matrix* (also known as the growth-share matrix) was created by the Boston Consulting Group as a way to determine whether a business unit was a cash producer or a cash user. It's a simple, four-cell matrix. The *X* axis is a measure of a business unit's relative market share. In a very general sense, market share is a proxy for its internal strengths and weaknesses. Relative market share is defined as the ratio of a business unit's market share compared to the market share held by the largest rival in the industry. If the ratio is greater than 1.0, then the business unit is said to have high relative market share. If it's less than 1.0, then the business unit has low relative market share. (Note that only if a business unit is the market leader in its industry will it have a relative market share greater than 1.0.) Some analysts have concluded that this 1.0 figure is too restrictive and have recommended using lower figures such as 0.75 or even 0.50.

The *Y* axis is a measure of the industry growth rate. Likewise, in a very general sense, industry growth rate is a proxy for the external opportunities and threats facing the business unit. We want to know whether this industry is growing faster than the overall economy as a whole. If it is, then industry growth rate is evaluated as high. If it's not growing faster, the industry growth rate is low.

Each of the organization's business units would be assessed according to these guidelines and placed as a circle in the appropriate cell on the matrix. The size of the circle would correspond to the size of the business unit, using some measure such as business unit proportion of total corporate revenues. Thus, the matrix will show the relative size of the organization's various business units—that is, some are bigger and some are smaller. A business unit's placement on the matrix provides strategic decision makers with information to determine appropriate strategic actions to take.

A business unit with low relative market share and low industry growth rate is classified as a *dog*. According to the BCG analysis, a dog offers few growth prospects and, in fact, may require significant investments of cash just to maintain its position. The strategic recommendation for a business unit evaluated as a dog often is to exit that industry by either divesting or liquidating. However, a strategy of harvesting—that is, gradually letting the business unit decline in a controlled and calculated fashion and using any excess cash flows to support other, more desirable business units—may be an option *if* the business unit is profitable. A business unit with low relative market share and high industry growth rate is classified as a *question mark*. The question marks are low in competitive strengths but they're in an industry where there's a lot of potential. The recommendation for a business unit evaluated as a question mark is that those with the weakest or most uncertain long-term potential should be divested. Why? Meeting the cash needs of too many business units may spread organizational resources too thin and result in none being able to achieve star status. Question marks are easy to sell, however, because of the attractiveness of the industries. Those question marks with more potential should be infused with cash to attempt to turn them into market leaders. A business unit with high relative market share and high industry growth rate is classified as a *star*. Stars are the leading business units in an organization's portfolio. Depending on how competitive the industry is, stars may take significant cash resources to maintain their market leadership position or they may take little cash if they're in an industry where competitive rivalry isn't high. The recommendation for a business unit evaluated as a star is to maintain its strong position while taking advantage of the significant growth opportunities in the industry. Finally, a business unit with high relative market share but low industry growth rate is a *cash cow*. Cash cows are strong cash providers. The positive cash flows from cash cows should be used to support those question marks with potential and to support the stars.

Although the BCG matrix is relatively simple to use, its simplicity is both its biggest advantage and its biggest drawback. The reliance on relative market share and industry growth rate to evaluate a business unit's performance and future potential is an extremely limited view. The fact that the BCG matrix is easy to use and understand is the main reason for its continued popularity as a portfolio assessment tool.

The *McKinsey–GE Stoplight Matrix* was developed by McKinsey and Company for GE. This nine-cell matrix (shown in Figure 7.7) provides a more comprehensive analysis of a business unit's internal and external factors. In this matrix, the X axis is defined as business strength–competitive position. What's included in this analysis? It's more than just relative market share! It includes an analysis of the internal resources and capabilities that are believed by strategic managers to be important for success in this business. For instance, it might include an analysis of economies of scale, manufacturing flexibility, workforce morale, product quality, company image, and so forth—whatever strategic managers think the business needs to be good at in order to be competitive. The evaluation scale used in this analysis typically ranges from 1 (very weak) to 5 (very strong). The Y axis is defined as industry attractiveness, which again provides a much broader analysis than the BCG's

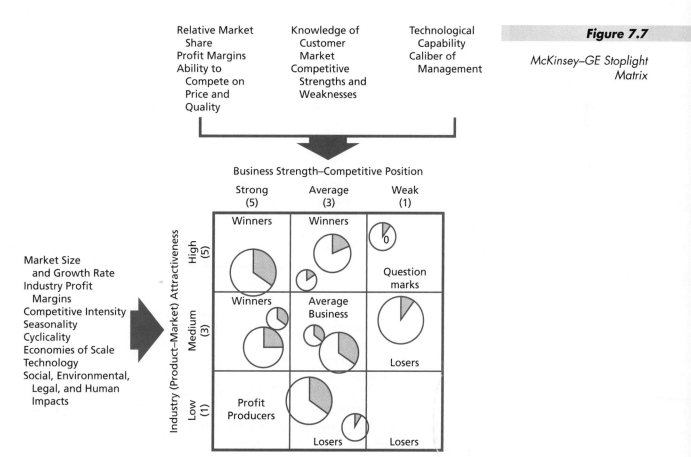

Figure 7.7

McKinsey–GE Stoplight Matrix

industry growth rate. Industry attractiveness might include such factors as average industry profitability, number of competitors, ethical standards, technological stability of the market, market growth rate, and so forth. Again, strategic managers would use a measurement scale from 1 (very unattractive) to 5 (very attractive) to evaluate the industry a business unit is in. An organization's business units would be plotted on the matrix using these two measures.

As with the BCG matrix, the number of circles on the McKinsey matrix corresponds to the number of business units. In this instance, however, the size of the circle corresponds to the relative size of the industry and the shaded wedge corresponds to the market share held by the organization's business unit. With this matrix, we have a little more information to judge a business unit's position. How should strategic managers evaluate the placement of the business units on the matrix?

The three cells in the lower right-hand corner of the matrix are evaluated as *losers*. These business units have weak competitive position–low industry attractiveness; weak competitive position–medium industry attractiveness; and average competitive position–low industry attractiveness. In the original GE stoplight matrix, these cells were colored red, indicating "stop investing in these business units." The three cells in the upper left-hand corner of the matrix are described as *winners*. These business units are evaluated as strong competitive position–high industry attractiveness; strong competitive position–medium industry attractiveness; and average competitive position–high industry attractiveness. As you can probably guess, these cells were colored green, indicating "go ahead, invest in, and grow these business units." Finally, the three cells along the diagonal in the matrix are evaluated as question marks (weak competitive position–high industry attractiveness), average businesses (average competitive position–medium industry attractiveness), and profit producers (strong competitive position–low industry attractiveness). These cells were colored yellow, indicating caution in strategic decisions about these business units. Obviously, the profit producers would be milked for their cash flows with the cash going to support the winners and those question marks with potential to turn into winners.

Although the McKinsey matrix overcame the problem of simplistic analysis that plagued the BCG matrix, its main drawback is the subjectivity of the analysis. Because the factors used to measure competitive position and industry attractiveness were created by an organization's decision makers (and because these individuals then rated business units on these factors), there was a risk that the analysis might be too subjective. Another drawback (also shared by the BCG matrix) is that the performance analysis is static. It's similar to what accountants often say about an organization's balance sheet—that it's a snapshot of the performance of business units at one point in time. Unless a series of "snapshots" are taken, strategic managers would have no way to interpret whether a business unit's performance is improving or declining. So even though the McKinsey matrix was an improvement over the BCG matrix, it still had its shortcomings.

The *product–market evolution matrix* was developed by C. W. Hofer and is based on the product life cycle, which serves as the *Y* axis. The six stages in the product life cycle include Development, Growth, Competitive Shakeout, Maturity, Saturation, and Decline. The *X* axis (internal analysis of the business unit) is the same analysis of competitive position as used in the McKinsey matrix.

Also like the McKinsey matrix, the size of the circles corresponds to the relative size of the industry, and the shaded wedge corresponds to the market share of that business unit. Business units are placed on the matrix according to their individual evaluation on competitive position and stage in the product life cycle. Once all business units are plotted on the matrix, strategic managers have an indicator of the range of business units in various stages of the product life cycle. Say, for instance, that most of the organization's business units were positioned in the maturity or even decline stages. The strategic managers here should be looking at ways to balance the organization's portfolio with some business units in earlier stages of the life cycle in order to provide long-run potential.

Although Hofer's product–market evolution matrix attempts to provide some semblance of the dynamic nature of an organization's business units by using the product life cycle, it still suffers from the same subjectivity biases that the McKinsey matrix does. In addition, there are many products that don't fit nicely and neatly into the industry life cycle, so this particular evaluation tool also has drawbacks that limit its usefulness.

As an evaluation tool, the portfolio matrices do provide a way to assess the performance of the organization's various business units. With this evaluation, an organization's strategic decision makers have information for deciding what to do with the various business units: Should they be supported and strengthened? Should they be sold? Do we need to start looking for businesses to acquire? Because every portfolio analysis technique suffers from drawbacks, each should be used with caution or at least in conjunction with other strategy evaluation measures.

What happens after evaluating the corporate strategy? If the evaluation indicates that performance results aren't as strategic managers had hoped, then strategic changes are in order.

Changing Corporate Strategies

If the evaluation of corporate strategies shows that they aren't having the intended results—growth objectives aren't being attained, organizational stability is causing the organization to fall behind, or organizational renewal efforts aren't working—then some changes are obviously needed. Then, strategic managers have to decide whether to act and what actions to take.

If it's determined that changes are needed, they might look at changing the functional and competitive strategies that have been implemented. Perhaps some modifications to those will be enough to bring about the desired results. On the other hand, strategic managers might decide that more drastic action is needed and the corporate direction itself should be changed. If so, changes might also be necessary in the way the corporate strategy is being implemented. For example, when Microsoft's strategic decision makers realized that the Internet had dramatically altered the world of computing, they did a complete about-face and changed the corporate direction with an all-out focus on this area. What did this corporate strategic change involve? Several actions: Microsoft acquired various Internet and Web startup companies, reshuffled administrative duties, redesigned software already under development, and basically did what it had to in order to build up its commitment to this new corporate direction.[30] Notice how, in this example, the corporate strategy change affected the organization's functional and competitive strategies, as well.

An organization's corporate strategy is important to establishing the overall direction the organization wants to go. As the chapter-opening case illustrated, strategic managers have to understand both the opportunities–threats and the strengths–weaknesses facing the organization in order to design appropriate strategies—ones that will develop or exploit the resources, distinctive capabilities, and core competencies the organization has in its various business units in order to realize a sustainable competitive advantage. Each level of the organization's strategies is linked through this all-encompassing effort to develop a sustainable competitive strategy. Each plays a different, but important, role in this process.

Learning Review: Learning Outcome 7.5

- Why is it important to evaluate corporate strategies?
- What are the four ways to evaluate corporate strategies?
- Describe each of the portfolio analysis matrices including how it's used, the cells in the matrix, and its advantages and drawbacks.
- Why might an organization's corporate strategy need to be changed?
- How might an organization's corporate strategy be changed?

the bottom line

Learning Outcome 7.1: Explain what corporate strategy is.

- *Corporate strategy* is a strategy that's concerned with the choices of what business(es) to be in and what to do with those businesses. One thing we need to know is whether the organization is a *single-business organization* (in primarily one industry) or a *multiple-business organization* (in more than one industry).
- The corporate strategy establishes the overall direction the organization hopes to go while the other organizational strategies (functional and competitive) provide the means for getting there. Each type of strategy is important to whether the organization does what it's in business to do and whether it achieves its goals.
- The three corporate strategic directions include moving an organization forward (growth strategy), keeping an organization where it is (stability strategy), and reversing an organization's decline (renewal strategy).

Learning Outcome 7.2: Discuss organizational growth strategies.

- A *growth strategy* is one that expands the products offered or markets served by an organization or expands its activities or operations either through current business(es) or through new business(es). There are five different ways for an organization to grow.
- *Concentration* is a growth strategy in which an organization concentrates on its primary line of business and looks for ways to meet its growth goals by expanding its core business. Three concentration options include: (1) product–market exploitation, which is selling more current products to current markets; (2) product development, which is selling new products to current markets; and (3) market development, which is selling current products to new markets. The advantage of concentration is that this is the organization's primary business and it knows it well. The main drawback is the vulnerability to industry and other external changes.
- The *vertical integration strategy* is one in which an organization grows by gaining control of its inputs (backward), its outputs (forward), or both. The benefits of vertical integration seem to slightly outweigh the costs.
- *Horizontal integration* is a strategy in which an organization grows by combining operations with competitors. It can be a good growth strategy as long as it enables the company to meet its growth goals, it can be strategically managed, and it satisfies legal and regulatory guidelines.
- The *diversification strategy* is a strategy in which an organization grows by moving into a different industry. *Related (concentric) diversification* is diversifying into a different industry that's related in some way to the organization's current business. *Unrelated (conglomerate) diversification* is diversifying into a completely different industry not related to the organization's current business.
- The final type of growth strategy is international in which an organization grows by taking advantage of potential opportunities in global markets or protecting its core operations from global competitors.
- The growth strategies can be implemented in three ways: (1) *merger* (legal transaction in which two or more organizations combine operations through an exchange of stock and create a third entity) or *acquisition* (outright purchase of an organization by another; if the organization being acquired doesn't want to be acquired, it's referred to as a *hostile takeover*); (2) *internal development* (organization grows by creating and developing new business activities itself); and (3) *strategic partnering* (two or more organizations establish a legitimate relationship [partnership] by combining their resources, distinctive capabilities, and core competencies for some business purpose). Types of strategic partnerships include: *joint venture* (two or more organizations form a separate independent organization for business purposes), *long-term contract* (a legal contract between organizations covering a specific business purpose), or *strategic*

alliance (two or more organizations share resources, capabilities, or competencies to pursue some business purpose but no separate entity is formed).

Learning Outcome 7.3: Describe the organizational stability strategy.

- A *stability strategy* is one in which an organization maintains its current size and activities. In most instances, it should be a short-run strategy.
- Times when the stability strategy is appropriate include: industry is in period of rapid change, industry is facing slow or no growth opportunities, organization has just experienced rapid growth, organization is large and in an industry that's in the maturity stage of industry life cycle, or organization is a small business whose owners are satisfied with staying as is.
- Stability strategy is implemented by not growing but also by not allowing organization to decline.

Learning Outcome 7.4: Describe organizational renewal strategies.

- *Renewal strategies* are used when an organization's situation is declining and strategic managers want to reverse the decline and put the organization back on a more appropriate path to achieving its goals.
- The main cause of performance declines can be traced to poor management although factors such as inadequate financial controls, uncontrollable or too high costs, new competitors, unpredicted shifts in consumer demand, slow or no response to significant external or internal changes, and overexpansion or too rapid growth also contribute.
- There are two main renewal strategies: (1) *retrenchment* (a short-run strategy designed to address organizational weaknesses that are leading to performance declines) and (2) *turnaround* (a strategy that's designed for situations in which organization's performance problems are more serious).
- These renewal strategies are implemented by cutting costs and restructuring. The amount and extent of these are determined by whether it's a retrenchment or turnaround.
- Restructuring actions include: (1) *divestment* (selling a business to another organization where it will continue as an ongoing business), (2) *spin-off* (setting up a business unit as a separate business by distributing its shares of stock), (3) *liquidation* (shutting down a business completely), (4) *downsizing* (individuals are laid off from their jobs), and (5) *bankruptcy* (failure of a business in which it's dissolved or reorganized under the protection of bankruptcy legislation).

Learning Outcome 7.5: Discuss how corporate strategy is evaluated and changed.

- There are four main techniques for evaluating corporate strategy: (1) corporate goals (were organization's goals achieved); (2) measuring *efficiency* (organization's ability to minimize resource use in achieving goals), *effectiveness* (organization's ability to reach its goals), and *productivity* (specific measure of how many inputs it took to produce outputs); (3) *benchmarking* (search for best practices inside or outside an organization); and (4) portfolio analysis, which is used to assess an organization's portfolio of businesses.
- Three main portfolio analysis techniques include the BCG matrix, the McKinsey–GE stoplight matrix, and the product–market evolution matrix.
- If the evaluation of corporate strategy shows it's not working, strategic managers might first change the functional and competitive strategies or they might take more drastic action and change the corporate direction.

YOU
as
strategic
decision
maker:
building
your
skills

1. Do some research on mergers and acquisitions. What were the five largest mergers–acquisitions last year? Make a list of the partners in each. What reasons were given for the merger–acquisition? Do you think these mergers–acquisitions made strategic sense? Explain.

2. Using the Internet (company's Web site, Hoover's, or other Web sites), research each of the companies listed below and answer the following questions:

   a. What corporate strategy(ies) does the company appear to be following? Explain your choice.

   b. Evaluate the company's performance using financial and other measures you choose.

   c. What changes might you recommend in the company's strategic direction? Explain why you did or did not recommend changes.

   Companies

   Cemex [**www.cemex.com**]

   United Technologies [**www.utc.com**]

   Google [**www.google.com**]

   Unilever [**www.unilever.com**]

   Toshiba [**www.toshiba.com**]

   Smith Corona [**www.smithcorona.com**]

3. A company growing at an annual rate of 35 percent will double in size in just two years. A company growing at an 18 percent rate will double in size in four years. A company growing by 12 percent will double in size in six years. Persistent long-term growth is most achievable in moderate rates. Do you agree? Why or why not? What are the challenges of rapid growth?

4. Find examples in current business publications (*Wall Street Journal, BusinessWeek, Fortune,* etc.) of each of the types of corporate strategy (i.e., each of the types of growth strategies, stability strategy, and each of the types of renewal strategies). Describe your examples. Be sure to provide your citation information.

5. "The acid test for any corporate strategy is that the company's businesses must not be worth more to another owner." What do you think this statement means? Do you agree with this statement? Explain.

6. Can corporate growth have a downside? Explain. How might drawbacks be addressed?

7. Research into corporate "bloopers" by Professor Sidney Finkelstein pinpointed some reasons why smart executives made bad decisions.[31] Some of these reasons included: CEO identifies too closely with his or her company; CEO is too distracted by involvement in personal and social causes; CEO and executive team are so overconfident and aggressive that it's hard to trust them; CEO believes all problems are public relations-related and can be handled by putting a "good spin on it"; and CEO missed clear market signals. Find three examples of bad decisions made by executives. Do any of your examples fit under the reasons listed above? What could other organizations learn from these mistakes? What are the implications for an organization's corporate strategy?

8. Companies often grow by doing one or more of the following: boosting capital spending on new technologies, launching new products, entering new markets, increasing marketing, and bolstering R&D.[32] Find an example of each of these. Describe what the company did. Were any strategic goals listed? If so, what was the goal? How might strategic decision makers evaluate the effectiveness of their company's growth strategy?

CASE #1: Changing the Menu

This Strategic Management in Action case can be found at the beginning of Chapter 7.

Discussion Questions

1. What examples of corporate strategies do you see in this situation? Explain.

2. What strategic challenges must CEO Rosenfeld deal with?

3. When an organization frequently changes its strategic direction, what problems can arise? (Think in terms of its functional and competitive strategies.)

4. What do you think of Rosenfeld's strategic initiatives?

5. What corporate strategy evaluation measures might you suggest that the company use? Explain your choices.

6. Update the information on Kraft Foods: revenues, profits, and strategic initiatives.

CASE #2: Time for Bread

From the heartland of America comes bread baked with heart. As a leader in the quick-casual dining business, St. Louis–based Panera Bread Company operates and franchises more than 1,200 bakery-cafés in some 40 states under the Panera Bread and St. Louis Bread Company brands. Its mission statement—A loaf of bread in every arm®—reflects the company's purpose and its passion.

Panera's beginnings can be traced to 1981 when CEO Ron Shaich cofounded Au Bon Pain Company, which operated bakery-cafés on the East Coast and internationally. Shaich and his management team were looking for a concept that combined Au Bon Pain's quality food with the potential for a broader appeal. In late 1993, Shaich met the owners of St. Louis Bread Company, which had 19 bake shops doing about $1 million in lunch business a year. St. Louis Bread had targeted suburban areas where real estate was less expensive, the competition was less intense, and the target customers lived. Shaich sensed an opportunity, seeing it as "our gateway into the suburban marketplace and backward into a manufacturing business." After studying the business inside and out, they decided to sell Au Bon Pain Company and purchase the St. Louis Bread Company. Their goal—turn the concept into a national brand under the Panera Bread name.

The management team at Panera (Latin for "time for bread") spent considerable time trying to figure out what this business should look like. They looked at restaurants, coffeehouses, and even retailers in an attempt to understand what it would take to be successful. One thing they discovered was that consumers were tired of the boring sameness of dining-out choices. Shaich said, "Customers are rejecting fast food. They want something better, something special." The new owners knew they would have to achieve that perception by paying careful attention to the details. They also used what they had learned in running Au Bon Pain—quality makes a real difference. In Panera's case, that means, among other things, making fresh dough every single day in 20 locations and trucking it to the cafés for baking.

During 2007, Panera opened 169 new stores, giving it over 1,200 stores total. Given the uncertain economic environment in 2009, the executive team now planned to pursue a more moderate rate of growth. Panera's locations, of which about 62 percent are owned by franchisees, sell custom sandwiches made with artisan breads, as well as soups and salads. Customers also can buy bread, bagels, pastries, and gourmet coffees to go. Panera has attracted customers and built significant loyalty by concentrating on the quality of their fresh-baked breads and other ingredients. Although the average customer check at a typical Panera store is $8.51, company executives recently implemented a "category management" strategy to redefine its menu structure and utilize store associates to change customer behavior. The goal was to increase gross profit per sales transaction. One important component of this strategy was a systemwide rollout of breakfast sandwiches that utilized many of the ingredients already in the stores and that were easy to make, meaning no increase in fixed labor costs.

Even in today's worrisome economy, the company appears to have tapped into a consumer phenomenon of affordable indulgences. Consumers want to "reward" themselves with small but good-quality products in a few categories that are important to them. Panera's premium sandwiches, bread, and pastries fit into this category. Maybe it really is Panera's "time for bread!"

Discussion Questions

1. What corporate, compelitive, and functional strategies is Panera using to realize its goal of turning the concept into a national brand under the Panera Bread name? Be as specific as possible.

2. How would you recommend Shaich and his management team evaluate whether the company is accomplishing its corporate strategy?

3. Panera Bread was on *BusinessWeek's* "hot growth companies" list for several years. What problems might arise if the company grows too fast? How might they know whether they were growing too fast?

4. The company depends heavily on franchising to fuel its growth. Do some research on franchising. What advantages and drawbacks might it present?

5. What other examples of affordable indulgences can you think of? What strategic risks are there to such a trend? How can Shaich ensure that Panera doesn't fall victim to those risks?

Sources: Based on M. R. della Cava, "Sweetening a Sour Economy," *USA Today*, February 24, 2009, pp. 1D+; "2008 Year in Review," *Nation's Restaurant News*, December 22, 2008, pp. 46–48; C. Walkup, "Bakery-café Chains Turn Up the Heat on Dinner, Catering," *Nation's Restaurant News*," September 29, 2008, pp. 4+; "Consumers' Choice in Chains: Sandwiches," *Restaurants & Institutions*, September 15, 2008, pp. 58+; P. Ziobro, "Panera Bakes Up Ways to Earn More Per Customer," *Wall Street Journal*, August 13, 2008, pp. B1+; and M. Arndt, "Giving Fast Food a Run for Its Money," *BusinessWeek*, April 17, 2006, pp. 62–64.

CASE #3: Speed Bump

What comes to mind when you think of NASCAR (National Association for Stock Car Auto Racing)? Fast cars, roaring engines, the smell of gasoline, beer-guzzling spectators? Those are images that Brian France, chairman and CEO, tried to change to appeal to new market segments by doing things such as adding late afternoon and night races, adding a foreign automaker (Toyota), and going after different demographics (upscale, Hispanics, and blacks). One of his major changes was trying to make the sport safer, especially after the death of driver Dale Earnhardt Sr. in 2001. However, by making the sport "safer" was it less appealing to the fans who watch races so they can experience vicariously in the stands or on television the speed, danger, and excitement of going really, really fast in a crowd of cars? Another major change (and the most criticized one) was the Car of Tomorrow program, which required race teams to use cars with identical specifications. "The program was meant to eliminate the ability of bigger, wealthier race teams to gain advantage by bankrolling separate cars

suited for different tracks." These changes didn't sit too well with race team owners who shoulder the biggest financial risks of investing in equipment and people. However, changing the image of NASCAR races and fans is the least of France's worries these days.

NASCAR was founded in 1948 by Brian's grandfather, Bill France Sr., as a place for ex–moonshine runners to show off their driving skills. During the early years, Bill tirelessly promoted the sport with the help of racetrack owners who wanted to make their stock car races official. The sport grew rapidly in the 1950s and 1960s. Racetrack owners responded by upgrading their facilities and building new paved tracks to replace the older dirt tracks. In 1971, NASCAR signed R. J. Reynolds Tobacco Company as a major sponsor and held the first Winston 500 race in Talladega, Alabama. The first televised race—the Daytona 500—aired on CBS in 1979. Cable sports network ESPN began airing races in 1981. The popularity of the sport "resulted in TV ratings second only to the National Football League, leading to a $4.4 billion TV contract with Disney's ABC and ESPN, Time Warner's TNT, and News Corporation's Fox and the Speed Channel" and which runs through 2014. Very little of this revenue is shared with race teams, and ticket sales revenues go mainly to the track owners. The untimely deaths of drivers Adam Petty and Dale Earnhardt Sr. served to heighten the appeal of the sport as exciting and dangerous. The company's top management team's goal was to "make the sport grow in a way that invigorated hard-core fans and made it attractive to people who might want to sample racing." But over the last couple of years, NASCAR hit a speed bump. Although it's still the second-most-watched sport after football, it's no longer the marketing phenomenon it used to be. Despite the company's prior broadcast successes, its regular-season TV ratings have fallen 21 percent since peaking in 2005, "a reversal from the prior five years, when they vastly outgrew all other professional sports in viewership." NASCAR is also suffering declines in attendance and sponsorships. "Attendance at 2008 races fell for a third straight year from 130,000 to 118,000." And race team sponsorships are drying up, maybe because of the economic climate, but also perhaps because of the sport's declining popularity. Other sponsors that are still committed to the sport have gravitated to winning teams. "The haves are pulling away from the have-nots." Team owners and managers say it's time for a major overhaul of the sport.

What many team owners want to see is a franchise system, similar to what is used in professional football and baseball. A fixed number of teams, maybe a dozen or so, would have three to four cars each. All drivers would automatically qualify for a race so that sponsors would know their brand would be represented at each race. However, the France family, which built NASCAR from a regional sport to a national marketing phenomenon, is opposed to such

a change. Its opposition stems from the belief that "A franchise system would likely create a system that values a franchise more than the need to perform each week at the racetrack. This, of course, runs counter to everything NASCAR is based upon." Others outside the France family say that the problem is that the France family doesn't don't want to give up control. However, with NASCAR's growth fading, Brian France and NASCAR are facing some tough choices.

Discussion Questions

1. What strategic challenges do you think Brian France faces as he guides his company? Using what you know about managing strategically, how might he respond to these challenges?

2. Look at the goal the top management team had for the company. What are the implications for corporate strategy? How about for the other organizational strategies (functional and competitive)?

3. The success of NASCAR depends on its ability to satisfy the race teams, the drivers, advertisers–sponsors, the drivers, and the customers. What are the implications for the company as it formulates appropriate strategies?

4. What corporate strategy evaluation tools might you recommend for NASCAR? Explain your choices.

Sources: Based on J. Gage, "Pileup," *Forbes*, March 2, 2009, pp. 82–86; S. Hamner, "NASCAR's Sponsors Hit by Sticker Shock," *New York Times Online*, December 14, 2008; R. Thomaselli, "Sponsor Exodus from Troubled NASCAR Nation," *Advertising Age*, December 8, 2008, pp. 1+; K. Linebaugh, "Toyota Finds NASCAR Fans Tough Crowd," *Wall Street Journal*, July 24, 2008, pp. B1+; J. Gage, "Pedal to the Metal," *Forbes*, June 30, 2008, pp. 146–151; M. Newsome, "NASCAR's Race Problem," *Condé Nast Portfolio*, February 2008, pp. 124+; S. Elliott, "Marketers Are Putting NASCAR on Different Kinds of Circuits," *New York Times Online*, February 15, 2008; and C. Isidore, "NASCAR Shifts into a Higher Gear," *CNNMoney.com*, December 1, 2006.

CASE #4: WaMu Who?

"We hope to do to this industry what Wal-Mart did to theirs, Starbucks did to theirs, Costco did to theirs, and Lowe's–Home Depot did to their industry. And I think if we've done our job, five years from now you're not going to call us a bank." Such was a statement made by Kerry Killinger, chief executive of Washington

Mutual in 2003. It was a prophetic statement but probably not in the way that Killinger intended.

Its customers called it WaMu for years and Washington Mutual, the Seattle-based financial services institution, finally embraced the nickname "as our brand name." One thing that WaMu always tried to do in its long history (it was founded in 1889) was to distinguish itself from its competitors. It did so by becoming one of the largest originators and servicers of residential mortgages in the United States. In 2003, WaMu came out with a slogan "The Power of Yes." It wasn't just an advertising pitch, however. It was how employees were expected to work. One former employee said, "WaMu came out with that slogan, and that was what we had to live by. We joked about it a lot. A [mortgage application file] would get marked problematic and then somehow get approved. We'd say: O.K.! The power of yes." Getting the job done meant lending money to just about anyone who asked for it. In San Diego, supervisors at a WaMu mortgage processing center saw "baby sitters claiming salaries worthy of college presidents and schoolteachers with incomes rivaling stockbrokers'." Nobody ever questioned it . . . WaMu was all about saying yes. However, it was that strategic decision that eventually led to WaMu's downfall.

Prior to the implosion, WaMu's vision was "to be the nation's leading retailer of financial services for consumers and small businesses." Its mission was "to build strong, profitable relationships with a broad spectrum of consumers and businesses, which it will do by delivering products and services that offer great value and friendly service and by adhering to our core values." Those core values included "being fair, caring, human, dynamic, and driven." As the largest thrift institution in the United States, WaMu once served more than 10 million customers. And serving those customers was always a high priority. As stated on its Web site, "We've always been about making things better for people—our customers, employees and neighbors." CEO Kerry Killinger positioned WaMu in key markets in California, Florida, Oregon, Texas, and Washington. In addition, he increased the company's presence in key cities including Atlanta, Chicago, Denver, Las Vegas, Phoenix, and Tampa. He wanted to reinvent how people thought about banking. His goal was to have WaMu thought of in the same category as Wal-Mart, Southwest Airlines, Best Buy, and Target. He said, "In every retailing industry, there are category killers who figure out how to have a very low cost structure and pass those advantages on to customers, day in and day out, with better pricing. I think we have a shot at doing that in this segment."

By 2006, WaMu already was facing challenges. In the company's Annual Report, Killinger described a difficult operating environment "characterized by rising short-term interest rates, a flat-to-inverted yield curve, declining credit spreads, and a weakening housing market, all of which had a negative impact on the year's results." The company didn't achieve the financial targets in its five-year strategic plan. Analysts say that some of WaMu's problems were "self-inflicted, such as picking poor locations amid the rush to open dozens of branches in new markets." In addition, WaMu's strategy of a "simpler, friendlier way of banking" was widely cloned. All the big retail banking rivals were also obsessively focused on taking care of customers. All of those factors in conjunction with the fact that it was opening branches at a pace "worthy of a fast-food chain" and lending money to practically anyone who asked for it eventually led to its collapse in September 2008, the biggest bank failure in American history. JP Morgan Chase & Company (Chase) stepped in quickly to "pick up the pieces . . . and promised to move quickly to clean up the wreckage of the thrift's troubled portfolio of mortgage loans."

Discussion Questions

1. What examples of corporate strategy do you see in this case? Explain.
2. How did WaMu's vision, mission, and core values affect its choice of corporate strategy? How about the effect on its competitive and functional strategies?
3. Why do you think WaMu's corporate strategy didn't work out as intended? What could it have done differently? How would a different corporate strategy have affected the company's other strategies?
4. Given WaMu's new strategic "life" as part of Chase, what strategy evaluation measures might be appropriate now? Explain.

Sources: Based on WaMu Web site [www.wamu.com/about], February 27, 2009; P. S. Goodman and G. Morgenson, "By Saying Yes, WaMu Built Empire on Shaky Loans," *New York Times Online*, December 28, 2008; R. Thurow, N. Casey, and J. Carlton, "With J. P. Morgan, Many WaMu Customers Relax," *Wall Street Journal*, September 27–28, 2008, p. B3; R. Sidel and D. Fitzpatrick, "J. P. Morgan Bets on the Consumer," *Wall Street Journal*, September 26, 2008, pp. B1+; D. DeSilver, "Feds Seize WaMu in Nation's Largest Bank Failure," *Seattle Times Online*, September 26, 2008; and J. R. Hagerty and A. Carrns, "WaMu Whiplash: Fast Expansion Yields Problems," *Wall Street Journal*, December 16–17, 2006, pp. B1+.

Endnotes

1. D. Lieberman, "Kraft Sees Benefits As Consumers Stay Home," *USA Today,* December 11, 2008, pp. 1B+; J. Jusko, "Kraft Crafts an Open Innovation Strategy," *Industry Week,* December 2008, pp. 60–61; M. Boyle, "Snap, Crackle, Pop At the Food Giants," *BusinessWeek,* October 6, 2008, p. 48; J. Jargon, "New Leaf for Sara Lee, Kraft: Salads," *Wall Street Journal,* March 26, 2007, p. A9; M. Boyle, "Better Eating through Genomics," *CNNMoney.com,* March 23, 2007; J. Jargon, "Kraft Sets Path for Overseas Expansion," *Wall Street Journal,* March 22, 2007, p. B4; R. M. Schneiderman, Market Scan, "Altria Gives Details of Kraft Spin-Off," *Forbes.com,* March 20, 2007; D. Carpenter, The Associated Press, "Kraft CEO's Pay in '06: $18.6 Million," *BusinessWeek Online,* March 13, 2007; L. Shepherd, The Associated Press, "Kraft Hopes to Take a Bite of Take-Out," *BusinessWeek Online,* February 26, 2007; "Kraft Plans to Invest More to Reignite Future Growth," *Wall Street Journal,* February 21, 2007, p. B4; A. Martin, "Kraft Chief Outlines Turnaround Strategy," *New York Times Online,* February 21, 2007; A. M. Heher, The Associated Press, *Springfield News-Leader,* February 21, 2007, p. 7B; Reuters, "Kraft Stirs Up New Strategies," *CNNMoney.com,* February 20, 2007; J. Adamy, "Cooking Up Changes at Kraft Foods," *Wall Street Journal,* February 20, 2007, pp. B1+; M. Arndt, "It Just Got Hotter in Kraft's Kitchen," *BusinessWeek,* February 12, 2007, p. 36; "Altria Profit Up: OKs Kraft Spinoff," *CNNMoney.com,* January 31, 2007; M. Arndt, "Kraft: Time to Sink or Swim," *BusinessWeek Online,* January 30, 2007; and V. O'Connell and J. T. Hallinan, "Table Clears for Kraft Spinoff," *Wall Street Journal,* January 26, 2007, p. A6.

2. J. McCracken and P. Lattman, "Apparel Chain Faces Closure Three Months After Rescue," *Wall Street Journal,* November 18, 2008, p. B1; E. Wilson, "Steve & Barry's, a Retailer, Files for Bankruptcy Protection," *New York Times Online,* July 10, 2008; J. McCracken and P. Lattman, "Steve & Barry's, Short of Cash, May Shut Stores," *Wall Street Journal,* July 1, 2008, p. B3; and P. Lattman and J. McCracken, "Steve & Barry's Faces Cash Crunch," *Wall Street Journal,* June 21/22, 2008, p. A4.

3. The discussion of these concentration strategy options has been slightly modified from information found in P. Kotler, *Marketing Management* (Upper Saddle River, NJ: Prentice Hall, 2000), pp. 74–75.

4. A. Pressman, "Ocean Spray's Creative Juices," *BusinessWeek,* May 15, 2006, pp. 88–90.

5. Beckman Coulter Inc., [**www.beckmancoulter.com**], February 21, 2009; and B. Upbin, "What Have You Invented for Me Lately?" *Forbes,* December 16, 1996, pp. 330–334.

6. Bose Corporation [**www.bose.com**], February 21, 2009; and W. M. Bulkeley, "How an MIT Professor Came to Dominate Stereo Speaker Sales," *Wall Street Journal,* December 31, 1996, pp. A1+.

7. G. C. Marcial, "Hail to CVS/Caremark," *BusinessWeek Online,* April 9, 2007, p. 84.

8. R. D'Aveni and D. J. Ravenscraft, "Economies of Integration versus Bureaucracy Costs: Does Vertical Integration Improve Performance," *Academy of Management Journal,* October 1994, pp. 1167–1206.

9. J. Leeds, "Big Promoter of Concerts to Acquire House of Blues," *New York Times Online,* July 6, 2006.

10. The Associated Press, "Journey Back With New Album, Tour Plans," *Springfield News-Leader,* January 21, 1997, p. 5B.

11. I. Rowley, "Way, Way, Off-Road," *BusinessWeek,* July 17, 2006, pp. 36–37.

12. L. E. Palich, G. R. Carini and S. L. Seaman, "Internationalization as a Moderator in the Diversification-Performance Relationship: An Empirical Assessment," *Academy of Management Proceedings on CD-Rom,* August 1996; I. Goll and R. B. Sambharya, "Corporate Ideology, Diversification and Firm Performance," *Organization Studies,* Vol. 16, No. 5, 1995, pp. 823–846; C. C. Markides and P. J. Williamson, "Related Diversification, Core Competencies, and Corporate Performance," *Strategic Management Journal,* Vol. 15, 1994, pp. 149–165; H. Singh and C. A. Montgomery, "Corporate Acquisition Strategies and Economic Performance," *Strategic Management Journal,* Vol. 8, No. 4, 1987, pp. 377–386; K. Palepu, "Diversification Strategy, Profit Performance, and the Entropy Measure," *Strategic Management Journal,* Vol. 6, No. 3, 1985, pp. 239–255; D. J. Lecraw, "Diversification Strategy and Performance," *Journal of Industrial Economics,* Vol. 33, No. 2, 1984, pp. 179–198; R. A. Bettis, "Performance Differences in Related and Unrelated Diversified Firms," *Strategic Management Journal,* Vol. 2, No. 4, 1981, pp. 379–393; R. Rumelt, 1974; and H. I. Ansoff, *Corporate Strategy* (New York: McGraw-Hill, 1965).

13. L. Palich, G. R. Carini, and S. L. Seaman, 1996; R. B. Sambharya, "The Combined Effect of International Diversification and Product Diversification Strategies on the Performance of U.S.-based Multinational Corporations," *Management International Review,* Vol. 35, No. 3, 1995, pp. 197–218; V. L. Blackburn, J. R. Lang, and K. H. Johnson, "Mergers and Shareholder Returns: The Roles of Acquiring Firms' Ownership and Diversification Strategy," *Journal of Management,* December 1990, pp. 769–782; B. W. Keats, "Diversification and Business Economic Performance Revisited: Issues of Measurement and Causality," *Journal of Management,* March 1990, pp. 61–72; and A. Seth, "Value Creation in Acquisitions: A Re-examination of Performance Issues," *Strategic Management Journal,* February 1990, pp. 99–115.

14. J. Birkinshaw, A. Morrison, and J. Hulland, "Structural and Competitive Determinants of a Global Integration Strategy," *Strategic Management Journal,* Vol. 15, 1995, pp. 637–655; "Competitors: Some Criteria for Success," *Business Horizons,* January–February 1988, pp. 34–41; and B. S. Chakravarthy and H. V. Perlmutter, "Strategic Planning for a Global Business," *Columbia Journal of World Business,* Spring 1985, pp. 3–10.

15. B. Villalonga and A. M. McGahan, "The Choice Among Acquisitions, Alliances, and Divestitures," *Strategic Management Journal,* December 2005, pp. 1183–1208; D. Henry, "Mergers: Why Most Big Deals Don't Pay Off," *BusinessWeek,* October 14, 2002, pp. 60–70; M. Arndt, "How Companies Can Marry Well," *BusinessWeek,* March 4, 2002, p. 28; L. Capron, "Historical Analyses of Three Waves of Mergers and Acquisitions in the United States: Triggering Factors, Motivations, and Performance," *Academy of Management Proceedings on CD-Rom,* August 1996; and M. H. Lubatkin and P. J. Lane, "Psst . . . the Merger Mavens Still Have It Wrong," *Academy of Management Executive,* February 1996, pp. 21–39.

16. P. Haspeslagh and D. Jemison, *Managing Acquisitions* (New York: Free Press 1991); E. R. Biggadike, *Corporate Diversification: Entry, Strategy, and Performance* (Cambridge, MA: Division of Research, Harvard Business School, 1983); G. S. Yip, "Diversification Entry: Internal Development versus Acquisition," *Strategic Management Journal,* Vol. 3, 1982, pp. 331–345; M. S. Salter and W. A. Weinhold, *Diversification Through Acquisition: Strategies for Creating Economic Value* (New York: Free Press, 1979); and H. L. Ansoff, *Corporate Strategy* (New York: McGraw-Hill, 1965).

17. "Happy 20th Birthday, NUMMI," *Industry Week,* March 2004, p. 15.

18. "L'Oreal, Nestle Team Up on Product Line," *Springfield News-Leader,* June 26, 2002, p. 6B.

19. "Clorox, P&G to Form Joint Venture," *Wall Street Journal,* November 15, 2002, p. A10.

20. M. Liedtke, The Associated Press, "Yahoo, eBay Join Forces in Partnership," *ABC News Online,* Mary 25, 2006.

21. C. Woodyard, "Honda, GE Build New Jet Engine," *USA Today,* February 17, 2004, [**www.usatoday.com**].

22. D. Durfee, "Try Before You Buy," *CFO,* May 2006, pp. 48–54; B. McEvily and A. Marcus, "Embedded Ties and the Acquisition of Competitive Capabilities," *Strategic Management Journal,* November 2005, pp. 1033–1055; R. D. Ireland, M. A. Hitt, and D. Vaidyanath, "Alliance Management as a Source of Competitive Advantage," *Journal of Management,* 2002, Vol. 28, No. 3, pp. 413–446; E. Krell, "The Alliance Advantage," *Business Finance,* July 2002, pp. 16–23; C. Ellis, "Making Strategic Alliances Succeed," *Harvard Business Review,* July–August 1996, pp. 8–9; C. M. Brown, "Partnering for Profit," *Black Enterprise,* June 1995, p. 43; R. Maynard, "Striking the Right Match," *Nation's Business,* May 1995, pp. 18–28; Roundtable Discussion, "Strategic Partnering," *Chief Executive,* November 1995, pp. 52–62; D. E. Gumpert, "Business 2000: Partnerships for Success," *Inc.,* December 1995, pp. 133–146; N. Templin, "More and More Firms Enter Joint Ventures with Big Competitors," *Wall Street Journal,* November 1, 1995, pp. A1+; N. S. Levinson and M. Asahi, "Cross-National Alliances and Interorganizational Learning," *Organizational Dynamics,* Autumn 1995, pp. 50–63; and J. Bleeke and D. Ernst, "Is Your Strategic Alliance Really a Sale?" *Harvard Business Review,* January–February 1995, pp. 97–105.

23. S. Parise and A. Casher, "Alliance Portfolios: Designing and Managing Your Network of Business-Partner Relationships," *Academy of Management Executive,* November 2003, pp. 25–39; Ireland, Hitt, and Vaidyanath, *Journal of Management,* 2002; M. Kotabe and K. S. Swan, "The Role of Strategic Alliances in High Technology New Product Development," *Strategic Management Journal,* Vol. 16, 1995, pp. 621–636; J. B. Barney and M. H. Hansen, "Trustworthiness: Can It Be a Source of Competitive Advantage?" *Strategic Management Journal,* Vol. 15, Special Issue, 1994, pp. 175–203; and C. W. L. Hill, "Cooperation, Opportunism, and the Invisible Hand: Implications for Transaction Cost Theory," *Academy of Management Review,* Vol. 15, 1990, pp. 500–513.

24. See J. M. Ivancevich, T. N. Duening, and W. Lidwell, "Bridging the Manager–Organizational Scientist Collaboration Gap," *Organizational Dynamics,* May 2005, pp. 103–117; C. Siafter, *Corporate Recovery: Successful Turnaround Strategies and Their Implementation* (Hammondsworth, England: Penguin Books), 1984; R. C. Hoffman, "Strategies for Corporate Turnarounds: What Do We Know About Them?" *Journal of General Management,* Vol. 14, 1984, pp. 46–66; D. Schendel, G. R. Patton, and J. Riggs, "Corporate Turnaround Strategies: A Study of Profit Decline and Recovery," *Journal of General Management,* Vol. 2, 1976, pp. 1–22; and J. Argenti, *Corporate Collapse: Causes and Symptoms* (New York: McGraw-Hill, 1976).

25. P. Lorange and R. T. Nelson, "How to Recognize—and Avoid—Organizational Decline," *Sloan Management Review,* Spring 1987, pp. 41–48.

26. C. C. Markides, "Diversification, Restructuring, and Economic Performance," *Strategic Management Journal,* February 1995, pp. 101–118; W. W. Lewis, "Strategic Restructuring: A Critical Requirement in the Search for Corporate Potential," in M. L. Rock and R. H. Rock, eds., *Corporate Restructuring* (New York: McGraw-Hill, 1990), pp. 43–55; and "Shifting Strategies: Surge in Restructuring is Profoundly Altering Much of U.S. Industry," *Wall Street Journal,* August 12, 1985, p. 1.

27. G. D. Bruton, J. K. Keels, and C. L. Shook, "Downsizing the Firm: Answering the Strategic Questions," *Academy of Management Executive,* May 1996, pp. 38–45; and W. McKinley, C. M. Sanchez, and A. G. Schick, "Organizational Downsizing: Constraining, Cloning, and Learning," *Academy of Management Executive,* August 1995, pp. 32–44.

28. D. L. Worrell, W. M. Davidson, and V. M. Sharma, "Layoff Announcements and Stockholder Wealth," *Academy of Management Journal,* Vol. 34, 1991, pp. 662–678.

29. Y. Chen, J. F. Weston, and E. I. Altman, "Financial Distress and Restructuring Models," *Financial Management,* Summer 1995, pp. 57–75; J. P. Sheppard, "Strategy and Bankruptcy: An Exploration Into Organizational Death," *Journal of Management,* Vol. 20, No. 4, 1994, pp. 795–833; and C. M. Daily, "Bankruptcy in Strategic Studies: Past and Promise," *Journal of Management,* Vol. 20, No. 2, 1994, pp. 263–295.

30. J. Markoff, "Tomorrow, the World Wide Web," *New York Times,* January 16, 1996, pp. C1+; and K. Rebello, "Inside Microsoft," *BusinessWeek,* July 15, 1996, pp. 56–67.

31. S. Finkelstein, *Why Smart Executives Fail and What You Can Learn from Their Mistakes* (New York: Penguin Books), 2003; and J. Merritt, "The ABCs of Failure," *BusinessWeek,* June 9, 2003, p. 126.

32. M. Arndt, S. Hamm, S. Rosenbrush, and C. Edwards, "Signs of Life," *BusinessWeek,* July 14, 2003, pp. 32–34.

Special Topics: International Strategies and Strategies for Entrepreneurial Ventures and Not-For-Profits

8

LEARNING OUTCOMES

8.1 *Explain the issues that arise as organizations go international.*

8.2 *Describe the important international strategic decisions.*

8.3 *Discuss the strategic management process and issues that face entrepreneurial ventures and small businesses.*

8.4 *Discuss the strategic management process and issues that face not-for-profit and public sector organizations.*

One Man's Junk—Another Man's Treasure

Eighteen thousand expired cans of sardines. A complete McDonald's McHappy Land play set. Fifty garden gnomes. A unicorn-shaped coffee table. A mechanical bull. A mortician's closet. That's just a sampling of some of the weird stuff that 1-800-Got-Junk? customers have asked the uniformed people in the freshly scrubbed blue trucks to haul away. Company founder and CEO Brian Scudamore discovered a lucrative niche between "trash cans and those big green bins dropped off by" the giant trash haulers. But even hauling people's junk, Scudamore is aware of the issues involved with strategically managing an entrepreneurial venture, especially as he positions his company for international growth.[1]

1-800-Got-Junk? is based in Vancouver, British Columbia, with a corporate staff numbering around 175. Scudamore says, "With a vision of creating the 'FedEx' of junk removal, I dropped out of university with just one year left to become a full-time JUNKMAN! Yes, my father, a liver transplant surgeon, was not impressed to say the least." By the end of 2008, however, the company had over 340 franchises in the United States, Canada, and Australia, and systemwide revenues of over $125 million. Since its founding in 1989, the company has grown exponentially. The next push may be the United Kingdom, where the company is exploring franchising opportunities. Scudamore was recently named to *Entrepreneur* magazine's Honor Roll of franchise businesses.

You may think that hauling junk is a simple business. Instead, Scudamore's company has been described as a "curious hybrid" that blends the old and new economies. Although its product—getting rid of trash—has been done for hundreds of years, it relies heavily on sophisticated information technology and has the kind of organizational culture that most people associate with high-tech startups.

Information systems and technology have been important to the company's growth. Scudamore says, "It has allowed us to expand all over North America. Our system has made the process easier." The company's call center does all the booking and dispatching for franchise partners. They also use a proprietary intranet (dubbed the JunkNet) to access schedules, customer information, real-time reports, and so forth. Scudamore's philosophy is that this approach lets them "work *on* the business" instead of "*in* the business." Needless to say, the company's franchise partners tend to be pretty tech-savvy.

In addition, the company's culture is a unique blend of fun and seriousness. There's a quote posted in the head office—which is affectionately known as the Junktion—that says "It's all about people." And those four simple words sum up Scudamore's philosophy: find the right people and treat them right. Since 2004, the company has been ranked by *BC Business* magazine as one of the best companies to work for in British Columbia. Grizzly, Scudamore's dog, comes to the office every day and helps employees relieve stress by playing catch anytime, anywhere. Each morning at exactly 10:55, all employees at headquarters meet for a five-minute huddle, where they share good news, announcements, metrics, and problems they're encountering. Visitors to the office are also expected to join in. The open-concept floor plan encourages communication among all levels of staff—from top to bottom, and embodies the importance of the team environment. One of the most conspicuous features of the Junktion—"the first thing one sees upon entering—is the Vision Wall," which contains "the fruits of Scudamore's brainstorms." And franchisees are encouraged to emulate the energy, initiative, and creativity so evident at the Junktion. For instance, the Toronto franchise has been known to take its fleet of blue trucks and proceed in a motorcade down Yonge Street through the heart of the city as a way to be noticed and to publicize its services. And, of course, they're wearing their blue wigs, a wardrobe staple for many franchisees.

The story of Brian Scudamore, who built a small business into one with revenues of over $125 million and who hopes to continue growing internationally, illustrates how important strategic management and managing strategically are to entrepreneurial organizations. His recognition of environmental opportunities, his strategic plan for exploiting the "junk" niche, and his company's use of franchising partnerships domestically and internationally are all examples of strategic management in action. Although we may think that competitive advantage, internal and external analysis, strategy formulation, and strategy implementation are important concepts for large business organizations, the fact is that these things are important for *all* organizations. Although we've used examples of international, entrepreneurial, and not-for-profit organizations in previous chapters as we discussed various strategy topics, in this chapter we want to focus exclusively on the challenges associated with strategically managing those organizations.

LEARNING OUTCOME 8.1
Explain the Issues That Arise As Organizations Go International

An annual study of global wine consumption predicts that the United States will overtake France as the world's largest wine market between 2010 and 2012. Not only will wine consumption continue to rise, the value of the wine market will continue to increase as consumers (especially in the United States and other industrialized countries) drink better and more expensive wines. In addition, Italy was forecasted to remain the second-largest market in terms of volume. But the biggest surprises were Russia and China, which both appeared in the top-ten markets in terms of consumption and were forecasted to continue growing.[2] What organizations might be most interested in this forecast and what strategic implications (opportunities and threats) might it have for those organizations?

The International Environment

Doing business internationally isn't new. Countries and organizations have been trading with each other for centuries. As we stated in Chapter 1, organizations are no longer constrained by national borders. Smaller organizations, such as 1-800-Got-Junk?, to larger organizations, such as heavy equipment maker Caterpillar, are finding ways to do business internationally and thus face advantages and challenges as shown in Table 8.1. Before doing business internationally, strategic managers need to know the important aspects of the international environment including the legal-political environment, the economic environment, and the cultural environment.

The Legal-Political Environment

The legal-political environment in the United States is stable. Changes are slow, and legal and political procedures are well established. The laws governing the actions of individuals and institutions are fairly stable. The same can't be said for all countries. Deutsche Bank's assessment of global political risk categorizes countries into different stability categories: maximum, high, moderate, low, and failed states. Some countries on the maximum stability list included Australia, Germany, Japan, Spain, and the United States. Some countries on the low stability list included Bosnia, Mozambique, Nigeria, and North Korea. Some countries on the failed state list included Haiti, Somalia, and Sudan.[3] Organizations wanting to do business in countries with low stability levels face greater uncertainty and strategic threats as a result of that instability. But even in countries with fairly stable political-legal environments, the fact that those environments differ is reason enough to understand the constraints and opportunities that exist.

The Economic Environment

There are several important factors to consider in the economic environment. One is currency exchange rates. If you've ever traveled to another country, you've probably experienced firsthand how these rates work as you've converted your home currency into the currency of the country where you were traveling. Businesses also have to convert currencies when they do business outside their home country. For instance, if they export goods to another country and receive payment in the currency of that foreign country, that payment must be

Advantages	Drawbacks	
• Could lower operational costs • Provides a way to supplement or strengthen domestic growth • Contributes to achieving benefits of economies of scale • Becomes a stronger competitor both domestically and internationally	• Poses greater economic, strategic, and financial risks • Process of managing strategically becomes more complex and challenging • Finding similarities in markets or operational capabilities is more difficult • Capturing and exploiting advantages is not easy or guaranteed	**Table 8.1** *Advantages and Drawbacks of International Expansion*

converted back to the home currency. Large international companies, such as GE or Avon, convert huge amounts of currency each year. The timing of that conversion can significantly affect a company's balance sheet and bottom line. A currency's value (which influences the exchange rate) adjusts as supply and demand for that currency changes. For instance, when the U.S. dollar is strong, imports seem less expensive, leading to increased demand for imported products. Also, when interest rates in another country are higher than those in the United States, demand for that foreign currency rises as people buy that currency in order to invest in the other country's securities. Likewise, a stronger dollar decreases exports because they appear more expensive to foreign consumers. While importers prefer a strong dollar, exporters prefer a weaker dollar. And although there are mechanisms in place to try to prevent a global economic meltdown, a currency crisis in one country isn't limited to just that country because the global economy is so interwoven.

Another economic factor to consider is inflation rates. Inflation means that prices for products and services are rising. But inflation also affects interest rates, exchange rates, cost of living, and the general confidence in a country's political and economic system. In most developing countries, consumer prices are rising more slowly than they were in the late 1990s, although inflation rates can, and do, vary widely.[4] For instance, *The 2009 World Factbook* shows country inflation rates ranging from a minus 3.6 percent (Nauru) to a whopping plus 11.2 million percent (Zimbabwe). Strategic managers need to monitor international inflation trends so they can make good decisions and anticipate possible changes in a country's monetary policies.

Finally, diverse tax policies should be monitored as some countries are more restrictive than others. About the only certainty is that tax rules differ from country to country. Thus, strategic managers need specific information on various tax rules to minimize their business's overall tax obligation.

The Cultural Environment

Legal, political, and economic differences among countries are fairly obvious. But cultural differences often aren't as easy to see. For instance, when a large global oil company found that employee productivity in one of its Mexican plants was down 20 percent, it sent a manager to find out why. After talking to several employees, the manager found out that the company used to have a monthly fiesta in the parking lot for all the employees and their families. Another manager had canceled the fiestas saying they were a waste of time and money. The message employees were getting was that the company didn't care about their families anymore. When the fiestas were reinstated, productivity and employee morale soared.[5] As this example points out, it's important that managers understand **national culture,** which is the values and attitudes shared by individuals from a specific country that shape their behavior and their beliefs about what is important. The FYI box "Understanding National Culture" describes two frameworks for assessing a country's culture. When there are cultural differences between countries in which an organization does business, it could affect what strategies are used and how that organization is managed.

Once strategic managers are familiar with the opportunities and threats found in the international environment, they can begin to look at strategies for doing business internationally.

Learning Review: Learning Outcome 8.1

- Explain the advantages and drawbacks of going international.
- Describe the legal-political, economic, and cultural aspects of the international environment.

FOR YOUR INFORMATION

Understanding National Culture

One of the most widely used approaches for understanding national culture was developed by Geert Hofstede. His research focuses on five dimensions of a country's culture: individualism versus collectivism (degree to which people in a country prefer to act as individuals or as members of groups), power distance (measure of the extent to which a society accepts that power in institutions and organizations is distributed unequally), uncertainty avoidance (degree to which people tolerate risk and prefer structured over unstructured situations), achievement versus nurturing (degree to which a country values assertiveness and competitiveness versus relationships and concern for others), and long-term versus short-term orientation (measure of a country's orientation toward life and work). For instance, using these five dimensions, the national culture of the United States is characterized as individualistic, small power distance, low uncertainty avoidance, strong achievement, and short-term orientation. On the other hand, the national culture of Japan is characterized as collectivistic, large power distance, high uncertainty avoidance, strong achievement, and long-term orientation.

Another framework for understanding national culture comes from the Global Leadership and Organizational Behavior Effectiveness (GLOBE) research project. GLOBE is an ongoing investigation of cross-cultural leadership behaviors and focuses more on the managerial and leadership implications of cultural differences. It uses many of the same dimensions as identified by Hofstede but expands the cultural analysis to nine dimensions including assertiveness, future orientation, gender differentiation, uncertainty avoidance, power distance, individualism/collectivism, in-group collectivism, performance orientation, and humane orientation. Information from the GLOBE findings appear to be most useful to managers who want to be effective leaders. Why might these approaches to understanding national culture be important to strategic decision makers?.

Sources: Based on J. S. Chhokar, Felix C. Brodbeck, and R. J. House (eds.), Culture and Leadership Across the World: The GLOBE Book of In-Depth Studies of 25 Societies (Mahwah, NJ: Lawrence Erlbaum Associates, 2007); R. T. Moran, P. R. Harris, and S. V. Moran, Managing Cultural Differences: Global Leadership Strategies for the 21st Century, 7th ed. (Oxford, UK: Elsevier, 2007); R. J. House, P. J. Hanges, M. Javidan, P. W. Dorfman, and V. Gupta, Culture, Leadership, and Organizations: The GLOBE Study of 62 Societies (Thousand Oaks, CA: Sage, 2004); and G. Hofstede, Culture's Consequences: International Differences in Work-Related Values, 2nd ed. (Thousand Oaks, CA: Sage, 2001).

LEARNING OUTCOME 8.2
Describe the Important International Strategic Decisions

McDonald's Corporation, the world's largest fast-food company, added rice burgers—fried beef slices served between two pressed rice cakes—to its menu in Singapore to appeal to local palates.[6] This example illustrates one of the first important strategic decisions that must be made: A multicountry approach or a global approach?[7] After we've discussed this, we'll look at different international strategy alternatives.

Multicountry Approach versus Global Approach

A multicountry approach is one in which an organization's strategies vary according to the countries in which it does business. This approach is based on developing a differentiation advantage. Products are tailored to fit consumer tastes and preferences. Marketing and distribution are adapted to local customs and cultures. Competitive actions are chosen to fit the unique circumstances of the market. Such local responsiveness is important when there are significant country-to-country differences. Although there may be some sharing of organizational capabilities and competencies, that's not the goal of the multicountry approach. On the other hand, the global approach is one in which the strategies are basically the same in all countries in which the organization does business. This approach is designed to help develop a low-cost advantage. There's more of an emphasis on globally integrating operations rather than on local market responsiveness. Products may have minor variations but this approach emphasizes coordination between functions and business units and more sharing of capabilities, competencies, and technologies across those functions and units.

International Strategy Alternatives

When a company decides to expand beyond its domestic borders, it has several alternatives it might use: exporting, importing, licensing, franchising, and direct investment. In *exporting,* an organization makes products in its home country and then transports those products to other countries to be sold there through an existing distribution channel. *Importing* involves selling products at home that are made in another country. *Licensing* is an arrangement in which a foreign licensee buys the rights to manufacture and market a company's product in that country for a negotiated fee. In *franchising*—which is mainly used by service and retailing providers—the company sells franchisees in other countries limited rights to use its brand name in return for a lump-sum payment and a share of the franchisee's profits. In *direct investment,* an organization actually owns assets, such as a manufacturing facility or a sales office, in another country.

● *Strategic Management in Action*

Sonia Seye, an immigrant from Senegal, is typical of many new entrepreneurs. She's young, she's female, *and* she's comfortable with doing business globally. Sonia runs a busy Los Angeles salon called Hair Universal, but wants to build a "bigger, more profitable future." One way she's doing this is by tapping into the global market, not to sell her products, but to find product suppliers. The product? Human hair extensions, which are popular. She found an import source in India, where there are many companies that sell "Indian women's fine long locks." And Sonia is not alone. Many small U.S. businesses are "increasingly looking to other countries to boost their businesses through the import of cheaper or better products." She says, "You don't have to be big to be global." Do you agree? Why or why not?

Source: Based on R. Richmond, "Entrepreneurs with Big Dreams Tap Global Market," Wall Street Journal, April 17, 2007, p. B6.

What are some examples of these international strategies? U.S. toymakers Mattel and Hasbro had never really pursued overseas markets because many toys that were popular in the U.S. market simply didn't appeal to other global customers. As American culture has spread, however, these companies found their products more in demand. Mattel now gets about 49 percent of its total revenues from international markets.[8] MTV Networks is another company growing internationally by tailoring its programming to specific markets. MTV is in over 88 million homes in the United States but in over 100 million homes in Southeast Asia. The company's international division, MTV Networks International, oversees more than 120 channels worldwide and is growing at a 20 percent-a-year rate. Then there's Domino's Pizza, which has over 3,700 international locations. Most of these stores have achieved several periods of same-store sales growth. How? Domino's "careful balance of central control and local flexibility."[9] The company knows what makes a Domino's pizza a Domino's pizza but they also understand what makes a pizza Japanese or Indian or British.

Although these examples describe companies that are using international strategies to grow, there's another type of international organization called a **born global firm,** which is an organization that chooses to go international from founding.[10] For example, Logitech International is a good illustration of a born global firm. Started by an Italian and a Swiss who met while studying computer engineering at Stanford University, the two student founders hoped to emulate in Europe the entrepreneurial spirit of California's Silicon Valley. Initially, the company's operations and R&D were split between Switzerland and California. Because its main focus was a computer mouse, it quickly expanded production to Ireland and Taiwan. Today, most of its high-volume manufacturing of mice and other computer peripherals is done in China. With 7,200 employees, Logitech's annual revenues now are around $2 billion. Logitech's experience is a prime example of both international and entrepreneurial strategies, which we're going to discuss next.

Learning Review: Learning Outcome 8.2

- Contrast the multicountry and the global approaches.
- What are the five international strategy alternatives?
- Describe a born global firm.

LEARNING OUTCOME 8.3
Discuss the Strategic Management Process and Issues That Face Entrepreneurial Ventures and Small Businesses

In this section, we want to look at strategic management in entrepreneurial ventures and small businesses. Before we can do that, however, we need to know what these organizations are.

What Is an Entrepreneurial Venture, and What Is a Small Business?

Many people think that entrepreneurial ventures and small businesses are the same, but they're not. The key differences are summarized in Table 8.2. Entrepreneurs create **entrepreneurial ventures**—organizations that pursue opportunities, are characterized by

Entrepreneurial Venture	Small Business
• Innovative strategic practices • Strategic goals are profitability and growth • Seeks out new opportunities • Willingness to take risks	• Independently owned, operated, and financed • Fewer than 500 employees • Doesn't emphasize new or innovative practices • Little impact on industry

innovative practices, and have growth and profitability as their main goals. On the other hand, a **small business** is an independent business having fewer than 500 employees that doesn't necessarily engage in any new or innovative practices and that has relatively little impact on its industry.[11] A small business isn't necessarily entrepreneurial because it's small; to be entrepreneurial means that the business is innovative and seeking out new opportunities. Even though entrepreneurial ventures may start small, they pursue growth. Some new small firms may grow, but many remain small businesses, by choice or by default.

Why Are These Types of Organizations Important?

Using any number of sources, you can find statistics on how many small businesses there are, how many workers they employ, and how much of the national economic output they're responsible for. For example, small businesses represent over 99 percent of all employers, employ over half of all private workers, and account for 50 percent of the private sector output.[12] The importance of these organizations can be shown in three areas: job creation, new start-ups, and innovation.

Job Creation

How important are these organizations to job creation? Statistics collected by the U.S. Small Business Administration (SBA) show that small firms generate 60 to 80 percent of all net new jobs annually.[13] Even with the challenging current economic environment, the creation of jobs by small businesses is expected to continue as new firms start small and grow.[14]

Number of New Start-ups

Entrepreneurship is important to every industry sector in the United States and in other global economies. People continue to start businesses, probably for a couple of reasons. First, continual changes in the external environment—competition, technology, consumer wants, and so forth—provide a fertile climate for entrepreneurial ventures because these organizations often are better able to respond quickly to changing conditions than are larger, more bureaucratic, and less flexible organizations. Also, many of the cost advantages that large organizations traditionally had because of their size (economies of scale) have been eroded by technological advances. This means that smaller organizations can compete against larger ones and aren't at a disadvantage because of their small size.

How many new start-ups are there? The latest figures show that some 644,000 business were started in 2005, 640,000 in 2006, and 637,000 in 2007.[15] Add these new start-ups to the large number of small businesses (estimated at over 5 million employer firms) already operating and you can begin to understand the economic importance of entrepreneurial ventures and small businesses.

FOR YOUR INFORMATION

Global Entrepreneurship Monitor (GEM)

What about entrepreneurial activity outside the United States? How extensive is it and what kind of impact has it had? An annual assessment of global entrepreneurship called the Global Entrepreneurship Monitor (GEM) estimates the level of involvement in early-stage entrepreneurial activity by looking at nascent entrepreneurs (individuals who have taken some action toward creating a new business) and new business owners (individuals who are active as owners-managers of a new business that has paid wages or salaries for more than three months but less than 42 months). The GEM 2008 Report covered 43 countries that were divided into three clusters—factor-driven economies, efficiency-driven economies, and innovation-driven economies. Study results showed that:

- There was an "overall decline in perceived opportunities to start a business." Countries showing the largest declines were Iceland, Chile, Ireland, Latvia, and Hungary.

- However, "perceived skills and knowledge to start a business were not affected by the business cycle." Thus, intentions to start a business don't seem to have declined as much as perceived opportunities.

- In factor-driven economies (which includes countries such as Bolivia, Colombia, Egypt, and India—you can find the whole list in the GEM report), the rate of involvement for early-stage entrepreneurial activity and established business activity is high.

- In efficiency-driven economies, Latin American countries have relatively high early-stage entrepreneurial activity whereas Eastern European countries have relatively low rates of early-stage entrepreneurial activity.

- In the United States, there is more early-stage entrepreneurial activity than in European Union (EU) countries and in Japan.

- Overall early-stage entrepreneurial activity in innovation-driven economies (which includes most of the economically developed countries) has been relatively stable over time.

The GEM report concludes that "the broad nexus between entrepreneurship, economic development and institutions is a critical area of inquiry for understanding entrepreneurship within or across countries." The intent is to provide policy makers with information that helps them understand how "different aspects of policy can affect productive entrepreneurship through the major phases of economic development."

Source: *Based on N. Bosma, Z. J. Acs, E. Autio, A. Coduras, and J. Levie,* Global Entrepreneurship Monitor 2008 Executive Report, *Babson College, Universidad del Desarrollo, and London Business School, 2009.*

Innovation

Finally, you can understand the especially important role of entrepreneurial ventures in innovation. Innovating is a process of creating, changing, experimenting, transforming, and revolutionizing. The "creative destruction" process of innovating leads to technological changes and employment growth.[16] Entrepreneurial firms are an essential source of new and unique ideas that might otherwise go untapped.[17] Statistics back this up. New entrepreneurial organizations generate 24 times more innovations per R&D dollar spent than do *Fortune* 500 organizations, and they account for over 95 percent of new and "radical" product developments.[18] In addition, the SBA's Office of Advocacy reports that small entrepreneurial firms produce 13 to 14 times more patents per employee than do large patenting firms.[19] Innovation is important to entrepreneurial firms globally as well. The GEM 2006 study reported that 19 percent of early-stage entrepreneurs in middle-income countries and 15 percent of early-stage entrepreneurs in high-income countries indicated their product was new to all customers.[20]

There's no doubt that entrepreneurial ventures and small businesses play a significant role in the U.S. and global economies—and their economic importance will continue. That's why we need to look at what it means to manage strategically in these organizations. In addition, both face unique strategic challenges. Before we look at these, we need to explain how the strategic management process might be used.

Patricia Karter is founder and CEO of Dancing Deer Baking, a company that makes all-natural sweets. Although customers rave about her great-tasting baked products, Karter also "often hears praise for the company's philanthropy, green packaging, and commitment to its employees and inner-city Boston." Because Dancing Deer isn't big enough to have much of a social impact, Karter focused on creating a successful brand and growing the company. Now that she has that successful brand, she's looking for ways to have more of an impact. She responded when asked by One Family, a group that helps homeless mothers continue their education, to create a house-shaped cookie it could sell to raise money. To date, Dancing Deer has donated more than $200,000 to One Family. Says Karter, "I always want to do better. Whenever I've had an opportunity and one route was more lucrative, I've always chosen the more interesting, less lucrative one. I've always chosen to chase my dreams." What do you think? Can an entrepreneur "chase a dream" *and* do good for society?

Source: Based on M. Hefferman, "Helping the Homeless with Cookies," Reader's Digest, August 2008 [**www.rd.com**]; and S. Perman, "Scones and Social Responsibility," BusinessWeek, August 21/28, 2006, p. 38.

The Strategic Management Process in Entrepreneurial Ventures and Small Businesses

How important is it to identify environmental opportunities? Consider the following: More than 4 million baby boomers turn 50 every year. Almost 10,000 turn 60 each day. More than 57.5 million baby boomers are projected to be alive in 2030, putting them between the ages of 66 to 84. The strategic decision makers at Zimmer Holding are well aware of those demographics. Why? Their company, which makes orthopedic products including reconstructive implants for hips, knees, shoulders, and elbows, sees definite marketing opportunities.[21] Exploiting such opportunities and developing a sustainable competitive advantage are important for entrepreneurial ventures and small businesses. As we've discussed previously, getting a sustainable competitive advantage means developing organizational resources and capabilities into distinctive capabilities and core competencies that competitors can't duplicate and that provide customers with products they desire. However, getting to that point isn't easy. But, that's the intent behind managing strategically—using the strategic management process to identify and assess important internal and external factors that influence appropriate strategic choices and decisions. What's different or unique about the way in which strategic managers in entrepreneurial ventures and small businesses do this?

Value of Planning

We first need to look at whether strategic decision makers in these organizations should do strategic planning. Is such planning valuable? Research that's looked at the value of general planning, and pre-start-up planning in particular, has shown mixed results. Several studies have shown positive links between planning and business performance.[22] Others have found no such relationship between planning and performance or have shown that the relationship depends on the industry.[23] What's our conclusion? Many entrepreneurship researchers now believe that instead of spending months (or even years) developing elaborate business plans, a "more practical approach (especially if not seeking external start-up financing) is to write a 'back-of-the-envelope' plan with basic financial projections, such as cash flow, and fine-tune the business model after launching the business."[24] In other words, don't spend a lot of time writing a business plan without knowing whether you have actual customers. Also, a recent study that compared businesses that started with formal business plans and those that didn't, found no statistical difference in success.[25] Although spending a lot of time preparing a start-up business plan may not be as critical as once thought, strategic planning is. How should strategic planning be done?

The Overall Approach to the Strategic Planning Process

Most researchers generally agree that the strategic planning process in small organizations should be far less formal than that in large organizations.[26] If the process becomes too formal, rigid, and cumbersome, an entrepreneurial venture or small business can lose the flexibility that's often crucial to its competitive success. In fact, the value of strategic planning for these organizations lies more in the "doing"—that is, in the process itself—than in the outcome of the process, a formal strategic "plan." And that value in "doing" comes from analyzing the external and internal environments—steps that are important to effective strategic planning.

External and Internal Analysis

Strategic decision makers in entrepreneurial ventures and small businesses need to know what's happening externally and internally. Why? One reason is that many aspects in an organization's external environment have been shown to influence performance, particularly in new entrepreneurial ventures.[27] However, even for established small businesses, external analysis provides important information for developing or exploiting a competitive advantage.

Another reason it's important to do an external analysis is to have information about changes in customer expectations, competitors and their actions, economic factors, technological advances, and other marketplace features.[28] As we discussed in Chapter 3, an external analysis provides information on potential opportunities and threats. If no external analysis is done, it's impossible to know what they are. The same thing holds true for an internal analysis. If employees don't assess an organization's strengths and weaknesses, it's difficult to know what strategies are needed to help develop or exploit the organization's competitive advantage. In other words, what resources, capabilities, and core competencies does the organization have and not have? Although it may be difficult for an entrepreneur or a small business owner to be totally objective in analyzing strengths and weaknesses, such an analysis *is* necessary.

Finally, the "boiled frog phenomenon," a classic psychological experiment, can help explain why environmental analysis is important to these organizations.[29] In the experiment, when a live frog is dropped in a pan of boiling water, it reacts instantaneously and jumps out. If a live frog instead is dropped into tepid water that's gradually heated to the boiling point, the frog doesn't react and so dies. The same concept can be seen in entrepreneurial ventures and small businesses. Research has shown that gradual negative changes in organizational performance don't trigger a serious response to do something or at least not until it's too late.[30] Therefore, both external and internal environments need to be analyzed in order to detect subtle, but potentially damaging, changes. Don't be like the frog that waits too long to jump out of the boiling water!

Strategic Management in Action

Andrew and Peggy Cherng founded Panda Express in 1983. From that first restaurant in the Galleria mall in Glendale, California, the company has grown to over 1,100 restaurants in 36 states and Puerto Rico. The company's revenues, which now have topped over $1 billion, are nearly triple the sales of its top two competitors combined. The company's best-seller? A lightly sweetened fried chicken dish called orange chicken. Future plans are to continue opening units.

Even as the company expands, however, "it keeps looking for ways to work out kinks in its formula." For instance, store locations will soon keep prepared dishes in woks rather than in flat-bottomed bins that smash the food at the bottom. And drive-in locations are being added to meet the needs of customers on the go.

Source: Based on E. Hessel, "Kung Pao Chicken for the Soul," Forbes, April 21, 2008, pp. 106–107; and M. Krantz, "Panda Express Spreads Chinese Food Across USA," USA Today, September 11, 2006, p. 4B.

Strategy Choices

Entrepreneurial ventures and small businesses can use most of the same strategies that large firms do with just a few exceptions. Let's look at the three different strategy levels to see what these differences are.

The main difference in functional strategies between small and large businesses is the extent or range of possible strategies. These organizations are limited in terms of the resources and capabilities that are available to implement their strategies.

At the competitive level, the strategy choices for entrepreneurial ventures and small businesses often are limited to focus strategies because of their small size and narrow competitive scope. It would be extremely difficult, even with technological advances, for a smaller organization to compete head-to-head in a broad market with a large organization on the basis of low costs, and probably even on differentiation. However, these organizations can compete successfully in narrow market niches by developing a low-cost or differentiation competitive advantage. Which competitive advantage strategic decision makers choose to develop depends on the resources, capabilities, and core competencies present in the functional areas of the organization. One thing that small firms want to avoid is pursuing both approaches. Research has shown that small firms that mixed efficiency (low-cost) and flexibility (differentiation) strategies significantly underperformed those firms that utilized one or the other.[31]

Finally, it may seem strange to talk about "corporate" strategies for an entrepreneurial venture or a small business, especially if you think of corporate strategy as encompassing a portfolio of businesses. However, strategic decision makers in these businesses do need a strategy that addresses the overall direction the organization wants to go. The possible strategic directions are the same as for a large organization: Is it going to grow, stabilize, or reverse a decline by renewing? Again, however, there are limits to the range of strategic options available to these organizations for each of these directions. For example, most entrepreneurial ventures will choose to grow using the concentration strategy because vertical integration, horizontal integration, or diversification may not be financially or operationally feasible. Organization renewal actions may be limited to cost cutting and simple restructuring activities. Despite the limited options, strategic decision makers still need a corporate strategy.

One final point we need to stress is that the whole process comes down to choosing what business to be in, the competitive advantages needed to be successful in that business, and the strategies necessary to get there. This encompasses the whole range of strategic activities from developing or exploiting organizational resources, capabilities, and core competencies to building or exploiting a sustainable competitive advantage in order to move the firm in the desired direction.

Strategy Evaluation

This phase of the strategic management process for entrepreneurial ventures and small businesses is similar to that in large organizations. The organization's strategies might be evaluated by measuring goal attainment at the various levels. Strategy evaluation might also include an assessment of certain performance trends and a comparison of the organization to its competitors. The organization's strategic decision makers need to know whether implemented strategies are working. If not, why not, and what changes might be necessary? The main difference between the strategy evaluation efforts of large and small organizations would be the extent of evaluation done.

All in all, the strategic management process in these organizations is similar to that used in larger organizations. Figure 8.1 illustrates this process. As we stated earlier, the main differences will be in terms of "how much" the small business or entrepreneurial venture can do these things. Because of limited resources and capabilities, strategic decision makers often

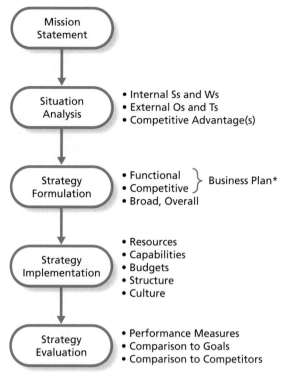

Mission Statement

Situation Analysis
• Internal Ss and Ws
• External Os and Ts
• Competitive Advantage(s)

Strategy Formulation
• Functional ⎫
• Competitive ⎬ Business Plan*
• Broad, Overall ⎭

Strategy Implementation
• Resources
• Capabilities
• Budgets
• Structure
• Culture

Strategy Evaluation
• Performance Measures
• Comparison to Goals
• Comparison to Competitors

*Business plan is typically needed when business is first starting up.

find their options limited. This doesn't mean that they don't—or shouldn't—do these things, however; it just means they don't have the range or extent of alternatives to choose from.

Specific Strategic Issues Facing Entrepreneurial Ventures and Small Businesses

Although the strategic management process for entrepreneurial ventures and small businesses is virtually identical to that for larger organizations, these organizations do face some unique strategic issues, including human resource management and innovation and flexibility considerations. Let's take a closer look at each.

The Grey Zone

How far should a business go in exploiting its competitive advantage? Popular social networking sites such as Facebook and MySpace have become an important communication link for many young adults. Although most of these sites have minimum age requirements (usually age 16), much-younger kids are setting up profiles with photos and personal—sometimes way too personal—information. What do you think about this? Discuss what ethical obligation, if any, these organizations have to users. Is there anything these organizations might do to counter criticisms that they're not doing enough to keep young children off the site? Explain.

Human Resource Management Issues

One of the most valuable resources and competitive advantages a small organization has is its employees. Yet, research indicates that recruiting, motivating, and retaining employees is one of the biggest problems for small organizations.[32] Human resource management (HRM) issues are among the most significant ones for entrepreneurial ventures and small businesses. A large organization typically enjoys a wider range of HR strategy options than does a smaller organization in terms of recruiting, selecting, training, appraising, and compensating employees. However, just because these organizations don't have the wide range of HR strategies doesn't mean they should just forget them. Quite the opposite, in fact! Strategic decision makers should recognize how important human resources are and commit whatever time and resources are necessary to develop appropriate strategies for attracting and keeping good people, just as Brian Scudamore from our chapter-opening case clearly did. It's something that entrepreneurial ventures and small businesses can't ignore.

Innovation and Flexibility Considerations

One of the primary competitive advantages that entrepreneurial ventures and small businesses can develop is being flexible and innovative.[33] Because large organizations are usually concerned with producing large quantities of products in order to take advantage of economies of scale, they often can't be as flexible. Their resource commitments often prevent them from responding to new and quickly changing markets as effectively as small, nimble businesses can. Therefore, strategic decision makers need to capitalize on this flexibility advantage and to be aware of and open to environmental changes (another good reason for doing an external analysis).

Also, these organizations have the potential—more so than large organizations—to come up with real innovations. Why? Larger organizations tend to concentrate on improving products they already have in order to justify large capital expenditures on facilities and equipment. Entrepreneurial ventures especially are in a better position to develop innovations in technology, markets, and products. Economist Joseph Schumpeter referred to this process in which existing products, processes, ideas, and businesses are replaced with better ones as **creative destruction**. These organizations are the driving force of change in the process of creative destruction. Developing and exploiting a sustainable competitive advantage may mean that strategic managers at these organizations need to be on the lookout for ways to "creatively destruct!"

⬤ *Strategic Management in Action*

Zingerman's Deli is an institution in Ann Arbor, Michigan. Opened in 1982 by Ari Weinzweig and Paul Saginaw, their deli-bakery-café-restaurant business has prospered by understanding its product, its customers, and its employees. Their business principles include the following:

- Customer service is what earns the profits because no one really needs what we sell.

- Customers who get a great product but poor service won't be as loyal as those who get an okay product but great service.

- Getting complaints by listening to people shows you care . . . and that's a good thing.

- Employees who are rewarded, respected, and well cared for will treat customers the same way.

These are two guys who understand the strategies it takes to be successful. What do you think of their business principles? How might these principles affect strategy choices? Do you think these could be applied to other businesses? Explain.

Source: *Based on G. Hamadey, "Big Man Off Campus," Every Day With Rachel Ray, July 2008, pp. 159–160; and D. Kiley, "Zingerman's Took the Road Less Traveled to Success," USA Today, October 1, 2003, p. 5B.*

- Contrast entrepreneurial ventures and small businesses.
- Why are these organizations important to the U.S. and global economies?
- Describe the strategic management process for these organizations.
- Discuss the specific strategic issues that face entrepreneurial ventures and small businesses.

LEARNING OUTCOME 8.4
Discuss the Strategic Management Process and Issues That Face Not-For-Profit and Public Sector Organizations

In this section we're going to look at strategic management in not-for-profit organizations. We'll start off by defining these organizational types and looking at how they're different from for-profit organizations. Then, we'll discuss the details of the strategic management process for these organizations and finish up with a discussion of some special strategic issues with which these organizations might have to contend.

What Are Not-for-Profit Organizations?

A **not-for-profit organization** is an organization whose purpose is to provide some service or good with no intention of earning a profit in order to meet the requirements of U.S. tax code Section 501(c)(3) as a tax-exempt organization. Note that "not-for-profit" doesn't mean "no revenue." Just because a not-for-profit (NFP) organization has no intention of earning a profit doesn't mean that it needs no source of income. An organization can't exist without some means of covering the expenses associated with providing a good or service. Where can an NFP's revenues come from? Figure 8.2 lists typical sources of revenue: taxes; dues; donations; product sales; permits, fees, and charges; and grants. In many instances, an

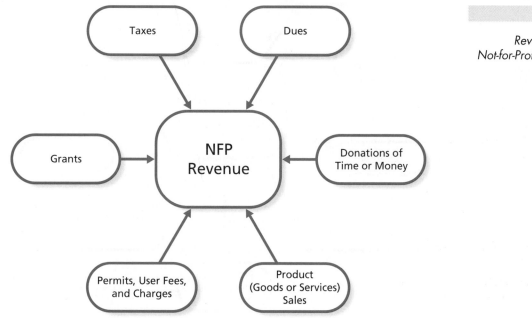

Figure 8.2

Revenue Sources for Not-for-Profit Organizations

NFP gets its revenues from a combination of these sources. What happens if an NFP's revenues actually *exceed* its expenses? Because an NFP can't earn a profit and retain its not-for-profit status, usually it will use any surplus to improve the goods or services it's providing or to reduce the price or fee charged for those goods or services. Also, it's not uncommon for an NFP to set aside a specified amount of funds in some type of reserve account to be used when revenues *don't* meet expenses.

Just as business (for-profit) organizations aren't all alike, neither are NFPs! There are a number of different types of NFP organizations. (See Figure 8.3.) One is the **public sector organization,** which is an NFP that's created, funded, and regulated by the public sector or government. These organizations include governmental units, offices, departments, agencies, and divisions at all levels—federal, state, and local. They provide public services that a society needs to exist and operate, such as police protection, paved roads and other transportation needs, recreation facilities, care and help for needy and disabled citizens, laws and regulations to protect and enhance life, and so forth.

Other types of NFPs include educational (public schools, colleges, and universities); charitable (United Way, American Cancer Society, and Children's Miracle Network); religious (churches, synagogues, and other religious associations); social service (American Red Cross, Camp Fire, Habitat for Humanity, Big Brothers–Big Sisters, and Mothers Against Drunk Drivers); cultural and recreational (theaters, museums, dance troupes, symphonies, parks, zoos, and other arts or recreation-oriented organizations); health service (hospitals, medical clinics, and other health care-related organizations); professional membership associations (American Bar Association, American Medical Association, and Academy of Management); cause-related (Save the Whales, Republican or Democratic National Parties, Nature Conservancy, and American Association of Retired Persons); and foundations (Rockefeller Foundation, Bill and Melinda Gates Foundation, college-university alumni foundations, and Foundation for the Health and Safety of American Firefighters).

Figure 8.3

Types of Not-for-Profit Organizations

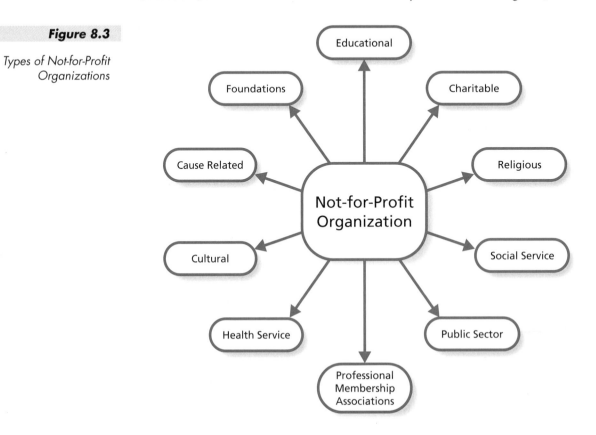

Figure 8.4

Employment—Percentage of Total	
NFPs	7.2%
Public Sector	14.5%

GNP—Percentage of Total	
NFPs	4.9%
Public Sector	11.3%

Economic Contributions of NFPs and Public Sector Oraganizations—2006

Both public sector organizations and other types of NFPs are important to society because they provide many of society's essential needs that either can't be or shouldn't be provided by for-profit businesses. For example, most individual citizens couldn't afford to pay for private police protection but instead rely on the government to provide this protection; the American Cancer Society provides funds for cancer research and to help educate people about cancer and its causes; and any child born with birth defects is eligible for help from the March of Dimes. Many of the services and goods that NFPs provide are important to the quality of life in society. NFPs also play a significant role in maintaining an economic, social, and political system that encourages, facilitates, and protects the development and continued existence of for-profit organizations. Although the vast array of laws and regulations may seem overly cumbersome and meaningless at times, most have been enacted with society's best interests in mind. Finally, NFPs are an important economic activity. Figure 8.4 shows that these organizations contribute a significant portion of the gross national product and employ a large number of individuals who, in turn, have income to pay taxes and to spend on goods and services.

You may not have realized the wide variety of NFPs, understood the extent of what they did, or recognized the economic significance of these types of organizations. These organizations *are* important to our society as well as to other societies around the world— one study of 37 nations found that the global nonprofit sector had total operating expenditures of over $1.6 trillion.[34] Other studies of the U.S. not-for-profit sector estimate that its total asset base "would make it the sixth largest economy in the world."[35] Strategically managing these organizations is also important and that's what we want to look at next.

The Strategic Management Process in NFPs

Because these types of organizations don't struggle to "make a profit," you may think that managing strategically isn't necessary or maybe even possible. However, developing and exploiting a competitive advantage *is* an important task for strategic decision makers. Why? Because NFPs also compete for resources and customers! For example, the American Heart Association competes with other social service, health service, and charitable and religious organizations for volunteers. A local community theater or symphony competes with other community arts organizations and with "entertainment" businesses for customers, volunteers, and corporate and private donations. A state university competes with countless other organizations for state funds, employees, and "customers" (that's you and the rest of your fellow students!). That means an NFP also needs to develop and exploit a competitive advantage—something that sets it apart and gives it a competitive edge. So, the strategic management process is clearly needed by these organizations.

Although most strategy research has been done in for-profit organizations, strategy researchers have recognized the need to look at strategic management in NFPs.[36] Just like for-profit organizations, there does appear to be a positive link between strategic planning efforts in NFPs and organizational performance.[37] So, what *does* the strategic management process involve for NFPs?

External and Internal Environmental Analysis

Both external and internal analyses can reveal important information for strategically managing NFPs. These organizations are facing increasingly dynamic environments, just as business organizations are. An external analysis provides an assessment of the positive and negative trends that might affect the NFP's strategic decisions. For example, economic trends are likely to influence the amount of tax revenues or the level of private and corporate donations an NFP might expect. Changing societal attitudes toward respect for others and individual responsibility can influence the willingness of individuals to volunteer or to make contributions to a particular cause. A new community arts organization (a new "competitor") can affect the program offerings and revenues of other community arts organizations. Even a long-running governmental monopoly like the U.S. Postal Service faces competition from technological advances such as e-mail, fax machines, and overnight package delivery services. It should be quite evident that strategic decision makers in NFPs must analyze external factors in order to determine opportunities and threats.

An internal analysis provides an assessment of the organization's resources and capabilities and its strengths and weaknesses in specific areas. What resources and capabilities does it have? Which ones are inadequate or absent? With this information, strategic decision makers can see what distinctive capabilities, core competencies, and competitive advantage(s) an NFP might have or might need to develop. The functional areas of an NFP are probably not the same as those in a for-profit organization, but the process of analyzing the functional areas *is* similar. Even in an NFP, the product or service must be produced and delivered to the "customer" and revenues must be accounted for in some way. What an internal analysis shows, as we well know, is how efficient and effective the organization is at doing these things. An internal audit would be an appropriate tool for assessing an NFP's resources and capabilities and where the organization's strengths and weaknesses are. The information from the SWOT analysis is used to assess various strategy options and choices for creating or exploiting a competitive advantage.

Strategy Choices

The idea that NFPs have strategic choices may seem strange. After all, NFPs aren't "selling" anything and aren't competing with other organizations, and they certainly aren't motivated to be efficient and effective in developing a competitive advantage because they don't have to make a profit to stay in business. These statements definitely are *not* true! Strategic

Strategic Management in Action

The U.S. military is well aware that it has to understand demographic and sociocultural trends when designing its recruitment strategies. For example, more than 90 percent of the army's target market is online at least once a week. So what better way to reach them than by designing a Web site that is sleek, loud, action-oriented, and features soldiers carrying big guns. They also have to tap into what's hot. When a professor at West Point saw how obsessed his students were with computer games, the army decided to create a game to use in recruiting. Then, the military realized that it would be important to "play to their audience." How? By sponsoring a NASCAR driver and putting up elaborate displays at every race to attract the largely white, working-class audience packed with potential recruits. To reach blacks, they designed the "Taking it to the Streets" tour with an "Army of One" Hummer fitted with a basketball hoop and blaring hip-hop. To reach Latinos, they're customizing a Hummer H2 with tricked-out rims. Will these new strategies work? Military recruiters hope so. What other external trends can you think of that might impact military organizations' strategies?

Sources: Based on T. Vanden Brook, "Military Recruiters Lure Extreme Sports Thrill Seekers," USA Today, May 24, 2006, pp. 1A+; J. E. Barnes, "The New Action Heroes," US News & World Report, November 21, 2005, pp. 53–54; D. Kiley, "Uncle Sam Wants You in the Worst Way," BusinessWeek, August 22/29, 2005, p. 40; and T. Mucha, "Operation Sign 'Em Up," Business 2.0, April 2003, pp. 44–45.

managers at NFPs *do* face similar constraints—limited resources, competition for customers and resources, performance measurement, and long-run survival—just as strategic managers at for-profit organizations do. Thus, at some point, an NFP's strategic decision makers must make some decisions about strategies the organization is going to use to fulfill its vision and mission(s). The strategic options are similar in many respects to those available to businesses.

At the functional level, the NFP or public sector organization must have strategies that allow it to do what it's set up to do—whether that's collecting taxes; imprisoning or rehabilitating convicted felons; developing and showcasing community art, dance, and music; or providing regional home health care assistance to elderly individuals. Every NFP needs resources and capabilities to deliver its service or to provide its products. As we know, the functional strategies are the ways an organization might choose to do these things. The main difference between the functional strategies of business organizations and NFPs is that NFPs don't have the wide variety of alternatives from which to choose because of scarce and limited resources or because of external constraints. Scarce and limited resources affect both public sector organizations and other types of NFPs, but external constraints are most common in public sector organizations, particularly in functional areas such as purchasing or employee hiring or firing. These constraints may limit strategic decision makers' discretion in choosing appropriate and feasible functional strategies.

Competition still exists even if an organization isn't profit-oriented. As we stated earlier, NFPs *do* compete for resources (financial and human) and customers (clients, users, members, etc.) just like business organizations do. These NFPs are competing with each other and, in many instances, with business organizations for resources and customers. Very little research has been done on specific competitive strategies that NFPs and public sector organizations use. One study of community arts organizations did show that these organizations competed on the basis of keeping costs low, being different, or focusing on a specific niche—in other words, Porter's cost leadership, differentiation, and focus strategies.[38] Another study of competitive strategies of religious organizations focused on explaining how these organizations compete and elaborated specific strategic management issues facing these organizations.[39]

◗ Strategic Management in Action   THE GLOBAL PERSPECTIVE

Welcome to the world of e-government! U.S. public agencies at all levels of government are putting an increasing variety of services online. As local, state, and federal agencies go online, millions of dollars are being saved on staffing and mailing expenses. However, declining costs of delivering services is only one benefit of online government services. There's also the convenience factor. For instance, motorists in most states can register a car and get new license plates via their home computer any time of the day or night. Residents of Georgia can purchase hunting, fishing, and boating licenses on the Internet. Parking tickets can be paid online in Boston, Indianapolis, and Seattle. College students can even apply for financial aid on an Education Department Web site. But wait, there's more!

E-government initiatives are going global. When the European Commission (EC), the governing body of the EU, established its eEurope Action Plan, it established aggressive targets for moving government services and information to the Web. The EC chose 20 common government services, including income taxes, car registration, and building permits, and challenged its member nations to put them online. Currently, 55 percent of overall EC services are online.

Yet, with all the progress in online governmental services, there's still a long way to go. Despite the advantages associated with going online, the biggest drawback may be the widespread lack of Internet access for many citizens. Often, those individuals lacking access are society's poorest and most disadvantaged. This is an aspect of this strategy that governmental decision makers will have to address as they look at future strategic actions.

Sources: Based on V. Alvord, "It's the Era of Big.gov-ernment," USA Today, August 19, 2004, p. 3A; Cisco Corporation, "E-Government Blooms in Europe," IQ Magazine, May–June 2003, p. 13; and A. Borrus, "Click Here to Pay Your Parking Ticket," BusinessWeek, January 17, 2000, pp. 76–78.

Even without much research on specific competitive strategies in NFPs and public sector organizations, we know that these organizations must develop and exploit a sustainable competitive advantage to ensure their continued existence. How strategic decision makers choose to do that is the essence of their organization's competitive strategy.

Finally, NFPs face the same types of corporate strategy choices as do businesses: Should it grow and what are its options for growth? Does it need to stabilize its operations? Or, does it need to correct declining performance and renew itself? The main difference between corporate strategies for business organizations and for NFPs is the limited range of strategic options. For instance, concentration is a frequently used growth strategy for NFPs, but diversification would be unusual. For example, strategic managers at Rotary International had to use a turnaround strategy to address its declining performance. Strategic actions involved cost cutting, restructuring, and re-establishing good relationships with member chapters throughout the United States. However, even if strategic alternatives are somewhat limited, NFPs *do* look at ways to grow, stabilize, or renew. They're faced with the same kinds of broad, comprehensive, and long-run strategic decisions that for-profit organizations face.

Strategy Evaluation

Once a strategy has been implemented, strategic decision makers must evaluate whether it had the intended effect and if not, to take corrective action. Even though we know it's important, this is the part of the strategic management process that's probably the most difficult for NFPs. Why? Primarily because there isn't a single performance measure, like profit, that accurately assesses success. Also, clearly stated performance standards (goals and objectives) aren't easy to develop for these types of organizations. Without clearly stated goals, strategy evaluation is more difficult. Instead, strategic managers may have to look at several measures of strategic performance. For example, what are some ways that a church's strategic performance could be measured? One measure might be whether member contributions increased. Another might be the increase (or decrease) in the number of members. The fact that strategic decision makers may have to look for different performance measures makes the process of strategy evaluation and control more challenging. Also, because it's often easier for strategic managers of NFPs to measure the resources coming into the organization (inputs) rather than the services or goods being provided (outputs), they often tend to focus more on the resources coming into the organization than on how the resources are being used—that is, how the organization is performing.[40] Again, this reflects the difficulties associated with developing appropriate ways to evaluate the strategies. Despite the difficulties associated with strategy evaluation in these organizations, strategic decision makers must assess the strategies being used to see whether they're doing what was intended.

Strategic Management in Action

At the Greater Chicago Food Depository (GCFD), considered by some to be America's best-run food bank, the challenge is providing meals to more than 500,000 needy people in and around Chicago. To do this, individual leadership and organizational skills were used to build the GCFD into a "formidable fighting machine in the war on poverty." Some of the strategies—adapted from the for-profit world and combined with old-fashioned military discipline—included "such concepts as training, branding, and competitive bidding."

As the former executive director said, "Even though we're a monopoly here, I want to be at the leading edge in our field. If Wal-Mart went into food banking, we'd out-compete them." Even given today's sometimes overwhelming demand for services, the food bank continues to fulfill its mission and build on its successful strategies.

Sources: *Based on J. Weber, "Waging War on Hunger," BusinessWeek, May 16, 2005, pp. 94–96; and W. Cole, "General Food," Time Inside Business, July 2004, p. IB2.*

Specific Strategic Issues Facing NFPs

Because of their unique purposes, NFPs often must deal with some specific strategic issues such as the misperception that strategic management isn't needed in or can't be applied to these types of organizations, the challenges of managing multiple stakeholders, and some unique strategies that not-for-profits have developed in response to environmental pressures.

Misperception About the Usefulness of Strategic Management

You'd probably agree that strategic management is useful to and necessary in for-profit organizations. Somehow, when "profit" is involved, the benefits of the process are clear, and yet, many people question the usefulness of strategic management for NFPs. Also, many not-for-profit managers themselves aren't aware of what strategic management is and why it's important. They don't understand why and how it should be used. Some even go so far as to say that management, in general, isn't needed. Their rationale: We're not a business, so why should we be worried about managing the organization like a business?

Of course, we know that such attitudes are simply misunderstandings about strategic management and its purposes. Managing strategically in order to develop a sustainable competitive advantage is a task that *all* strategic decision makers face. Doing so requires tasks such as developing an organizational vision and mission(s), analyzing positive and negative external trends, assessing internal resources and capabilities, and designing appropriate programs and services. As academic research and media stories on well-managed and successful NFPs are published, these misperceptions about the usefulness of strategic management should change.

Multiple Stakeholders

We know that strategic decision makers in business organizations must cope with multiple stakeholders. However, this issue is magnified in not-for-profit organizations, and especially public sector organizations, which are closely intertwined with politics and the political process. Strategic managers in these organizations may find their plans and strategies ignored by political leaders who may be interested only in getting reelected. In addition, in the United States, our fundamental assumption about government is that individual citizens *are* the government—government of the people, by the people, and for the people, as our Constitution so eloquently states. Public sector organizations, then, are "owned" by all citizens, and strategic managers may find that their decisions and actions are more closely monitored. Public sector managers also may find their actions scrutinized by oversight agencies such as

---

● *Strategic Management in Action*

What would happen if a not-for-profit organization suddenly had more money than it knew what to do with it? That's the nice "problem" the Salvation Army found itself facing when the late Joan Kroc, widow of McDonald's founder Ray Kroc, bequeathed it at least $1.5 billion. A Salvation Army spokesperson said the charity is aware of no larger gift by an individual to a single charity, although there have been larger gifts. (Microsoft founder Bill Gates and his wife, Melinda, for instance, donated $28.8 billion to their foundation.) In announcing the donation, Salvation Army National Commander W. Todd Bassett said, "This blends beautifully with Joan's desire to see the lives of people strengthened, enriched, and made full." What were the plans for the money? It will be used to build and operate more than two dozen community centers across the country modeled after the one in Kroc's hometown of San Diego. What strategic challenges would such a gift present to an NFP? How would you recommend an organization that received such a gift use strategic management to help it use the funds wisely?

Source: *Based on S. Strom, "New Wealth, and Worries, for the Salvation Army," New York Times Online, August 4, 2006; J. Hopkins, "A Philanthropic Powerhouse," USA Today, June 27, 2006, pp. 1B+; and T. A. Fogarty, "Joan Kroc Leaves Salvation Army $1.5 Billion," USA Today* [**www.usatoday.com**]*, January 21, 2004.*

---

courts, legislative bodies, and political commissions. They may find their strategic decisions "second-guessed" by individuals who feel they have the right to voice their opinions.

Just as strategic managers in public sector organizations face multiple and often conflicting stakeholder demands, strategic managers in other types of NFPs may find themselves dealing with multiple stakeholders who have different agendas. For instance, think of a public school superintendent and the various stakeholder groups he or she must consider when making decisions and taking actions, or think of the executive director of a local Red Cross organization and the many stakeholders that might influence strategic decisions and actions. The challenge of coping with multiple stakeholders is compounded if the NFP relies on these stakeholders for revenues. You can begin to imagine how difficult that might be! Multiple stakeholders do represent a unique strategic issue with which NFP and public sector decision makers have to deal.

Unique Strategies Used by Not-for-Profit Organizations

Because NFPs often rely on variable and unpredictable revenue sources, they have developed some unique strategies to cope with changing environmental conditions—both external and internal. Three of these strategies are: (1) cause-related marketing, (2) marketing alliances, and (3) strategic piggybacking.

Many not-for-profit organizations use cause-related marketing activities. **Cause-related marketing** is a strategic practice in which for-profit businesses link up with a social cause that fits well with their products. For instance, Avon Products, Inc. (the cosmetics company) developed the Avon Breast Cancer Crusade [**www.avoncrusade.com**]. Its mission has been to provide women, particularly those who are medically underserved, with direct access to breast cancer education and early detection screening services. The Avon Breast Cancer Crusade in the United States is one of several Avon-sponsored programs in countries around the world that support women's health. These programs are supported by the Avon Foundation, which has raised over $660 million to "improve the lives of women, globally." The company sees these as a way to fund causes that are meaningful to its target customers. Cause-related marketing can, and does, benefit the NFP through public exposure and corporate donations, but the primary intent of the strategy is to enhance the image of the supporting company.[41] Although cause-related marketing may be designed for the strategic advantage of the sponsoring corporation, NFPs can also benefit from the marketing link, and many have chosen to participate in these types of activities.

Some NFPs have taken cause-related marketing a step further and actively pursue alliances between themselves and corporate partners. These **not-for-profit marketing alliances** are strategic partnerships between an NFP and one or more corporate partners in which the corporate partner(s) agrees to do marketing actions that will benefit both the NFP and the corporate partner(s).[42] These marketing alliances are an extension of cause-related marketing, with the main difference being that the NFP is the one that proposes and initiates the alliance. Figure 8.5 illustrates the three different types of these marketing alliances.

The transaction-based promotion is an alliance in which the corporate partner donates a specific amount of cash, food, or equipment in direct proportion to sales revenues, typically up to a certain limit. For example, American Express's Celebrity Chefs Dinner is an example of this type of not-for-profit marketing alliance. In this program, American Express sells ticket packages to this dinner and donates the proceeds to the Chefs for Humanity fund.

The joint-issue promotion is an alliance in which the partners agree to tackle a social problem through actions such as advertising and distributing products and promotional materials. For example, *Glamour* magazine and Hanes Hosiery teamed up with the National Cancer Institute, the American College of Obstetricians and Gynecologists, and the American Health Foundation to distribute health materials and magazine articles about breast cancer to young women between the ages of 18 and 39.

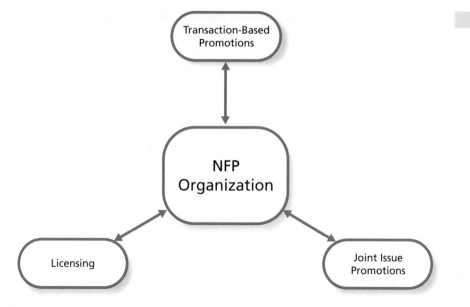

Figure 8.5

Types of NFP Marketing Alliances

The last type of not-for-profit marketing alliance involves licensing names and logos of NFPs in return for a fee or percentage of revenues. For example, the Arthritis Foundation allowed McNeil Consumer Products, a division of Johnson & Johnson, to market a line of pain relievers called "Arthritis Foundation Pain Relievers." In return, the foundation receives a minimum of $1 million annually to fund research. Another good example of licensing you might be more familiar with is that of a university's name and logo for use on clothing and other types of merchandise. In return for allowing its name and logo to be used, the university or college receives licensing fees. In fact, some universities generate significant funds through these licensing arrangements.

These marketing alliances can be an excellent way for NFPs to cope with uncertain revenue sources. However, strategic decision makers *do* need to ensure that the marketing alliance doesn't waste scarce organizational resources, reduce other types of donations, bring about restricted flexibility in decision making, or establish partnerships with unethical or questionable corporate partners.

The last unique strategy we want to look at is **strategic piggybacking,** or when an NFP develops a new activity to generate revenue.[43] For instance, when the Special Olympics organization sells clothing and other related merchandise, it's generating revenue through strategic piggybacking. A community symphony may decide to sell cookbooks or other types of merchandise to supplement revenue from symphony memberships. One cautionary note regarding strategy piggybacking is that the Internal Revenue Service watches these activities very closely. If an NFP engages in a business "not substantially related" to its exempt purposes, it may jeopardize its tax-exempt status. Obviously, strategic managers would want to monitor these activities closely.

Learning Review: Learning Outcome 8.4

- List the typical sources of revenues for NFPs.
- What are the main types of NFPs?
- Describe the strategic management process for these organizations.
- Explain how functional, competitive, and corporate strategies might be used in NFPs and public sector organizations.
- Describe the specific strategic issues that face NFPs.

Learning Outcome 8.1: Explain the issues that arise as organizations international.

⊙ Advantages for organizations that go international range from lowering operational costs and contributing to economies of scale to supplementing domestic growth and becoming a stronger competitor. Drawbacks include the greater risks and complexity of managing strategically.

⊙ Strategic decision makers should know about the legal-political environment (laws and regulations and political stability), the economic environment (currency exchange rates, inflation rates, and tax policies), and the cultural environment (the *national culture:* the values and attitudes shared by individuals from a specific country that shape their behavior and their beliefs).

Learning Outcome 8.2: Describe the important international strategic decisions.

⊙ One strategic decision is whether to use a multicountry (strategies vary across the countries where an organization does business) or global approach (strategies are basically the same in all countries where an organization does business).

⊙ Five international strategy alternatives include (1) exporting—making products in the home country and transporting them for sale to other countries, (2) importing—selling products that are made in another country in the home country, (3) licensing—an arrangement in which a foreign licensee buys the right to manufacture and market a company's product in that country for a fee, (4) franchising—an arrangement in which a business sells franchisees in other countries limited rights to use its brand name in return for a lump-sum payment and share of profits, and (5) direct investment—when an organization owns assets in another country.

⊙ Although many organizations use international strategies to grow, some organizations are *born global firms* that choose to go international from founding.

Learning Outcome 8.3: Discuss the strategic management process and issues that face entrepreneurial ventures and small businesses.

⊙ An *entrepreneurial venture* is an organization that pursues opportunities, is characterized by innovative practices, and has growth and profitability as its main goals. A *small business* is an independent business having fewer than 500 employees that doesn't necessarily engage in new or innovative practices and has little impact on its industry.

⊙ These organizations are important because they contribute to job creation, the number of new start-ups, and innovation.

⊙ Although strategic decision makers should plan, the strategic planning process is a lot less formal and rigid in smaller organizations. The benefit is more in the process itself rather than the outcome—a formal strategic plan.

⊙ Both external and internal analyses are important in determining opportunities and threats and strengths and weaknesses. The "boiled frog" phenomenon helps explain why.

⊙ Strategy choices for these types of organizations are pretty much the same as for larger organizations, although they face some limitations in terms of what and how much they can do.

- Strategy evaluation is also important, although there are some limitations as far as the extent of evaluation done.

- Two main strategic issues facing these organizations include human resource management and innovation and flexibility considerations. Entrepreneurial ventures are particularly well suited to *creative destruction,* the process in which existing products, processes, ideas, and businesses are replaced with better ones.

Learning Outcome 8.4: Discuss the strategic management process and issues that face not-for-profit and public sector organizations.

- A *not-for-profit organization (NFP)* is one whose purpose is to provide some service or good with no intention of earning a profit in order to meet the requirements of U.S. tax code Section 501(c)(3). Although it can't earn a profit, it must have revenues, which can come from taxes, dues, donations of time or money, product sales, permits/user fees/charges, or grants.

- There are different types of not-for-profit organizations such as educational, charitable, religious, social service, professional membership association, health service, cultural, cause related, foundation, or public sector.

- A *public sector organization* is an NFP created, funded, and regulated by the public sector or government.

- These organizations are important because they serve many of society's essential needs that can't be or shouldn't be provided by for-profit businesses.

- These organizations also are an important economic activity.

- Strategic planning is important because there appears to be a positive link between strategic planning efforts and organizational performance.

- Both external and internal analyses are important in determining opportunities and threats and strengths and weaknesses.

- Strategy choices for NFPs are similar to for-profit organizations with some exceptions. For instance, diversification growth strategies would be unusual for NFPs.

- Strategy evaluation is important, although it is challenging for NFPs, primarily because there's not a single performance measure, like profit, that's used for business organizations. Also, it's not as easy to develop clearly stated performance goals.

- Three main strategic issues facing NFPs include the misperception that strategic management isn't needed or useful, the challenges of managing multiple stakeholders, and the use of some unique strategies by NFPs.

- These unique strategies include *cause-related marketing* (a strategic practice in which for-profit businesses link up with a social cause that fits well with their products), *not-for-profit marketing alliances* (strategic partnerships between an NFP and one or more corporate partners in which the corporate partners agree to do marketing actions to benefit both), and *strategic piggybacking* (in which an NFP develops a new activity to generate revenue).

1. The American Lung Association (ALA) [**www.lungusa.org**] is facing strategic challenges. First established to combat tuberculosis (TB), the organization has done such an effective job in educating individuals about TB and eradicating the disease that the ALA no longer has a visible identity or a cause to rally people around. Its annual Christmas Seal campaign, the organization's revenue generator, is floundering because of the economic climate and because donors have so many "attractive" causes from which to choose. Log on to the organization's Web site and familiarize yourself with its mission and activities. You might even want to contact the local chapter for more information. With the information you get, do a brief SWOT analysis. Then, come up with some strategies that the ALA could use to make itself more appealing to potential donors.

2. Jim Collins, author of many best-selling business books, said his advice to new entrepreneurs would be "don't obsess on finding the great idea." He said his research showed that many of the greatest businesses started with either no great idea or even with failed ideas. Would you agree with his assessment? What are the implications for strategically managing an entrepreneurial venture?

3. In order to cope with dwindling budgets and growing maintenance backlogs, many state parks have become entrepreneurial. How? In Ohio, for example, campers who don't own their own gear or who don't want to haul their gear around can rent cots, coolers, cook stoves, and even teepees at many of the state parks. In New York, the state park system serves Coke products as its "official" soft drink thanks to an alliance with the Coca-Cola Company. Many park administrators believe that they don't have any choice but to pursue revenues on their own. Park attendance, especially at national parks, is increasing, but higher operating costs and budget shortfalls have forced service cutbacks. What strategic options do these managers have? What do you think? Are "entrepreneurial" activities okay and what types of issues might arise? What recommendations would you make for strategically managing in the environment that national and state parks face?

4. Trends can be a powerful source for entrepreneurial ideas. However, how do you know when something is really a trend and not simply a fad? For instance, think of the "clear" colas. Why did these turn out to be a fad? Do some research on trends and fads. Write up a report that includes suggestions for strategic decision makers about understanding trends and fads.

5. The Sierra Club [**www.sierraclub.org**] is a well-known environmental organization. In fact, it's the world's oldest, largest, and most influential grassroots environmental organization, with over 1.3 million members and a multimillion-dollar budget. What is the Sierra Club's mission? What stakeholders do you think the Sierra Club might have to contend with? What are its strategic goals and policies? If you were the club's president, how would you use the strategic management process to help you strategically manage this NFP? Be specific.

6. "The best growth strategy for an entrepreneurial venture or a small business is a well-planned one." What's your interpretation of this statement? Do you agree? On a piece of paper, make two columns with one listing reasons why this statement is a good description of growth strategy and the other listing reasons why it isn't. Be prepared to debate both sides in a class discussion.

7. A survey of professionals who help troubled companies cited the top reasons why most businesses fail: too much debt, inadequate leadership, poor planning, failure to change, inexperienced management, and not enough revenue. What are the implications of each of these for managing strategically? How could strategic management help prevent or resolve each?

8. Charitable events involving outdoor participation (walkathons, bikeathons, and charity runs) have doubled since the late 1990s. Charity dollars raised in running and walking events continue to climb as well. However, these fundraisers pose particular challenges to cities because they create traffic snarls and block access to businesses and even homes. Should they even be allowed? Come up with some possible strategies that might satisfy the multiple stakeholders.

CASE #1: One Man's Junk—Another Man's Treasure

This Strategic Management in Action case can be found at the beginning of Chapter 8.

Discussion Questions

1. Would you call 1-800-Got-Junk? a small business or an entrepreneurial venture? Explain your choice.

2. What examples of managing strategically do you see in this case?

3. What strategic challenges might Brian Scudamore face as his company goes international?

4. Which part of the strategic management process do you think might be most important to small businesses and entrepreneurial ventures? Explain your answer.

CASE #2: Delivering a Turnaround

The U.S. Postal Service (USPS) is a large organization and you may not realize just how large it is. Revenues in fiscal year 2008 were $74.9 billion, an amount that would have put them 26th on the *Fortune* 500 list. Also, with its career workforce of more than 684,000 employees, the USPS is the third-largest employer in the United States, after the U.S. Department of Defense and Wal-Mart. The U.S. Postmaster General and CEO of this not-for-profit organization, John E. Potter, faces strategic issues that would challenge even the most effective private sector manager.

One issue is that total mail volume is declining. In 2008, the USPS delivered some 202 billion items, which is an enormous amount needless to say, but it was about 9.5 billion items fewer than in 2007, making it the largest single volume decline in the organization's history. Dwindling volume coupled with rising costs sent the USPS into the red by $2.8 billion.

Another thing that makes Potter's job so challenging are the constraints on operating freedom he has to deal with. The USPS is an independent agency of the U.S. government and is subject to oversight control by the Congress, which has never been shy about expressing or exercising its will. The quasi-governmental organization also reports to an 11-member Board of Governors, which sets policy, procedure and postal rates for services rendered, and has a role similar to a corporate board of directors. However, new legislation has given the USPS some flexibility to introduce new products and adjust prices in response to changing market conditions.

Even given all the constraints posed by these various factors, the biggest lack of self-determination is that the USPS can't pick and choose its markets and services. Its mandate is to provide universal service at a uniform price. This universal service obligation encompasses multiple dimensions such as geographic scope, range of products, access to services and facilities, delivery frequency, affordable and uniform pricing, service quality, and mail security. Competitors (such as FedEx and United Parcel Service) can select target markets and customers who represent the best potential profits. The USPS doesn't have this luxury. Other strategic challenges facing Potter include (1) quick, flexible competitors who continue to slice away at USPS markets; (2) an overly bureaucratic organizational structure; (3) no excess revenues; and (4) severe cost pressures—for instance, a USPS official said in an interview that for every penny increase in the national average price of gasoline, the USPS spends an extra $8 million to fuel its fleet of delivery vehicles.

The USPS has responded to these challenges with various strategies. One is its commitment to providing excellent service and to earning customers' trust. The 2008 Letter from the Postmaster General and CEO and the Chairman of the Board of Governors stated that "This is the heart of our brand." According to a survey by the Ponemon Institute, the USPS remained the most trusted government agency and among the top 10 most trusted organizations—public or private—in the United States. Another strategic goal for the organization was reducing costs by $1 billion during 2008. That target was met and exceeded as work hours were reduced, thus cutting the amount of overtime. In addition, more than 20,000 career positions were eliminated through attrition. From the marketing front, for the first time the USPS is offering online savings and other pricing incentives for shipping services. It also combined product development, product management, and sales into a new Mailing and Shipping Services Division hoping to strengthen its position in an extremely competitive marketplace. The new Customer Relations division will be managing pricing and key consumer and business customer relationships. Finally, in the technology area, the Postal Service is implementing two technologies that promise to enhance the value of mail and increase its effectiveness. The first, Intelligent Mail services, will provide information about printing logistics, verification, acceptance, payment, processing, diagnostics, routing, transportation, and delivery. The second, the Flats Sequencing System, will automate the sorting of flat-size mail (magazines, catalogs, large envelopes) and thus improve efficiency. Finally, a strategic option the USPS is considering would involve a major change to its operations. In testimony before Congress, Potter said that if current trends continue (declining mail volume and rising costs), the USPS might experience a $6 billion or more net loss during 2009. He has asked lawmakers to consider changing the requirement that mail be delivered six days a week. Said Potter, "It is possible that the cost of six-day delivery may simply prove to be unaffordable . . . The ability

to suspend delivery on the lightest delivery days could save dollars in both our delivery and our processing and distribution networks." In addition, the USPS announced that it would cut management staff by 15 percent.

Discussion Questions

1. What evidence of strategic management, if any, do you see in this organization? Explain.

2. What types of constraints do strategic decision makers at the USPS face?

3. What should an external analysis for the USPS include? Be specific.

4. What types of strategic evaluation might you recommend that the USPS use? Be specific.

5. Go to the USPS's web site [**www.usps.com**]. Look for the Five-Year Strategic Plan called Vision 2013. What strategic goals and initiatives is the organization pursuing? How might these strategies be measured and evaluated?

Sources: *United States Postal Service* [**www.usps.com**]; *March 13, 2009; R. E. Schmid, "Postal Service Looks for Ways to Cut Losses," The Associated Press, Springfield, Missouri, News-Leader, March 22, 2009, p. 1E; D. Cauchon, "A Part of Americana Seeks to Weather Economic Storm," USA Today, February 3, 2009, pp. 1A+; and R. E. Schmid, Associated Press, "Mail Week May Shrink," Springfield, Missouri, News-Leader, January 29, 2009, p. 4B.*

CASE #3: The Sky's the Limit

Its goal was to be the "Checker Cab of the skies." Eclipse Aviation of Albuquerque, New Mexico, wanted to change the face of aviation with its Eclipse 500 aircraft. The company was founded by Vern Raburn, a former Microsoft executive who formerly was president of Microsoft's consumer products division consumer products division and who is a pilot. His company used revolutionary propulsion, manufacturing, and electronics systems to produce an aircraft that cost less than a third of other small jet aircraft, was significantly safer and easier to operate, and had the lowest cost of ownership ever achieved in a jet aircraft. Eclipse's goal was to make air travel "personal" by making it possible for passengers to move directly between cities on a quick, affordable,

and convenient basis rather than having to rely on the big airlines' scheduled service. That dream was embodied in the Eclipse 500, the company's twin-engine microjet. This six-seater could fly about 400 miles per hour and had a flight range of approximately 1,500 miles. With orders for more than 2,500 jets, Eclipse thought it was cleared for take-off.

What had made the Eclipse possible was a handful of technological breakthroughs, the most critical being an engine with the highest thrust-to-weight ratio of any commercial jet. Also, in building the aircraft, Eclipse pioneered the use of innovative manufacturing processes to speed up production and lower costs. For instance, technologies such as friction stir welding, which replaces more than 60 percent of the rivets in assembling the aircraft, dramatically reduces assembly time while producing stronger (and safer) joints on the aluminum aircraft. That aluminum skin was also an innovation that saved manufacturing costs. Raburn also chose to merge navigation and weather systems into digital displays and to replace the units that control the plane's flaps and gears with computers that do it at a fraction of the weight. Operating costs for the jet have been estimated at 56 cents per mile. And at a selling price of $1.5 million, the Eclipse cost less than two of its biggest competitors—the Cessna Mustang, which cost about $2.6 million, and the Adam A700, with a sticker price of $2.25 million.

Bringing the Eclipse jet to life was the result of several strategic supplier partnerships. For instance, one supplier provided the three-function antennas, which meant reducing the number of antennas from three to one. Other partners supplied the aircraft's computer system and manufactured the complete wing assembly of the Eclipse 500. Eclipse was very strict about its partnerships and not all the original supplier partners made it through to actual manufacturing assembly. Eclipse dropped one after discovering reliability and usage problems during test flights of the first preproduction plane. Another was dropped when it could not meet its commitments to Eclipse.

Assembly of the Eclipse 500 began in May 2004 with the first test flights in 2004 and most of 2005. The FAA certified the jet in 2006 and the first jet was delivered in January 2007 to co-owners David Crowe, a private owner, and Jet Alliance, a shared jet ownership company in Westlake Village, California. Vern Raburn's vision of helping bring corporate jets to the masses seemed to be opening up lots of opportunities

and the sky seemed to be the limit. Then, along came the economic crisis. Demand for multimillion-dollar business jets plummeted. Corporate jets were getting less use as global business activity declined and companies cut back on perks like private jet travel. Tightened credit markets froze corporation's plans for purchasing the planes. One large Eclipse customer, Florida-based DayJet, an air-taxi start-up, liquidated in November 2008, canceling orders for nearly 1,400 Eclipse jets. Not long after that startling development, Eclipse filed for Chapter 11 bankruptcy protection. The company's largest shareholder, Europe's Atirc Aviation, indicated that it planned to acquire Eclipse's assets and continue manufacturing the jets.

1. Would you call Eclipse Aviation a small business or an entrepreneurial venture? Explain your choice.

2. What examples of strategic management do you see in this case? Be specific.

3. Could Eclipse Aviation have done anything differently to keep from ending up in bankruptcy? Discuss.

4. Which part of the strategic management process is most important to small businesses and entrepreneurial ventures? Explain your answer.

Sources: D. Reed, "Economy, Corporate 'Fat Cat' Label Hit Aircraft Makers Hard," USA Today, March 3, 2009, pp. 1B+; A. Keeton and M. Gutschi, "Business-Jet Demand Is Stalling," Wall Street Journal, January 21, 2009, p. B3; A. Pasztor, "Jet Maker Eclipse Files for Chapter 11," Wall Street Journal, November 26, 2008, pp. B1+; S. McCartney, "Here Come the Mini Jets," Wall Street Journal, September 30–October 1, 2006, pp. P1+; A. Barrionuevo, "Taking the Taxi to Higher Heights," New York Times Online, July 26, 2006; M. L. Wald, "FAA Says Era of the Air Taxi Is at Hand," New York Times Online, March 1, 2006; and R. Karlgaard, "Small-Jet Market Heats Up," Forbes, February 27, 2006, p. 37.

CASE #4: Tata's Time

It holds the number 6 spot on the list of the world's most reputable companies. The Tata Group, based in Mumbai, India, is the largest conglomerate in that country. Its latest revenues are estimated at $62.5 billion, of which 61 percent is from business outside India. Tata has more than 95 companies in seven main business groups: chemicals, communications and IT, consumer products, energy, engineering,

materials, and services. Its two largest businesses are Tata Steel and Tata Motors. Its Tata Tea, which owns the valued Tetley brand, also is one of the largest tea producers in the world. Ratan Tata, Tata Group's chairperson, has forged a strategy that encompasses the globe. In 1999, he issued a "clarion call to push outside India with acquisitions and exports." One of the company's executive directors recalled, "We didn't know what to expect, to be honest."

Today, Tata controls many businesses ranging from Eight O'Clock Coffee Co. in the United Sates to the Taj Group of hotels, which took over management of the landmark Pierre Hotel on Central Park in New York City. Tata made its boldest global strategic push, however, in October 2006 when Tata Steel formally proposed buying British steelmaker Corus Group PLC for about $8 billion USD. Corus, which was formed by a merger of British Steel and Hoogovens, was three times the size of Tata Steel. The buyout offer soon turned into a bidding war when Tata Group discovered another company, Companhia Siderúrgica Nacional of Brazil (CSN), was also preparing a bid and therefore upped its opening offer to $9.2 billion; CSN then raised the stakes by offering to pay $9.6 billion. A Tata Group spokesman said that the company's attempt to acquire Corus was "based on a compelling strategic rationale." Ratan Tata explained further by saying, "The revised terms deliver substantial additional value to Corus shareholders." The increased takeover bid did not impress investors as the company's share price fell 6 percent after the news was announced. Analysts and investors both "expressed concern that Tata is overpricing Corus, whose operating costs are among the highest of any steel maker—something that would affect its profitability and its plans to expand in India." However, Ratan Tata knew that the acquisition could catapult Tata Steel from its mid-50s ranking in the global steel list to the sixth-largest industry competitor. He said, "Analysts were taking a short-term, harsh view of the deal. Hopefully the market will look back and say it was the right move." By the end of January 2007, the U.K. Takeover Panel called an auction in order to end the bidding war and "presided over the contest that started on Tuesday, January 30." The "contest" continued for several hours until CSN pulled out. Tata Steel won its coveted prize for $12.2 billion—a 22 percent premium over what it had originally offered. That acquisition represented the latest consolidation in the global steel industry. The combined Tata-Corus can produce 25 million tons of steel a year. The deal also represented the largest foreign acquisition by an Indian company and made the diversified Tata Group the largest company in India.

In 2008, Tata made an even bigger global splash, at least in terms of recognized consumer brand names. It acquired the Land Rover and Jaguar brands from Ford for an estimated $2.3 billion. Has Tata's time on the global stage just begun or will it be the moment before the curtain falls? What will happen to Tata Group if the global economy continues its downward spiral?

Discussion Questions

1. Discuss the advantages and drawbacks of going international using Tata Group's experiences.

2. What strategic challenges do you think Ratan Tata might face as he guides his company? Using what you know about managing strategically, how might he respond to these challenges?

3. Do some research on India's economic and political-legal environments. What opportunities and threats do you see? In light of these, do you think Ratan Tata's strategy of pushing outside India makes sense? Explain.

4. Do some research on the Tata Group [www.tata.com]. What is its purpose? How would its core values influence strategic choices? Does its international strategy approach seem to be working?

Sources: Based on Tata Group [www.tata.com], March 14, 2009; S. Choudhury, "Tata Hopes Tiny Car Is a Big Hit," Wall Street Journal, March 21/22, 2009, p. B5; "Tata's Strategic Retreat," Business Week, October 20, 2008, p. 10; S. Silke Carty, "Tata, Jaguar/Land Rover Not Such an Odd Couple," USA Today, May 28, 2008, pp. 1B+; "In Pictures: Most Reputable Global Companies," Forbes.com, June 4, 2008; S. Hamm, "IBM vs. Tata: Which Is More American?" Business Week, May 5, 2008, p. 62; J. Elliott, "Passage from India," Fortune, February 19, 2007, p. 13; R. David, "Ratan Tata Basks in the Corus Glow," Forbes.com, February 2, 2007; S. Rai, "Tata Steel Buying Corus for $12 Billion," New York Times Online, January 31, 2007; S. Rai, "2 Rivals Make Higher Bids for Big European Steel Maker," New York Times Online, December 12, 2006; H. Clark, "The World's Most Respected Companies," Forbes.com, November 21, 2006; H. Timmons, "Indian Conglomerate Looks Beyond Purchase of Corus," New York Times Online, October 21, 2006; S. Rai and H. Timmons, "Indian Steel Maker Is Ready to Acquire Much Larger British Rival," New York Times Online, October 20, 2006; E. Bellman and J. Singer, "Tata Steel Offers $8 Billion for Corus," Wall Street Journal, October 18, 2006, p. A6; A. Giridharadas and S. Rai, "An Indian Company Wants to be Everywhere," New York Times Online, October 18, 2006; and P. Wonacott and J. Singer, "Ratan Tata Builds Indian Behemoth Into Global Player," Wall Street Journal, October 7–8, 2006, pp. B1+.

Endnotes

1. B. Scudamore, "All You Need Is Tough Love," *Profit,* December 2008/January 2009, p. 19; "Best Places to Work," *BC Business,* December 2008, p. 85; P. Severinson, "Interview with Launi Skinner," *BC Business,* September 2008, pp. 155–156; J. Straczewski, "Turning Up the Heat: Seeking a Solution to the Energy Price Squeeze," *Franchising World,* September 2008, pp. 40–43; S. Kilcarr, "Small Players, Big Ideas," *Waste Age,* September 2008, pp. 44–50; "Honor Roll," *Entrepreneur,* July 2008, p. 100; J. Johnson, "1-800-Got Growth," *Waste News,* June 9, 2008, p. 3; B. Scudamore, "Changing of the Guard," *Profit,* June 2008, p. 22; J. Hainsworth, The Associated Press, "Canadian Company Finds Treasure in People's Trash," *Springfield, Missouri, News-Leader,* April 24, 2006, p. 5B; G. Stoller, "Rubbish Boy Turned Junk Into His Career," *USA Today,* June 13, 2005, p. 7B; and J. Martin, "Cash from Trash," *Fortune Small Business,* November 2003, pp. 52–56.

2. Reuters, "U.S. Set to be Largest Wine Market—Study," *CNNMoney.com,* January 30, 2007.

3. World Economic Forum, "Global Risks 2008: A Global Risk Network Report," [**www.weforum.org**], 2008; Think Tank of Deutsche Bank Group, "The Risks for Firms; Activities in Emerging Markets," [**www.ial.it/pdf/Global_Outlook**], May 2007; and I. Bremmer, "Managing Risk in an Unstable World," *Harvard Business Review,* June 2005, pp. 51–60.

4. Central Intelligence Agency, *The World Factbook 2008* (Washington, DC: Potomac Books), [**www.cia.gov/cia/publications/factbook**].

5. T. Raphael, "Savvy Companies Build Bonds with Hispanic Employees," *Workforce,* September 2001, p. 19.

6. Reuters, "McDonald's Goes Local in Asia," *CNNMoney.com,* January 3, 2006.

7. P. Ghemawat, "Regional Strategies for Global Leadership," *Harvard Business Review,* December 2005, pp. 98–108; and P. Ghemawat, "The Forgotten Strategy," *Harvard Business Review,* November 2003, pp. 76–84.

8. F. Armer and C. Palmeri, "Overseas Adventure for U.S. Toys," *BusinessWeek,* November 3, 2003, p. 12.

9. J. Esty, "One Pizza, United . . . but Open to Interpretation," *Fast Company,* February 2004, p. 32.

10. A. Kudina, G. S. Yip, and H. G. Barkema, "Born Global," *Business Strategy Review,* December 2008, pp. 38–44; O. Moen, R. Sørheim, and T. Erikson, "Born Global Firms and Informal Investors: Examining Investor Characteristics," *Journal of Small Business Management,* October 2008, pp. 536–549; M. Gabrielsson, V. H. Manek Kirpalani, P. Dimitratos, C. A. Solberg, and A. Zucchella, "Born Globals: Propositions to Help Advance the Theory," *International Business Review,* August 2008, pp. 385–401; G. A. Knight and S. T. Cavusgil, "A Taxonomy of Born-Global Firms," *Management International Review,* vol. 3, 2005, pp. 15–35; S. A. Zahra, "A Theory of International New Ventures: A Decade of Research," *Journal of International Business Studies,* January 2005, pp. 20–28; and B. M. Oviatt and P. P. McDougall, "Toward a Theory of International New Ventures," *Journal of International Business Studies,* January 2005, pp. 29–41.

11. "Frequently Asked Questions," *U.S. Small Business Administration* [**www.sba.gov/advo**], September 2008; T. L. Hatten, *Small Business: Entrepreneurship and Beyond* (Upper Saddle River, NJ: Prentice Hall,1997), p. 5; L. W. Busenitz, "Research on Entrepreneurial Alertness," *Journal of Small Business Management,* October 1996, pp. 35–44; and J. W. Carland, F. Hoy, W. R. Boulton, and J. C. Carland, "Differentiating Entrepreneurs from Small Business Owners: A Conceptualization," *Academy of Management Review,* vol. 9, no. 2, 1984, pp. 354–359.

12. J. Hopkins, "Small Businesses Again Gain Ground in Overall U.S. Employment," *USA Today,* October 9, 2006, p. 2B; and "United States Business Facts, September 2006," *U.S. Chamber of Commerce Statistics and Research Center,* U.S. Chamber of Commerce Web site [**www.uschamber.org**], April 16, 2007.

13. News Release, "Small Business Creates America's Jobs," *U.S. Small Business Administration* [**www.sba.gov/advo/press**], October 25, 2007; "Frequently Asked Questions," *U.S. Small Business Administration* [**www.sba.gov/advo**], September 2008; and P. Coy, "Small Business: Right Place, Right Time," *BusinessWeek,* October 13, 2003, pp. 82–88.

14. E. Caroom, "Dueling Statistics on Small Business Hiring," *Inc.com,* February 5, 2009; "The Third Millennium: Small Business and Entrepreneurship in the 21st Century," *U.S. Small Business Administration* [**www.sba.gov/advo**], April 16, 2007; and P. Hise, "Everyone Wants to Start a Business," *CNNMoney.com,* March 26, 2007.

15. "Frequently Asked Questions," *U.S. Small Business Administration* [**www.sba.gov/advo**], September 2008.

16. "The Third Millennium: Small Business and Entrepreneurship in the 21st Century."

17. P. Almeida and B. Kogut, "The Exploration of Technological Diversity and Geographic Localization in Innovation: Start-up Firms in the Semiconductor Industry," *Small Business Economics,* vol. 9, no. 1, 1997, pp. 21–31.

18. R. J. Arend, "Emergence of Entrepreneurs Following Exogenous Technological Change," *Strategic Management Journal,* January 1999, pp. 21–31.

19. U.S. Small Business Administration Office of Advocacy, "Frequently Asked Questions," *Small Business Administration* [**www.sba.gov**], April 16, 2007.

20. N. Bosma and R. Harding, *Global Entrepreneurship Monitor 2006 Results,* (Babson College and London Business School), p. 19.

21. J. W. Elphinstone, "Universal Home Design is Accessible for All Ages and Attitudes," *Dallas Morning News* [**www.dallasnews.com**], November 13, 2008; "Facts for Features," *U.S. Census Bureau Newsroom,* January 3, 2006; and M. Arndt, "Zimmer: Growing Older Gracefully," *BusinessWeek,* June 9, 2003.

22. C. Schwenk and C. B. Shrader, "Effects of Formal Strategic Planning on Financial Performance in Small Firms:" A Meta-Analysis," *Entrepreneurship Theory and Practice,* vol. 17, no. 3, 1993, pp. 53–64; J. Bracker, B. Keats, and J. Pearson, "Planning and Financial Performance Among Small Firms in a Growth Industry," *Strategic Management Journal,* vol. 9, 1988, pp. 591–603; J. Bracker and J. Pearson, "Planning and Financial

Performance of Small, Mature Firms," *Strategic Management Journal,* vol. 7, 1986, pp. 503–522; R. Ackelsberg and P. Arlow, "Small Businesses Do Plan and It Pays Off," *Long Range Planning,* vol. 18, no. 3, 1985, pp. 61–67; C. Orpen, "The Effects of Long-Range Planning on Small Business Performance," *Journal of Small Business Management,* January 1985, pp. 16–23; R. Robinson and J. Pearce, "Research Thrusts in Small Firm Strategic Planning," *Academy of Management Review,* vol. 9, 1984, pp. 128–137; P. Wood and R. LaForge, "The Impact of Comprehensive Planning on Financial Performance," *Academy of Management Journal,* vol. 22, 1979, pp. 516–526; R. Robinson, "Forecasting and Small Business: A Study of the Strategic Planning Process," *Journal of Small Business Management,* vol. 17, no. 3, 1979, pp. 19–27; P. Karger and R. Mali, "Long Range Planning and Organizational Performance," *Long Range Planning,* vol. 8, no. 6, 1975, pp. 61–64; D. Herold, "Long Range Planning and Organizational Performance: A Cross-validation Study," *Academy of Management Journal,* vol. 15, 1972, pp. 91–102; and H. I. Ansoff, et. al., "Does Planning Pay? The Effect of Planning on Success of Acquisition in American Firms," *Long Range Planning,* vol. 3, no. 2, 1970, pp. 2–7.

23. K. K. Spors, "Do Start-Ups Really Need Formal Business Plans?" *Wall Street Journal,* January 9, 2007, p. B9; C. B. Shrader, C. Mulford, and V. Blackburn, "Strategic and Operational Planning, Uncertainty, and Performance in Small Firms," *Journal of Small Business Management,* October 1989, pp. 45–60; R. Robinson and J. Pearce, "The Impact of Formalized Strategic Planning on Financial Performance in Small Organizations," *Strategic Management Journal,* vol. 4, 1983, pp. 197–207; W. Lindsay and others, "Strategic Planning: Determining the Impact of Environmental Characteristics and Uncertainty," *Academy of Management Journal,* vol. 25, 1982, pp. 500–509; R. Hogarth and S. Makridakis, "Forecasting and Planning: An Evaluation," *Management Science,* vol. 27, no. 2, 1981, pp. 115–138; M. Leontiades and A. Tezel, "Planning Perceptions and Planning Results," *Strategic Management Journal,* vol. 1, 1980, pp. 65–76; R. Kudla, "The Effects of Strategic Planning on Common Stock Returns," *Academy of Management Journal,* vol. 23, 1980, pp. 5–20; R. Fulmer and L. Rue, "The Practice and Profitability of Long-Range Planning," *Managerial Planning,* May–June 1974, pp. 1–7; and S. Thune and R. House, "Where Long Range Planning Pays Off," *Business Horizons,* vol. 13, no. 4, 1970, pp. 81–87.

24. Spors, 2007.

25. Ibid.

26. T. J. Callahan and M. D. Cassar, "Small Business Owners' Assessment of Their Abilities to Perform and Interpret Formal Market Studies," *Journal of Small Business Management,* October 1995, pp. 1–9; C. B. Shrader and others, *Journal of Small Business Management,* 1989; L. R. Smeltzer, G. L. Fann, and V. N. Nikolaisen, "Environmental Scanning Practices in Small Businesses," *Journal of Small Business Management,* July 1988, pp. 56–62; S. W. McDaniel and A. Parasuraman, "Practical Guidelines for Small Business Marketing Research," *Journal of Small Business Management,* January 1986, pp. 1–9; and S. W. McDaniel and A. Parasuraman, "Small Business Experience With and Attitudes Toward Formal Marketing Research," *American Journal of Small Business,* Spring 1985, pp. 1–6.

27. S. Shane and L. Kolvereid, "National Environment, Strategy, and New Venture Performance: A Three-Country Study," *Journal of Small Business Management,* April 1995, pp. 37–50.

28. A. Bhide, "The Questions Every Entrepreneur Must Answer," *Harvard Business Review,* November–December 1996, pp. 120–130; S. I. Mohan-Neill, "The Influence of Firm's Age and Size on Its Environmental Scanning Activities," *Journal of Small Business Management,* October 1995, pp. 10–21; T. J. Callahan and M. D. Cassar, *Journal of Small Business Management,* October 1995; J. Masten, G. B. Hartmann, and A. Safari, "Small Business Strategic Planning and Technology Transfer: The Use of Publicly Supported Technology Assistance Agencies," *Journal of Small Business Management,* July 1995, pp. 26–37; and A. Shama, "Marketing Strategies During Recession: A Comparison of Small and Large Firms," *Journal of Small Business Management,* July 1993, pp. 62–72.

29. S. D. Chowdhury and J. R. Lang, "Crisis, Decline, and Turnaround: A Test of Competing Hypotheses for Short-Term Performance Improvement in Small Firms," *Journal of Small Business Management,* October 1993, pp. 8–17.

30. Ibid.

31. J. Ebben and A. C. Johnson, "Efficiency, Flexibility, or Both? Evidence Linking Strategy to Performance in Small Firms," *Strategic Management Journal,* December 2005, pp. 1249–1259.

32. S. P. Deshpande and D. Y. Golhar, "HRM Practices in Large and Small Manufacturing Firms: A Comparative Study," *Journal of Small Business Management,* April 1994, pp. 49–56.

33. See T. M. Hatten, *Small Business: Entrepreneurship and Beyond,* pp. 17–18.

34. R. Foroohar, "Where the Money Goes," *Newsweek,* October 31, 2006, pp. E18–E20.

35. Appraisal Institute Online, "FASB Issues Exposure Drafts on M&A for Not-for-Profit Organizations," *VFR in Focus,* October 2006.

36. S. L. Durst and C. Newell, "The Who, Why, and How of Reinvention in Nonprofit Organizations," *Nonprofit Management & Leadership,* Summer 2001, pp. 443–457; S. Espy, *Marketing Strategies for Nonprofit Organizations* (Chicago, IL: Lyceum Books, 1993); K. Ascher and B. Nare, "Strategic Planning in the Public Sector," in *International Review of Strategic Management,* vol. 1, 1988, D. E. Hussey (ed.) (New York: John Wiley and Sons), pp. 297–315; M. S. Wortman, Jr., "Strategic Management in Nonprofit Organizations: A Research Typology and Research Prospectus," in *Strategic Management Frontiers,* J. H. Grant (ed.) (Greenwich, CT: JAI Press, 1988), pp. 425–442; J. W. Harvey and K. F. McCrohan, "Strategic Issues for Charities and Philanthropies," *Long Range Planning,* December 1988, pp. 44–55; D. Harvey and J. D. Snyder, "Charities Need a Bottom Line, Too," *Harvard Business Review,* January–February 1987, pp. 14–22; I. Unterman and R. H. Davis, *Strategic Management of Not-for-Profit Organizations* (New York: Praeger, 1984); J. M. Stevens and R. P. McGowan, "Managerial Strategies in Municipal Government Organizations," *Academy of Management Journal,* vol. 26, no. 3, pp. 527–534.

37. J. Collins, *Good to Great and the Social Sectors* (New York: HarperCollins, 2005); Durst and Newell, 2001; A. Howard and J. Magretta, "Surviving Success: An Interview with the Nature Conservancy's John Sawhill," *Harvard Business Review,* September–October 1995, pp. 108–118; P. V. Jenster and G. A. Overstreet, "Planning for a Non-Profit Service: A Study of U.S. Credit Unions," *Long Range Planning,* April 1990, pp. 103–111; and G. J. Medley, "Strategic Planning for the World Wildlife Fund," *Long Range Planning,* February 1988, pp. 46–54.

38. M. Coulter, "Competitive Strategies of Community Arts Organizations," working paper from a research study of community arts organizations in the Midwest, 1996.

39. F. Warner, "Prepare Thee for Some Serious Marketing," *New York Times Online*, October 22, 2006; W. C. Symonds, "Earthly Empires," *BusinessWeek*, May 23, 2005, pp. 78–87; and K. D. Miller, "Competitive Strategies of Religious Organizations," *Strategic Management Journal*, May 2002, pp. 435–456.

40. R. M. Kanter and D. V. Summers, "Doing Well While Doing Good: Dilemmas of Performance Measurement in Nonprofit Organizations and the Need for a Multiple-Constituency Approach," in *The Nonprofit Sector: A Research Handbook*, W. W. Powell, (ed.) (New Haven, CT: Yale University Press, 1987).

41. See, for example, N. Lublin, "Jurassic Park Syndrome," *Fast Company*, March 2009, p. 50; G. Smith and R. Stodghill II, "Are Good Causes Good Marketing?" *BusinessWeek*, March 21, 1994, pp. 64–65; G. Levin, "Green Marketing Gets Cautious," *Advertising Age*, July 5, 1993, p. 4; "Cause-Related Marketing," *Inc.*, July 1991, p. 72; and "Marketing: Cause-Related Marketing," *Wall Street Journal*, February 19, 1987, p. B1.

42. A. R. Andreason, "Profits for Nonprofits: Find a Corporate Partner," *Harvard Business Review*, November–December 1996, pp. 47–59.

43. R. P. Nielsen, "Piggybacking Strategies for Nonprofits: A Shared Costs Approach," *Strategic Management Journal*, May–June 1986, pp. 209–211; R. P. Nielsen, "Piggybacking for Business and Nonprofits: A Strategy for Hard Times," *Long Range Planning*, April 1984, pp. 96–102; and R. P. Nielsen, "SMR Forum: Strategic Piggybacking—A Self-Subsidizing Strategy for Nonprofit Institutions," *Sloan Management Review*, Summer 1982, pp. 65–69.

Appendix 1

How to Do a Comprehensive Case Analysis

Case analysis is a major component of the strategic management course at most schools. In this part of the book, we're going to look at how to do a comprehensive case analysis so that when it's time for you to do one, you'll feel comfortable with what's involved. One thing you need to understand is that a comprehensive case analysis is not like the end-of-chapter minicases that you may have completed as you read the chapters in this textbook; that is, there are no discussion questions at the end of the case to guide you as to which strategic issues are important. Instead, you'll be using what you've learned by reading and studying the various aspects of strategic management in action to analyze the case.

WHAT IS A CASE?

A case is simply a story about a company and the strategic issues its strategic decision makers are facing. In order to identify and address those issues, you put yourself in the position of being one of those decision makers. You analyze the information that's provided about the company in the case. In some instances, your professor may provide you with additional information that's not specifically provided in the case. With this information (from the case itself and any additional information that's provided), you'll do your SWOT analysis. Then, based on your analysis, you should be able to identify the major strategic issues facing the company and formulate the strategic alternatives you think would best address those issues. Going through the process of analyzing a case can be a wonderful way to "practice" the skills of being a strategic decision maker, especially if you remember to put yourself in the role of being that decision maker by asking the following questions: *What information do I have? What information do I need? Based on my analysis of that information, what do I need to do now?* Given this, what specifically should a case analysis include?

WHAT SHOULD A CASE ANALYSIS INCLUDE?

A case analysis typically includes six parts: external analysis, internal analysis (including financial analysis), strategic issues, strategic alternatives, recommendations, and implementation. Let's look at what's included in each of these areas.

External Analysis

The external analysis section includes a description of the opportunities and threats found in the specific and general external environmental sectors. The specific sector includes the industry and competitive forces. The general sectors include economic, demographic, sociocultural, political–legal, and technological forces. We discussed in Chapter 3 how you do an external analysis and what you look for in each of these sectors. Based on your analysis of these sectors, then, you should describe *what* opportunities and threats you see in each area and explain *why* you see these as opportunities and threats.

Internal Analysis

The internal analysis section includes a description of the strengths and weaknesses found in the organization's internal functional areas, which typically include production–operations, marketing, human resource management, research and development, information systems, and financial–accounting. The internal analysis should also include an assessment of other internal organizational aspects such as strategic managers (top management team and board of directors), organizational culture, and organizational structure. In Chapter 4, you learned how to do an internal analysis and what to look for in each of these areas. Based on your analysis of these internal areas, you should describe *what* strengths and weaknesses you see in each area and explain *why* you see these as strengths and weaknesses.

The internal analysis section also usually includes a thorough financial analysis. An organization's financial data represent the results or outcomes of its past or current strategies. Strategic decision makers must and do use some form of financial analysis to make good decisions. In preparing your financial analysis, be sure to examine and analyze any financial information that's included in the case material such as exhibits, tables, graphs, appendices, and so forth.

The financial analysis should cover four parts: (1) ratio analysis and comparison to industry trends and company trends and an explanation of what is happening in the ratios (see Exhibit 1 for a description of the four major categories of ratios); (2) graphs and charts outlining the company's sales, profits, and other important financial measures; and comparisons of the company's numbers to industry averages; (3) listing and explanation of company's financial strengths and weaknesses; and (4) a statement of the company's overall financial condition (weak, fair, or strong) and written support of how you came to that conclusion.

Strategic Issues

Once you've completed the SWOT analysis, you're ready to identify the critical strategic issues facing the company. What are "typical" issues? They're critical weaknesses that need to be corrected, opportunities that the company wants to take advantage of with its strengths, distinctive competencies the company wants or needs to develop from its strengths, or possibly threats the company wants to steer away from or buffer against. In describing the strategic issues, focus on describing *what* the issue is as well as *why* you see it as an issue. Supporting "why" you see something as an issue should come from the information you've included in your SWOT analysis.

Strategic Alternatives

Once you've identified the critical strategic issues, you'll need to develop strategic alternatives to address those issues. How many alternatives do you need to develop? Your professor may have guidelines for you on developing alternatives. If not, however, a general guideline is to propose at least two alternatives to address each issue. In fact, some issues may have only two alternatives—to either change or to stay as is. However, other issues may have numerous alternatives that could be proposed to resolve them.

Exhibit 1 *Financial Ratios*

Category	Ratio	How Calculated	What It Measures
Liquidity	Current ratio	$\dfrac{\text{Current assets}}{\text{Current liabilities}}$	A measure of the organization's ability to meet short-term obligations
	Acid test	$\dfrac{\text{Current assets minus inventories}}{\text{Current liabilities}}$	A more accurate measure of liquidity when inventories turn over slowly or are more difficult to sell
Leverage	Debt ratio	$\dfrac{\text{Total debt}}{\text{Total assets}}$	Indicates what percentage of an organization's assets are financed by debt
	Debt–equity ratio	$\dfrac{\text{Total debt}}{\text{Total equity}}$	Indicates the organization's use of equity compared with its use of debt
	Times interest earned	$\dfrac{\text{Profits before interest and taxes}}{\text{Total interest charges}}$	Measures how many times the organization can cover its interest payments with its gross operating income
Activity	Inventory turnover	$\dfrac{\text{Sales}}{\text{Inventory}}$	A measure of efficiency that indicates how many times the organization has "sold" its inventory
	Total asset turnover	$\dfrac{\text{Sales}}{\text{Total assets}}$	A measure of how efficiently the organization is using its total assets to generate sales
	Fixed asset turnover	$\dfrac{\text{Sales}}{\text{Fixed assets}}$	A measure of how efficiently the organization is using its fixed assets to generate sales
Profitability	Profit margin	$\dfrac{\text{Net profit (after taxes)}}{\text{Sales}}$	Indicates the percentage of profit being generated from each dollar of sales
	Return on assets (ROA) (also called return on investment, or ROI)	$\dfrac{\text{Net profit (after taxes)}}{\text{Total Assets}}$	Indicates the rate of return on organization is generating from its assets
	Return on equity	$\dfrac{\text{Net profit (after taxes)}}{\text{Total Equity}}$	Indicates the rate of return the organization is earning for its shareholders

What should your description of alternatives include? Again, your professor may have specific guidelines for you. But if not, one approach is to describe what, how, who, when, and where. *What* is the strategic alternative being proposed? The possible strategic alternatives are the functional, competitive, and corporate strategies we discussed in Chapters 5, 6, and 7. *How* will the alternative be done? This is an important part of describing your proposed alternative and should explain in detail—step-by-step—what needs to happen in this alternative. *Who* will be responsible for doing the alternative? What individuals or groups will be involved in the alternative? *When* will the alternative need to be done? Is it something that needs to happen immediately, in the short run, or is it more long-term? And finally, *where* will the alternative need to be done? Think in terms of the location(s) where the alternative will take place.

Recommendations

Once you've developed your issues and proposed strategic alternatives, you're ready to make some choices. Which alternatives are you choosing and why? Which alternatives are you rejecting and why? You can choose as many of your alternatives to "resolve" your issue as you want, as long as they're not mutually exclusive. You want to also explain how your chosen alternative(s) will resolve the strategic issue.

Implementation

One drawback of case analysis is that you can't really put your proposed ideas into action. To overcome this limitation, however, your case analysis should provide a description of what changes would have to take place if your chosen strategies were implemented. One approach to implementation involves describing the proposed changes in organizational structure, the proposed changes in organizational culture, and the source of funding for implementing the chosen strategies. In other words, how would the organization's structure and culture have to change if this alternative were implemented, and where would the money come from to implement the alternative?

Important Note: The format for a case analysis that we just described—external analysis, internal analysis, strategic issues, strategic alternatives, recommendations, and implementation—is just one approach. Keep in mind that your professor may have another specific format for you to follow, rather than the approach that's described here.

FINDING INFORMATION TO DO A CASE ANALYSIS

Doing a case analysis involves getting and evaluating information. Where do you find the information to do a case analysis? The obvious place to start is the written case itself. You'll want to read through the case initially to familiarize yourself with the company and the situation. Then, go back through the case and start noting certain statements and whether they describe internal or external factors. For instance, does the information relate to marketing, production–operations, research and development, and so forth? Or, does the information seem to describe the external sectors such as industry–competition, demographic, economic, and so forth? It may take you a couple of times reading through the case to be able to determine the categories under which the information might eventually fit. And, keep in mind that not every piece of information included in the written case is going to be important to your analysis. But you won't be able to determine that unless you've studied the case by reading through it more than once.

If your professor allows it, you might also want to look at other sources of information about the company and the external environment it's facing (such as company Web sites, governmental Web sites, company and industry reference sources, and even general business and news periodicals). One precaution, however, is that you need to keep within the same time frame as the case. For instance, if your case ends in 2008, you couldn't use news events that happened in 2009 because those events wouldn't have happened yet. To get the most educational benefit from doing a case analysis, you have to "arm" yourself with the information the company's strategic decision makers would have had and address the case under those conditions. However, keep in mind that your professor may ask you to update the case to the present time period, which you would do by finding current information on the company, the industry, and the general external environment.

What then? Once you have your information, you're ready to evaluate it by identifying strengths, weaknesses, opportunities, and threats. The SWOT analysis should help you in identifying the relevant strategic issues facing the company and serve as the basis for formulating appropriate strategic responses to the issues.

PRESENTING CASE ANALYSIS INFORMATION

You've completed your analysis of the case information. Now what? You'll need to present the information in a written format, as an oral presentation, or maybe both. What do you need to know about presenting information as a written report or as an oral report?

Written Case Analysis

Your written report should cover the six parts of a case analysis. This information could be presented in a bulleted item format or in a paragraph format. Your professor will tell you what he or she prefers. Either way, label your case sections clearly and carefully check your spelling and grammar. If you have used information from another source, you will need to cite that information. Again, your professor will tell you the preferred format (e.g., as in the text itself, at the end of the report, or some other way) for doing this. Also, you should include a cover page with pertinent information. You may even want to include a table of contents (with page numbers) if your report is lengthy. Pay careful attention to what your professor outlines as the specific requirements for a written case analysis and follow those requirements to the letter!

Oral Presentation

You may also be required to present your case analysis information in an oral presentation. Again, your professor may have specific requirements for an oral presentation. Be sure that you prepare your materials in accordance with those specific requirements. Exhibit 2 offers some suggestions for good oral presentations.

• Get the audience's attention immediately by opening with, for instance, an interesting piece of information about the company, an audience participation survey, video clips, or examples of the company's products.

Exhibit 2

Suggestions for Good Oral Presentations

- Get the audience's attention immediately by opening with, for instance, an interesting piece of information about the company, an audience participation survey, video clips, or examples of the company's products.
- Present all the required parts. Your professor will let you know what these are.
- Provide explanations of your analysis but don't provide so much detail that you lose your audience.
- As each person starts his or her part, state your name and what you will be covering.
- Use good transitions between speakers.
- Stay within the allotted time frame.
- Use visuals to present information when appropriate. For example, audience members likely will better understand financial and other quantitative information when it is presented in a visual format.
- Make sure visuals have no grammatical or spelling errors.
- Make your visuals simple and attractive.
- Display examples or samples of the company's products, if appropriate.
- Make good eye contact with different members of the audience—you don't want to always look at your professor.
- Practice the presentation before actually doing it.
- Enjoy giving your presentation, or at least act like you're enjoying it. If you act bored or uninterested, your audience is likely to respond in the same way.
- Vary the tone of your voice so it doesn't sound like you're speaking in a monotone.
- Don't use "umm" or "uhh" as you speak.
- Wear appropriate business-professional dress.
- Use note cards or a professional-looking folder to hold your typed notes.
- If using a PowerPoint presentation, do not talk to the computer screen in front of you or to the display screen behind you.
- Be sure to turn off cell phones, beepers, or pagers.

Appendix 2
Sample Case Analysis

Here is a sample case analysis that one of my student groups prepared. This analysis covers the following: an executive summary; external analysis; internal analysis; financial analysis; and strategic issue, alternatives, recommendation, and implementation. The company has been disguised and the analysis includes only selected brief portions of each section so that you can see content and format. Again, keep in mind that any case analysis you do should follow the format that your professor requires.

Mary Coulter

EXECUTIVE SUMMARY

Big Loud Motorcycles Inc. (BLM) has had three consecutive years of revenue and profit increases. During the case years studied (2006–2009), revenue increased 8 percent each year and profits grew 12 percent. Although the company was able to maintain its dominant 42.1 percent share of the U.S. market during this period, its push into international markets has not been as effective as planned.

Company Vision/Mission

As stated on its Web site, BLM's vision is to "build the world's best motorcycle product so that customers can experience the joys of motorcycling." Its mission is to "continue expanding its extensive line of motorcycles and accessories and to continue developing product features that help make motorcycling enjoyable and safe."

Company Goals

- Achieve sales and profit growth of at least 4 percent a year.
- Foster a sense of connection and community among our dealers and customers.
- Continually innovate new safety features in our motorcycles and our motorcycling accessories.
- Increase global revenues from 8 to 10 percent of annual revenues.

Company Policies/Values

- Our employees are the reason behind our success and we value their contributions.
- BLM is committed to environmental responsibility.
- We are dedicated to providing our customers with outstanding product value and product service.

Corporate and Competitive Strategies Being Used

BLM is pursuing a corporate growth strategy using concentration through product and market development. The company's competitive strategy can be described as a defender strategy. It's a well-established company with the dominant market share. However, in "defending" its market share, BLM also uses differentiation in order to provide its customers with the best products possible.

EXTERNAL ANALYSIS

Industry/Competition—Five Forces

Current Rivalry Opportunities

- **Strong industry sales growth.** According to the Motorcycle Industry Council, motorcycle sales in the United States have been increasing steadily since 2004. This is an opportunity because competitors won't compete as fiercely for a share of the market.

Current Rivalry Threats

- **High exit barriers.** Manufacturing motorcycles to consumers' expectations requires specialized and expensive machinery and a skilled workforce. This is a threat because these specialized assets are tailored to this industry, making it difficult for competitors to leave the industry.

Potential Entrants Opportunities

- **Government regulation.** Many government entities have noise regulations governing the manufacture and sale of motorcycles. This is an opportunity because it creates a barrier for potential entrants into the industry.

Potential Entrants Threats

- None found.

Bargaining Power of Buyer Opportunities

- **Products purchased are differentiated and unique.** Consumers aren't making purchase decisions only on price. There are many different elements about motorcycles that make them unique and desirable to consumers. This is an opportunity for the industry to be innovative in creating new designs and features to attract consumers.

Bargaining Power of Buyer Threats

- **Buyers have full information.** The Internet has made information readily available to consumers. Each industry competitor has its own Web site to inform the public about its products. This is a threat to the industry because consumers can use this information to compare competitors' products and bargain for the best deal.

Bargaining Power of Supplier Opportunities

- **Suppliers do not have ability to do what buying industry does.** Suppliers of materials such as metal, rubber, and plastic do not have the ability to manufacture motorcycles. This is an opportunity because industry competitors do not have to fear that, if they don't agree to the suppliers' terms, the supplier will decide to manufacture the product.

Bargaining Power of Supplier Threats

- ***Suppliers' products are an important input to industry.*** Materials such as metal, rubber, and plastic are necessary inputs for the motorcycle manufacturing industry. This is a threat because without these resources, there would be no motorcycles.

Substitute Products Opportunities

- None found

Substitute Products Threats

- ***There are several substitutes.*** Consumers can satisfy their need for transportation in numerous ways: automobiles, car pooling, public transit, bicycles, walking, etc. As automobile manufacturers continue to focus on improving mileage efficiency and [overall] safety, the motorcycle industry may lose one of its major product selling points.

General External Environment

Economic Opportunities

- ***Personal disposable income is around $37,682 and is forecasted to continue increasing.*** This is an opportunity because it means consumers have more available funds to spend on products that are not necessities.

Economic Threats

- ***Unemployment levels are currently rising and are forecasted to continue increasing as the economy slows down.*** Although the U.S. unemployment level was at 8.2 percent, economic analysts are predicting it could rise to 9 percent as companies continue to downsize. This is a threat because unemployed individuals don't have enough disposable income to purchase nonnecessity products.

Demographic Opportunities

- ***The U.S. population is increasingly diverse.*** Data released by the U.S. Census Bureau in mid-2006 reported that about one-third of the U.S. population was a minority. Hispanics continued to be the largest minority group (43.6 percent of all minority groups) as well as the fastest-growing minority group (growing at a rate of 3.3 percent). This is an opportunity for motorcycle manufacturers to broaden their target market to encompass these minority groups. In addition, experience marketing to different minority groups could prove beneficial in the global market.

Demographic Threats

- ***Cost of higher education continues to increase, as does the amount of student financial aid.*** Information from The College Board indicated that the average tuition and fees at four-year public colleges was up 35 percent from 2002. Also, total student financial aid increased by 3.7 percent but that amount didn't keep pace with inflation. This is a threat because college graduates will be paying off their student loans limiting the amount of disposable income they might have to spend on products such as motorcycles.

Sociocultural Opportunities

- *More "gold-collar" employees (knowledge workers) in the workforce.* Today's organizations are composed of more gold-collar workers (designers, researchers, analysts, engineers, etc.). These employees are highly skilled individuals who are creative and talented problem solvers. This is an opportunity because they represent a potential target market that's likely to have more disposable income.
- *The increasing popularity of "green" issues.* People are becoming more concerned with green issues, looking for ways to be more environmentally friendly. This is an opportunity for the industry to promote how its products are better for the environment.

Sociocultural Threats

- *Public image of motorcycle riders is not always positive.* The Hells Angels image still haunts the motorcycle industry. Motorcycle riders are often perceived as scary, black-leather- and chain-wearing reckless outlaws. Although this is far from reality, this is a threat the industry faces. It is a threat because this perceived image potentially could prevent people from buying motorcycles.

Political–Legal Opportunities

- *State helmet laws.* Only four states have no helmet restrictions. Twenty states have full helmet regulations. The remaining states say helmets must be worn with some exceptions; most typically the restriction deals with the age of the driver. This is an opportunity because people may be more likely to purchase a motorcycle depending on their state's helmet laws.

Political–Legal Threats

- *State helmet laws.* Helmet laws are also a threat because these laws may prevent some people from purchasing a motorcycle.

Technological Opportunities

- *Increased use of robotics in manufacturing.* Sales and shipments of robots for use in manufacturing have topped the $1 billion mark annually. Such robots can be used in many different situations. This is an opportunity because a manufacturer can use such technology to become more efficient.
- *Online purchasing.* The number of online purchases is skyrocketing. This is an opportunity because, as the number of customers looking for customized motorcycles continues to grow, the Internet can be a tool to help them try out different options and features.

Technological Threats

- None found.

INTERNAL ANALYSIS

Strategic Managers' Strengths

- ***BLM's CEO is very hands-on.*** Every week, the CEO meets with a small group of BLM employees to discuss the company's products and to hear what types of issues they're dealing with. This is a strength because it provides the top decision maker with employees who are dealing daily with products and customers.

Strategic Managers' Weaknesses

- ***BLM's CEO is very hands-on.*** The CEO is meeting weekly with employees. This is a weakness because these meetings take a lot of time that he could be using to address more important corporate strategic issues.

Corporate Structure Strengths

- ***Organized into different product divisions.*** BLM's structure is organized around two different divisions: motorcycles and accessories. This is a strength because it allows the company to develop resources and capabilities for each important product division.

Corporate Structure Weaknesses

- ***Company is not organized around geographic markets.*** Although BLM has said it wants to grow internationally, it doesn't have a structure in place that supports that [goal]. This is a weakness because the company may not be able to achieve its goal of expanding its global revenues.

Corporate Culture Strengths

- ***BLM employees believe in the products.*** Over 70 percent of the employees own one of the company's motorcycles. This is a strength because it shows that employees believe in and support the company and what it stands for.

- ***Company is very people-oriented.*** As stated in its company values, BLM values the contributions of its employees. This is a strength because it shows the company is aware of how important its people are to its success.

- ***Company emphasizes open communication.*** Managers are encouraged to maintain open lines of communication with their employees in all matters. In addition, the company uses its Web site, customer forums, and charity rides to communicate with its customers. This is a strength because good communication is essential to a company's ability to keep employees and customers.

Corporate Culture Weaknesses

- None found.

Production–Operations Strengths

- ***Most of the company's production facilities are less than seven years old.*** A major updating of the company's production facilities was completed within the last seven years. This is a strength because during this updating the company reconfigured the layout to be more efficient.

Production–Operations Weaknesses

- ***Company has a large number of suppliers.*** BLM's supply network consists of well over 100 suppliers. This is a weakness because this network must be coordinated to ensure that materials are available when and where needed. In addition, a problem with any of the suppliers could result in a production slowdown.

Marketing Strengths

- *Company's logo.* BLM's open-road logo is well known and easily recognizable. This is a strength because it helps establish a strong brand identification for the company's products.
- *Repeat customers.* A high percentage (42 percent) of BLM customers are repeat customers. Such customer loyalty is a definite strength because it indicates that BLM knows its customers and what they want. Also, customer loyalty means that customers are buying your product and not your competitors' products. This is a definite strength!

Marketing Weaknesses

- *Target market is narrow.* Marketing research has shown that BLM's average customer is a married white male in his mid-forties who makes around $79,000 a year. This is a weakness because the company has not been able to expand its product appeal to segments [in which] there may be additional opportunities, especially the female demographic group and a younger demographic group.
- *Global marketing has not been effective.* BLM has not been able to secure a larger share of the European or the Asian markets in which it is competing. This is a weakness because the company has set of goal of increasing its global revenues but the marketing approach it is currently using does not appear to be effective.

R&D Strengths

- *Current expansion of R&D facility.* BLM is currently expanding its R&D facility by adding an additional 165,000 square feet to the 300,000-square-foot facility. This is a strength because R&D is critical to success in this industry. BLM recognizes this and has invested in ensuring that it continues to be on the cutting edge of innovations in motorcycling technology.

R&D Weaknesses

- *No global R&D facility.* Currently, BLM conducts all R&D in its facility in Tennessee. Although this keeps all R&D efforts under one roof, it is a weakness because it also means that global R&D efforts may not receive the amount of attention needed to know how those markets are changing.

Human Resource Management Strengths

- *Educational benefits offered to employees.* BLM employees can use tuition reimbursement to pursue additional educational training. This is a strength because BLM is investing in the knowledge, skills, and abilities of its employees. BLM plainly states on its Web site that "its employees are the reason behind our success." Thus, to continue being successful means investing in those employees, which BLM is doing.

Human Resource Management Weaknesses

- *Assembly work on custom-ordered motorcycles is precise and demanding.* A large percentage of BLM's production is for custom orders. Producing these large numbers of custom-ordered products requires close attention to detail so that product quality remains high. This can be considered a weakness because employees may experience job stress from such precise work.

Information Systems Strengths

- ***Numerous forms of communication with employees and customers.*** Employees have monthly work forums and access to a company intranet where information is updated weekly (or more often as needed). Customers have access to online catalogs, magazine catalogs, direct mail pieces, and company-sponsored events throughout the year. This is a strength because the company is committed to making sure that two important stakeholder groups—employees and customers—are well informed.

Information Systems Weaknesses

- ***Web site is only in English.*** BLM's Web site currently can be viewed in only one language. This is a weakness because the company has committed to growing its international markets. If it wants to do this, its Web site needs to be offered in different languages.

FINANCIAL ANALYSIS

Author's note: Appendix 1 (see p. 260) identified what a thorough financial analysis includes. Because your own professor is likely to have specific instructions on how the financial analysis should be done, I did not include financial analysis data in this sample case analysis.

STRATEGIC ISSUES

Strategic Issue #1

What is the Issue?

One important issue facing BLM is the fact that **its target market is very narrow**. The company's research shows that its average customer is a married white male in his mid-forties who makes around $79,000 a year.

Why is this an Issue?

BLM is missing out on significant marketing opportunities as the U. S. Census shows that about 51 percent of the population is female. There are some significant marketing opportunities being missed. BLM needs to come up with strategies to attract this potential target group.

Strategic Alternatives

Alternative #1

What: Offer more bikes that are tailored to fit women. Most of the company's bikes are heavy and designed to fit men. We need to design and develop completely new products that are designed for women.

How: The first step in this alternative is to find out what female riders want in a motorcycle. We propose they do this in a couple of ways. First, do an online survey of a selected sample of its current female customers. Ask them several questions about their experiences with our products. Then, conduct a focus group survey of a selected sample of women who are not currently customers. This research should look at what product features these women would look for in purchasing a motorcycle.

Once this information has been gathered and analyzed, a cross-functional group will be formed with seven employees—two each from R&D, production, and marketing, and one from the financial area. This group will be asked to study the information and develop a list of possible product ideas that BLM might pursue. Once this group has completed its task, the information will be presented to BLM's top management team, who will make the final decision regarding which ideas are the most feasible.

When that idea (or ideas) has been selected, the top management team will develop a plan for implementing the idea. This plan will cover product R&D (researching all aspects of design, building prototypes, product testing), production-operations (preparing to launch production of the new product), marketing (creating a total marketing campaign for the new product), human resource management (determining [whether] additional employees will be needed or if current employees will need additional production training), and financial (putting together the financials for this product).

Who: Individuals from the marketing area will be responsible for creating and administering the surveys. The analysis of the information will be done by the marketing research department. The cross-functional team will be formed by the director of marketing. BLM's top management team will be involved with assessing the team's ideas selecting which one(s) will be pursued, and developing the implementation plan.

When: This alternative should be started immediately. The demographic opportunities are there and we need to exploit those opportunities. The total time frame for doing this alternative is expected to be 18 months.

Where: This alternative will be done in the U.S. market and will involve input from headquarters staff in Tennessee. The implementation plan will indicate whether the new product will be produced at the Tennessee or the Arkansas facility.

Alternative #2

What: BLM should advertise and promote its current line of motorcycles to women.

How:

Who:

When:

Where:

Alternative #3

What: Acquire an established motor scooter manufacturer. A motor scooter is a two-wheeled vehicle with a step-through frame. They are typically lighter weight and highly maneuverable with styles and designs that might have strong appeal to women.

How:

Who:

When:

Where:

Recommendation

We are recommending that BLM pursue Alternative #3. There are several small motor scooter manufacturers that have developed products that have proven to be quite popular. An added benefit to this alternative is that it has the potential to not only attract women but an older demographic, as well. As the average age of baby boomers continues to increase, a smaller, lighter-weight motorized product such as a motor scooter might appeal to them. Such an arrangement could be beneficial to both BLM and the motor scooter manufacturer. BLM would have ready access to R&D and production. The motor scooter manufacturer would have access to a wider market. This alternative will resolve this strategic issue because it allows BLM to add products to its line that are more suitable for the female market. With such products, BLM should see its sales revenues increase.

We are recommending that BLM reject Alternatives #1 and #2. Although Alternative #1 would provide BLM with complete control of the product from design to sale, there are too many uncertainties associated with this alternative. Alternative #2 has some serious drawbacks because even by developing a targeted marketing campaign, the current products still have some drawbacks for the female customer.

Implementation

Changes in Organizational Structure: BLM's organizational structure will change when this motor scooter company is acquired. Those employees will now be part of BLM's employee team. In addition, BLM may need to add some additional employees to its marketing staff as they make this push into the female market.

Changes in Organizational Culture: The company's culture is not likely to change all that much although there will now be an emphasis on the female customer perspective. The cultural challenge is likely to be in ensuring that the employees of the newly acquired company are welcomed as employees of BLM and are made aware of the values and philosophies that have made BLM so successful.

Funding: Funds will be needed for the actual acquisition of the motor scooter company as well as the transition of that company as a subsidiary of BLM. These funds will come from two sources. The funds needed for the actual acquisition will come from long-term debt. Because BLM's debt ratio is favorable (50 percent), there should be no problem getting that funding. The funds needed for the transition will come from BLM's $500 million cash reserves. As revenues increase (as expected), the long-term debt will be paid off.

Strategic Issue #2
What is the issue?

Why is this an issue?

Strategic Alternatives
Alternative #1

What:

How:

Who:

When:

Where:

Alternative #2

What:

How:

Who:

When:

Where:

Recommendation

Implementation

Appendix 3

Comprehensive Cases for Analysis

In this section, you'll find three comprehensive cases for analysis. These cases—McDonald's, Southwest Airlines, and Ford Motor Company—cover a range of industries and strategic issues to consider.(Additional cases can be found on the Web site at www.prenhall.com/coulter.) Although a significant amount of information is provided, you may want to find and use additional outside information, *if* your professor allows you to do so. After gathering your information, use the guidelines outlined in Appendix 1 for doing a comprehensive case analysis, unless your professor has specific directions for you to follow. I hope you have as much fun reading and analyzing these cases as I did writing them!

Mary Coulter

McDonald's Corporation

The first decade of the twenty-first century has been one of ups and downs for McDonald's Corporation. In the early part of the decade, bad and poorly executed strategic decisions and the untimely consecutive deaths of two competent, experienced, and passionate CEOs (Jim Cantalupo in April 2004 and Charlie Bell in January 2005) led to a number of strategic challenges. Since that time, however, McDonald's golden arches have been shining bright!

A LOOK BACK

What had happened at the world's number one fast-food company when things weren't looking so good? For years, McDonald's had been at the forefront of the fast-food industry (or as it's also known, the quick-service restaurant industry). It was the best known of the fast-food chains and had changed the way Americans ate (issues of healthy eating aside). Millions of teenagers got their first taste of working for a paycheck at a McDonald's. The company prided itself on its consistent product and restaurant experience. Customers knew what to expect. They knew they would have the same product quality and restaurant experience at a McDonald's in downtown Detroit as one in Birmingham, Alabama, or Birmingham, England. However, the company's golden arches had become a little tarnished by 2000. A brand that was synonymous with fast and friendly service and consistent product quality had become known more for slow, surly service and poor product quality. In fact, McDonald's ranked last in a national survey done in 2001 of nearly 50,000 customers who ate frequently at fast-food chains. As one of the researchers said, "Most consumers have a pretty low perception about food at McDonald's." In another survey of repeat customers, many respondents said they ate at McDonald's simply because there wasn't a better alternative. That survey also showed that for the first time in 15 years, more people disliked the brand than liked it. As if the company's own problems weren't enough of a strategic challenge, the industry also faced some major issues during this time period. A price war with a "how-low-can-you-go" approach had taken a toll on all fast-food restaurants. Savvy value-seeking consumers recognized that they could get a really cheap meal by purchasing a full-size burger or sandwich for a dollar and stopped buying the value meal deals, which typically required purchasing the more profitable fries and soft drink.

What had gone wrong at McDonald's and how did it respond? Poorly planned product changes, ineffective marketing plans, and changing consumer attitudes toward fast food forced a major restructuring of its U.S. operations in 2001. During this restructuring, corporate jobs were eliminated and service regions consolidated. But even those drastic steps didn't lead to desired performance improvements. So in 2002, additional corporate jobs were cut and some 175 underperforming stores closed. The corporate performance tipping point came at the end of 2002 when the company had its first quarterly profit loss ever. That was a huge wake-up call for the company. So by early 2003, the CEO was out and longtime veteran company employee Jim Cantalupo was brought in as CEO. He took over a company with serious problems. However, McDonald's board of directors felt that Cantalupo's 30 years of experience in the company, as well as his hands-on, back-to-basics leadership style, was exactly what was needed to fix things and fix them fast.

Cantalupo obsessed over the basics—fast service, hot food, and clean restaurants. He was known for walking into any of the chain's stores unannounced, and after looking around, handing the store manager a scorecard that just happened to be printed on the back of his business card. And quite often, that score was frank and critical. He said, "When I see something wrong, someone's gonna hear about it." Cantalupo had a plan for turning around the company he loved, a plan he dubbed the Plan to Win. His plan for refocusing and redirecting the company's strategies was built on three components.

The first component was operational excellence. The company implemented this through a consistent restaurant-specific review and measurement process including mystery diners. It also made changes to increase the speed of service by taking actions such as better organizing the kitchen, front counter, and drive-through areas and simplifying the restaurant environment by eliminating certain sizes and slow-selling items. In addition, the company reemphasized hospitality, accuracy, and cleanliness through new employee training and incentive programs.

The second component in the Plan to Win was to retake the lead in marketing, which McDonald's did by reconnecting with customers using a more hip and contemporary global marketing direction. The company chose to use a global brand message in advertising, packaging, and restaurant experiences, instead of having different messages for different locations. What it developed was the popular Justin Timberlake "I'm lovin' it" campaign (which it still uses). That campaign was more than a global marketing effort. It reflected an attitude that employees were to embrace and display as they served customers.

The final component in the Plan to Win was innovation. The company refocused its efforts on being an innovator. Its goal was to feature a variety of value, premium, and wholesome product options and to deliver the right products at the right price to customers.

In addition to its Plan to Win, McDonald's worked hard to improve individual restaurant profitability by leveraging economies of scale and by being more efficient. To this end, it expanded the use of labor-saving equipment and it streamlined processes.

All these strategic changes had a positive effect on performance. The company posted steady sales increases through most of 2003 and early 2004. Then, tragedy struck. In April 2004, at a worldwide convention for McDonald's franchisees in Orlando, Florida, Cantalupo died unexpectedly of an apparent heart attack. The company's board met and quickly named Charlie Bell as CEO. Bell was Cantalupo's right-hand man and one of the most forceful proponents of change at McDonald's. Bell continued the strategic realignment that he and Cantalupo had started. However, one month after being named CEO, another tragedy hit. Bell was diagnosed with cancer and underwent radical surgery. A recurrence of the cancer led to Bell's resigning his CEO position in November 2004. Not long after (January 2005), Bell lost his battle with cancer. Jim Skinner, the company's vice-chairperson, was named CEO. Today, Skinner is building on the foundation put in place by both Jim Cantalupo and Charlie Bell. The Plan to Win is still the strategic cornerstone of McDonald's business today.

McDONALD'S TODAY

"Our Plan to Win, with its strategic focus on 'being better, not just bigger,' has delivered even better restaurant experiences to customers and superior value to shareholders." This statement, found on the company's Web site, summarizes the results of McDonald's varied strategic efforts. In a recent annual report, CEO Skinner stated, "I am proud to report that since early 2003, when we announced comprehensive plans to revitalize our business and initiated our Plan to Win, we have struck the balance between immediate and longer-term objectives better than at any time in our history. Our success has been a total system effort, with McDonald's owner/operators and Company employees and suppliers aligning fully to serve more customers, more often, more profitably than ever before." It's clear that McDonald's strategic plan with its emphasis on the key business drivers—people, products, place, price, and promotion—is the foundation for its future strategic choices. What are some of the strategies the company, which now has almost 32,000 outlets worldwide, is pursuing today?

Marketing

McDonald's has long recognized the importance of promoting its brand and has one of the world's best-known and most valuable brands. In the 2008 ranking of best global brands by *BusinessWeek* and Interbrand Corporation, it ranked eighth on the list of the 100 most powerful brands. In another global survey of the 100 most valuable brands by market research firm Millward Brown, McDonald's was ranked as the eighth most valuable brand, although it was rated number one in the fast-food segment. In 2006, 2007, and 2008, the company was honored with Effie awards, which recognize outstanding advertising campaigns. One promotional approach the company used was putting real people on its packaging. The company's chief marketing officer said, "People are really interested in reality. It's about real people connecting with our brand." Advertising industry experts say that for companies like McDonald's, "packaging has become an increasingly important opportunity to connect with consumers who may not be spending as much time watching television commercials." In today's economic environment, however, the company's promotional push has focused on value. McDonald's has relentlessly reminded consumers about its dollar menu, which has been around for a number of years. Although the company has been careful "not to overuse value messaging," it added the tagline "Now more than ever" to its ads during the second half of 2008. McDonald's promotional strategies appear to be hitting the mark, but the company's marketing strategies don't just revolve around promoting their brand.

The company always has been and continues to be on the forefront of product innovations. McDonald's basic product strategy is to "offer relevant menu variety to appeal to a broad range of customers." It carefully searches the market for new products and spends months testing those products in heavily monitored field tests to ensure that customers will purchase its new products. Some recent menu additions include Premium Roast Coffee, grilled Snack Wraps, a Southern-style chicken sandwich and biscuit, and the specialty Southwest Salad, all of which have been extremely popular with consumers so far. Seeing a market opportunity, the company is currently pushing its McCafe espresso coffee line. All U.S. restaurants will have the product by mid-2009. A company spokeswoman said, "We are very aggressive and very bullishly adding this new line of coffees to all of our existing restaurants."

Although new product development is an important strategy, the company also relies heavily on old classics like the Big Mac and French fries. These products are on company menus around the world and account for more than 75 percent of annual revenues. In addition, McDonald's recognizes the importance of appealing to local tastes and offers a broad selection of food and beverages tailored to those preferences. For instance, in Japan, it offers the Ebi Filet-O (a shrimp burger similar to the Filet-O-Fish). In the Middle East, there's the McArabia (available with either grilled chicken or grilled kofta). Aussies can order a McOz (similar to a Quarter Pounder with beetroot, tomato, lettuce, and fresh onions). And doughnuts are a fixture on menus at British, Dutch, and German McDonald's locations. As the company states, it has "a global commitment, but a local approach."

One issue that McDonald's has been addressing is that its products have been the target of an ongoing negative publicity campaign aimed at what critics call its low nutritional quality (films and books such as *Super Size Me* and *Fast Food Nation*). However, as one analyst said, "McDonald's is not responsible for the way Americans eat. But the inescapable fact is that it serves an enormous number of them every day." That's why it's likely to remain the "top target for the food police." And that's why the company continues to introduce healthier menu items and is working to meet changing consumer expectations and needs as far as nutrition and balanced lifestyles. One way it's doing this is by focusing on its Balanced, Active Lifestyles (BAL) efforts that are designed to provide customers with tools to help them make informed lifestyle choices. For instance, it was the first restaurant chain to place nutrition information in an easy-to-read graphic format on product packaging. It also introduced high-tech, minigyms for kids called R Gyms (named for Ronald McDonald) to replace the familiar PlayPlaces. These gyms encourage kids to be physically active and feature everything from stationary bicycles with kid-friendly video screens to mini–basketball courts that give electronic feedback to participants to video dance pads where kids dance to moves programmed on video screens.

One restaurant owner/operator located in California who installed an R Gym said that business at his store was up considerably and he planned to install them at his other stores. McDonald's also created a Global Moms Panel with 10 moms from seven countries who will provide input and guidance on how best to meet the needs of moms and families around the world. It also relies on a Global Advisory Council of top academic researchers and fitness experts from around the world to give advice on a diverse range of BAL issues. Because the company has always used numbers to communicate results (we've all seen the big signs stating "billions served"), here are some interesting numbers from a recent year. McDonald's served over 433 million pounds of vegetables and 16 million gallons of fruit juice worldwide. And here's one that might surprise you: as the leading purchaser of apples in the United States, McDonald's served over 34 million pounds.

Beyond Burgers

In an attempt to move beyond its reliance on burgers, McDonald's has tried different strategies. For instance, it developed a McKids line of clothing and toys to build on its strong brand name. However, only a few products remain in this line including toys, interactive videos, and books, some of which can be found online at Amazon.com, Wal-Mart.com, and Target.com. A more significant push beyond burgers was the company's investment in different restaurant formats including the Chipotle Mexican Grill (in 1998) and the Boston Market chains (in 2000). In 2006, it spun off Chipotle through an initial public offering (IPO). Then, in 2007, it sold its Boston Market U.S. locations, and in 2008, sold its minority interests in the United Kingdom–based Pret A Manger. These strategic actions should allow McDonald's to concentrate on its flagship brand.

Taking Care of Its People

McDonald's commitment to its employees has been a focus since Ray Kroc founded the company in 1955. He said, "Take good care of those who work for you, and you will float to greatness on their achievements." The company's belief is that "only satisfied people can satisfy our customers."

Despite its stated commitment to its employees, McDonald's has been criticized for its "dead-end McJobs" work environment and its high employee turnover (restaurant crews turn over entirely within a year, on average). In response, the company says, "Work at McDonald's meets various needs. For some people, it's a starting point … for others, it's a way to earn money while pursuing other interests." Forty percent of the top management team (20 of 50) started in a McDonald's restaurant, including the CEO, who joined the company in 1971 as a manager trainee. For the company to achieve its goal of being the world's best quick-service restaurant, it realizes the importance of providing the best experience for all McDonald's employees. These beliefs have been formalized into its strategic initiative called People: Learning for Life. At the heart of this initiative are its five people principles, as follows: (1) resources and recognition—managers treating employees as they would want to be treated; respecting and valuing employees; and formally recognizing employees for good work performance, extra effort, teamwork, and customer service; (2) values and leadership behavior—all acting in the best interest of the company; all communicating openly and valuing diverse opinions; all accepting personal responsibility; and all engaging in coaching and learning; (3) competitive pay and benefits—paying at or above local market salary levels; and having employees value their pay and benefits; (4) learning, development, and personal growth—giving employees work experiences that teach skills and values that last a lifetime; and providing employees the tools they need to develop personally and professionally; and (5) resources to get the job done—giving employees the resources they need to serve the customer; and adequately staffing restaurants to allow for a good customer experience and to provide schedule flexibility, work–life balance, and time for training.

Training is at the core of McDonald's people strategies. Its training mission is "to be the best talent developer of people with the most committed individuals to Quality, Service, Cleanliness, and Value in the world." The company and its owners/operators spend over $1 billion a year on training and development programs worldwide. More than 300,000 people have graduated from Hamburger University (U), the company's Center of Training Excellence. At Hamburger U, employees are immersed in training on restaurant operations procedures, service, quality, and cleanliness. When they complete their Hamburger U training, they are said to leave with "ketchup in their veins."

The company has been recognized worldwide for its workforce practices. In 2008 the Great Place to Work Institute® ranked McDonald's as one of the best places to work in Latin America. It has received similar honors in more than 20 countries including Australia, Canada, France, Germany, Hong Kong, and the United Kingdom. Also, the company trains more women and minorities than any other U.S. employer. In recognition of that, McDonald's received the Freedom to Compete Award from the U.S. Equal Employment Opportunity Commission in 2006 for its diversity and inclusion initiatives.

Operational Excellence

"Serving customers is job #1 at McDonald's." Doing so efficiently and effectively is the goal of every single restaurant throughout the company. That's why McDonald's relentlessly focuses on all details of its restaurant operations. Many of the operational strategic initiatives introduced in the Plan to Win continue today. For instance, the Global Restaurant Operations Improvement Process evaluates how effectively company restaurants are meeting McDonald's standards and identifies opportunities to improve performance. Also, since more than half of its revenues come from its drive-through windows, the company continually upgrades and improves that product delivery format by using things such as double drive-through lanes. And it continues to develop products that are easy to eat, easy to prepare so they can be made quickly, and appealing to customers. But McDonald's also is implementing some new operational strategies. Recognizing the 24/7 lifestyles of many consumers, one major strategic shift has been the move to a round-the-clock schedule. There was a time when lunch used to be the busiest time at a McDonald's restaurant. However, when the Egg McMuffin was introduced in 1975, the breakfast hours (typically 6 a.m.–10:30 a.m.) became the big revenue generator. The company is evaluating the possibility of offering breakfast items at any time during the day. And it wants to be there for customers the rest of the day as well! Today, some 24,500 of the company's restaurants offer extended or 24-hour service. Now, both the night owls and the early birds can indulge their McDonald's cravings! And in Singapore, Egypt, and several countries in Asia and the Middle East, customers can get food orders delivered to their homes or offices.

Another operational strategy initiative has been a total redesign of its restaurant format. "The last major change at McDonald's restaurants was the introduction of PlayPlaces for children in the early 1980s." The company focused on two aspects with this redesign. One was an operational system encompassing production, customer service, and support with flexible components that could be "plugged in" to customize the operations and menu to specific restaurant needs. Even with this customization, the critical need for standardization wasn't ignored. Every component of the production system has been designed to ensure that products are easy to prepare and can be prepared fast. The other aspect of the redesign was "the look." Although coming up with an efficient design was critical, the company didn't overlook the importance of visual appeal. It eliminated the "heavy, plastic look" and replaced it with a more "clean and simple design"—something that it feels matches the new "contemporary, welcoming image the company wants to present."

The uncertain economic environment has led company executives to prepare for the "what ifs" that come with uncertainty. One thing it's doing is installing computerized systems in more locations that allow price adjustment based on consumer demand. For instance, in China, some restaurants cut the price of certain combo meals at lunch by as much as one-third. This increasing focus on customer data "measuring everything from whether customers are trading down to smaller value meals or dropping Cokes from their order to exactly how much they're willing to pay for a Big Mac" can only help McDonald's. As the company's president, Ralph Alvarez, said, "I love numbers. I think data used well really tells a story."

Other operational strategies include the company's emphasis on energy efficiency and an efficient supply chain. McDonald's has implemented a global energy management strategy to optimize energy use. In a pilot program in North and Latin America, restaurants were able to cut their energy consumption by more than 10 percent. This program is now being introduced to other locations. In 2007, the U.S. Environmental Protection Agency named McDonald's an Energy Star Partner of the year for its energy efficiency program. The company also realizes how important an efficient supply chain is to its ability to provide customer value. To that end, it collaborates with suppliers to ensure a "reliable supply of high quality food at predictable, competitive prices."

Doing Business Responsibly

"For us at McDonald's, corporate responsibility is about who we are and how we operate in the diverse communities we serve." The philosophy of doing good and giving back is an important part of the company's heritage. It's always been at the heart and soul of McDonald's business. And with its Worldwide Corporate Responsibility Report, McDonald's "opens the doors to share what's behind the Golden Arches ... not just what we do well, but our challenges too." McDonald's commitment to corporate responsibility can be seen in four areas: community, environment, marketplace, and people.

Its community responsibilities focus on local development by supporting local schools, youth sports, and other community programs. For example, one of its most widely known programs, the Ronald McDonald House charities, provides health care and help to children and families around the world. Its environmental responsibilities reflect its long-standing commitment to environmental protection. They have developed innovative programs for recycling, resource conservation, waste reduction, and now, energy conservation. The company's marketplace responsibilities involve working with suppliers and expert advisers to improve animal handling practices, helping preserving the effectiveness of antibiotics, ensuring the safety and quality of products and restaurant environments, and promoting the protection of workers' healthy, safety, and human rights. Finally, its people responsibilities, as shown by its workforce management policies and practices, revolve around integrating diversity in business operations and planning.

INDUSTRY CHARACTERISTICS

The restaurant industry is an interesting one. It's highly competitive, although there is significant growth potential as an increasing portion of consumers' food dollars is being spent on eating out, both in the United States and globally. According to industry analysts, the global fast-food market is forecast to increase by 7.6 percent through 2012. And the U.S. Department of Agriculture reports that consumption of food away from home accounted for 48.9 percent of total food expenditures in 2007. With the increase in dual-income families, single-parent families, and numerous moderately priced restaurant choices, dining out is a convenient option. Although the casual dining sector had been profiting from this trend, the declining global economic environment has seemed to favor the fast-food industry as consumers look for ways to stretch their dollars. In addition, fast-food chains must continue to cater to consumers' demands for healthier food alternatives. Not only will this help attract customers, it's important for deflecting potential obesity-related lawsuits.

Another trend affecting the fast-food industry is the rapidly fragmenting market with different ethnicities that have made once-exotic foods like sushi and burritos everyday meal options. In addition, quick meals of all kinds can be found in many locations including supermarkets, convenience stores, and even vending machines.

Finally, the fast-food industry is coping with other companies trying to slice away pieces of its market, especially the lucrative breakfast market. According to a fast-food research firm, 11 percent of business is done at breakfast. That's why Starbucks rolled out hot breakfast sandwiches in various areas of the country. Even Panera and Subway are now offering breakfast sandwiches.

WHAT NOW?

McDonald's golden arches are gleaming brightly again. Amazingly, the company feeds 58 million people every day and added about 2 million customers in 2008. Ever since posting that first-ever quarterly loss in 2002, the company has logged consecutive quarterly sales increases (through the end of the first quarter of 2009). Results for 2008 showed systemwide sales of $23.5 billion up 3 percent globally and net income of $4.3 billion, up over 80 percent. However, where does McDonald's go from here? Its Plan to Win is driving results and has played a primary role in the company's strategic direction. Now, the strategic imperative is "to be better, not just bigger." CEO Skinner stated, "Our customer-centric Plan to Win continues to drive sustained momentum and is generating broad-based growth in our business. Our performance confirms that our emphasis on improving the McDonald's restaurant experience on the 5 P's of People, Products, Place, Price, and Promotion is the right strategy for our customers and McDonald's. One of our two separate but equally important goals is to stay sharply focused on the here and now and to run day-to-day operations with maximum efficiency and productivity. The other is to ensure that the right people and processes are concentrating on the future, and developing new innovations that can sustain profitable growth over the long haul."

Sources: Based on McDonald's [**www.mcdonalds.com**], March 15, 2009; Millward Brown, 2008 *BRANDZ: Top 100 Most Powerful Brands,* [http://www.millwardbrown.com/Sites/Optimor/Content/KnowledgeCenter/BrandzRanking.aspx], March 15, 2009; EFFIE 2007 and 2008 Awards, [**www.effie.org**], March 15, 2009; T. Sellen, "Coffee Connoisseurs Sniff Out Cheaper, No-Frills Fix," *Wall Street Journal,* March 16, 2009, p. C6; J. Adamy, "McDonald's Seeks Way to Keep Sizzling," *Wall Street Journal,* March 10, 2009, pp. A1+; M. Krantz, "Restaurants Struggle as Consumers Eat at Home," *USA Today,* February 23, 2009, p. 4B; E. Bryson York, "McD's Secret Sauce: It Embodies Value," *Advertising Age,* February 2, 2009, pp. 3+; J. Adamy, "McDonald's to Expand, Posting Strong Results," *Wall Street Journal,* January 27, 2009, pp. B1+; G. Charles, "McDonald's Is On-Message," *Marketing,* November 5, 2008, p. 14; J. Adamy, "McDonald's Pitches Iced-Coffee Campaign," *Wall Street Journal,* May 1, 2007, p. B7; B. Horovitz, "Fast Food Rivals Suit Up for Breakfast War," *USA Today,* February 20, 2007, p. 3B; M. Arndt, "McDonald's 24/7," *BusinessWeek,* February 5, 2007, pp. 64–72; J. Adamy, "For McDonald's It's a Wrap," *Wall Street Journal,* January 30, 2007, p. B1+; A. Martin, "McDonald's Says Latest Results Are Strongest in 30 Years," *New York Times Online,* January 25, 2007; and J. Adamy, "How Jim Skinner Flipped McDonald's," *Wall Street Journal,* January 5, 2007, pp. B1+.

Simple, fun, and *profitable.* These three words sum up Southwest Airlines. Yet, behind these words lies the heart and soul of a company's strategies that have helped it achieve an enviable record in the intensely competitive airline industry—36 consecutive years of profitability. As Southwest continues to grow, can it maintain its commitment to simplicity, fun, and profitability?

BACKGROUND

Southwest Airlines began service in June 1971, with three planes flying between three Texas cities: Houston, Dallas, and San Antonio. Herb Kelleher, the colorful character who cofounded the company and who now serves as chairman emeritus, recalls, "A lot of people figured us for road kill at that time." Why? Because the company's strategic approach was unlike anything the other major airlines were doing at that time. Air service in the early 1970s could best be characterized by high airfares, inconvenient flight schedules, complicated ticketing, and long and inconvenient flying experiences (from driving to the airport, parking, and finally reaching your destination). Southwest wanted to change that! It began with a simple notion—get your passengers to their destinations when they want to get there, on time, at the lowest possible fares, and make sure they have a good time doing it. To deliver this type of service, Southwest's strategy was to fly short-haul routes where the fares were competitive with driving. In these short-haul markets, speed and convenience would be essential to marketplace success. Therefore, Southwest's overall strategy was to minimize total travel time for customers, including ticketing and boarding, and to provide service out of airports convenient to doing business or vacationing in a city. Simple, yet effective, even today. Southwest has had a dynamic and impressive corporate history. The company has earned the respect of other airline competitors as well as other businesses around the world. An entertaining description of various highlights in the company's history can be found on its Web site [**www.southwest.com**].

CURRENT OPERATIONS

Southwest Airlines bills itself as the nation's low-fare, high customer satisfaction airline. It serves primarily short- and medium-haul routes with single-class service targeted at business and leisure travelers. Its approach has been to focus primarily on point-to-point, rather than hub-and-spoke, service in markets. This point-to-point system provides for more direct nonstop flights for customers and minimizes connections, delays, and total trip time. Approximately 79 percent of Southwest's customers fly nonstop, with an average passenger trip length of about 846 miles. Despite the challenges facing the airline industry—high fuel costs, dire economic conditions, and enhanced security measures—2008 was another year of accomplishments for Southwest, including its 36th consecutive year of profitability (an airline-industry record) and continued leadership in customer satisfaction as it once again received the fewest customer complaints of all airlines. Several strategic factors can be identified as the keys to Southwest's success.

Low-Cost Advantage

Historically, Southwest has enjoyed a significant cost advantage compared to the other traditional carriers, and low operating costs continue to be one of its competitive strengths. How does Southwest keep its costs low? One important element is its use of a single type of aircraft—the Boeing 737—that allows for simplified scheduling, operations, maintenance, and training. The planes have identical configurations, making them easy for crews to operate, maintain, and service. In 2009, Southwest had a fairly young fleet of more than 530 Boeing 737 aircraft with an average age of nine years. Planes on order will replace older ones in the fleet and will add additional capacity as needed. Each plane flies an average of about seven flights per day, with an average daily utilization of about 13 hours. The company also has outfitted its fleet with fuel-saving, performance-enhancing blended winglets (appendages on the wings). These winglets extend flight range, save fuel, and reduce engine maintenance costs and takeoff noise.

For several years, Southwest benefited from fuel hedging in which it paid upfront for the right to buy fuel at certain (in this instance, lower) prices. Although it still pays less for fuel than its competitors, Southwest's average fuel price rose from an average of 72 cents per gallon in 2003 to $2.44 in 2008. (A 737 plane can hold about 7,000 gallons.) In 2008, Southwest's fuel bill rose more than $500 million, an amount nearly equal to its 2007 profits. To cut fuel costs, Southwest is power-washing jet engines to get rid of grime, carrying less water for bathroom faucets and toilets, and replacing passenger seats with lighter models.

Another operational strategy that has allowed Southwest to keep costs low is the use of technology, especially automated processes. Early on, Southwest recognized the benefits of automation. It was the first airline to offer a ticketless travel option (in 1994), eliminating the need to process and then print a paper ticket. In 2007, online bookings reached 74 percent, compared to approximately 70 percent in 2006. In 2005, Southwest further exploited technology by introducing DING!, a downloadable desktop application that alerts customers to exclusive deals.

Southwest also has relied on automation to facilitate the implementation of increased security requirements put in place after 9/11 and again after the thwarted London terrorist plot in 2006. It also has invested significant sums in facilities, equipment, and technology to efficiently process customers, who now have plenty of options to acquire boarding passes and who don't have to wait in lines at ticket and gate counters. Baggage tags are computer generated, as are automated boarding passes, and customers can access both at multiple points throughout the airport. Southwest also has self-service rapid check-in boarding pass kiosks where customers can check their bags and obtain transfer boarding passes. Customers can also check in and get their boarding passes online at Southwest's Web site. In 2007, approximately 70 percent of Southwest customers checked in online or at a kiosk. Not only do such options benefit the customer, they benefit the company as well, because fewer employees are needed to provide these services.

The company's Web site has benefited it in other ways, as well. As one of the first airlines to establish a Web site, southwest.com continues to be the number one airline Web site for sales and revenues. In 2007, the company's SWABIZ, a free online booking tool for business persons to plan, purchase, and track business travel, increased sales by 19 percent. As this percentage has continued to increase over the years, it's clear that the Web site has been and will continue to be a vital part of Southwest's strategy for generating passenger revenue.

Southwest also has chosen to operate out of conveniently located satellite or downtown airports, which are typically smaller and less congested than other airlines' hub airports that are usually located quite a distance from a city's main business district. This operating strategy allows for high asset utilization because gate turnaround is quick (currently, Southwest's turnaround time is approximately 25 minutes) and the planes can get back in the air transporting more customers to their destination. As Kelleher used to point out, you don't make money sitting on the ground. Quick turnaround also means that the company doesn't need as many aircraft or gate facilities. In 2009, Southwest is veering away from this strategy by flying out of New York's LaGuardia and Boston's Logan airports. This strategic shift is part of the company's plan to target new markets. CEO Gary Kelley says, "There are opportunities to tap that we haven't taken advantage of."

Legendary Customer Service

Southwest gives customers what they want—great service at low prices. Southwest isn't just attracting large numbers of passengers (it carries more domestic passengers than any other airline), it's keeping them happy. For 14 years running, the American Customer Satisfaction Index has ranked Southwest first among airlines for highest customer service satisfaction. In 2007, Southwest rated highest among all major airlines in the U.S. Department of Transportation's (DOT) customer satisfaction and on-time performance surveys. This honor is in addition to Southwest's continual ranking at the top of DOT's Air Travel Consumer Report for receiving the fewest customer complaints. In addition, another industry survey, the Airline Quality Rating report, said that Southwest is "consistently the company with the lowest customer complaint rate in the industry."

Southwest has formalized its dedication to customer satisfaction by adopting a comprehensive plan called Customer Service Commitment, which outlines actions the company is taking to promote the highest quality of customer service. This plan covers the gamut of possible customer concerns from baggage handling and passenger safety to delays and cancellations and getting a refund. The company is so committed to customer service that it has a person whose formal job title is senior manager of proactive customer communications. This person spends his or her "12-hour work days finding out how Southwest disappointed its customers and then firing off homespun letters of apology."

The company's mission (as found on its Web site) establishes the foundation for its commitment to serving customers: "The mission of Southwest Airlines is dedication to the highest quality of Customer Service delivered with a sense of warmth, friendliness, individual pride, and Company Spirit." This mission statement influences the way Southwest employees do their work. It emphasizes the company's strong desire to serve its customers and provides guidance to employees when they make service-related decisions. In fact, employees are continually reminded that Southwest is in the customer service business—and its business just happens to be airline transportation. The goal is getting customers from Point A to Point B and doing so in a way that is simple and fun for the customers and profitable for the company.

Southwest currently flies to 65 destinations in 32 states throughout the United States with over 3,300 flights a day. In 2005, Southwest introduced its first code-share arrangement with ATA Airlines. In code-share arrangements, airlines market and sell tickets for certain flights on each other's routes. Such code-sharing alliances are quite common among the other major U.S. airlines. Although ATA went out of business in 2008, the arrangement was so beneficial that Southwest began looking at other alliances, especially beyond U.S. borders. A code-sharing agreement with Canada's WestJet Airlines is scheduled to commence in 2009 and an alliance with Mexico's Volaris D.F. will start in 2010. And the company is actively pursuing code-sharing deals with foreign carriers in Europe and Asia in order to expand its markets beyond North America. With the high frequencies of flights and extensive route system that's continuing to expand, customers have convenience and reliability with lots of options to get where they want to go, when they want to go. The combination of low fares, convenient and frequent schedules, and friendly customer service means that Southwest dominates the majority of the markets it serves.

A Black Eye for the Company—Plane Maintenance and Inspection Troubles

In the first quarter of 2008, Southwest faced serious allegations about its plane maintenance program. Two Federal Aviation Administration (FAA) officials who had noticed problems with the company's planes and Southwest's failure to do required inspections said they were pressured by Southwest executives to keep the serious problems hidden. In the wake of these allegations, the company grounded 8 percent of its fleet due to safety concerns until required inspections of the planes could be completed. In addition, Southwest suspended three employees and pledged to "fix any deficiencies in its internal controls." After receiving the results of an internal investigation, CEO Kelly said he "was concerned with some of our findings related to maintenance compliance." He went on to say that he has "insisted that we have the appropriate maintenance organizational and governance structures in place to ensure that the right decisions are being made." In March 2009, Southwest Airlines announced that it had resolved all outstanding issues with the FAA and would continue to work together with the agency to ensure the highest degree of flight safety for the public.

SOUTHWEST'S CULTURE AND PEOPLE

A major reason behind Southwest's success has been its culture and its people. Southwest has one of the most unique cultures among those of all major U.S. corporations. It's a high-spirited, often irreverent culture, much like its legendary cofounder Herb Kelleher. At company headquarters, the walls are covered with more than 10,000 picture frames containing photos of employees' pets, of Herb dressed like Elvis or in drag, of flight attendants in miniskirts, and caricatures of Southwest planes gnawing on competitors' aircraft. There are teddy bears and pink flamingoes. There's lots of laughter, and few, if any, neckties to be found. Even the CEO, Gary C. Kelley, normally a mild-mannered former accountant, shocked coworkers by showing up at a company Halloween party dressed—makeup and all—as Gene Simmons, front man for the rock group Kiss. On flights, flight attendants have been known to dress up as the Easter Bunny or to wear Halloween masks on those respective holidays. They've hidden in the overhead baggage compartments and jumped out at passengers who first opened them. However, no matter how fun and goofy it may get, no one at Southwest loses sight of the fact that the focus is on customers. This was plainly evident in the weeks after 9/11, when the laughter stopped. And it didn't take a memo from company headquarters to tell employees how to handle themselves during this difficult period. Employees understood that the normal gags played on passengers and the jokes and Halloween costumes were inappropriate. However, after about six months, passengers indicated through e-mails and comments that they were once again ready for Southwest's brand of fun. But even now, employees are sensitive to customers' concerns and know when to tone it down.

On its company's Web site, the company describes its culture from the perspective of "living the Southwest way, which involves a warrior spirit, a servant's heart, and a fun-LUVing attitude." In addition, employees are expected to get excellent results by focusing on safety, low costs, and high customer service and by demonstrating integrity in all actions.

In April 2006, Southwest went where no other airline had gone—the blogosphere. Playing the role of maverick once again, it launched its blog, Nuts About Southwest, "which allows customers to take a peek inside the culture and operations of Southwest Airlines." The corporate blog has employee bloggers representing a mix of frontline and behind-the-scenes employees—flight attendants, pilots, schedule planners, mechanics, and more. The blog offers customers a great venue for open dialogue. Southwest Air's now-retired president, Colleen Barrett, said, "When we first started the blog, I often told folks that I considered it to be a great customer service laboratory, if you will, but it has evolved into much more than that." Check it out at [**www.blogsouthwest.com**]. Southwest also has been tweeting since July 2007 and was recently named one of the 40 Best Twitter Brands. The company's social media specialist says that success in the micro-blogging arena requires being "honest, real, quick, and FUN."

Southwest recognizes that its success is due to its people and emphasizes that its people are its most valuable asset. The company has deep concern for its employees and seeks to provide fun and challenging jobs. It also takes care of its employees. Southwest was the first U.S. airline to offer a profit-sharing plan (in 1974). Employees own approximately 10 percent of the company's stock. Southwest's employees are known for their commitment to the company and to the Southwest spirit, which isn't surprising considering that the company has a reputation as a great place to work. The number of resumés it receives every year (over 329,000 in 2007) is further proof that Southwest is perceived as a great place to work. At the end of 2008, Southwest had over 35,000 employees with approximately 40 percent in flight operations; 6 percent in maintenance; 41 percent in ground, customer, and fleet service; and 13 percent in management, accounting, marketing, and office support positions.

The company, of course, wants the best of the best. Job applicants endure a rigorous interview process that can take as long as six weeks. Once hired, about 20 percent of new hires fail to make it through the training period. "We don't keep them if they don't fit into our culture. A lot of people think we're just relaxed, loosey-goosey, but we have a lot of discipline." Those employees who do make it are provided the support they need to succeed. Southwest has always had the approach of trusting employees and empowering them to make decisions effectively as they perform their jobs.

Many people assume that Southwest's outstanding relationship with its people is because it's nonunion but nothing could be further from the truth. More than four out of five employees at Southwest (approximately 86 percent) are union members. However, even during the times when other heavily unionized airlines were laying off employees and asking for sizable pay cuts from their employees, Southwest was negotiating new contracts and trying to keep its strategy of no layoffs and using employee furloughs as "a last resort." The company is proud of its reputation as a great place to work and acknowledges that its people are wonderful. They want to honor them, to treat them with respect, and to reward their productivity. However, Southwest also understands the importance of maintaining its low-cost structure. If that is lost, the company's future could be jeopardized.

FINANCIAL HIGHLIGHTS

To achieve 36 consecutive years of profitability in an industry that's known to be challenging and competitive is quite an accomplishment. During 2008, revenues were up 11.8 percent to a little over $11 billion, but net income was down 72.4 percent to $178 million. Considering the state of the economy, however, the ability to even post a net income is a testament to Southwest's strategies. Complete financial information can be found on the company's Web site at [**www.southwest.com**].

COMPANY AWARDS AND RECOGNITIONS

When you do outstanding work, you get recognized and Southwest Airlines is no exception. Here are a few of the company's many awards from 2008 and 2009:

- One of the most admired companies in *Fortune* magazine's annual ranking of Most Admired Companies for the 13th year in a row. In 2009, it ranked number seven.
- Named in 2007 to *BusinessWeek's* first-ever list of Customer Service Champs. (In 2009, however, it was JetBlue, not Southwest, that was named to the list.)
- Cited by *Chief Executive* magazine on its list of "Best Companies for Leaders" for 2008. Southwest ranked number seven out of twenty.
- Named in 2009 as one of America's Most Shareholder Friendly Companies by *Institutional Investor Magazine*.
- Ranked third in 2009 on the list of Best College Internship Programs, just behind Google and Microsoft.
- Southwest Airlines Cargo was honored in 2009 as Airline of the Year for its excellence in air cargo delivery service.
- For seven years, listed by *Hispanic* magazine on the Hispanic Corporate 100 for leadership in providing opportunities for Hispanics.

THE AIRLINE INDUSTRY AND MAJOR COMPETITORS

The airline industry is intensely competitive. Numerous external factors influence each competitor's profitability. One major uncertainty now facing the industry is fuel prices. Airlines need fuel to operate and are severely impacted by changes in jet fuel prices. Southwest has substantial fuel-hedging positions until 2009 at $50 per barrel, which gives them ample protection against jet fuel price spikes. These prices are higher than during the last several years, however, when fuel prices were $36 per barrel or lower.

Other industry uncertainties included economic conditions in the United States and the resulting customer demand and continued vulnerability to exogenous events (such as a terrorist attack) that had the potential to adversely affect air travel. Other characteristics that make the airline industry vulnerable include:

- It is tremendously capital intensive.
- There are enormous fixed costs.
- It is fuel intensive, and with alternative energy sources unlikely, is subject to global political events.
- It is labor intensive and there are fewer and less experienced workers available to fill jobs.
- There is no product inventory or shelf life—an unfilled seat on a flight can't be put in inventory and sold later.
- It is quite cyclical as much of passenger travel demand is discretionary.
- It is heavily regulated and taxed.

Competitors are also nipping at Southwest's wings. Although several have tried in the past to duplicate Southwest's formula, with little success, competitors such as JetBlue and AirTran have caught the attention of Southwest's management team. Both are strong, innovative, and low-cost. AirTran Holdings, based in Orlando, Florida, has been growing fast, operating primarily out of its Atlanta base. And JetBlue had managed to generate a lot of positive buzz in the industry until its customer service fiasco in February 2007 when its operational systems couldn't handle the aftermath of an ice storm. Now, it has its own set of problems to deal with. Despite this, Southwest is well aware that it needs to keep an eye on both JetBlue and AirTran. Other mainline carriers (e.g., American, Delta, and United) have been addressing many of their fundamental problems by cutting costs, although they still have a long way to go to pose a major threat.

THE FUTURE

Southwest Airlines has been an anomaly among airlines. Its performance has consistently been among the industry's best. However, Southwest faces some serious challenges as it seeks to maintain its competitive leadership position. Severe cost pressures have led the company to implement some aggressive measures to improve productivity. These measures included no longer paying commissions on flights booked by traditional travel agents, consolidating its reservations operations centers, and motivating employees to continue to look for innovative ways to better run the business. Even though Southwest continues to have some of the lowest costs in the industry, costs continue to climb. Keeping costs under control and keeping its culture alive are just two of the key challenges facing Southwest as it continues to expand and to reinforce its role as a leading prime-time industry player.

Sources: Based on Southwest Airlines [**www.southwest.com**], March 26, 2009; B. D. Bowen and D. E. Headley, "2008 Airline Quality Rating," [**http://aqr.aero/aqrreports**], March 26, 2009; American Customer Satisfaction Index [**http://www. theacsi.org**], March 26, 2009; M. Esterl, "Southwest Airlines CEO Flies Uncharted Skies," *Wall Street Journal*, March 25, 2009, pp. B1+; Southwest Airlines 10-K, [**www.southwest.com**], February 2, 2009; D. Reed, "Southwest Amps Up Its Strategy," *USA Today,* December 26, 2008, p. 1B; M. Maynard, "To Save Fuel, Airlines Find No Speck Too Small," *New York Times Online,* June 11, 2008; "Southwest's Fuel Bill Takes Off," *CNNMoney.com,* April 11, 2008; A. Pasztor, "Southwest's Cozy Ties Triggered FAA Tumult," *Wall Street Journal,* April 3, 2008, pp. A1+; D. Griffin and S. Bronstein, "FAA Inspectors: Southwest Tried to Hide Safety Problems," *CNN.com,* April 3, 2008; A. Pasztor and M. Trottman, "Southwest Rethinks Plane Retirement, Shelves Outsource Plan," *Wall Street Journal,* March 17, 2008, p. A2; A. Pasztor and M. Trottman, "Southwest Suspends Workers Amid Probe," *Wall Street Journal,* March 12, 2008, p. A4; and "Southwest Grounds 41 Planes on Safety Concerns," *CNNMoney.com,* March 12, 2008.

Ford Motor Company

Ford Motor Company (Ford), like other global car manufacturers, is at a critical juncture in its history. In 2008, it suffered its worst loss ever—$14.8 billion on total revenues that had dropped 15 percent to $146 billion. And 2009 started off badly as sales plunged 40 percent in January, 48 percent in February, 41 percent in March, and 31 percent in April. Once the world's second largest automaker, Ford is now number three behind Toyota and General Motors. The first decade of the twenty-first century has been a tough one for Ford. The company is coping with declining market share, an industry going through dramatic changes, and an uncertain future. CEO and president Alan Mulally faces a challenge in turning around this corporate icon. His plan can be summed up by statements he made in the company's 2009 Outlook: "Although business conditions have deteriorated rapidly on a global scale, our ONE FORD plan is more right than ever; we are focused on swift and decisive actions to stay on course with the four elements of our plan; and we are working on longer term restructuring actions on a global basis and managing all of the elements that we control to respond to changing economic conditions."

HISTORY

With much sentimental fanfare and hoopla, Ford celebrated its 100-year anniversary in June 2003. In the early 1900s, Ford "began a manufacturing revolution with its mass production assembly lines." From the production of the first Model T in 1908 to the 500hp GT racer with a price tag of $150,000, Ford has had some fabulous successes in product design. The Mustang, first introduced in 1964, is one of the company's best ever products. The car made the company a lot of money as it ignited Detroit's obsession with the baby boomer market, a preoccupation that has been difficult to let go. Ford sold one million Mustangs in 24 months, an incredible product launch for a new model, even by today's standards. Then, there was the Ford Explorer, the first sport utility vehicle (SUV) designed for the consumer market. It proved to be extremely popular and started a product craze that other car manufacturers soon followed as consumers clamored for more. Other big product successes for Ford Motor included the Taurus and the popular and best-selling F-Series truck. But it's also had some notable failures as well. For example, there was the Pinto and its exploding gas tanks. And the Edsel (1958–1960) was a car with an unusual design that never really caught on with consumers. More recent (2000–2001) was the Firestone tires–Ford Explorer fiasco, which some have suggested may have been the start of the company's current struggles.

In 1998, when family member William Clay Ford Jr. (who prefers to be called Bill) became chairman of the company (a position in which he wouldn't have to be heavily involved with the "strategy stuff"), Ford was riding high. Sales and market share were strong and the company was well positioned to exploit its strengths. However, the CEO at that time, Jacques Nasser, had grand plans to transform Ford from a simple car manufacturer to a consumer brand company. He planned to take the company into diverse businesses such as Internet ventures, car retailing, repair shops, and even junkyards. Not surprisingly, these businesses flopped and, perhaps even more damaging, distracted Ford executives from their core business of designing, building, and selling cars. Then, the Firestone tire recall spun out of control. With the company's worldwide operations floundering, the board of directors fired

Nasser in October 2001 and Bill took on the additional responsibility of CEO, a position he was reluctant to assume. However, as the great-grandson of founder Henry Ford and the fourth generation of his family to lead the company, Bill understood and accepted his family responsibility.

The burden was on Bill to fix the company and drive it into its second century. And this was a company in crisis, having lost close to $6.4 billion total in 2001 and 2002. Although the company posted a profit of $495 million in 2003 and $1.4 billion in 2005, it's been downhill ever since and is still a long way from the $7 billion level that Bill pledged the company's profits would be by mid-decade. In light of the challenging industry and economic conditions, that goal was not achieved.

INDUSTRY AND COMPETITORS

The global car industry is one characterized by fierce competition; fickle customers; manufacturing overcapacity worldwide; maturity stage of the industry life cycle, especially in the large industrialized countries; and declining demand for cars in an anemic global economy. Technology continues to drive rapid change in products and processes. In addition, more market segments and new products are leading to intensified competition. The once-dominant U.S. car manufacturers have been displaced by strong, smart, and aggressive global competitors. In fact, in 2008, Toyota took over the title of the world's number one automaker from General Motors. In addition, Toyota and the other Japanese car companies have made an all-out assault on the European market—a market that had been dominated by the U.S. car companies. In May 2007, DaimlerChrysler announced it would sell a controlling interest in its struggling Chrysler Group to a private equity firm, Cerberus Capital Management of New York. In early 2008, Ford announced the sale of its Land Rover and Jaguar lines to India-based Tata Motors. Then, in late 2008, as the economy situation worsened and car sales volumes continued to decline, both Chrysler and General Motors took bailout money from the U.S. government. Ford was the only U.S. car manufacturer that did not take any government monies, saying that it had enough cash on hand to get through 2009.

Consumer demand for cars, especially in the U.S. and European markets, tends to follow the state of the economy. During good economic times, consumers are more willing to buy cars and other expensive products. However, uncertainty—economic, social, global, or political—makes consumers more hesitant to buy new cars. To stimulate demand, car companies often try incentives such as rebates, no money down, and free financing for extended time periods to pull customers into dealers' showrooms. Although these incentives can be good for consumers, they tend to have a disastrous effect on a car company's bottom line. Because of the intense competition in the industry, when one car company introduces an incentive, others usually must follow suit or risk losing potential buyers. Also, U.S. car manufacturers have had to deal with the threat of the ever-strengthening foreign car companies, especially the Japanese.

For years, the Japanese car manufacturers have used flexible manufacturing systems, which allow multiple models to be built on the same assembly line and enable faster product changeovers. Although U.S. car manufacturers had lagged behind Japanese competitors in terms of manufacturing costs and efficiency, they are making progress. A key annual manufacturing efficiency study (the Harbour Report) showed that in 2008, Chrysler and Toyota both had an average 30.37 manufacturing labor hours per vehicle; GM averaged 32.29 hours per vehicle and Ford was at 33.88 hours. Another area where Ford was outpaced by foreign auto companies was in labor costs. Ford's union labor costs were about $22 an hour more than nonunion labor at U.S. plants of foreign makers. These manufacturing realities have made it difficult for U.S. car companies, especially Ford, to be competitive. However, Ford remained committed to transforming its assembly plants into lean and flexible centers of manufacturing excellence, although it was still trying to catch up.

FORD MOTOR COMPANY TODAY

As Ford's financial condition worsened in 2006, Bill went to the company's board of directors and said he wanted to "readjust the company's management structure." Bill "handpicked his successor as CEO, gambling that Alan Mulally's team-building skills and industrial savvy would inspire and embolden employees enough to revive the hard-up automaker." Mulally joined Ford Motor in September 2006 from Boeing, where he also led a successful turnaround effort. Mulally's first move was to "immediately dust off his Boeing playbook" as he looked to implement many of the same strategies that had worked in turning around Boeing. Although he recognized the massive problems facing the company in achieving strategic competitiveness and profitability, he was determined to take the dramatic, painful steps and to "plow through gut-wrenching change" to transform the company and return it to global prominence. Guiding his initial efforts was the Way Forward plan that was first announced in January 2006 and the implementation of which was accelerated in September 2006 when Mulally was appointed CEO. This comprehensive plan addressed seven areas where strategic changes would be focused: bold leadership; customer focus; strong brands; bold, innovative products; great quality; clear pricing; and competitive costs and capacity. Mulally also identified four key priorities: (1) aggressively restructure the company to operate profitably at the current real demand and changing model mix; (2) accelerate product development with new products that customers really want and value while achieving manufacturing excellence by reducing complexity and improving quality; (3) obtain financing to do these things and improve the balance sheet; and (4) work together with accountability with all partners. In addition to the Way Forward plan, Mulally fashioned a strategic effort dubbed ONE FORD in an attempt to "fully leverage the tremendous worldwide resources of Ford." In his remarks to shareholders at the 2008 annual meeting, Mulally had this to say: "We operate in a fiercely competitive global industry. To achieve profitable growth we have to make the best use of our human resources and take advantage of every potential economy of scale and best practice we can find. That means operating as one team around the world, with one plan and one goal … ONE FORD … profitable growth for all." These efforts and priorities affect several functional areas within the company.

Manufacturing and Product Design

Ford is first and foremost a manufacturing company. However, the stark reality is that the Japanese and Korean car companies outearn Ford on each car made by delivering more features for lower cost. To have any chance of turning its business around, Ford would have to focus on its manufacturing strategies.

As the Way Forward plan indicated, Ford's goals in manufacturing were competitive costs and capacity. A central part of the strategy for achieving those goals was the decision to close 16 plants and eliminate 44,000 jobs by 2012, with nine of the plants closed by 2008. But Ford also had to continue to make its remaining manufacturing plants as efficient and effective as possible by stressing manufacturing strategies and processes to maximize operational quality and efficiency.

Ford already had several strategic initiatives in place to reduce costs. During 2003, for instance, it achieved cost reductions of $3.2 billion, part of which came from its quality improvement and waste elimination methodology called consumer-driven Six Sigma. Since the implementation of this quality improvement program, Ford completed more than 9,500 projects that saved a total of $1.7 billion worldwide. These quality improvements also led to a dramatic reduction in the number of car recalls and drove down warranty spending by 18 percent. Currently, the quality of Ford, Lincoln, and Mercury vehicles has matched that of Toyota and Honda, as evidenced by quality surveys. It's an accomplishment of which the company is understandably proud. In addition to the quality improvements, Ford also is the industry safety leader, with more five-star crash ratings than any other brand or company. It also is working collaboratively with suppliers to find additional areas for performance improvement. Another step in the right direction was the new agreement with the United Automobile Workers union announced in mid-March 2009. This agreement reduces workers' hourly rate (including salary and benefits) to $55, an amount that will save the company at least $500 million a year and bring its labor costs more in line with that of foreign competitors' plants in the United States.

Under the Way Forward plan, Ford is continuing efforts to reduce material costs by at least $6 billion by 2010. Achieving such cost reductions will require continued efforts to reduce manufacturing complexity and to improve quality in products and in processes. Although the company has made progress, it hasn't been an easy thing to do.

When Mulally came on board, he scrambled to familiarize himself with Ford's vehicles. He began driving a different Ford car to and from work each day. He discovered that the switches for lights, wipers, and so on, were often in different locations. Such variations are unnecessary and costly. Mulally "demanded that product engineers create uniform parts that most Fords can share," an action he believed would lead to leaner and more reliable production. At another meeting, Mulally laid out 12 different metal rods used to hold up a vehicle's hood. "He wanted to demonstrate that this kind of variation is costly but doesn't matter to consumers." By sharing vehicle architecture, components, and best practices from around the world, the company could leverage its scarce resources for the greater good of the entire company.

Another element in changing Ford's manufacturing strategy was to right-size its capacity. Although the announced plant closings have played a major role, Mulally also wanted to emphasize a capacity strategy that was in line with customer demand—a more "customer-driven strategy versus a fill-the-plant strategy." Although the goal was to reduce capacity by 26 percent by the end of 2008, the dire economic situation and plummeting demand for cars forced an unplanned reduction in capacity.

Mulally also realigned the organizational structure to put additional focus on markets and customers and to better leverage global assets and capabilities. The automotive operations, which include Ford North America, Ford Europe, Volvo, Ford South America, Ford Asia/Pacific & Africa, now report directly to him. The company is in "preliminary discussions" with several parties interested in acquiring the Volvo unit.

Mulally also created a single global product development organization. This new structure enabled the company to "work together more effectively to continuously improve quality, productivity, and speed of product development." The global product head was working to create a "Ford feel" for all its vehicles, much like

---

BMW has. He said, "When you get into a Ford vehicle, you should know immediately it's a Ford by the feel." Many of these strategic changes are impacting the company's marketing strategies as well.

Marketing

Great automotive products have always been important to Ford. The company's auto brands include Ford, Lincoln, Mercury, Volvo, and Mazda (in which it has a 13 percent stake). Many of these brands are quite successful. For instance, in 2008, the Ford F-series was the best-selling truck in America for the 32nd year in a row and the best-selling vehicle of any type for the 27th year in a row. In 2007, Ford South America sales were up 19 percent and Ford China sales were up 26 percent. However, plummeting global demand during 2008 negatively affected the company's sales, which declined 15.2 percent. And 2009 was not off to a good start and was going to be another challenging year.

Ford's marketing strategies will again play an important role in turnaround efforts. Mulally hired James Farley, a former Toyota executive, as Ford's chief global marketing executive. They decided that the company's brands needed to be more focused. Thus, Lincoln now will focus on premium sedans and SUVs; Mercury will sell premium small cars and crossovers; and the Ford brand will continue to offer the broadest range of products and options. Mulally also said that by 2010, 100 percent of the company's products would be "refreshed or new." For instance, one of Ford's most popular models, the Taurus, which was relaunched during the summer of 2007, has been totally revamped for rollout in summer 2009.

In continuing its aggressive move to global vehicles, Ford announced in early 2009 that Elena Ford (great-great-granddaughter of company founder Henry Ford) was hired for the newly created position of director of Global Marketing, Sales, and Service Operations. In this position, she will implement the company's "ONE FORD" marketing vision. Enhancing the global marketing efforts is the next step in the ONE FORD plan to integrate Ford's worldwide operations and leverage its scale and expertise. This marketing approach follows the company's consolidation of global product development in 2006 and global purchasing operations in 2008. Within the next five years, the plan is to have common Ford vehicles competing in global segments. In 2010, the new Ford Focus global car will be introduced simultaneously in North America, Europe, and Asia. That product launch is building on lessons learned from the launch of the Fiesta, the company's first global product under its ONE FORD vision. Farley said, "Our new products are being recognized for excellence around the world, and they are leading the competition in quality, fuel efficiency, safety, and smart technologies. Now, our job is to more effectively and efficiently connect these great products with our customers and build on Ford's strength as one of the world's most admired companies and brands."

Another marketing change Ford made was to its advertising. The company used a "more combative strategy that it hoped would put its vehicles back on America's shopping list." The Ford Challenge advertising campaign asked consumers to compare Ford vehicles to their toughest competitors. The first ads showed consumers favorably comparing the Ford Fusion midsize sedan against a Toyota Camry and a Honda Accord. This "push" accelerated the model's sales by almost 33 percent. Ford also ran ads that compared the safety record of its popular F-150 truck with that of competitors, especially taking a jab at Toyota's Tundra truck that received only a four-star safety rating.

Ford is committed to its products and customers. The company's vision, mission, and values can be found on its Web site [**www.ford.com**]. Its values statement is particularly enlightening: "The customer is Job 1." Ford understands how important strong customer relationships and innovative, high-quality, high-value products are to its business and its ultimate success.

Ford's dealers are an important element in the success of the company's marketing efforts. Together, the dealers and the company must provide customers (current and potential) with products and a buying and service experience that meet and exceed their expectations. It's a relationship that hasn't always been pleasant—especially now, as Ford and the auto industry are going through extremely challenging circumstances. In 2008, the number of U.S. auto dealers (all manufacturers, not just Ford) declined 4.2 percent because of fewer people purchasing cars. However, one automotive magazine writer stated that "Ford dealers I've talked with show a pride of dealership that belies some of the troubles they and Ford have seen lately from sluggish sales and lost market share." Ford is committed to working together closely as partners and providing dealers with outstanding new products and trucks so everyone experiences a successful and profitable outcome.

Some of Ford's newer models have been good performers; for instance, the Edge, which was introduced in December 2006, and the Fusion (introduced in October 2005). The company had high hopes for the Flex, which went on sale in summer 2008 as a 2009 model. It's described as a "modern station wagon that bears a strong resemblance to Toyota's Scion xB and the Honda Element." In 2009, unlike the other car manufacturers, Ford was taking an aggressive stance by introducing three new models: the Fusion, with either a hybrid or conventional engine; the new Taurus sedan; and the Transit Connect van.

In addition to its automotive products, Ford's other main business is its finance subsidiary, Ford Motor Credit, which provides financial services and is the number one auto finance company in the United States. Also, until 2005, it owned Hertz, the rental car company, but sold it to focus on its automotive divisions.

Employees

The struggles Ford is facing have not been easy for its employees. Despite the difficult conditions, Ford cares about its people. The top management team is experienced and firmly committed to turning around this proud company. Its workforce is dedicated and talented. The company understands that its future success depends on its people. As it says in its Code of Basic Working Conditions (which can be found on the company's Web site), "The diverse group of men and women who work for Ford are our most important resource." This code outlines universal values that serve as the cornerstone of the company's relationship with employees and covers important people issues such as child labor, compensation, forced labor, collective bargaining, harassment and discrimination, healthy and safety, and work hours.

As stated earlier, a major component of the Way Forward plan was the elimination of 44,000 jobs by 2012. To accomplish this, Ford used buyout offers to persuade hourly workers to retire early or to give up their jobs, hoping to get 35,000 hourly workers to leave. More than 37,000 accepted the deals, but Ford announced in April 2007 that about 2,000 hourly workers had changed their minds about accepting incentives to leave. But that merely put Ford back to its original goal. Additional workforce reductions are coming from the elimination of salaried positions through early retirements, voluntary separations, and even involuntary separations, as needed.

Another major personnel problem facing Ford is its increasing health care-related expenses. In 2006, its health care expenses for U.S. employees, retirees, and their dependents were $3.1 billion, 58 percent of that going to retirees' health care costs. Ford, like many other companies, has shifted a higher portion of health care costs to its employees and retirees, but still expects its health care costs to continue to increase. This commitment will continue to affect the company's ability to meet its profitability goals. The newly signed agreement between the company and its union should go a long way to helping the company better control its total labor costs.

Corporate Culture

Having a CEO with no experience in the industry is always a gamble. However, even Bill Ford says that Mulally's progress in "shaking up a calcified culture has thus far kept Ford independent and away from" the government's bailout. Another industry consultant said that, "The speed with which Mulally has transformed Ford into a more nimble and healthy operation has been one of the more impressive jobs I've seen. It probably would have been game over for Ford already but for the changes he has brought."

With its long and exceptional heritage, Ford believes strongly in the values that have guided the company over the years. But that heritage also made needed changes more difficult. A professor of management at Wharton said he was "concerned that Ford's corporate culture might be getting in the way of Mr. Mulally. As you walk into Ford or even General Motors these days, the culture feels different. It does not have that drive for perfection, the focus on continuous improvement, the attention paid to the small things that Toyota does." Ford employees may be finding it difficult to change their "mental mapping" instilled when the company was reaping millions in profits from its SUVs and pickup trucks and not wanting to recognize the dire circumstances and tough choices faced today. The new message at Ford is that "the bigger-is-better worldview that had defined it is being replaced with a new approach: less is more."

What did Mulally have to deal with? Initial discussions between Bill Ford and Mulally were pretty candid. Bill shared one key insight: "Ford is a place where they wait for the leader to tell them what to do." His point? Ford executives weren't sufficiently involved in the decision making. By the time Mulally came on board, he had met with every senior executive and asked a lot of questions. Not all of them liked the "Way Forward Plan," especially the part that had the company moving to vehicles that could be sold in different markets. Mulally knew that to work the plan, he would have to change Ford's culture.

The changes haven't been easy for Ford's hourly workers or for its management team. One of Mulally's first moves when he came onboard was instituting the same Thursday meetings he had used at Boeing. These meetings were a tool for formulating business plans. "At those weekly meetings, cell phones, BlackBerrys, side conversations, mean jokes, personal opinions, turf battles, and bathroom breaks (unless urgent and quick) were out. In were candor, data, results, more data, and applause for executives who showed progress." The first Thursday meeting, as expected, went badly. When Mulally asked each division head to present his or her results and forecasts, he said that the numbers didn't make sense. He asked, "Why don't all the pieces add up for the total corporate financials?" One manager replied, "We don't share everything." Instead, executives had run their units without integrating with other divisions, even occasionally holding back information. Mulally was astounded. He told the associates, "Data can set you free. You can't manage a secret."

After that first disastrous meeting, one thing Mulally tackled was a culture that "loved to meet and where managers commonly held 'pre-meetings' where they schemed how to get their stories straight for higher-ups." Mulally was determined to have a constant stream of current data that would give his team a "weekly snapshot of Ford's global operations and hold executives' performance against profit targets." Now it's become difficult for managers to hide unpleasant facts because numbers are being constantly updated. In the data operation rooms at Ford's headquarters, the walls are covered with color-coded tables, bar charts, and line graphs that represent what's going on in every corner of Ford's world. Divisions not living up to profit projections are red; those hitting their numbers are green; and yellow means results could go either way. Even though executives were held accountable, most began believing in the power of information when they saw how Mulally used the data. For instance, the executive team decided to delay the launch of the F-Series truck by about six weeks, cycle down fourth-quarter production, and clear out last year's F-Series trucks when inventory had piled up.

Another thing Mulally changed was Ford's approach to grooming managers. Previously, Ford executives were cycled into new jobs every few years. No one was ever in a job long enough to feel accountable or like they could make a difference. Under Mulally, executives were kept in jobs and as one said, "I've never had such a consistency of purpose before."

One final important aspect of Ford's culture is something that Bill Ford is known for: his strong and unwavering commitment to environmental responsibility. And Mulally supports those efforts. He said, "Bill Ford and I share the same vision of building fuel efficient, environmentally friendly vehicles that protect their passengers and our planet." Although the company backed off its headline-grabbing promise in 2000 to improve the fuel economy of its SUVs by 25 percent in five years, its commitment to the environment hasn't wavered. In fact, Bill likes to point out his pet project—an eco-friendly manufacturing plant that opened in Dearborn, Michigan, in 2004. As fuel oil prices continue to be an issue for consumers, environmentally friendly products will continue to be attractive options. Ford maintains its commitment to being a green company. Descriptions of its environmental efforts can be found in the 2007/08 Sustainability Report. As government-mandated fuel-economy standards continue to get tougher, Ford is looking at several ideas from the past for boosting gas mileage and slashing emissions. For instance, its 2011 Ford Explorer will use green technology such as lighter-weight steel body parts and "direct injection" engine technology, a technology that dates back to the 1940s.

Financial

Ford's executives are well aware that the company has a long, difficult road ahead of it and that its financial health is a long way from where it once was and where it needs to be. Mulally's goal of making money in 2009 will not be achieved. In fact, the best he's hoping for is to break even during 2011. Complete company financial information can be found on its Web site [**www.ford.com**].

FORD MOTOR COMPANY—THE FUTURE

In the company's 2009 Outlook, Alan Mulally reiterated his commitment to ONE FORD. "In a global market, success flows from having ONE TEAM working on ONE

PLAN with ONE GOAL in mind." The ONE TEAM concept means including everyone with a stake in the outcome in the decision-making process. The ONE PLAN concept means changing the way the company has been run as largely autonomous business units to a more aligned and globally integrated organization and leveraging worldwide resources. The ONE GOAL is to build more of the products that people really want and value. Is Ford going down the right road with its Way Forward plan? How will a prolonged economic downturn affect Mulally's ability to continue the company's turnaround and to keep it from tapping into government bailout monies? It's something that he wants to avoid in an attempt to distance Ford from its Detroit rivals.

Sources: Based on Ford Motor Company [**www.ford.com**], March 24, 2009; C. Isidore, "Ford Sales Plunge," *CNNMoney.com,* April 1, 2009; Dow Jones, "Ford Confirms Talks with Parties Interested in Volvo," [money.cnn.com], March 25, 2009; D. Kiley, "Ford's Savior," *BusinessWeek,* March 16, 2009, pp. 30–34; M. Dolan, "UAW Says Ford Workers Ratified Concessions," *Wall Street Journal,* March 10, 2009, p. B3; C. Isidore, "Ford's Sales Plunge 48%," *New York Times Online,* March 3, 2009; B. Vlasic, "Ford Bucks Detroit Trend with 3 New Car Models," *New York Times Online,* March 2, 2009; D. Kiley, "Ford Sees the Future, and It's Retro Tech," *BusinessWeek,* February 23, 2009, p. 64; Ford Motor Company Press Release, "Ford Strengthens Global Marketing Function as Next Step in Implementing 'ONE FORD' Vision," [**www.ford.com**], January 27, 2009; K. Marr, "Toyota Passes General Motors as World's Largest Carmaker," *Washington Post Online,* January 22, 2009; "Ford's F-Series Reigns as America's Best-Selling Truck and Best-Selling Vehicle in 2008," Reuters Newswire [**www.reuters.com**], January 5, 2009; A. R. Carey and S. Ward, "Automakers' Pay Gap," *USA Today,* December 31, 2008, p. 1A; Oliver Wyman News Release, "Lean Improvements: Worker Buyouts Bring Detroit Three Productivity Closer to Asian Rivals," [**http://www.oliverwyman.com/ow/automotive.htm**], June 5, 2008; M. Landler and M. Maynard, "Chrysler Group to Be Sold for $7.4 Billion," *New York Times Online,* May 14, 2007; R. K. Farrell, "Shareholders Give Ex-Chief Blame for Ford Woes," *New York Times Online,* May 11, 2007; M. Maynard, "Ford Chief Sticking to His Road Map for Turnaround," *New York Times Online,* April 5, 2007; S. Finlay, "Ford Dealers a Loyal Bunch," *Ward's Dealer Business* [**wdb.wardsauto.com**], March 1, 2007; M. Maynard, "Ford Chief Sees Small as Virtue and Necessity," *New York Times Online,* January 26, 2007; M. Longley, "Inside Mulally's 'War Room': A Radical Overhaul of Ford," *Wall Street Journal,* December 22, 2006, pp. A1+; "Ford CEO Offers Glimpse of Turnaround Plan," *CNNMoney.com,* December 22, 2006; Bloomberg News, "Ford Reorganizes Executives," *New York Times Online,* December 13, 2006; and J. R. Healey, "Ford's Famous Filly Turns 40," *USA Today,* April 16, 2004.

Index

Note: Letters n, f, and t denote notes, figures, and tables, respectively.

Innovation Network Inc., 45
Intangible resources, 103
Intangible sectors, 40
Integrated low cost–differentiation
    strategy, 170–171
Intelligent Mail services, 253
Intelligentsia Coffee, 169
Internal analysis, 102–108
    defined, 102
    doing, 108–120
    importance of, 120–121
Internal audit approach, 109–111,
    113–115t
Internal development, 200, 200f
Internal Revenue Service, 247
International Monetary Fund
    (IMF), 16
International strategies, 198
Internet, 19, 74
    e-government, 243
Internet Diamonds, 153
Intranet, 19
Intuit, 206
InVision Technologies, 199
I/O view. See Industrial organization
    (I/O) view
Ireland, R. D., 29n15, 60n3, 201, 224n22,
    224n23
Isidore, C., 221, 298, 299
Isla, Pablo, 32
iTunes Store, 57–58
Ivancevich, J. M., 224n24
Iwata, E., 29n12

J. C. Penney, 97
J. Crew, 8
Jargon, J., 223n1
Javidan, M., 229
Jaworowski, K., 98n1
Jayson, S., 99n19, 99n20
Jemison, D., 224n16
Jennings, D. F., 187n8
Jenster, P. V., 257n37
JetBlue Airways, 126–127, 164
Jikoda, 136
Job creation, 232
Jobe, L. A., 29n3
Johnson, A. C., 29n3, 257n31
Johnson, G., 29n14
Johnson, J., 256n1
Johnson, K., 60n1
Johnson, K. H., 223n13
Johnson & Johnson, 71, 247
Johnston, Jerry, 26
Joint venture, 200–201
Jone, Dow, 146
Jones, G. R., 188n23
Jones, J., 187n1
Jones, T. O., 144
Jones Apparel Group, 76
Jordan, Michael, 185
JP Morgan Chase & Company
    (Chase), 222
Jung, Andrea, 24–25
Junior Achievement survey, 50
Juniper Networks, 81
Junk removal, 225
Junktion, 226
Jusko, J., 9, 29n12, 223n1

Kabanoff, B., 187n8
Kaihla, P., 5
Kale, P., 133n2
Kamenetz, A., 27
Kamenev, M., 60n1
Kane, Y. I., 58
Kanter, R. M., 258n40
Kapner, S., 130
Karger, P., 257n22
Karlgaard, R., 254
Karnitschnig, M., 24
Karter, Patricia, 234
Kavilanz, P. B., 96, 98n17, 187n1
KaZaA, 57
Keats, B. W., 223n13, 256n22
Keels, J. K., 224n27
Keenan, F., 166
Keeton, A., 254
Keighley, G., 116
Kelleher, K., 133n12
Keller, K. L., 156n4
Kellwood, 76
Kelly, K., 98n1
Kennedy, K., 26
Kessler, S., 35
Ketchen, D. J., Jr., 29n3, 29n11, 98n13,
    187n5–7
Keveney, B., 24
KFC. *See* YUM! Brands
Khermouch, G., 132
Kiesling, L., 72
Kilcarr, S., 256n1
Kiley, D., 168, 238, 242, 298, 299
Killinger, Kerry, 221–222
Kim, E., 188n22
Kim, T., 188n18
Kimberly-Clark's Kleenex, 116
Kimelman, J., 47
Kinard, D., 87
Kinko, 8
Kirkpatrick, D., 61n15
Kirpalani, V. H. Manek, 256n10
Kmart, 3–4, 206
Knauss, Donald, 26
Knight, G. A., 256n10
Knight, Phil, 184–185
Knox, N., 98n16
Knudstorp, Jørgen Vig, 11
Koenig, D., 8, 97
Kogut, B., 256n17
Kohl's Corporation, 96–97
Kolk, A., 49
Kolvereid, L., 257n27
Koots Green Tea, 165
Koppelman, Charles A., 130
Korberg, C. S., 99n30
Kotabe, M., 224n23
Kotha, S., 99n32, 188n22, 188n25
Kotler, P., 133n19, 156n4, 187n3, 223n3
Kraft General Foods, 189–190, 192, 193,
    194, 207
    concentration strategy, 193, 194
Krantz, M., 235, 283
Krell, E., 201, 224n22
Kriger, M. P., 61n21
Krishnan, M. S., 133n2
Kroc, Ann, 245
Kroc, Ray, 245
Kroger Company, 8

Kroll, M., 60n3, 188n23
Kudina, A., 256n10
Kudla, R., 257n23
Kuka Robotics, 194
Kurlantzick, J., 30n23

La Monica, P. R., 142
La Prairie, 168
Labaton, S., 30n28
Laboratoires Inneov, 201
Lado, A. A., 60n3, 156n6
LaForge, R., 257n22
Lahart, J., 79
Laise, E., 61n27
Lamiman, K., 96, 97
Lancaster Colony Corporation, 198
Landler, M., 30n18, 299
Lane, P. J., 30n17, 223n15
Lang, J. R., 223n13, 257n29
Large organizations, external analysis, 87
Larwood, L., 61n21
Lattman, P., 223n2
Laudon, J., 156n11
Laudon, K., 156n11
LaVallee, A., 57
Lawrence, P. R., 98n5
Layoffs, 142
Lazaridis, Mike, 162
Learned, E. P., 11
Leask, G., 98n13
Lecraw, D. J., 223n12
Lee, S. M., 61n19
Leeds, J., 223n9
Legislation, 83
LEGO, 11
Leibs, S., 61n15
Leinwand, D., 75
Lemonick, M. D., 61n13
Lend Lease Corporation, 15
Lengnick-Hall, C. A., 60n4, 98n6
Leonhardt, D., 8, 98n1
Leontiades, M., 257n23
Lerner, L. D., 61n26
Levi Strauss, 19
Levie, J., 233
Levin, A., 98n17
Levin, G., 258n41
Levine, R., 24, 57, 98n1
Levinson, N. S., 224n22
Levitas, E., 61n32
Lewan, T., 98n1
Lewis, A., 61n29
Lewis, P., 57, 187n1
Lewis, W. W., 224n26
Lexus, 168
Licensing, 230
Lidwell, W., 224n24
Lieberman, D., 98n15, 223n1
Liebs, S., 30n26
Liedtke, M., 187n1, 224n20
Liepert, Berndt, 194
Lin, T. W., 132
Lindsay, W., 257n23
Linebaugh, K., 221
Linebaugh, L., 156n1
Linens 'N Things, 78
Lipton, 202
Liquidation, 207
Litschert, R. J., 187n8

Reactor strategy, 165–166
ReadyMop, 166
RealNetworks, 35
Reason, T., 30n28
Rebello, K., 224n30
Recording Industry Association of
America (RIAA), 57
Reed, D., 127, 254, 290
Regal Entertainment Group, 63
Reimann, B. C., 61n16
Reingold, J., 59
Related (concentric) diversification,
196–197, 197f
Render, B., 156n3
Reputations. *See* Corporate reputations
Research and development (R&D),
136, 139
Resource-based view (RBV), 33, 34–37
comparison with I/O and guerrilla
views, 33t, 37–38
Resources. *See also specific resources*
and competitive advantage, 162
defined, 35
environment as source of, 66–67,
67t, 88
exploitation of, 36–37
financial, 103
human resource, 103, 238
imitation of, 36
organizational, 102–105
physical, 103
rare, 36
role of, 162
structural-cultural, 103
uniqueness, 36f
valuable, 35–36
Restructuring, 207–209
Retrenchment strategy, 206
Rhino Entertainment Company, 169
Rhodes, Bill, 28
Riccitello, John, 56, 57
Richardson, K., 26
Richmond, R., 230
Richtel, M., 57, 142, 162
Riggs, J., 224n24
Rindova, V. P., 3, 60n4
Rivlin, G., 154
Roberts, D., 132
Roberts, J. H., 187n9
Roberts, P. W., 61n27
Robinson, R. B., 188n21, 257n22, 257n23
Robinson, W. T., 188n28
Robison, J., 61n6
Rockwood, K., 155
Rohwedder, C., 8, 60n1
Rosenbloom, S., 97
Rosenbrush, S., 224n32
Rosner, B., 133n21
Rotary International, 244
Rothaermel, F. T., 29n3
Routines and processes, 104, 106–107
Rowley, Cynthia, 130
Rowley, I., 156n1, 223n11
Royal Caribbean, 70
Royal Typewriter Company, 195
Rue, L., 257n23
Ruefli, T. W., 60n4
Rugman, A. M., 60n3
Ruimin, Z., 131, 132

Rumelt, R. P., 29n9, 29n10, 60n3,
223n12

Sacks, D., 133n15
Safari, A., 257n28
Saginaw, Paul, 238
Salancik, G. R., 98n6
Salierno, D., 30n26
Salter, M. S., 224n16
Salvation Army, 245
Salwen, K. G., 86
Samakh, E., 11
Sambharya, R. B., 223n12, 223n13
Saminather, N., 60n1
Sanchez, C. M., 224n27
Sanders, P., 29n1
Sanson, M., 6
Saporito, B., 153, 211
Sapsford, J., 98n7
Sarbanes-Oxley Act, 17
Sarnin, P., 29n14
Sasser, W. E., 144
Sauer, P. J., 133n1
Scanlon, J., 11, 40
Scannell, K., 30n28
Schatz, R., 3
Schaubroeck, J., 156n6
Schendel, D. E., 29n7, 29n9, 29n10, 98n13,
224n24
Schick, A. G., 224n27
Schlesinger, L. A., 144
Schlosser, J., 130
Schmid, R. E., 253
Schneiderman, R. M., 223n1
Schoemaker, P. J. H., 60n3
Schubert, S., 84, 194
Schulze, Dick, 94–95
Schumpeter, Joseph, 238
Schwartz, N. D., 11
Schwenk, C., 256n22
Scudamore, B., 225–226, 256n1
Seaman, S. L., 187n8, 223n12, 223n13
Sears, 166, 173, 206
Section 404, of Sarbanes-Oxley Act, 17–18
Sedensky, M., 133n1
Seelye, K. Q., 146
Segev, E., 187n8
Selden, L., 118
Sellen, T., 283
Service-providing industries, 40
Serwer, A., 133n22
Seth, A., 223n13
Severinson, P., 256n1
Sewell, D., 26
Seye, Sonia, 230
Shaich, Ron, 219
Shalfi, M., 155
Shama, A., 257n28
Shane, S., 257n27
Shanghai World Financial Center, 159
Shanley, M., 187n5
Sharfman, M. P., 29n4
Sharma, V. M., 224n28
Sharper Image, 78
Shcere, R. F., 61n14
Shenhar, A., 187n8
Shepherd, L., 223n1
Sheppard, J. P., 224n29
Shimizu, K., 60n3

Shimizu, N., 156n1
Shook, C. L., 224n27
Short, J. C., 29n3, 98n13, 187n6
Shortell, S. M., 187n8
Shrader, C. B., 29n3, 256n22, 257n23,
257n26
Siafter, C., 224n24
Sidel, R., 222
Siekman, P., 156n2
Siklos, R., 29n1
Sikorsky Aviation, 107
Silke, S., 255
Silkos, R., 24
Silver, S., 47
Silvers, D. I., 61n20, 61n22
Simison, R. L., 156n1
Simon, D. G., 60n3
Simon, H. A., 98n4
Simrany, J. P., 165
Sinegal, Jim, 154
Singapore Airlines (SIA), 174
Singer, A. E., 61n30
Singer, J., 255
Singh, H., 223n12
Singh, J. V., 133n2
Singh, Manmohan, 228
Single-business organization, 190–191
Sinha, I., 187n8
Situation analysis, 5, 7
Sizzler International Inc., 166
Ski industry, 73
Skype Technologies, 197
Slawsky, R., 138
Small business, 232
Smaller and medium-sized
organizations, 86
Smaller organizations, 86
Smallwood, N., 133n17
Smeltzer, L. R., 257n26
Smith, C., 153
Smith, E., 58
Smith, G., 248n41
Smith, J. M., 60n1
Smith, K. G., 3
Snow, C. C., 163, 164, 187n5, 187n7
Snyder, J. D., 257n36
Social networking sites, 237
Sociocultural sector, evaluation of, 81–82
Soderquist, Don, 211
Soft drink industry, current rivalry, 68–70
Solberg, C. A., 256n10
Solomon, D., 30n28
Soma, 185
Song, M., 187n8
Sørheim, R., 256n10
Sormunen, J., 99n28
Southwest Airlines, 104–105, 106–107,
140, 164
background, 283–284
company awards and recognitions,
288–289
culture and people, 287–288
current operations, 284–287
financial highlights, 288
future, 290
industry and major competitors,
289–290
legendary customer service,
285–286